M000290857

UNDERSTANDING
THE DIACONATE

UNDERSTANDING THE DIACONATE

Historical, Theological, and
Sociological Foundations

W. SHAWN MCKNIGHT

Foreword by David W. Fagerberg

THE CATHOLIC UNIVERSITY OF AMERICA PRESS
Washington, D.C.

Copyright © 2018
The Catholic University of America Press
All rights reserved
The paper used in this publication meets the minimum requirements
of American National Standards for Information Science—
Permanence of Paper for Printed Library Materials,
ANSI Z39.48-1984.
∞

Design and composition by Kachergis Book Design

Cataloging-in-Publication Data available
from the Library of Congress

ISBN 978-0-8132-3035-1

In gratitude to God the Father,

who sent his Son to redeem us

and pours out his Spirit

to strengthen us

CONTENTS

FOREWORD

David W. Fagerberg

One can find histories of the diaconate. One can find theologies of the diaconate. One can find pastoral treatments of diaconal ministry. But one very rarely finds these all within the same covers, and one never finds them integrated by an insightful hermeneutic stemming from the social sciences. The combination of these four dimensions—history, theology, pastoral practice, and an approach that sees the deacon as social intermediary and symbol of *communitas*—makes this an extraordinary book that will advance the objectives of Vatican Council II when it called for the restoration of the permanent diaconate. *Lumen Gentium*, no. 29, refers to deacons as those "upon whom hands are imposed 'not unto the priesthood, but unto a ministry of service.' For strengthened by sacramental grace, in communion with the bishop and his group of priests they serve in the diaconate of the liturgy, of the word, and of charity to the people of God."[1] Or, as Pope Paul VI says in *Ad Pascendum*, "The permanent diaconate should be restored as an intermediate order between the higher ranks of the Church's hierarchy and the rest of the people of God ... as a driving force for the Church's *diaconia* towards the local Christian communities, and as a sign or sacrament of the Lord Christ himself, who 'came not to be served but to serve.'"[2] Have we even begun to fully understand the ministry of this restored, permanent order in the Latin rite?

Fr. Shawn and I were co-participants in a conference on the diaconate where I heard him present a paper titled "The Uniqueness of the Deacon." It seemed to me then, as it still does now, the appropriate place to begin. The

---

1. Here the Dogmatic Constitution cites: "*Constitutiones Ecclesiac aegyptiacae*, III, 2: ed. Funk, *Didascalia*, II, 103; Statuta Eccl. Ant. 371: 3, 954."
2. The Apostolic Letter cites Mt 20:28.

challenge faced by deacons is that we do not recognize their unique identity and ministry, but rather mistake them to be "quasi-priests," or men who "did not go all the way." This definition by negation will not disappear until a positive definition takes its place. And in his conclusion to this book Fr. Shawn identifies this as the motive for making this the subject of his dissertation at Sant' Anselmo. "An inadequate role description for Latin rite deacons hampers the effectiveness of their ministry. For the diaconate to become successful it must have a specialized ministry that is well defined and important to the life and mission of the Church." I asked for a copy of that dissertation after our conference together, printed it out, read it with great profit and much underlining, planned to steal a chapter or two for my annual "Orders and Ministry" course, and was then delighted to learn that the Catholic University of America Press would publish it so that it receives the audience it so richly deserves.

I said that within these covers the reader will find history, theology, pastoral questions, and the social sciences. Why is it important that a study contains them all?

First, there is a long and complicated *history* of the diaconate, and Fr. Shawn serves as a conversant tour guide through it. He summarizes the attention that the meaning of "diakonia" has lately received, scriptural sources, the patristic foundational practices, the little-known phenomenon of the medieval archdeacon, and the effect that scholastic sacerdotal theology had upon the transitional diaconate. It is a rich and complex history, necessary for making theological conclusions. He writes of his research, "At the start of our inquiry I had no clear means of determining which roles were appropriate for diaconal charisms and which were not. The historical forms of the diaconate are a mixture of consistent patterns and divergent irregularities."[3]

When I was received as an adult into the Catholic church, someone made the comment, with a smile, that the church is like grandma's house, where nothing is ever thrown away but only stored in a cluttered attic in case we ever need it again. I smiled back, because I had already come to appreciate that the Catholic church is not a rigid monolith, stiff-jointed with old age, and therefore always behind the times. Rather, she is flexible and agile when adapting to needs. Chesterton had already convinced me of this. "It is only by the analogy of animal bodies that we suppose that old things must be stiff. It is a mere metaphor from bones and arteries. In an intellectual sense old things are flexible.... A thing as old as the Catholic Church has an accumulated armoury

3. Page 255.

and treasury to choose from; it can pick and choose among the centuries and brings one age to the rescue of another."[4] The inherent plasticity of the diaconate imposes two demands on us. The first is to study the various forms the diaconate has assumed in the past as a resource for how this ministry should be structured by the church today. Paul VI said that the diaconate is an expression of the needs and desires of the Christian communities today, that is, the church responding to particular needs. She can check her armory for what has helped in the past.

Second, the diaconate must be approached *theologically*. The people of God want to know why and how deacons are important. That is a question about the church, and it is therefore a theological question. The permanent diaconate is an ecclesiological issue (in addition to an ecclesiastical one), and its theology therefore sends ripples across numerous other fronts in ecclesiology: appreciating that deacons are genuine clerics will dilate our theology of ordination beyond merely sacerdotal categories; intimately connecting the ministry of the deacon to the ministry of the bishop creates a broader understanding of the episcopacy; seeing the deacon work beyond the parish expands the boundaries of the church in our mind to its diocesan measure; the existence of a deacon conditions our understanding of the presbyterate; the freedom the deacon has to bear the presence of Christ to those on the margins of society and the church models the outreach of the hierarchy to all persons; and we perceive how inseparably joined are word, liturgy, and charity when we see these united in the person of the deacon.

A theology of the diaconate sheds light on the hierarchy of the church as it exists above this order and below it. On the one side, the identity of those ordained to priesthood (bishop and presbyter) is further clarified when juxtaposed with one who is ordained to ministry. And, in turn, they are reminded of the foundational identity they were given when ordained to the state of cleric. On the other side, the vocational call of the laity is illuminated by the service the deacon gives them. John Paul II says the central mystery is God's plan to bring all things under the headship of Christ, and if all the baptized are predestined for this, he then wants to know what is the specific dimension of the service of deacons. He answers, "The sacramental grace of his ordination is meant to strengthen him and to make his efforts fruitful, even as his secular occupation gives him entry into the temporal sphere in a way that is normally

---

4. G. K. Chesterton, *The Catholic Church and Conversion* (San Francisco, Calif.: Ignatius Press, 2006), 113–14.

not appropriate for other members of the clergy.... The service of the deacon is the Church's service sacramentalized."[5]

Third, any discussion of the diaconate must consider its *pastoral* expression. This is why Fr. Shawn is so attentive to the Magisterial documents of the church, ranging from constitutions of the Second Vatican Council to the Code of Canon Law. He brings the experience of a presbyter familiar with pastoral ministry; he has served as head of the USCCB's Secretariat for Clergy, Consecrated Life and Vocations; he worked with seminary formation while teaching at the Pontifical College Josephinum; and he has served on the faculty of St. Meinrad Permanent Deacon Formation Program. From this experience in ministry, administration, and formation comes a very different sort of book than if someone had written it in an ivory tower with a theoretical understanding alone. The history and theology arrives at suggestions for new frontiers of ministry by the diaconate for the reader to ponder and develop.

Fourth, Fr. Shawn's special contribution is the incorporation of the human sciences into this theological investigation. One would be cautious, or even skeptical, about a ham-handed application of sociology conducted in the hands of an amateur to dilute the vertical theological verities with horizontal social sciences, or substitute the latter for the former. Fr. Shawn describes more clearly than most people I have read how the church is a social body as well as a mystical one. The church is more than a social reality, but we must also say the church *has* a social reality. The famous eighth paragraph of *Lumen Gentium* establishes this for us. On the one hand, the church is an entity with visible delineation, a society of hierarchical organs, and a visible assembly; but on the other hand, the church is a community of faith receptive to Christ's communicated truth and grace, a mystical body, and a spiritual community enriched with heavenly things. And the main conclusion of the paragraph is that these "are not to be considered as two realities.... Rather, they form one complex reality which coalesces from a divine and a human element." If so, then our understanding of the diaconate benefits from a theological discussion of the divine element *and* a sociological examination of the human element. Fr. Shawn's work therefore adds the resources of sociology and anthropology to the theological sources of scripture, liturgy, patristic-era texts, theologians, and Magisterial teachings to conclude that the deacon can be understood as "social intermediary and symbol of communitas" who serves the participation

---

5. Pope John Paul II, *Meeting with the Men Ordained to the Permanent Diaconate* (Detroit), September 19, 1987; available at www.vatican.va.

of the laity in the life and ministry of the church. This research proposes "that intermediate structures are necessary to ensure the sufficient distribution of knowledge and power. Intermediate institutions satisfy the need to legitimate authority within a given society when they are effective in making the leadership aware of the needs of the people and when they communicate the concern of the leadership back to the people."[6] The deacon serves the role of an intermediary figure between (a) the bishop and the people, and (b) between the people of God and the individual in need. Thus diaconal ministry places deacons in many concrete contexts of pastoral importance; the deacon does more than simply "help out at Mass."

This book will be exceedingly useful in the formation of permanent deacon candidates. But in addition, transitional deacons will better understand the service identity that lays the foundation for their presbyteral identity, the laity will appreciate their own vocational call in the world when they find a cleric accompanying them into the temporal sphere, the bishop will receive one more tool from grandma's attic with which to care for his flock, and a world that is sick unto death will find the church's healing arms reaching out to it in word, liturgy, and charity. This divine *diakonia* will be given special witness when it is sacramentalized by the ordained permanent deacon. This book makes us appreciate the uniqueness of the deacon.

6. Page 257.

ACKNOWLEDGMENTS

I am indebted to those whose professional guidance improved the quality of this work and made possible its completion, especially Fr. James F. Puglisi, David W. Fagerberg, John B. Martino, and Paul Higgins.

ABBREVIATIONS

AAS   *Acta Apostolicae Sedis Commentarium Officiale*

ACO   *Apostolic Church Order*

ACW   Ancient Christian Writers

ANF   *The Ante-Nicene Fathers*

AS   *Acta Synodalia*

AT   *The Apostolic Tradition of Hippolytus*

BEM   *Baptism, Eucharist and Ministry* (WCC)

CCSL   Corpus Christianorum, Series Latina

CD   *Christus Dominus*

CECDC   *Commentario Exegético al Código de Derecho Canónico*

CIC   *Codex Iuris Canonici* (Code of Canon Law) (1983)

CIC 1917   *Codex Iuris Canonici* (Code of Canon Law) (1917)

CLSAC   *The Code of Canon Law: A Text and Commentary* (CLSAC)

DA   *Didascalia Apostolorum*

Denz.   *Sources of Catholic Dogma* (ed. Denzinger)

GIRM   *General Instruction of the Roman Missal*

LG   *Lumen Gentium*

LS   Leonine Sacramentary

NABRE   *The New American Bible Revised Edition*

NE   *The New English Bible*

NJB   *The New Jerusalem Bible*

NJBC   *The New Jerome Biblical Commentary*

NPNF   *A Selected Library of the Nicene and Post-Nicene Fathers of the Christian Church, First and Second Series*

NRSV   *New Revised Standard Version*

OEPD   *De Ordinatione Episcopi, Presbyterorum et Diaconorum*

PL   *Patrologia Cursus Completus, Series Latina* (ed. Migne)

ROBPD   *Rites of Ordination of a Bishop, of Priests, and of Deacons*

SC   *Sacrosanctum Concilium*

SEA   *Statuta Ecclesiae antiqua*

TDNT   *Theological Dictionary of the New Testament*

PART 1

Theological Foundations
of the Diaconate

CHAPTER 1

Biblical *Diakonia*

In order to articulate as clearly as possible a theology of the diaconate, a proper understanding of the teaching of the Second Vatican Council on the deacon is indispensable. It was the Second Vatican Council that called for the restoration of the permanent diaconate, and the Council's Magisterial teachings are the most authoritative in recent times to speak about the deacon. So, to grasp what the church intends when she uses the words "deacon" or "diaconal ministry," we have to concentrate on the Council's dogmatic teaching. However, we should keep in mind that the mentions of the ministry of the deacon are brief, and so we cannot expect a full theological description of the nature of the diaconate. What the Council did supply was a theological foundation from which a developed articulation of the nature and ministry of the deacon could be fashioned. In light of this foundation, the authorities within the church have made concrete decisions in their process of reestablishing the permanent diaconate in the years since Vatican II. In the post-conciliar documents we sometimes see a more concrete and detailed description of the deacon than in the conciliar decrees themselves. One can therefore rightfully speak of a general development in the theology of the deacon over the last fifty years in these later texts, but this cannot be supposed in every case.

Three passages of Council documents concern the reestablishment of the diaconate as a permanent state. First, in the decree on the Eastern Catholic churches, *Ecclesia Orientalium*, the Council stated its ardent desire for the restoration of the diaconate in the East, "so that the ancient discipline of the sacrament of orders may flourish again in the eastern churches."[1] Second, in the

---

1. Vatican Council II, *Ecclesia Orientalium*, November 21, 1964, no. 17. Unless otherwise cited, all conciliar decrees (including English translations) are from *Decrees of the Ecumenical Councils*, ed. Norman Tanner (Washington, D.C.: Georgetown University Press, 1990); translation from ibid., 2:905.

decree on the missions, *Ad Gentes* (no. 16), the Council gave its mandate to restore the permanent diaconate in the West, teaching that men who already perform diaconal functions would be strengthened by the sacrament of orders and bound more closely to the altar. The third and most significant teaching of the Council on the diaconate is found in the Dogmatic Constitution on the Church, *Lumen Gentium* (hereafter LG).[2]

The theological kernel of the conciliar teaching on the diaconate is found in just two concise sentences in LG 29, the Council's initial mandate for the reestablishment of the diaconate as a permanent state in the Latin West: "At a lower degree of the hierarchy stand the deacons, on whom hands are imposed 'not for the priesthood [*sacerdotium*], but for the ministry [*ministerium*].' For strengthened by sacramental grace, they are at the service of the people of God in the ministry of liturgy, the word and charity, in communion with the bishop and his presbyterium."[3] This text captures quite succinctly the theological "fundamentals" of the Latin rite diaconate. In this passage, the Council describes the diaconate as follows: (1) as a rank of the ordained ministry intended for service; (2) which is exercised in the three areas of liturgy, word, and charity; (3) in communion with the bishop and his presbyterate; (4) for the benefit of the people of God. A thorough investigation of the phrase "not for the priesthood, but for the ministry" is worthwhile. My analysis of this phrase will lead to the consideration of a more ancient and complete formula found in the *Apostolic Tradition* attributed to Hippolytus.[4] The nuance between *sacerdotium* and *ministerium* needs to be brought out clearly, for it is within these words that the distinction between deacon and presbyter lies. A study of the phrase can also help us see how the deacon's service is "in communion with the bishop and his presbyters" toward the people of God.

Yet, before we begin a study of the phrase that has roots going back to the third century, we should ask why the Council used the words *diaconi* and *diaconia* in describing the deacon and his ministry. It is not as obvious as it may seem. These are the Latinized forms of the Greek words διάκονοι and διακονία. Why did the Council use these loan-words instead of the Latin equivalents *ministri* and *ministerium*? The Council fathers evidently wanted to root the renewed diaconate in the biblical witness. We see a similar move in LG 24, where the fathers made this direct connection in their statement referring to the office of the

2. Vatican Council II, *Lumen Gentium*, November 21, 1964; available at www.vatican.va.

3. *Decrees* (ed. Tanner), 2:874.

4. Alphonse Borras, "Le diaconat exercé en permanence: restauration ou rétablissement?," *Nouvelle revue théologique* 118, no. 6 (1996): 824–25.

bishop: "This office which the Lord entrusted to the shepherds of his people is a true service, and in holy scripture it is significantly called '*diaconia*' or ministry."[5]

The use of the biblical word *diaconia* is often repeated in the post-conciliar documents on the permanent diaconate, most especially in the joint publication by the Congregation of Catholic Education and the Congregation for the Clergy. I shall therefore turn my attention firstly to a study of the use of διακονία (*diakonia*) and διάκονος (*diakonos*) in the New Testament so that we may then arrive at a nuanced understanding of the phrase "in the ministry of liturgy, the word, and charity."

Diakonia in the New Testament

There is a direct link between the English word "deacon" and the Greek title *diakonos*. The cognate words of the Greek noun, in contrast, did not become part of English by transliteration. The verb *diakonein* did not become "to deacon" but "to minister," from the Latin *ministrare*. We see the difference most clearly in 1 Timothy 3:13, where we read of those "who minister as deacons": here both "minister" and "deacons" are *diakon*-words in Greek. There has always been a need for a special title for the deacon lest his diaconate be confused with other types of ministry or service designated in the Christian scriptures as διακονία.[6] Given this intimate historical and linguistic link, the definition commonly accepted of these Greek words will naturally bear upon the assessment that is made of the deacon and his office today.

A Paradigm Shift: From "Waiter" to "Go-Between"

Diakonia and other members of the *diakon*-word group in Greek are commonly read as "humble service," a meaning that can be traced back to early twentieth-century German scholars Wilhelm Brandt and Herman Beyer.[7] In Beyer's estimation the sphere of meaning that the ancient Greeks attributed to

5. *Decrees* (ed. Tanner), 2:868.

6. John N. Collins, *Diakonia: Re-interpreting the Ancient Sources* (New York: Oxford University Press, 1990), 41.

7. Herman Beyer, διακονέω, διακονία, διάκονος," in *Theological Dictionary of the New Testament*, trans. Geoffrey W. Bromiley (Grand Rapids, Mich.: Eerdmans, 1964–76), 2:81–93 (hereafter TDNT); Wilhelm Brandt, *Dienst und Dienen im Neuen Testament* (Gütersloh: Bertelsmann Verlag, 1931). The original dissertation was titled *Diakonie und das Neue Testament* (PhD diss., University of Münster, 1923), as cited in Collins, *Diakonia*, 265.

the *diakon*-word group involved: (1) something to do with waiting or attending on a person; (2) service that was common, ordinary—that is, there was nothing special about it; and (3) that the service involved menial tasks.[8] These characteristics can be summarized in the image of a "waiter." This meaning, according to Beyer, was then transformed by Christ's act of sacrificial love to leading, preaching, caring for the sick and poor, or organizing projects.[9] This "humble service" understanding of deacon has had a profound influence on how Christian ministry in general has been conceived since the Second Vatican Council. To cite an influential (although controversial) theologian, Hans Küng described *diakonia* as "a completely ordinary, non-religious word with a somewhat humble flavor that suggests no connotations of officialdom, authority, domination, positions of dignity or power."[10]

But this long-held view has been rejected by a 1990 study of John Neil Collins, *Diakonia: Re-interpreting the Ancient Sources*, that exhaustively reexamines the Hellenic background of the *diakon*-word group in Greek non-Christian sources. Collins finds that the primary meaning of *diakonos* in those sources is technically a "go-between," one who acts at his master's bidding to convey messages and to perform tasks that require immediate attention, mobility, and speed. Often this was in association with the service of a god. The Greek god Hermes was himself known as a *diakonos*, or "herald of the gods." The service rendered by the *diakonos* could be on behalf of an individual or a group. Thus the term could also signify an emissary or representative between various groupings of individuals.[11]

While menial table service has commonly been accepted as the *diakon*-word group's sphere of reference, Collins finds that the term is never restricted to, and does not even normally designate, waiters at table. Even when used in the context of a meal, the title *diakonos* is usually an attendant at a cultic banquet, rather than the modern notion of a waiter in a restaurant. When it is used of a waiter during a cultic meal, it connotes not attention and solicitude toward the guests, but the swiftness and efficiency of one who quickly passes back and forth between kitchen and dining room. Thus *diakonos* denotes a servant who

---

8. Beyer, "διακονέω," 82.

9. Ibid., 84–88.

10. Hans Küng, *Why Priests?*, trans. Robert Collins (Garden City: Doubleday, 1972), 39.

11. In the Greek Septuagint, the verb *diakonein* is never used. The common noun *diakonos* occurs seven times, most often in the Book of Esther. The abstract noun *diakonia* occurs three times. In the few instances that it is used, *diakonos* connotes an attendant or servant, usually in the royal sense. See Collins, *Diakonia*, 77–132.

is "on the move." The term *diakonos* also acquires connotations of officialdom when it is used for an ambassador or diplomat. A *diakonos* would not normally signify "one who performs a menial task," but rather describe someone of an elevated status. *Diakonia* calls to mind the service rendered, either in the delivery of a message or in actions, between the authority who gives the mission or mandate and the person or group of persons to whom the service is rendered.[12]

Collins's study, which has generally been well-received among those scripture scholars who have discussed it, does preserve some portions of the older understanding of *diakonia* as "humble service."[13] Both recognize the personal nature of the service it signifies. Both also recognize that the content of the service can be either the spoken word (in the case of a messenger) or deeds (serving as an intermediary between kitchen and table). However, the new understanding adjusts the older one in a variety of respects that have implications for our contemporary ministry of the diaconate. First, the sense "to serve at table" has been replaced by the "go-between," which does not necessarily involve the idea of "humble activity." Secondly, *diakonia* does not mean a service of "inferior value," but rather something special, even dignified. The notion of a "service of love" is confirmed, but also specified by the idea of "mission" or "mandate." Third, the biblical notion of *diakonia* is largely the same as that of the ancient Greek world: the service performed by one who is commissioned by another for a particular, often mediating responsibility. The *diakonos* was not principally a servant at table, but an intermediary: one entrusted with a message or commission by another. Consequently, the fourth change of perspective centers on who performs *diakonia*. If the root meaning is the service rendered by a "go-between," then only those individuals with a mandate or commission perform *diakonia*. The implications of this last point of difference are important for our understanding of Christian ministry today: does *diakonia* as any "service of love" apply to all the baptized, or does it only refer to those with a mandate to perform a particular mission within the church?

12. See ibid., 73–191.

13. Collins has continued to publish other works since this book—see especially *Diakonia Studies: Critical Issues in Ministry* (New York: Oxford University Press, 2014)—and his conclusions have been recognized and incorporated by several authors of the Sacra Pagina series, such as *Dictionary of Paul and His Letters*, ed. Gerald F. Hawthorne et al. David L. Bartlett, in his *Ministry in the New Testament*, acknowledges the validity of Collins's thesis in at least some, if not all, New Testament passages concerning *diakonia* and ministry. No one to date has successfully contested the heart of Collins's thesis as to the issues of grammar, syntax, usage, and social and literary contexts that contribute to the meaning of the *diakon*-word group.

Of course, the Council did not have the benefit of Collins's later scholarship when they used the terms *diaconia* and *diaconi*. Hence, it would be anachronistic to ascribe this "emissary" understanding to the Council fathers. On the other hand, it seems dubious to posit that the Council fathers would have recommended adhering to any particular biblical interpretation against a more thorough and accurate understanding of the diaconate in the Bible. Rather, by rooting the new diaconate in the Bible, they left the door open for a greater understanding of the biblical texts to illuminate the contemporary ministry of the deacon. With these considerations in mind, I will start with one of the central claims of the older "waiter" understanding of *diakonia;* that the *diakon* words underwent a change in meaning under the shadow of the cross. I shall therefore consider first the passages that reveal the *Christological* character of the *diakon*-word group. Next, I will look to the use of *diakonia* in the Pauline corpus to understand its *pneumatological and ecclesial* natures. Having considered those three characters—Christological, pneumatological, and ecclesial—I will then focus on two passages in the Pauline corpus and one in the Book of Acts that have been commonly associated with the particular "office" of deacon. Working through the careful details of the biblical texts, we will see that the New Testament does provide a foundation for understanding the contemporary ministry of the deacon, but not with all of the clarity that we may want the texts to provide.

The Christological Character of New Testament *Diakonia*

In the image of Jesus in the New Testament, and his teachings about service, it is apparent that the Christian life entails a "service of love." One of the key features of the New Testament understanding of Jesus is the manner in which the various intermediary functions occurring in the Old Testament are synthesized in Jesus—"Son of Man," messiah, prophet, servant.[14] Of these, none is more basic and interpretative of the others than is that of the Suffering Servant, which is quite clearly used in reference to the servant hymns of the Book of Isaiah.[15] Je-

---

14. Joachim Jeremias, *New Testament Theology*, trans. John Bowden (New York: SCM Press, 1971), 272–99.

15. These passages are commonly ascribed to "Deutero-Isaiah," on the widely-held theory that different portions of the book were composed at different times. Joachim Jeremias, "παις Θεου," TDNT 5:654–717, esp. 698–713. See Roland E. Murphy, "Second Isaiah: The Servant of the Lord," *Catholic Biblical Quarterly* 9 (1947): 273–74.

sus's ministry was viewed by the early church as service, a service which realized the expectations expressed in the Old Testament servant ideal.[16]

The context of Jesus's mission is portrayed poetically in Paul's letter to the Philippians. In this letter Paul incorporated a Christological hymn that expresses quite beautifully the humble way of Jesus for us. Paul wrote (2:5–8):

> Let the same mind be in you that was in Christ Jesus,
> who, though he was in the form of God,
> did not regard equality with God
> as something to be exploited,
> but emptied himself [*ekenosen*],
> taking the form of a slave [*doulos*],
> being born in human likeness.
> And being found in human form,
> he humbled himself
> and became obedient to the point of death—
> even death on a cross.

The Christ hymn presents the incarnation in terms of servanthood. The way of Jesus Christ is the way of *kenosis*, self-emptying. Through his *kenosis* Jesus became *doulos* (a slave) for us. This is the course Jesus would continue to follow throughout his earthly life and ministry.

Jesus made a deliberate choice at the very beginning of his earthly ministry about what kind of messiah he would be. The temptation stories are commonly read in this light. The devil tempted Jesus, first to be a messiah who would satisfy his own physical hunger; second, to be a miracle-working messiah; and third, to be a political messiah (Mt 4:1–11, Lk 4:1–13). Jesus rejected these temptations of domination, choosing to accept the role suggested by the divine commission at his baptism (Mt 3:13–17, Mk 1:10–11, Lk 4:21–22). As Jesus came out of the water, "a voice came from heaven, 'You are my Son, the Beloved; with you I am well pleased'" (Mk 1:11). These words of the Father reflect the servant's commissioning in Isaiah 42:1.[17] In remaining faithful to his mission, Jesus sought to fulfill the needs of others rather than his own. Not only did Jesus remain faithful to the will of the Father, he also commanded his disciples to be faithful to their call. The fidelity of Jesus in his humble service

---

16. Bernard Cooke, *Ministry to Word and Sacraments: History & Theology* (Philadelphia: Fortress Press, 1976), 343.

17. Kevin Giles, *The Patterns of Ministry among the First Christians* (Melbourne: Collins Dove, 1989), 51–52.

becomes the new standard to live by, a standard contrary to the way of the world.

John's Gospel incorporates a parable-in-action of Jesus at the Last Supper. In order to demonstrate what service means, Jesus "got up from the table, took off his outer robe, and tied a towel around himself. Then he poured water into a basin and began to wash the disciples' feet and to wipe them with the towel that was tied around him" (Jn 13:4–5). Jesus assumed the role of a slave (*doulos*) by undressing and washing the feet of his disciples. Jesus goes on to say: "If I, your Lord and Teacher, have washed your feet, you also ought to wash one another's feet. For I have set you an example, that you also should do as I have done to you" (Jn 13:14–15). In no uncertain terms Jesus taught that faithful service is an essential, a *sine qua non*, of the Christian life. Those who were to be apostles were to recognize their life as a mission to provide service to others.

The synoptic Gospels show that the apostles were slow to develop this mindset, as they are depicted as bickering over who was greatest. Jesus's response is recorded in three related passages; Matthew and Mark place this saying of Jesus during the ascent of him and the Twelve to Jerusalem, while Luke places the saying during the Last Supper:

You know that among the Gentiles those whom they recognize as their rulers lord it over them, and their great ones are tyrants over them. But it is not so among you; but whoever wishes to become great among you must be your servant [*diakonos*], and whoever wishes to be first among you must be slave of all. For the Son of Man came not to be served [*diakonethenai*] but to serve [*diakonesai*], and to give his life a ransom for many.[18]

The kings of the Gentiles lord it over them; and those in authority over them are called benefactors. But not so with you; rather the greatest among you must become like the youngest, and the leader like one who serves [*ho diakonon*]. For who is greater, the one who is at the table or the one who serves [*ho diakonon*]? Is it not the one at the table? But I am among you as one who serves [*ho diakonon*].[19]

In rebuking the arrogance of the Twelve, Jesus presents a counter-cultural ethical teaching of service to one's neighbor. He identifies himself as "one who serves," and expresses in both Luke and Mark (along with Mathew's parallel passage of Mark) the idea that the disciples must be least, lowly or last as "one who serves."

In the statements "the Son of Man came not to be served but to serve" and

18. Mk 10:42–45.
19. Lk 22:25–27.

"I am among you as one who serves," Jesus identifies himself as a *diakonos*. This claim is made in the context of an ethical teaching about how his followers—in particular those who will be leaders among them—are to exercise their authority. On this point, Beyer's comment is therefore justified:

> Jesus' view of service grows out of the OT command of love for one's neighbor, which He takes and links with the command of love for God to constitute the substance of the divinely willed ethical conduct of His followers ... Jesus' attitude to service is completely new as compared with the Greek understanding. The decisive point is that He sees in it the thing which makes a man his disciple.[20]

In the saying about the Son of Man, Mark does indeed contrast the status of the wealthy and powerful of this world, surrounded by attendants, and the work of the Son of Man, who goes about carrying out the tasks assigned to him by the Father. As the model for his disciples, Jesus abolishes in advance all privileges of clerical triumphalism. The church's leaders are not to be attended by servants, who may be ordered around at will. The critical question for us, however, is not whether Jesus called his disciples to follow the form of service that is self-emptying, but whether or not the new ethical teaching of Jesus is rooted in the specific word choice of the *diakon*-word group in these related passages by the Gospel writers, or is *diakon* meant to convey something more? While Beyer sees only humble service here, Collins sees more.

Specifically, Collins sees not only an ethical but also a theological component. In this passage from Mark, Jesus recognizes that he is fulfilling a mission from the Father.[21] The *diakon*-words refer to this virtue of fidelity or obedience in one who is sent. His suffering and death would result from remaining faithful to the mission he received from the Father to preach the kingdom. Here is the connection between the *diakonia* of Jesus and the humble nature of his salvific death. It is not because the service of Jesus is humble that the writer used the *diakon*-word group, but rather because *obedience* to the mission Jesus received from the Father would necessarily involve his salvific death. He came not to have attendants waiting on him, but to fulfill his charge from the Father, which required suffering and death.

The final passage that I shall consider in the examination of *diakonia* in the context of the shadow of the cross is a pericope unique to the Gospel of Mat-

---

20. Beyer, "διακονέω," 84.

21. Collins, *Diakonia*, 251. "The infinitive itself, no less than the title 'the Son of man' and the prophetic verb 'came,' speaks of a particular personal commission under God, and from this point of view the statement is at once more theological than ethical."

thew. In the famous final judgment scene (Mt 25:31–46), Jesus preaches the ultimate value of compassion and genuine concern for one's neighbor as the criteria for final judgment, thus demanding a very different standard than the religious leaders of his day, and than the world which pays more attention to the rich and powerful.[22] In the first section (vv. 31–40) Jesus speaks to the just and lists the actions which would render them worthy to enter the kingdom: feeding the hungry, giving drink to the thirsty, welcoming the stranger, clothing the naked, caring for the sick, visiting prisoners. In the second section (vv. 41–46) the same acts are listed again when Jesus speaks to the wicked about their failure in living up to his standard as judge. The wicked respond to Jesus and ask, "Lord, when was it that we saw you hungry or thirsty or a stranger or naked or sick or in prison, and did not take care [diakonesamen] of you?" (v. 44).

Thus, the list of "good deeds" seem to be summarized under the verb diakonein. Are we to understand, as Beyer does, that this passage reveals the kind of service (i.e., humble service) intended by the diakon-word group?[23]

Collins's interpretation of this passage turns on a couple of points that might normally be missed in a cursory reading of the text. First of all, it is important to notice that Jesus and the just only speak of "giving," "clothing," "welcoming," "caring," and "visiting"; they do not use diakonein. It is only the wicked who use the verb diakonein, while never using the verbs of the different forms of the service of love. Is this a form of shorthand, in which diakonein would signify the same thing as the services of love mentioned previously? Collins sees the matter differently from Beyer. He suggests that we should recognize that the wicked are trying to talk their way out of a sticky situation by using a word, "minister," which is appropriate to a court setting.[24] Thus even in this passage, where at first glance diakonia seems to signify simple humble service, it more than likely bears a more nuanced meaning: humble service as a result of fidelity to the divine commission.

From my study of the scriptural passages concerning the image of Jesus as diakonos and his teaching of humble leadership, we can see that the opinion of Collins can be affirmed: the diakon-word group technically signifies not hum-

---

22. See David C. Sim, *Apocalyptic Eschatology in the Gospel of Matthew*, Society for New Testament Studies: Monograph Series 88 (Cambridge: Cambridge University Press, 1996), 123–26.

23. Beyer, "διακονέω," 85.

24. Collins, *Diakonia*, 65. "Might we not take a clue from the awesome solemnity of an occasion when a devastating judgement has been handed down by a king and anticipate some deviousness, born of despair, on the part of those against whom the judgement has gone? In other words we should perhaps view the wicked at this moment as fawning upon the king and in their appeal using an appropriate term from the language of the court, 'minister.'"

ble service, but the performance of deeds in the fulfillment of a mandate. In the case of Jesus, this is the divine commission that he received in his baptism at the Jordan from the Father. But we can also affirm with Beyer that for Christians, leadership in the church can never take the form of self-service. Thus, while technically signifying the service of one acting on behalf, or by authority of another, *diakonia* in the New Testament can never be conceived apart from the model and teaching of Jesus: fidelity in the service of God always includes serving the needs of others. Rooted in the very nature of Jesus's ministry, an authentically Christian *diakonia*, or better yet, an "apostolic *diakonia*" concerns how power and authority from God are to be exercised among the community of believers: for the good of others and not in self-service. As such, to affirm the core of Collins's thesis does not require one to exclude selfless service in biblical *diakonia*. There are many types of "service"—*diakonia* perhaps being only one category of them—but all Christian service, rooted in its Christological principle, necessarily involves love for neighbor as well as love for God. It is therefore important that we recognize the biblical context of the type or genre of service that *diakonia* technically indicates. The significance of this double affirmation will be kept in mind, as we proceed to review the use of the *diakon*-word group in the Pauline corpus.

The Pneumatological and Ecclesial Character of *Diakonia*

The Pauline texts present a variety of undifferentiated uses of *diakonia* and its cognates, with the single office like that of the diaconate today being only one of many.[25] It has often been stated that there is a tension in some New Testament passages between the ideal that all believers are to partake in *diakonia* of some sort, and the reality that some are "ministers" in a special sense. The fundamental text is 1 Corinthians 12:4–6, where Paul asserts that there are varieties of "gifts" (*charismaton*), varieties of "services" (*diakonion*), and varieties of "activities" (*energematon*), but the same Spirit, Lord and God. The other text we will consider is from Ephesians 4:11–12, where the author of the epistle expresses his understanding of the goal for which some have been given special functions among the community of believers. It is acknowledged that all members of the body of Christ have some contribution to make, but in what way does *diakonia* signify a particular kind of service, as Collins claims?

25. Here I refer to all material in the tradition of Paul, whether authored by him or not.

1 Corinthians 12

The twelfth chapter of Paul's letter to the Corinthians is famous for its discussion of the spiritual gifts and the unity of the "body of Christ" in light of those gifts, against those who would be proud of their gifts or envious of others. ("Gift" is the usual translation of the word the Greek word *charisma*.) Anyone within the community who disdains the gifts given to any other member disdains the work of the Spirit. The one God, working through the Spirit, is the common source of all the gifts. The exercise of the gifts that have been given is the way in which each Christian serves one and the same Lord. Present in the Christian, these gifts are the means by which God acts within the community. Paul uses what we identify as verses 12:4–6 to introduce this argument:

> Now there are varieties of gifts [*charismaton*], but the same Spirit;
> and there are varieties of services [*diakonion*], but the same Lord;
> and there are a varieties of activities [*energematon*], but the same God
> who activates all of them in everyone.

The three verses constitute a rhetorical *partitio*: that is, they divide the argument that will follow. Mention of the spiritual gifts (v. 4) anticipates the discussion of these gifts (vv. 7–11). Mention of the single Lord (v. 5) prepares for the discussion of the body of Christ (vv. 12–26). Finally the working of God (v. 6) prepares for the third section of the chapter, where the charisms are identified as coming from God (vv. 28–32).[26]

Later on (v. 7) Paul reaffirms: "To each is given the manifestation of the Spirit for the common good." Thus everyone has been given some gift of the Spirit, though not the same for everyone, and they are all for the benefit of the one body.[27] Thus there are apparently three parallel statements in verses 4–6. Are they total parallels, or do they express a contrast? Some scholars claim a Trinitarian unity in the threefold parallel. If gifts are associated with the Spirit (Πνεῦμα) in verse 4, services associated with Jesus, the Lord (Κύριος) in verse 5, and activities are associated with the Father, God (Θεος) in verse 6, this must have been intended by Paul to say that each of these three words (gifts, services, activities) are equivalent.[28] We can describe this common "complete-

---

26. Raymond F. Collins, *First Corinthians*, Sacra Pagina 7 (Collegeville, Minn.: Liturgical Press, 1999), 449.

27. Ibid.

28. Archibald Robertson and Alfred Plummer (eds.), *A Critical and Exegetical Commentary on the First Epistle of St. Paul to the Corinthians*, 2nd ed. (Edinburgh: T. and T. Clark, 1911–71), 262.

ly parallel" interpretation with an equation: gifts = services = activities. If this is the equation that Paul wanted to put forward, then indeed all in the church have gifts, all perform services (which could also be translated "ministries"), and all are equipped for "activities." Thomas O'Meara describes the relationship between them in his *Theology of Ministry*: "The horizon of the Spirit in baptized men and women is a life which is charismatic in terms of its source, but diaconal in terms of its goal. Spirit leads to ministry."[29]

On the other hand, what appear to be interchangeable words in this pericope may in fact be something else. Collins holds that *charismata* is the genus, and that services [*diakoniai*] and activities [*energemata*] are different species of *charismata*.[30] Instead of the equation given above, this view point is expressed diagramatically as follows:

FIGURE 1.1

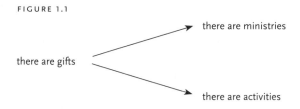

there are gifts

there are ministries

there are activities

Paul's point in this whole section of his letter, after all, is the unity-in-diversity of divine gifts, not their identity. Collins observes that the church "would be endangered if its members thought all members had every gift, and in particular if its members thought they were all ministers."[31] Later on in verse 19 Paul asks the Corinthians, "If all were a single member, where would the body be?"

This interpretation leads to a very different understanding of the word *diakonia*. If *charismata* = *diakoniai* and *diakoniai* = *energemata*, then a very broad understanding of the *diakon*-word is to be accepted. If, however, *diakoniai* are a species of *charismata*, then it is possible that the *diakon*-word group has a particular meaning distinct from the rest. But it is important to realize that even if 1 Corinthians 12 is referring to *diakoniai* as a special mandate for ministry, distinct from *energemata*, they are still *charismata*, gifts to the church from God. Here we have the pneumatological principle of *diakonia*.

29. Thomas O'Meara, *Theology of Ministry* (New York: Paulist Press, 1983), 61.

30. John N. Collins, "Forum: God's Gifts to Congregations," *Worship* 69 (1994): 246.

31. John N. Collins, "A Ministry for Tomorrow's Church," *Journal of Ecumenical Studies* 32 (1995): 173.

Ephesians 4:11–12

The ecclesial character of *diakonia* is found in Ephesians 4, which has themes of the unity of the body of Christ and the diversity of God's gifts that parallel 1 Corinthians 12. Here the "gifts" of God are quite explicitly, in chapters 11 and 12, various functionaries within the church: "And he gave some as apostles, others as prophets, others as evangelists, others as pastors and teachers, to equip the holy ones for the work of ministry [*diakonias*], for building up the body of Christ."[32] Notice that many functionaries are listed, but "the deacon" is not one of them. Rather, "the work of ministry [*diakonias*]" is related to the activity that the apostles, prophets, evangelists, and pastors and teachers are doing. But there is some debate about how it is related. The older interpretation, which Collins aims to revive, would put a comma between "to equip the holy ones" and "for the ministry." Commas, we should remember, are not part of the original Greek text but are rather inserted to help make sense of the text—they are already interpretations. Adding a comma would essentially read an implied "and" in this statement: that is, God gives us these ministers both (a) to equip the holy ones and (b) for the work of ministry, all with the end goal of building up the body of Christ.[33] For Collins, his interpretation of *diakonia* in this passage as a function necessarily exclusive to teachers requires him to read the first two phrases as two separate objectives.[34] But he is not alone even among recent scholars.[35]

On the other hand, all of the most recent English translations do not include a comma between the two phrases.[36] The footnote on this verse for

---

32. *New American Bible Revised Edition* (hereafter NABRE).

33. See Maximillian Zerwick and Mary Grosvenor, *A Grammatical Analysis of the Greek New Testament* (Rome: Editrice Pontificio Istituo Biblico, 1996), 585.

34. Collins, *Diakonia*, 233–34.

35. Rudolph Schnackenburg, *The Epistle to the Ephesians: A Commentary*, trans. Helen Heron (Edinburgh: T. and T. Clark, 1991), 183–84: "Contrary to the majority of interpreters and translations which opt for the combination 'to prepare the saints for a work of service,' the preference would then deservedly be given to the interpretation that Christ entrusted the people mentioned in v. 11—who were to prepare, to encourage the saints (perhaps even: in view of)—with a work of ministry, had in fact "given" them to his Church for the very purpose of building-up his Body with their help and in the combined activity of all the faithful. No exceptional position is thereby given to the 'office-bearers.' If in v. 7 each single individual in the Church is awarded a gift of grace by Christ and only in vv. 8–11 is special consideration given to the leading members, these are included in the general guarantee of grace which serves the building-up of Christ's Body. Only their special ministries in the Church and for the Church are emphasized, for reasons which are more clearly recognisable in vv. 13f."

36. *New Revised Standard Version* (hereafter NRSV): "some should be apostles, some prophets,

NABRE puts it well: "The ministerial leaders in Eph 4:11 are to equip the whole people of God for their work of ministry." This reading may be influenced by Beyer and the "humble service" view of *diakonia.*

The dispute boils down to how to relate the first and the second phrases in verse 12, "for a work of ministry," with "for the equipment of the saints." If the two phrases express two objectives—"for the equipment of the saints [and] for the work of ministry"—then the work of ministry refers to the multiple "teachers" previously listed, but not all the "holy ones." If they express only one objective—"to equip the saints for the work of ministry"—then the author implies that all the holy ones are meant to exercise *diakonia.*

Whichever interpretation is correct, the goal of *diakonia* is clear: the building up of the body of Christ. There need be no contradiction between the "special ministries" of the leaders and the "gifts" of each single individual in the church. Special consideration is given to the leading members by the author of the letter to the Ephesians, as they are part of the general guarantee of grace for the maturation of the Christian community. Seeing a special role for leaders in the building up of Christ's body echoes Paul's statement in 2 Corinthians 10:8, where he writes: "Now, even if I boast a little too much of our authority, which the Lord gave for building you up and not for tearing you down, I will not be ashamed of it." Thus, it is understood that the work of the "leading members" is to "make complete, strive for perfection, to prepare" every member of the church.[37] In bringing to fruition the gifts (mentioned in v. 7) of all "the saints," the unity of faith and knowledge of the Son of God is ensured. In this manner *diakonia* is understood in the ecclesial context: both the church as a whole has a mission to accomplish—to attain "the fullness of Christ"—and the "leading members" have a special mandate within this overall task of the church, namely, to help bring to fruition the faith of the other members. The ministers serve to build up the body of Christ by placing their unique spiritual charisms in service to the mission of the entire church.

---

some evangelists, some pastors and teachers, to equip the saints for the work of ministry." *The New English Bible* (hereafter NEB): "to equip God's people for work in his service." *The New Jerusalem Bible* (hereafter NJB): "to knit God's people together for the work of service." The Vulgate is ambiguous: "ad consummationem sanctorum in opus ministerii in aedificationem corporis Christi."

37. Barclay Newman Jr., *A Concise Greek-English Dictionary of the New Testament* (Stuttgart: Deutsche Bibelgesellschaft, 1993), 95.

The Office of Deacon in the New Testament

The word *diakonos* in the New Testament stands for more than a "deacon" in the modern sense. Within the New Testament there are three general headings for the various *diakonoi:* (1) spokesmen and emissaries of heaven, (2) emissaries in the church, and (3) commissions under God, church, and Spirit. Under "spokesmen and emissaries of heaven," we can include Paul (1 Cor 3:5; 2 Cor 3:6, 6:4, 11:23; Col 1:23, 25), Apollos (1 Cor 3:5), the collaborators Tychicus (Eph 6:21) and Epaphras (Col 1:7, 4:7), and the angels (Heb 1:14) as ministers of heaven. In all of these accounts, *diakonos* signifies messengers, on assignment from God or Christ, mediating between heaven and earth.[38] Under "emissaries in the church" there are Paul (Acts 11:29, 12:25; Rom 15:25, 31; 2 Cor 8:4, 19, 20, 9:1, 12, 13), Stephanas (1 Cor 16:15) and Phoebe (Rom 16:1). The function of the *diakonoi* here concerns primarily the affairs between the various churches. The collection for the Jerusalem church is a prime example. Under "commissions" there are two special occurrences. One is the Roman government (Rom 13:4) and Christ (Gal 2:17 and Rom 15:8). The other is commissions within the church, and we find the Seven (Acts 6:1–2), and Timothy (1 Thes 3:2). In this category, ministry is performed by way of delegation or "commissioning" by those in authority within the Christian community.

Is there a similar use of *diakonos,* where the diaconate can be found as a separate and distinct office in the New Testament? Where do we find a *diakonos,* when the Vulgate has the word *diaconus* instead of *minister,* that can appropriately be translated "deacon" into English?

Acts 6:1–6

The text of Acts 6:1–6, the appointment of the Seven by the apostles with prayer and the laying on of hands, has been considered from the time of Irenaeus of Lyons as the scriptural institution of the office or order of deacon, and of Stephen as the first deacon.[39] Irenaeus's interpretation of Acts 6, however, is

38. For a more exhaustive listing of persons implied as *diakonoi,* see William F. Moulton and Alfred S. Geden, *A Concordance to the Greek New Testament* (New York: Charles Scribner's Sons, 1897–1957), 203.

39. Joseph Lécuyer, "Les diacres dans le nouveau testament," in *Les diacre dans l'Eglise et le monde d'aujourd'hui,* ed. Joseph Lécuyer, Paul Winninger, and Yves Congar, Unam Sanctam 59 (Paris: Cerf, 1966), 24–25. Lécuyer notes that there are exceptions to the tradition begun by Irenaeus, including John Chrysostom, the Synod of Trullo (692 A.D.), and the Greek canonists of the twelfth century who commented on the canons of this council.

considered anachronistic by modern scholars. The importance of this passage in the understanding of the diaconate throughout history makes it worthwhile to recall here:

[1] At that time, as the number of disciples continued to grow, the Hellenists complained against the Hebrews because their widows were being neglected *in the daily distribution* [*en te diakonia te kathemerine*]. [2] So the Twelve called together the community of the disciples and said, "It is not right for us to neglect the word of God *to serve at table* [*diakonein trapedzais*]. [3] Brothers, select from among you seven reputable men, filled with the Spirit and wisdom, whom we shall appoint to this task, [4] whereas we shall devote ourselves to prayer and *to the ministry of the word* [*diakonia tou logou*]. [5] The proposal was acceptable to the whole community, so they chose Stephen, a man filled with faith and the holy Spirit, also Philip, Prochorus, Nicanor, Timon, Parmenas, and Nicolas of Antioch, a convert to Judaism. [6] They presented these men to the apostles who prayed and laid hands on them.

This passage is followed by the account of Stephen's successful ministry, his arrest, defense before the Sanhedrin, and his martyrdom (Acts 6:8–8:3). After the martyrdom of Stephen comes the account of Philip's ministry in Samaria, with the incidents of Simon Magus and the conversion of the Ethiopian eunuch (Acts 8:4–40).

The placement of this passage within Acts is somewhat awkward. Luke begins the story of Stephen and Philip with an abrupt change of mood. Without any explanation, a whole new class of Christians appear, "the Hellenists," as distinct from "the Hebrews."[40] For the first time Luke uses the term "disciples" (*matheton*) (v. 1) for Christians, and the only use of "the Twelve" (*hoi dodeka*) (v. 2) for the apostles.[41] Scholars therefore think that the pericope on the institution of the Seven came from a historical source that had circulated independently of Luke's tradition.[42] Luke joined this independent narrative about the institution of the Seven Hellenists to the Stephen and Philip episodes, which follow to form the present unified cycle. This does not mean that it should be seen as less reliable than other portions of Acts; indeed, it

40. Richard J. Dillon, "Acts of the Apostles," in *The New Jerome Biblical Commentary*, ed. Raymond Brown, Joseph Fitzmyer, and Roland Murphy (Englewood Cliffs, N.J.: Prentice-Hall, 1968 and 1990), 739 (hereafter NJBC).

41. Ernst Haenchen, *The Acts of the Apostles: A Commentary* (Philadelphia: Westminster Press, 1971), 260, 262.

42. See Charles K. Barrett, "Preliminary Introduction and Commentary on Acts I–XIV," *A Critical and Exegetical Commentary on the Acts of the Apostles* (Edinburgh: T. and T. Clark 1994), 1:305–6; Joseph T. Lienhard, "Acts 6:1–6: A Redactional View," *Catholic Biblical Quarterly* 37 (1975): 228–30; James D. G. Dunn, *The Acts of the Apostles*, Epworth Commentaries (Peterborough: Epworth, 1996), 79.

seems that "it had earned its own place in the tradition."[43] We can take away these basic facts from the text: a dispute arose within the early community; the Hellenists and the Hebrews were the two opposing parties in this dispute; the dispute was resolved by the appointment of the Seven, whose names are preserved, to an office within the community.[44]

In Acts, Luke is primarily concerned with recording the history of how the church overcame obstacles, resulting in the growth and spread of the church.[45] Acts emphasizes certain aspects of the original source in order to communicate that (1) a minor deficiency in administration was immediately set right, and that (2) this led to the emergence of a new group of devoted Christians.[46] Luke is more concerned with telling the story of the origin of the Hellenist Christians and the expansion of the church beyond Jerusalem, rather than the specific origin of the diaconate order. Luke's thin description of the details has left scholars to ponder and debate those things Luke chose not to amplify. Some scholars argue that the source of tension within the Jerusalem community went beyond that of the "daily distribution," involving tensions sprung from the sociological and linguistic distinction of the Hellenized Jews returned from the diaspora.[47]

Whatever the problem may have been, Luke simplifies it into a problem with what the NRSV and NABRE call the "daily distribution." The imperfect verb *paretheorounto* suggests a continuous "overlooking" of the widows in the past.[48] The "daily distribution" therefore was a function that preceded the institution of the Seven.[49] As the daily service was taking place previous to

---

43. Lienhard, "Acts," 230.

44. Ibid., 236.

45. Haenchen, *The Acts*, 100.

46. Barrett, *A Critical*, 303.

47. Beyer, "διακονέω," 85. Beyer suggests that the dispute was not over petty partiality, but over a radical difference of opinion on whether the Hellenist should be admitted to the fellowship and therefore whether they really belonged to the community. For him the committing of this service to the Hellenistic Seven implies more than a purely external release of the leaders of the community from administrative duties. See also Dunn, *The Acts of the Apostles*, 82; Haenchen, *The Acts*, 267. James D. G. Dunn and David A. Fiensy, "The Composition of the Jerusalem Church," in *The Book of Acts in its Palestinian Setting*, ed. Richard Bauckham, The Book of Acts in its First Century Setting 4 (Grand Rapids, Mich.: Eerdmans, 1995), 213–36, gives a detailed analysis of the culture and linguistic plurality in the early Jerusalem community.

48. Haenchen, *The Acts*, 268.

49. Barrett, *A Critical*, 310. Barrett remarks that *diakonia* defined as *kathemerine* recalls the Jewish custom of relieving the poor, in two ways. There was a daily distribution, consisting of basic foodstuffs given to the casual poor, and a weekly dole of food and clothing, given to poor members of the community. The relief described in Acts does not correspond precisely to either of these, as the widows were resident members of the community, yet the distribution was daily.

the institution of the Seven, there may have been an already existent group of Hebrew-speaking persons with whom the Hellenistic Seven joined in their task, whatever it may have been.[50] If we assume that Luke is correct in estimating the number of believers at an earlier time at about five thousand (Acts 4:4), and if the apostles had no other administrative helpers before the appointment of the Seven, then they would have reached the stage much sooner of complaining that their administrative work was getting in the way of their primary task of preaching the word of God.[51] This passage, consequently, may not have been about the *first* deacons, even with the assumption that the office held by the Seven was that of deacon.

Collins criticizes the NRSV translation, claiming that what is signified here is probably "public and even ritual performance of duties in the community" and not strictly the distribution *of food*.[52] In this passage Collins clearly restricts himself to the Greek understanding of the *diakon*-word group, which prevents him from seeing anything close to a "menial" task for the Seven. The main difference, to Collins, is to be found in the "daily" character of the ministry of the Seven, as opposed to that of the apostles. It is quite possible, therefore, that the duties of the Seven included ministry of various kinds, but having in common a residential or local character.

There is yet further reason to doubt that the office held by the Seven was that of deacon as it came to be understood later. Although it is true that the words *diakonein* (in v. 2 for "to wait at table") and *diakonia* (in vv. 1 and 4 for "daily distribution" and "service of the word") occur, the very term *diakonos* is not used in the description of the Seven. Nor does the rest of the New Testament ever call these men *diakonoi*. It would be unusual to set out to give an

---

50. Lécuyer, "Les diacres," 23.

51. Robert Nowell, *The Ministry of Service: Deacons in the Contemporary Church* (New York: Herder and Herder, 1968), 18.

52. All of the standard English translations share the same meaning as the NRSV in this instance. Collins, *Diakonia*, 231: "They [the apostles] are saying that their appointed ministry is not to be at tables … when they are at the command of the ministry of the word. Thus the only members of the sacred community who thus far have been instituted in an office, and by the Lord himself, choose to speak of 'ministering' at the moment when they are authorising the first church-made office. Whether the duties to be performed occur at tables where people eat or at those where people receive financial assistance is not said. The Twelve call the task 'duty,' which is a further indication of how much the passage is about commissioned roles. The duty is the *diakonia* of 6:1. So named, it is a public function under someone's direction already existing in the community; it is a 'daily' ministry in contrast with the ministry of Acts 1, which is to take the Twelve 'to the ends of the earth.' As ministry it is indeterminate, and we have to make our own estimates of the kind of care extended to the widows; the word says more about Luke's conception of a community with official structures than about how the community cared for its widows."

account of the origin of the diaconate without calling its first holders deacons. Furthermore, five of the seven named in Acts 6 are not mentioned again in the New Testament. The subsequent recorded careers of the other two, Stephen and Philip, have nothing to do with the care of the neglected Hellenistic widows for whom they were appointed, nor do their careers correspond to the office of deacon that we meet later in the church's early history. The activities of Stephen and Philip went well beyond the area of material service, to the point of appearing as apostles in preaching and evangelizing.

While we should doubt that the Seven were equivalent to contemporary "deacons," they are clearly implied to be *diakonoi* because of the character of their commissioning and the use of the *diakon*-word group to describe their function. And in this line of reasoning the Seven are *diakonoi* insofar as the apostles are too, for the Twelve also have *diakon*-words designating their own ministry. The only further distinction that can be made is that the "commission" for the apostles comes immediately from God, whereas the Seven are commissioned by the election of the community, prayer and laying on of hands by the Twelve. Whether the Seven receive a "heavenly commission," as opposed to a simple commission from the community, cannot be adduced from the text. Simply because the commissioning of the Seven involved election by the community, it does not necessarily follow that their authority comes merely from the community. This ambiguity further clouds the perception the identity of the Seven and the functions they performed.

Instead of finding the origin of the diaconate in Acts 6, it is perhaps more accurate to see an example of how the division of office arose in the early church. What can be gleaned from the text is that early in the history of the primitive community in Jerusalem, certain members of that community were authoritatively appointed to an office.[53] It is the first example of a new pattern for special ministry within the primitive church, in which specialization and subsidiarity were found necessary to make God's grace available to all.[54]

The creation of community officers illustrates how the apostles interpreted the command of Jesus to make themselves servants of all. It is clear from the New Testament that the Twelve did not perpetuate their own position as the Twelve, a privilege which would always remain unique and unrepeatable.[55]

---

53. Lienhard, "Acts," 236.

54. James M. Reese, "Patterns of Ministry in the New Testament as Interpreting the Role of the Permanent Diaconate," *American Ecclesiastical Review* 166, no. 3 (1972): 179.

55. See Raymond Brown, *Priest and Bishop: Biblical Reflections* (New York: Paulist Press, 1970), chap. 2.

The first leaders of the apostolic church, therefore, introduced flexibility in the structure for the sake of building up the community of believers—which is indeed what Luke says happened as a consequence.

Philippians 1:1

Paul's opening greeting in his letter to the Philippians (ca. 57–63 A.D.) is claimed by many scholars to be the earliest reference to the office of deacon.[56] This letter was written, in part, as a note of thanks for the material assistance that was sent to Paul by the Philippians.[57] In his greeting Paul states, "To all the saints in Christ Jesus who are in Philippi, with the bishops and deacons [*sun episkopois kai diakonois*]" (v. 1). As these titles appear without introduction or explanation, it is difficult to ascertain what they mean. Some have argued that the terms *episkopois kai diakonois* refer not to specific offices, but more generally to those who performed certain functions that made them particularly responsible for the collection.[58] Taking note of the plural forms of both terms, others hold an even broader interpretation, claiming that Paul is referring to "leaders who serve," or simply to "a group of leaders and helpers," of an unofficial nature.[59] But these explanations seem unlikely. The most natural meaning of the words suggests there were two special categories of persons in the church at Philippi who were known as *episkopoi* and *diakonoi*.[60]

Though we can be fairly certain that Paul is referring to specific ministers in this passage, we cannot be at all certain from the text as to what their functions were. Paul does not say anything about them in the remainder of his letter. Nonetheless we can deduce some points. First, their appearance at the

56. See Weiser, "διακονέω," 303; Beyer, "διακονέω," 89; Mary Ann Getty, *Philippians and Philemon* (Dublin: Veritas Publications, 1980), 9; Richard M. Gula, "Theology of the Diaconate—Part One," *American Ecclesiastical Review* 169 (1975): 624; Edward P. Echlin, "The Origins of the Permanent Deacon," *American Ecclesiastical Review* 163 (1970): 102; Brendan Byrne, "The Letter to the Philippians," in NJBC, 793; Lécuyer, "Les diacres," 19.

57. Getty, *Philippians*, xi, 5.

58. Marvin R. Vincent, *The Epistle to the Philippians and to Philemon*, The International Critical Commentary (Edinburgh: T. and T. Clark, 1972), 42.

59. Gerald F. Hawthorne, *Philippians*, World Biblical Commentary 43 (Waco, Tex.: Word Books, 1983), 9–10; and Kenneth Grayston, *The Letters of Paul to the Philippians and to the Thessalonians* (Cambridge: Cambridge University Press, 1967), 13 (respectively). See also Dunn's argument that, "although *diakonos* ('servant, minister') is beginning to function as a title, at this stage it still seems to be descriptive of an individual's sustained commitment (like 'fellow worker') and not yet the title of a clearly defined 'office,'" in *The Theology of Paul the Apostle* (Edinburgh: T. and T. Clark, 1998), 584.

60. Lécuyer, "Les diacres," 19, and Collins, *Diakonia*, 235–37.

beginning of the letter without further mention suggests that they occupied a well-understood position within the church at Philippi.[61] Presumably, everyone knew those to whom Paul was referring when he mentioned the *diakonoi*. The fact that they were singled out is in itself a strong indication that they were recognized officials. Second, the deacons are linked with the *episkopoi* and are named subsequent to them. It is apparent that the deacons are associated with the *episkopoi* in the leadership of the church, a characteristic that is in common with the notion of deacon today. Collins considers it significant that the deacons are listed after the *episkopoi*, suggesting that the former were subordinates to the latter as their agents.[62] Such a statement, however, is not precise enough to be of real assistance. Are the *diakonoi* here serving a commission from the *episkopoi*, the church, or God? These are questions that biblical scholarship has yet to answer, if indeed an answer will ever be possible from the text. As such, Philippians seems to raise more questions than answers concerning the office of deacon in the New Testament.

1 Timothy 3:8–13

Whether or not Paul uses a title for officers of the *episkopoi* in Philippians, we meet such officers in 1 Timothy 3 whom we can more confidently call deacons. In order to identify the function of the deacon, however, we need to distinguish usage in this passage, where the deacon is principally characterized by association with the *episkopoi*, from usage elsewhere in the pastoral letters where it refers variously to the following: the special apostolic ministry of the apostle (1 Tm 1:12); participation in the mission by Mark (2 Tm 4:11); Timothy's office (2 Tm 4:5) and function (1 Tm 4:6) as head and teacher of a local church; and Onesiphorus carrying out indeterminate church functions (2 Tm 1:18). With the possible exception of the last instance, these uses refer to activity in the direct interest of the Gospel by those with a commission of a missionary or local nature. No single item in this section necessarily points to duties of deacons in an evangelizing or in any other recognizable capacity. This letter, one of three pastoral epistles attributed to Paul but commonly understood as being composed after his death, has been dated from the end of the first to the beginning of the second century.[63]

61. Lécuyer, "Les diacres," 19.

62. Collins, *Diakonia*, 236. While Collins sees the *diakonoi* as agents of the *episkopoi* in this passage, the thrust of his entire book seems to indicate that they could just as well be "ministers of the Gospel" in some way.

63. The dating of this and the other pastoral letters of 2 Timothy and Titus depends in part on

The author gives us no direct information about the functions of the deacons, but does indicate the qualifications necessary in the aspirants to this noble office. After the description of the qualifications for an *episkopos* (noticing the change from the plural form of *episkopoi* in Philippians to the singular in 1 Timothy), we find:

[8] Similarly, deacons [*diakonous*] must be dignified, not deceitful, not addicted to drink, not greedy for sordid gain, [9] holding fast to the mystery of the faith with a clear conscience. [10] Moreover, they should be tested first; then, if there is nothing against them, let them serve as deacons [*diakoneitosan*]. [11] Women, similarly, should be dignified, not slanderers, but temperate and faithful in everything. [12] Deacons [*diakonoi*] may be married only once and must manage their children and their households well [*teknon kalos proïstamenoi kai ton idion oikon*]. [13] Thus those who serve well as deacons [*kalos diakonesantes*] gain good standing and much confidence in their faith in Christ Jesus.

Once again the offices of the *episkopos* and deacons are mentioned together, indicating their close connection as they developed in the church. The qualifications for both offices are nearly identical, with only minor differences.

It should also be noted that the offices of *episkopoi* and *diakonoi* are the only ones found in the principally Pauline material.[64] They probably originated in the Hellenistic Pauline communities, whereas *presbuteroi* (as seen later in 1 Tm 5:1–2, 17, 19; Ti 1:5) probably originated in the Jewish-Christian communities, particularly Jerusalem.[65] The limitations of this study do not allow for a thorough investigation of what is meant by *episkopoi* and *presbuteroi* in the Pauline corpus of writings. The issue is complicated by the seemingly interchangeable use of the two terms, especially with the term "presiding presbyters" (*proestotedz presbuteroi*) in 1 Timothy 5:17. All that we can conclude from current research is that nothing for certain is known about the relationship between the *episkopoi* and the *presbuteroi* in the New Testament.

In view of the qualifications for one aspiring to the diaconate mentioned

---

whether one considers Paul to be the direct author. For the case for Pauline authorship, and therefore an earlier date (ca. 62–65 A.D.), see John N. D. Kelly's *A Commentary on the Pastoral Epistles: 1 Timothy, 2 Timothy, Titus* (New York: Harper and Brothers, 1963), 34–36, and William Barclay, *The Letters to Timothy, Titus and Philemon*, rev. ed., The Daily Study Bible (Edinburgh: St. Andrew Press, 1975), 13. Anthony T. Hanson takes the more common view that the pastorals were written after Paul's death, in the first years of the second century in his *The Pastoral Letters*, Cambridge Bible Commentary (Cambridge: Cambridge University Press, 1966), 7–14.

64. Barnett, *Diaconate*, 34.

65. Bartlett, *Ministry*, 25. Günther Bornkamm, "πρεσβυτερος," in TDNT 6:651–83, notes that the term was used for civic leaders in Sparta, thus establishing the possibility of Hellenic origins.

in 1 Timothy 3, we must take into account the considerable evidence that most of them are not of Christian origin, but were in general use in the Hellenistic world.[66] A Hellenistic code of behavior clearly underlies the teachings of duties in 1 Timothy 3. This explains why so little is mentioned that would especially characterize a bishop or deacon. The specifically Christian element is missing.[67] This background helps to explain why the fullest account of the closest thing we have to the "diaconate" in the New Testament draws no parallel or analogy between the deacon and Jesus himself.[68] Nonetheless we do find here the mention of a class of officers who work under the *episkopos*, accompanied by a testing or screening process for entry.

We want to ask whether we have the office of "deacon," as we know it today, that is, a particular kind of "officer" of the bishop who is ordained and given the gift of the Holy Spirit? As it is evident that *diakonia* signifies a genre of all ministry that has something to do with a "go-between," we have to recognize the possibility that a multitude of different types of *diakonoi* could be the subject matter of this passage. Could not the *diakonoi* here refer to all the church's officials, in a general way, whose task is to assist the *episkopos* in his work? Recognizing that there are multiple types of *diakonoi* within the New Testament, and even among the pastoral letters themselves, leaves us in doubt. The mention of women in verse 11 makes this question even more important, for if the writer is in fact addressing "deacons" in our sense today, then the implications of this passage for women in the ordained ministry would be great. Once again we see that the scriptures raise more questions than answers concerning the New Testament office of deacon.

Conclusion

The New Testament, as we have seen, does not provide the clear role description that we seek for the deacon. Indeed, prior to the studies of John N. Collins, we may have been able to follow the main line of twentieth-century exegesis and subsequent theology, for instance Hans Küng's influential works on ministry, and accepted the notion that the biblical concept of *diakonia* is one of lowly, non-authoritative service. But Collins shows us that the biblical concept

---

66. George A. Denzer, "The Pastoral Letters," in NJBC, 354; Hanson, *The Pastoral Letters*, 39–40; Barnett, *Diaconate*, 34.

67. Martin Dibelius and Hans Conzelmann, *The Pastoral Epistle: A Commentary on the Pastoral Epistles* (Philadelphia: Fortress Press, 1972), 51.

68. John L. Houlden, *The Pastoral Epistles* (London: Penguin, 1976), 79.

of *diakonia* has richer connotations, those of an emissary or go-between, an exalted form of service rooted in a kingly or divine commission. Although this thesis has not permeated scripture commentaries and theologies of ministry in the twenty-five years since its initial publication, it has been praised by too many reviews and biblical commentators to be ignored.

Despite this still-unsettled state of biblical scholarship, we can glean valuable fruit from this exploration of the biblical meaning. We need not accept all of Collins's theological conclusions uncritically; we can also point out where the application of his biblical research to the contemporary theology of ministry may in fact be erroneous. First of all, it seems rather prudent to accept the nuanced understanding of Collins that *diakonia* signifies, not primarily humble service, but the notion of intermediary or go-between: a messenger between heaven and earth, and even between different parties within the church itself. Second, one can prudently accept that *diakonia* does not generally apply to every believer in the New Testament. It designates all activity that has to do with the general idea of being an agent, emissary, herald, attendant, and by commission of another. Accepting these two points does not require a major shift in the theology of ministry, but it will require a further nuance. Certainly, we must hold that there is biblical evidence for a distinct ministry *among others*, which at its root does not simply have the church as the commissioner, but God, Christ, or the Spirit in some way.

One thing that cannot be accepted at this point is Collins's theological conclusion that because *diakonia* does not generally refer to everyone in the church by way of membership, we should not think of "ministry" as applying to everyone in the church today. This is a mistake in the order of semantics. We should adhere to a balanced application of the three "characteristics" of Christian *diakonia*—Christological, pneumatological, and ecclesial—that I have derived from the New Testament, and that are even found in one of Collins's own works.[69] The charismatic as well as ecclesial characters of *diakonia* are contradicted by the claim that "ministry" only refers to those with a special, and indeed, divine "commission." What about the divine commission that pertains to the church as a whole? If we recognize that biblical *diakonia* is distinct, but nonetheless only one type of *charismata*, and if we hold that the goal is to build up the body of Christ by bringing to fruition or perfection the gifts of "the saints," then removing "ministry" from the "laity" is not precisely

69. Collins, "A Ministry," 170. George Tavard provides a similar threefold structure to explain the *ministerium* of the church in an ecumenical context, in *The Church, Community of Salvation: An Ecumenical Ecclesiology*, New Theology Studies 1 (Collegeville, Minn.: Liturgical Press, 1992), 138–42.

what should be sought. Granted that there needs to be a recovery of the notion of the distinct ministry of those with a "commission" among "the holy ones," it cannot be conceived apart from the ecclesial context. What we need is a nuanced way of articulating the unique ministry of "ministers" among the people of God without implicitly rejecting the right and obligation of all the faithful to put their gifts at the service of the mission of the church as a whole.

Furthermore, we need to balance Collins's description of ministry as a noble charge with its also being a humble service. These two are not contradictory but complementary, because Christian *diakonia* has a Christological character. Jesus has already set the pattern of ministry, a pattern attested again and again in the scriptures. While Son of God, as commissioned by his Father, he humbled himself, so much so that we can dare to claim that the humble nature of Jesus is normative to the point of being a mark of an apostolic community. The "greatest as the servant of all" is an identifying characteristic of authentic Christian ministry: it conforms the minister to the way of the Lord Jesus, the self-emptying gift of self, rather than self-filling. This notion of Christian ministry is biblically based and well-fortified in the Christian tradition.

In summary, I will succinctly state the conclusions from my study of διακονια in the New Testament:

1. Biblical *diakonia* essentially signifies the function of an intermediary; one who has been commissioned by either a heavenly authority or the church to perform personal deeds of service or heraldry.

2. Biblical *diakonia* has three characteristics:
   • Christological: patterned after the self-emptying and obedient ministry of Christ in the salvation of humankind.
   • Pneumatological: a gift of the Spirit that is distinct from other *charismata* in terms of a unique mandate or commission.
   • Ecclesial: the goal of *diakonia* is to perfect and build-up the body of Christ.

3. The biblical "office" of deacon is largely indeterminate, except that there is always a close association with the *episkopos*, and in a subordinate manner in the Pauline letters. It is very likely that the deacon served in some capacity as the go-between of the *episkopos*.

I am now ready to begin an investigation of the teaching of the Second Vatican Council, incorporating this nuanced understanding of biblical *diakonia*.

CHAPTER 2

The Theology of the Deacon
in *Lumen Gentium*

The biblical understanding of *diakonia* explored in the previous chapter allows us to return to some of today's questions concerning the nature and ministry of the deacon. Three questions present themselves:

1. From whom does the deacon receive his distinct mandate for ministry: the bishop, the church, or God?
2. What distinct mission, duty, or charge does the deacon fulfill in the church?
3. What are the Christological, pneumatological, and ecclesial characteristics of his ministry?

With these questions in mind, I shall further explore the teaching of the Second Vatican Council on the diaconate in this chapter. We have already seen the Second Vatican Council describe the deacon's ministry in terms of *diaconia liturgiae, verbi et caritatis.* My biblical study has shown that *diakonia* is used broadly to mean "ministry" (specifically that of a "go-between") and not solely to an activity that only deacons do. The Council, after all, refers to the office of the bishop as a *diakonia.* To interpret the Council's use of *diakonia* for the deacon requires therefore a more complete consideration of the Council's teaching on the nature and ministry of the deacon.

In order to discern the nature of the deacon's charge, I turn again to the first two sentences of LG 29, but this time in more detail. First I will consider the significance of the Council's teaching that the deacon is a member of the hierarchy. Second, the quality of this degree of the hierarchy will be explored, highlighting the relationship of the deacon to the bishop and his priests. What did the Council mean when it stated that the deacons stand at "an inferior degree," ordained "not to the priesthood, but to the ministry," and serve "in communion with the bishop and priests"? Third, I will explore the exact nature of the ministry that the deacon shares with the bishop and his presbyterate in service to the people of God. My analysis in three parts will provide an organized method for the illustration of fundamentals in the theology of the deacon drawn from the teaching of the Second Vatican Council. In light of the Council's brevity on the subject, I will explore the conciliar sources and references to post-conciliar documents, as necessary, to illuminate the theology of the deacon more precisely. In this way, the pneumatological, ecclesial, and Christological dimensions of the deacon's *diakonia* will be brought out into the open.

The Deacon Is Ordained

The first sentence of LG 29 states: "At a lower degree of the hierarchy stand the deacons." This phrase significantly expresses both continuity and distinction among the threefold ecclesiastical ministry. The deacon is affirmed as an ordained member of the people of God, a member of the hierarchy on whom hands are imposed.

The unity of the ecclesiastical ministry is emphasized in the use of the singular "sacrament of order," rather than the plural "sacrament of orders." *Ordo* is a Christian term that has been borrowed from ancient Latin. Its original sphere was not religious, but had to do with civic institutions. The term signified a well-defined social body that was distinct from the rest of the people. In the life of a city an *ordo* was a body of those who governed. Because the word *ordo* had no intrinsically pagan connotations, Christians were not averse to using it to describe the situation of the clergy among the people of God. In the Latin literature of the third century composed by Christians, the words *ordinare* and *ordinatio* are used for the process by which a candidate is installed in the *ordo ecclesiasticus*. The *ordo ecclesiasticus* is constituted "by the act of designation for a charge: the conferring of a mandate or function (*ordinare*)."[1]

In the beginning, the word *ordo* was used of the clergy as a whole, but it soon came to designate the various hierarchic strata into which the clergy was divided: the order of deacons or of subdeacons, the order of presbyters, and the episcopal order.[2] In Christian antiquity the word always referred to

1. Edward J. Kilmartin, "Ministry and Ordination in Early Christianity against a Jewish Background," *Studia Liturgica* 13 (1979): 61.

2. See Bernard Botte, "Collegiate Character of the Presbyterate and Episcopate," in his *The Sacrament of Holy Orders* (Collegeville, Minn.: Liturgical Press, 1962), 75–97.

a collectivity; it was therefore a matter not so much of *receiving* an order as of *entering* an order, of being received into it. With the scholastics came the distinction of *ordo* as having to do with the sacramental aspect of the priesthood, and *dignitas* having to do with the non-sacramental aspect of the episcopacy. From this developed the medieval distinction between the "power of order" and the "power of jurisdiction."[3]

At Rome *ordinatio* was the technical term for the appointment of officials. It could therefore be taken over unchanged by Christians to signify the choice made of someone to carry out an ecclesiastical function.[4] The highest ecclesiastical functions, being liturgical in nature, required a consecration or blessing. The term *ordinatio* soon came to signify also the rite of consecration or blessing. As early as the opening years of the fifth century, St. Jerome applied it to the imposition of hands on clerics.[5] Over the years the meaning of *ordinatio* shifted from the entire process for the transmission of office, to the liturgical act of the imposition of hands.[6]

It must be emphasized that the ordained are among the faithful, not apart from them. The relationship between the initiation sacraments of baptism, confirmation, and eucharist discloses the organic structure of the church, in which every member has a particular role to play in the eucharistic assembly. Baptism is a *sine qua non* for ordination. Baptism's fundamental gifts of uncreated grace and created graces make the Christian capable of receiving further outpourings of the Spirit by way of the other sacraments.[7] LG 10 refers to the "common priesthood" of believers, a concept similar to the Eastern notion "*of baptism and confirmation* as being essentially an ordination."[8] Every Christian

---

3. James Puglisi, *The Process of Admission to Ordained Ministry*, vol. 1: *Epistemological Principles and Roman Catholic Rites, A Comparative Study*, trans. Michael S. Driscoll and Mary Misrashi (Collegeville, Minn.: Liturgical Press, 1996), 213.

4. Pierre Jounel, "Ordinations," in *The Church at Prayer*, vol. 3: *The Sacraments*, ed. Aimes G. Martimort et al. (Collegeville, Minn.: Liturgical Press, 1992), 140.

5. Ibid.

6. Puglisi, *Epistemological Principles*, 213.

7. The scholastic explanation of the necessity of baptism for the reception of orders (as exhibited in Aquinas's *Summa Theologiae* III, supp., q. 35, a. 3) distinguishes baptism as the conferral of a passive power to receive the other sacraments, and orders as the conferral of active power to dispense the sacraments. Pope John Paul II, *Codex Iuris Canonici Auctoritate Ioannis Pauli PP. II Promulgatus* (Vatican City: Libreria Editrice Vaticana, 1989); English translation, *Code of Canon Law Latin-English Edition, New English Translation* (Washington, D.C.: Canon Law Society of America, 1999) (hereafter CIC), c. 1024 states: "Sacram ordinationem valide recipit solus vir baptizatus."

8. John Zizioulas, *Being as Communion: Studies in Personhood and the Church* (Crestwood, N.Y.: St. Vladimir's Seminary Press, 1985), 216. LG states: "The common priesthood of the faithful and the

becomes a member of a particular *ordo* in the eucharistic assembly through the sacraments of initiation. It is from this lay *ordo* that certain members are called to become members of other *ordines* in the eucharistic assembly.

Let there be no mistake: the lay *ordo* (or common priesthood) is the basis for all other *ordines*. It is not the other way around. The ecclesiastical orders presuppose and are dependent upon the primary *ordo* that springs from baptism. Without the ecclesial *ordo*, there would not be the ecclesiastical *ordines*. On the other hand, each believer needs organization, leadership, and inspiration in order to fruitfully and harmoniously exercise the charisms received in baptism. It is the duty of the ecclesiastical *ordines*, above all the bishop as head, to serve the unity of the church through the coordination and encouragement of the faithful's baptismal charisms. For these reasons, the ordained ministry cannot be understood, either in terms of its nature or purpose, apart from baptism. Any distinctions that are made concerning the ecclesiastical orders must always be kept in tension with the fundamental reality of the church as the people of God.[9]

The deacon is an ordained member of the people of God. In LG 28, the Council's understanding of the hierarchy is given, in which the transmission of the one ecclesiastical ministry occurs among three orders:

> Christ, whom the Father sanctified and sent into the world (see Jn. 10, 36), has through his apostles made their successors, the bishops, share in his consecration and his mission, and these have legitimately handed on the office of their ministry in varying degrees to various subjects in the church. In this way the divinely instituted ecclesiastical ministry is exercised in different orders by those who right from ancient times are called bishops, priests and deacons.[10]

The Council fathers clearly express their conviction that the diaconate is an order of the ecclesiastical ministry. They implicitly assert that there is no contradiction between the apostolic structure of the early church and the ministerial structure of the church today. Deacons have a share, in some degree,

---

ministerial or hierarchical priesthood, though they differ in essence and not simply in degree, are nevertheless interrelated: each in its own particular way shares in the one priesthood of Christ" (no. 10). While recognizing the real distinction between the ordained and the lay faithful, the concept of the "common priesthood" puts to rest any notion that the church is primarily her clergy.

9. Pope John Paul II, *Crossing the Threshold of Hope*, ed. Vitorrio Messori, trans. Jenny McPhee and Martha McPhee (London: Jonathan Cape, 1994), 14, citing St. Augustine's often repeated phrase, "Vobis sum episcopus, vobiscum christianus," John Paul II adds, "On further reflection, *christianus* has far greater significance than *episcopus*, even if the subject is the Bishop of Rome."

10. *Decrees* (ed. Tanner), 2:872.

in the consecration and mission of that which Christ received from the Father. The one divinely instituted ecclesiastical ministry is exercised by various orders.

Thus there is not the intention by the Council to teach that Christ himself established the threefold ministry as we see it exist today. According to Karl Rahner's essay, "The Theology of the Restoration of the Diaconate," it is "impossible to suppose that the tripartition of this office in the Church (i.e., the episcopal office, the sacerdotal office and the office of deacon) goes back directly to the explicit will of the historical Jesus before or after the Resurrection."[11] Where is the connection, then, between the mission of Christ and the mission of the ecclesial ministers? St. Clement argues in his letter to the Corinthians (ca. 96 A.D.) that it is in the appointment of the apostles under the guidance of the Holy Spirit:

The apostles received the Gospel for us from the Lord Jesus Christ; Jesus Christ was God's ambassador. Thus Christ (is sent) from God and the apostles from Christ; both these dispositions originated in an orderly way from God's will. Having thus received their mandate and fully convinced by the resurrection of (our) Lord Jesus Christ, and committed to the Word of God, they went forth with the full assurance of the Holy Spirit, announcing the good news that the Kingdom of God was close at hand. Preaching from country to country and from city to city, they established some of their first followers as "*episkopoi*" and "*diakonoi*" of the future believers, after having tested them by the Spirit.[12]

While the offices of the church certainly emerged within a concrete social and historical context of the Jewish and Hellenistic world, it is the teaching of the church that their origins are rooted in the power of the Spirit of Christ alive in the church. By virtue of the pneumatic nature of the apostolically ordered church, the ecclesiastical offices are themselves the fruit of the Spirit, and not simply the result of sociological growth. The role of the Spirit, after the death and resurrection of Christ, was to perfect and complete the work of Christ through his body, the church, and to make the risen Christ more fully present and active in the church of every age. In this sense, the offices of the church are also divine, because in them the will of Christ is made manifest to us through

11. Karl Rahner, "On the Diaconate," in his *Foundations for the Renewal of the Diaconate*, trans. David Bourke (Washington, D.C.: United States Conference of Catholic Bishops, 2003), 145.

12. In Josef Neuner and Jacques Dupuis (eds.), *The Christian Faith in the Doctrinal Documents of the Catholic Church*, rev. ed. (New York: Alba House, 1982), chap. 42 (492). This letter is dated in Maxwell Staniforth, *Early Christian Writings: The Apostolic Fathers* (New York: Dorset Press, 1968), 17.

the power of his Spirit. We can therefore say that the diaconate has been divinely established.[13]

The Council of Trent taught that the divinely instituted ecclesiastical ministry had more variations than bishop, priest, and deacon. In canon 6 of the decree on the sacred ministry we read: "If anyone denies that there exists in the catholic church a hierarchy consisting of bishops, priests and ministers [*ministris*], instituted by divine appointment: let him be anathema."[14] The intent of the fathers at Trent was to defend the contemporary structure of the ministry as legitimately apostolic, not to teach that it was the only structure that the church could have. As such, Trent defended even the minor orders below the deacon as "divinely instituted." While the Council of Trent used the term *ministris* to include all the minor orders as well as the orders of subdeacon and deacon, the Second Vatican Council refers only to deacons. Thus the hierarchy, as it stands today, consists of bishops, presbyters, and deacons, no more and no less.[15]

In summary, we see that the deacon receives a share in the ministry of Christ himself through the imposition of hands and the prayer of the church. The deacon is not merely delegated by the bishop or the church to perform a certain function, but neither is he independent from the church or the higher clergy, who also share in the mission of Christ but in a different way. The deacon functions according to the charisms received directly from the Spirit in the process of ordination. There is no conferral of the charisms for the diaconate office apart from the petition of the church. While the deacon receives a charge from heaven, it is mediated in, by, with, and through the church.

Non ad sacerdotium, sed ad ministerium

Now that we have a general understanding of the significance of the deacon as a sharer, to some degree, in the mission and consecration of Christ, I will explore the particular nature of his participation in the one ecclesiastical ministry. The Council describes the diaconate as sharing "in a lower degree"

13. Patrick Crowley, "The Diaconate for the Present Age: A Theological Assessment," *Clergy Review* 59 (1974): 788–89.

14. Council of Trent, *On the Sacrament of Order*, c. 6; *Decrees* (ed. Tanner), 2:744.

15. Pope Pius XII confirmed the teaching of the diaconate as a sacramental order in his Apostolic Constitution *Sacramentum Ordinis* (November 30, 1947), *Acta Apostolicae Sedis Commentarium Officiale* (hereafter AAS) 40 (1948): 5–7, defining the form and matter of the diaconate as the words of consecration and the imposition of hands.

(*inferiori*) in this one ecclesiastical ministry. Such language does not exactly appeal to our modern sense of equality, but how are we to understand its use concerning the deacon? The theology of the scholastics, most notably Thomas Aquinas, espoused a linear hierarchy, wherein the order of the ecclesiastical ministry focused upon the central action of consecrating the eucharist.[16] The diaconate was merely a transitional step toward priesthood. In this schema, the deacon would serve as the liturgical assistant to the priest, lacking a direct relationship with the bishop or to the rest of the church. But is this what the Second Vatican Council intends with the word "inferior"? No. The fact that the deacon serves "in communion" with the other two orders does not allow for this interpretation. In order to come to a more nuanced understanding of the place of the deacon within the hierarchy of the church, we must turn our attention to the phrase that describes more precisely the office conferred through the imposition of hands on a candidate for the diaconate.

The crucial phrase "not for the priesthood, but for the ministry" was lifted by the Council from the *Constitutiones Ecclesiae aegyptiacae* (*Egyptian Church Order*) of the fourth century. It appears equally in the *Didascalia apostolorum*, also of the fourth century, and the *Statuta Ecclesiae antiqua* of the fifth century. This mysterious phrase is considered almost unintelligible unless we look to its earlier source in a document scholarship has commonly called the *Apostolic Tradition of Hippolytus* (hereafter AT).[17] The *Egyptian Church Order* is accepted as a later version of this important document.[18] The *Apostolic Tradition*, once attributed to Hippolytus, provides a considerable body of extremely valuable information on the hierarchical organization of the church. It pro-

---

16. St. Thomas Aquinas provides the most extensive theological treatment of the deacon in the medieval period. This notion of hierarchy was especially based on the writings of Pseudo-Dionysius, an influential sixth-century neo-Platonist who Thomas (and all theologians of his time) took to be Paul's convert Dionysius the Areopagite from Acts 17:34. Thomas's writings exerted enormous influence on the theology of the diaconate until the Second Vatican Council. See his *Summa Theologiae* III, q. 64, a. 1; q. 67, a. 1; q. 71, a. 4; q. 82, a. 3; III, supp., q. 35, a. 2; q. 37, aa. 2, 4, 5; q. 40, a. 7.

17. Bernard Botte, *La Tradition Apostolique de saint Hippolyte. Essai de reconstitution*, ed. Albert Gerhards and Sabine Felbecker, 5th ed. (Münster: Aschendorff, 1989), 10. Two of the Council fathers asked for the removal of the phrase for they thought it too ambiguous. See "*Modorum expensio* (oct.-nov. 1964) c. III," in *Constitutionis Dogmaticae Lumen Gentium: Synopsis Historica*, ed. Giuseppe Alberigo and Franco Magistretti (Bologna: Istituto per le Scienze Religiose, 1975), 537.

18. The Council officially cites *The Egyptian Church Order*, an early liturgical treatise which, as a result of the research of Richard H. Connolly, *The So-called Egyptian Church Order and Derived Documents*, Texts and Studies 8.4 (Cambridge: Cambridge University Press, 1916), and Eduard Schwartz, *Über die Pseudoapostolischen Kirchenordnungen* (Strasbourg: K. J. Trubner, 1910), is now commonly identified as the *Apostolic Tradition of St. Hippolytus*.

vides, among other things, a description of the ordination and functions of the deacon of the post-apostolic church.

The text has a complicated history.[19] Most versions of the AT are very much reworked and interpolated, except for the Latin which appears to be a quite literal fourth-century translation.[20] The Latin text, however, contains lacunae that require the consultation of the other translations. The ambiguity of the text itself requires caution against attributing to Hippolytus of the third century what may have been a later interpolation.[21] But for our purposes, it is enough to be aware of the textual variations and to accept the AT as the precursor to the *Egyptian Church Order* for the purpose of interpreting the phrase *non ad sacerdotium, sed ad ministerium*.

Recall again the first sentence of LG 29: "At a lower degree of the hierarchy stand the deacons, on whom hands are imposed 'not for the priesthood, but for the ministry.'" Deacons are those *on whom hands are imposed*. Today, "ordination" usually stands for the liturgical act of the imposition of hands. As we have already seen, the original meaning of the word was much broader. *Ordinatio* stands for "the process by which a Christian is chosen and installed in an ecclesiastical office."[22] Remembering that the AT was originally in Greek, the AT is witness to an effort at establishing a technical terminology in Greek concerning ordination. The author of AT made a distinction between "ordination" and "institution" in an ecclesial office. In secular Greek, an official was said to be "instituted" or "established" in his office (*kathistasthai*); he could also be said to be "designated" (*cheirotonia*). Both terms are applied to ecclesiastical offices, but this text limits the use of the second to ordination in the strict sense, that is, to offices that make the chosen person a member of one of the three levels in the hierarchic structure, and for which a consecration is required.[23] The ritual gesture used in this consecration was the imposition of

19. Johannes Quasten, *Patrology*, vol. 2: *The Ante-Nicene Literature after Irenaeus* (Westminster, Md.: Newman Press, 1953–64), 180–82. The text was considered lost until the beginning of the twentieth century, but it is now believed that translations of the original Greek (ca. 215 A.D.) are extant in Coptic, Arabic made from the Coptic, Ethiopic made from the Arabic, Sahidic, Bohairic, and Latin.

20. William Jurgens, *The Faith of the Early Fathers* (Collegeville, Minn.: Liturgical Press, 1970), 166.

21. Basil Studer, "Liturgical Documents of the First Four Centuries," trans. Edward Hagman in *Introduction to the Liturgy*, in *The Pontifical Liturgical Institute Handbook for Liturgical Studies*, ed. Anscar Chupungco (Collegeville, Minn.: Liturgical Press, 1997), 1:203–4. Studer presents a succinct description of the contemporary controversies surrounding the origin and authorship of the *Apostolic Tradition*. That Hippolytus was not the actual author of this text has been generally accepted upon the scholarship of Paul F. Bradshaw, Maxwell E. Johnson, and L. Edward Phillips, *The Apostolic Tradition: A Commentary*, ed. H. W. Attridge, Hermeneia (Minneapolis, Minn.: Fortress Press, 2002).

22. Puglisi, *Epistemological Principles*, 214.

23. Jounel, "Ordinations," 140.

hands (*cheirotonein*), which was developed from the description of the pastoral epistles.[24] Thus, while a lector is "instituted" in the AT without the imposition of hands, the deacon, as well as the bishop and presbyter, are "ordained."[25]

The origin of this gesture is disputed. Some argue that the laying on of hands, as described in the AT, has its origins in a Pharisaic model of appointment operative in Jerusalem before the fall of the Temple.[26] Others argue against any Jewish origins for the laying on of hands in the early Christian community in Jerusalem.[27] But by whatever means, the practice of laying on hands in commissioning one for ministry in the church became widespread by the second century. During the second century, the laying on of hands gained prominence because of the conviction that ecclesiastical responsibility is grounded on the gift of the Spirit, communicated in ordination, which empowers the minister for certain specific functions.[28] The cultic act of the imposition of hands, the *cheirotonia*, expresses the bestowal of a mandate through the gift of the Spirit. It signifies a gift of the Holy Spirit, a gift not common to all the baptized but held only by those who hold one of the three offices in the *ekklesia*. This particular gift of the Spirit empowers the ordinand for certain fundamental functions, both pastoral and liturgical, in the community. The "gift of God" (*charisma tou theou*) is never conferred for the sole benefit of the person, but in view of service toward others.[29] Thus it is not far afield to write that the imposition of hands in the AT signifies the conferral of a divine commission, with all the Christological, pneumatological, and ecclesial characteristics associated with biblical *diakonia*.

In the AT the conferral of the Spirit, charisms, and office takes place together. The word *pneuma* is used to signify both the person of the Holy Spirit

24. Kilmartin, "Ministry," 54.

25. *Apostolic Tradition*, no. 2, text and translation in Botte, *La Tradition*, 30–31; Jounel, "Ordinations," 140. Neither do widows (AT 10), virgins (AT 12), or subdeacons (AT 13) receive the imposition of hands; they are merely installed.

26. Kilmartin, "Ministry," 63. Kilmartin believes that the Jewish Christians brought this custom with them into the Pauline communities, as represented in the pastoral letters, when they fled Jerusalem following the destruction of the Temple. The non-Pauline communities only later adopted the gesture in the development of a liturgy of ordination, but not necessarily as a direct result of influence by the Pauline tradition.

27. Lawrence Hoffman, a scholar of Jewish liturgy, denies that the laying on of hands was ever part of the Jewish ordination ceremony before the year 200. He claims that the evidence purported to indicate the practice of laying on hands within Jewish circles is either a matter of reading too much into the text, or mistaking a discussion on the proper way to offer sacrifice for a discussion on ordination. See Lawrence A. Hoffman, "Jewish Ordination on the Eve of Christianity," *Studia Liturgica* 13 (1979): 11–41.

28. Kilmartin, "Ministry," 64.

29. Puglisi, *Epistemological Principles*, 35.

and the charisms, and it is not by accident that we find there the first evidence of the liturgical salutation "and with your spirit" (*kai meta tou pneumatos sou*).[30] In the ordination of a bishop in the AT, the new bishop addresses a first salutation to the *ekklesia*, and the *ekklesia* answers that he has, from his very ordination, a "spirit" that is a special charism within the *ekklesia*.[31] It is noteworthy that the deacon today receives the same response to his salutation and before his proclamation of the Gospel and the Easter *Exsultet*.

The section concerning the ordination of a deacon in AT (8) contains an instruction (or rubric) with an explanation of the diaconal ordination, as well as the ordination prayer itself:

Over a deacon, then, (the bishop) shall say thus: God, who created all things and ordered them by your Word, Father of our Lord Jesus Christ, whom you sent to serve your will and make known to us your desire, give the Holy Spirit of grace and caring and diligence to this your servant whom you have chosen to serve your Church and to present in your holy of holies that which is offered to you by your appointed high-priest to the glory of your name; that serving blamelessly and purely, he may attain the rank of a higher order, and praise and glorify you through your Son Jesus Christ our Lord; through whom be glory and power and praise to you, with the Holy Spirit, now and always and to the ages of ages. Amen.[32]

In the prayer of ordination, we see the image of the deacon as servant of God. He is given the charge by a gift of the Holy Spirit to serve the church. The only specific task mentioned in the prayer is a liturgical one, "to present the gifts to be offered to the bishop." To fulfill the task of building up the body of Christ, the candidate for the diaconate receives the "Spirit of grace and caring and diligence." His service is accomplished for the praise and glory of God. The deacon receives these gifts in becoming himself a gift from God to the church.

The prayer of ordination associates the ministry of the deacon to that of Christ. As the Father sent Christ to serve his will and make known to us his plan, so the church beseeches the Father to send again the Spirit so that the

---

30. AT 4; P. M. Gy, "Ancient Ordination Prayers," *Studia Liturgica* 13 (1979): 82.

31. Willem C. van Unnik, "*Dominus Vobiscum*: The Background of a Liturgical Formula," in *New Testament Essays: Studies in Memory of Thomas Walter Manson*, ed. Angus J. Higgins (Manchester: Manchester University Press, 1959), 270–305; Bernard Botte, "L'Esprit Saint et l'Église dans la *Tradition Apostolique* de S. Hippolyte," *Didascalia* 2 (1972): 221–33.

32. AT 8; trans. Geoffrey J. Cuming, *Hippolytus: A Text for Students*, Liturgical Study 8 (Bramcote: Grove Books Limited, 1976), 13. After "to present," the Latin text breaks off. Botte and Dix supply most of the rest of the prayer from the later Ethiopian version.

deacon may faithfully serve the church. Here we see a strong correlation with the Christological character of New Testament *diakonia*. Christ revealed the love of the Father in his self-emptying service. The deacon represents this Christ within the *ekklesia* by fulfilling his charge "blamelessly and purely." The gifts of the Spirit conform the particular ministry of the deacon to the pattern established by the Lord Jesus. It is through the divine charge of the deacon that the commission of Christ to reveal the love and plan of the Father continues in a particular way through space and time.

It is in the rubric section of the AT, however, that we find the precursor to the phrase "not to the priesthood, but to the ministry" (*non ad sacerdotium, sed ad ministerium*) used in LG 29. In the explanatory section we read:

In the ordination of a deacon, the bishop alone shall lay on hands, because he is not being ordained to the priesthood, but to the service of the bishop, [*non in sacerdotio ordinatur, sed in ministerio episcopi*] to do what is ordered by him [*ut faciat ea quae ab ipso iubentur*]. For he does not share in the counsel of the clergy, but administers and informs the bishop of what is fitting; he does not receive the common spirit of seniority in which the presbyters share, but that which is entrusted to him under the bishop's authority.[33]

The AT provides a broader context by which we may understand this phrase in its original setting. First of all, we recognize the qualification of the type of ministry for which the candidate for the diaconate is ordained. He is not ordained to the *sacerdotium*. That the bishop was perceived in the AT as high priest of the *ekklesia* is without question.[34] The priestly and leadership figures are united in the AT.[35] The power of the Spirit first transmitted to the Son for his messianic and prophetic mission, then transmitted by Christ to the apostles for their evangelical mission, is now given to the bishop for the sake

---

33. Ibid.

34. The prayer for the ordination of a bishop asks for the office of a high priest, and relates to his pneuma the power of remitting sins: "bestow upon this your servant, whom you have chosen for the episcopate, to feed your holy flock and to exercise the high-priesthood before you blamelessly, serving night and day; to propitiate your countenance unceasingly, and to offer to you the gifts of your holy Church; and by the spirt of high-priesthood to have the power to forgive sins according to your command, to confer orders according to your bidding, to loose every bond according to the power which you gave to the apostles" (3).

35. The bishop exercises a pastoral ministry (as head) and a sacerdotal ministry (as high priest) in the church. Presidency and offering are two functions that go together. See Puglisi, *Epistemological Principles*, 56, and Herve-Marie Legrand, "The Presidency of the Eucharist According to the Ancient Tradition," *Worship* 53 (1979): 413–38, esp. 421: "The bishop, who presides over the Church by virtue of an ordination conferring an apostolic charism, presides at the Eucharist as high priest."

of the church, in every place, for the glorification of God. Within the church the new bishop must tend the flock, exercise his priesthood, and build up the church to help them give glory to God. To fulfill this ministry, the bishop is given the power (*exousia*) of the Spirit to forgive sins, to confer orders, to free all bonds. This power is not his personally, but is dependent upon the Spirit of the sovereign priesthood. The charism of the priestly ministry is given to the bishop not for his personal gain, but to build up the church, in which God is praised and glorified.[36] Clearly the ministry of the bishop in AT blends together the pneumatological, Christological, and ecclesial dimensions of biblical *diakonia*.

The ministry of the presbyterium involves the sacerdotal dimension of the bishop's ministry, and only the bishop, as head of the presbyterium and head of the *ekklesia*, has the "spirit" to ordain.[37] This is why the presbyters do not impose hands at the ordination of a deacon, underscoring the direct relationship between bishop and deacon.[38] Thus it is clear that while presbyters are ordained to the priesthood, the deacons are not. The deacon is not ordained for priestly mediation between God and people; he is not to preside over the community. He does not share in the counsel of the clergy, nor receive a spirit of seniority.

But the deacon is ordained *in ministerio episcopi, ut faciat ea quae ab ipso iubentur*. What is meant by the words *in ministerio episcopi*? The word *episcopi* could be understood in the objective sense—that the deacon is ordained to minister to the bishop, or in the subjective sense—that he is ordained to the bishop's ministry. With the former, the object of the deacon's ministry is the bishop himself. With the latter, the community is the object of the bishop's ministry, and therefore, the object of the deacon's ministry. The phrase *ut faciat ea quae ab ipso iubentur* might lead one to believe that ministry or service to the bishop is intended, as the deacon is "to do what is ordered by" the bishop. If this be the

---

36. From the prayer for the ordination of a bishop (AT 3). See Puglisi, *Epistemological Principles*, 52–54.

37. "For a presbyter has authority only to receive; he has no authority to give. For this reason, he does not ordain the clergy" (AT 8). Puglisi, *Epistemological Principles*, 46, states: "The presbyter is ordained to the priesthood in order to help the bishop accomplish his pastoral office (AT 8, 3), to offer the oblation, and in view of liturgical service (AT 10)."

38. It is not that the bishop acts alone in the ordination of a deacon. Primarily it is God who is acting. We see in AT 2 that ordination involves the participation of the entire assembly. The ordinand is to be chosen by all the people, and they are to keep silent, "praying in their hearts for the descent of the Spirit." The bishop fulfills the unique function of the presider and head of the community. Thus he alone imposes hands and says the prayer of ordination out loud.

case, then how should we take into account the ordination prayer which states, "give the Holy Spirit ... to this your servant whom you have chosen *to serve your Church*"? There is no contradiction between what is meant by service to the bishop and service to the church in the example given in AT 34: "Each deacon, with the subdeacons, shall attend on the bishop. They shall inform him of those who are ill, so that, if he pleases, he may visit them. For a sick man is greatly comforted when the high-priest remembers him." The deacon is ordained to the ministry of the bishop in the subjective sense; that is, the deacon's direct ministry to the church is under, and in the context of, the presiding ministry of the bishop. In this manner, the unity of the one ecclesiastical ministry is maintained while recognizing the deacon's distinct participation in that ministry.[39]

In like manner, the association of the ministry of presbyters to the pastoral ministry of the bishop is what explicates their ministry as priestly.[40] There are not two priesthoods, one for the bishop and one for the presbyters, but one priestly ministry exercised in two degrees. We can therefore understand the ordination phrase to mean "not unto the priesthood of the bishop, but to the ministry of the bishop." The bishop alone, as head of the *ekklesia*, has the primary responsibility, among the various ministers, for helping the local church to praise and glorify God. As the presbyters have a share in the charge of priestly ministry given to the bishop, so deacons have a share in the charge of ministry held by the bishop.

The main import of the phrase is to clarify that though the deacon shares in the bishop's ministry, the deacon's ministry lacks sacerdotal quality. The ministry of the deacon does not, however, make him merely a personal servant of the bishop. They are not in his personal service but are ordained for the ministry for which the bishop is responsible, which has the community as its object. We find confirmation of the theology of ministry in the AT in LG 20: "The bishops, therefore, have undertaken along with their fellow-workers, the priests and deacons, the service of the community." How then are we to interpret the phrase *ut faciat ea quae ab ipso iubentur*? As the bishop is primarily responsible for the ecclesial ministry in its totality, he alone, as high priest and president of the assembly, has the responsibility of distributing the work of the church among its members according to their specific charisms. Consequently, the deacon must do "that which is ordered by the bishop." The deacon's particular ministry to the people of God is within the unity of the one ecclesiastical

---

39. Alphonse Borras and Bernard Pottier, *La grâce du diaconat: Questions actuelles autour du diaconat latin* (Bruxelles: Cerf, 1998), 25–26.

40. Puglisi, *Epistemological Principles*, 66.

ministry. There is no contradiction between the deacon attending the bishop as head of the local *ekklesia* and his charge of service to the church at large. The deacon receives the gift of the Spirit and a share in the one charge given to Christ by the Father, and then by Christ to the apostles, and now by the Spirit to the bishop. He works with the bishop, under his presidency, to build up the church in a particular place for the praise and glory of God. It is therefore not unreasonable to say that the deacon in the AT has a share in the bishop's apostolic office, which has as an objective to safeguard and promote the apostolic identity of the local church. It is the divine charge of the bishop to keep watch over the apostolicity of the church so that the church is always recognized as a gift of God.[41]

What, then, are the duties of the deacon that are not priestly or presidential functions? What service does the deacon render to the local assembly under the auspices of the bishop? Within the ordination prayer itself, we see a specific function of the deacon, namely, service at the altar: "to present in your holy of holies that which is offered to you by your appointed high-priest to the glory of your name."[42] The deacon assists the high priest in his offering at the altar, but does not offer the gift itself, shying away from such a priestly function. We also remember the duty of the deacon to inform the bishop of those who are sick in AT 34. The deacon's charge includes various services to the community (AT 24, 25, 28, and 39), and in AT 21 and 22 we see his liturgical assistance at baptism and eucharistic celebrations.[43] In the AT the deacon works closely with the bishop in providing liturgical and pastoral assistance so that the ministry as a whole might be accomplished.

In conclusion, let us summarize the theology of the diaconate as presented in the *Apostolic Tradition* attributed to Hippolytus:

1. The pneumatological character: the deacon, upon whom the bishop alone imposes hands, receives the gift of the Holy Spirit. He is ordained to a ministry that requires more than personal gifts and talents.

2. The Christological character: conformed to the pattern of Christ through the gift of the Spirit, the deacon continues the mission of Christ to reveal the love of the Father. He is an icon of Christ, the faithful servant, among the people of God.

---

41. Borras and Pottier, *La grâce du diaconat*, 26–28.

42. This liturgical function of the deacon preparing the gifts is repeated in AT 23.

43. E.g., providing relief to the sick; lighting of lamps for the Christian household; attend at communal meals; and with the presbyters, catechize the faithful.

3. The ecclesial character: as a servant of God, the deacon is a gift of God to the church. Through the imposition of hands the deacon is received into an order that has in common with the bishop and his presbyters the ministry of helping the *ekklesia* praise and glorify God. The deacon shares in the bishop's ministry, but not in his priesthood. The quality of the deacon's ministry is neither sacerdotal nor presidential. He is closely associated with the bishop, providing liturgical and pastoral assistance. The deacon is in service to the apostolic identity of the local church.

4. Continuity with *diakonia* in the NT: we can justly call the deacon's ministry a biblical *diakonia*. The deacon receives a share of the mission of Christ, by the imposition of hands of the bishop and prayer of the assembly. In his liturgical and pastoral assistance, the deacon functions as an agent of the bishop, often functioning as his intermediary to those in need.

Having arrived at a nuanced understanding of the phrase *non ad sacerdotium, sed ad ministerium*, I now return to the teaching of the Second Vatican Council that the deacon stands "at a lower degree."

The ancient text of the *Apostolic Tradition* is one of the fundamental theological sources for the conciliar teaching on the diaconate. The description of the deacon and his ministry, articulated ever so briefly in the first two lines of LG 29, is in view of the image of the deacon presented in the AT. The teaching of the Second Vatican Council illustrates the unique place of the deacon within the ecclesiastical ministry by negative qualifications and positive assertions.

The negative qualifications are that the deacon is of "a lower degree," and that he is not ordained "for the priesthood." He performs neither presidential nor priestly activities in administrative or liturgical functions. In the words of the Council, the deacon stands "at a lower degree," not because he carries out inferior work, but because his share of the ministry is not all-encompassing. He does not share, by way of ordination, in the mission of Christ in the same way as either the bishop or his presbyters. The Council's description of the deacon at a "lower degree" does not therefore make him a flunky of the bishop or the presbyters for their personal affairs. The phrase *in communione* may be read as the only corrective now available to the notion of the hierarchy as rungs of a ladder to be climbed up.[44] The office of the deacon, like that of a presbyter

---

44. Herbert Vorgrimler, "The Hierarchical Structure of the Church, with Special Reference to the Episcopate, Article 29," in *Commentary of the Documents of Vatican II*, ed. Herbert Vorgrimler, in his

but in another way, is a restricted participation in the one, whole ministerial office, the fullness of which is found in the bishop. The relation between the various orders is thus seen in a descending rather than ascending perspective, centered on the bishop and not the presbyter.

To Serve the People of God

Turning to the positive assertions of the deacon, we see more clearly what is at the heart of the diaconate. The positive theological qualities given by the Council are that the deacon is: (1) ordained by the imposition of hands and (2) ordained "for the ministry." The imposition of hands, linked with the gift of the Spirit, signifies that the deacon is made a member of the ecclesiastical order and that he is "strengthened by sacramental grace." In this statement the Council affirmed the sacramental nature of the diaconate in such a way as not to cast a slur on venerable theologians who questioned it.[45] The reality of "sacramental grace" was taken up again by the Council in *Ad Gentes* (no. 16, a passage I will consider shortly) as the very reason for the restoration of the permanent diaconate in missionary territories. No further details are given concerning the charisms received in diaconal ordination; especially lacking is their relation to the threefold office (*tria munera*) of the bishop. We shall soon see that this ambiguity has led to much confusion over the role of the deacon *vis-à-vis* the bishop, presbyter, and the laity. "At a lower degree," nonetheless, the deacon has critical functions to perform for the life and mission of the church. For the fulfillment of these important functions, the church does not simply rely on the Christian's personal qualities, talents, and skills but requires a special gift of the Spirit for their accomplishment.

As the deacon is ordained "to the bishop's ministry," diaconal ministry correlates directly with the episcopal ministry. As we consider in greater detail the ministry for which the deacon is ordained today, it behooves us to consider the ministry of the bishop as articulated by the Council.[46] In LG 18–27 the Council set forth its most authoritative teaching on the office of the episcopa-

---

Das Zweite Vatikanische Konzil, Dokumente und Kommentare, trans. Lalit Adolphus, Kevin Smyth, and Richard Strachan (New York: Crossroad, 1967–89), 1:229.

45. Gérard Philips, *La chiesa e il suo mistero. Storia, testo e commento della <<Lumen gentium>>* [The Church and its Mystery: History, text and commentary of *Lumen gentium*] (Milan: Jaca, 1975–93), 329; Vorgrimler, *Commentary*, 229.

46. Obviously, an exhaustive study of the bishop's ministry cannot be done within the parameters of this chapter. For an extensive bibliography, see Christopher O'Donnell, "Bishops," in *Ecclesia: A Theological Encyclopedia of the Church* (Collegeville, Minn.: Liturgical Press, 1996), 56–57.

cy. The decree on the pastoral office of bishops in the church, *Christus Dominus* (hereafter "CD"), considers the pastoral implications of the teaching in LG, but adds nothing to the doctrinal understanding of the bishop's ministry. We shall therefore follow the dogmatic teaching in LG, integrating pertinent concrete examples as articulated in CD.

The main interest of the Council in LG rests in three central themes: the sacramental nature of the episcopacy (21), the intrinsic connection of the various *munera* of the bishop (21), and the function and dignity of the college of bishops (22).[47] In LG 18–20 the Council explores the significance of the Catholic teaching that the college of bishops has taken the place of the college of apostles as pastors of the church by divine institution. The language of "sacred power" is used to describe the transmission of authority and grace that comes by way of the apostolic succession through the imposition of hands (LG 21). The "fullness of the sacrament of order," called the "supreme priesthood," is received through the episcopal consecration that confers the offices of teaching, governing and sanctifying.[48] In an eminent and visible way, bishops take on the functions of Christ and act in his person. This sacred ministry is entrusted to the bishops, in whom the apostolic tradition is "manifested and safeguarded" (LG 20). With priests and deacons as their helpers, bishops receive the charge of the community "presiding in the place of God over the flock, whose shepherds they are, as teachers of doctrine, priests of sacred worship and ministers of government" (LG 20).

Every bishop, as a member of the college of bishops, has responsibilities to the universal church, as well as to the local church in which he is "the visible principle and foundation of unity" (LG 23). Our concern lies primarily in the ministry of the bishop as it pertains to the local church, in which deacons assist him. The description of the bishop's ministry in the local church is structured along the lines of the three offices, the *tria munera* of teaching (prophet), sanctifying (priest), and governing (king).[49]

47. Rahner, *Commentary*, 186. It is noted that the Council only "teaches" the doctrine of the sacramental nature of the episcopacy without proposing a solemn definition.

48. Bernard Cooke gives five different definitions for the term "priesthood" used by the Council, sometimes without discrimination, in "'Fullness of Orders': Theological Reflections," *Jurist* 41 (1981): 153.

49. According to Rahner, *Commentary*, 188, the doctrine of the three offices of Christ was only developed fully in Catholic theology in the nineteenth century, particularly by canonists, along the lines suggested by Protestant models. See, for example, John B. Franzelin, *Theses de Ecclesia Christi* (Rome: Typographia Polyglotta, 1887), esp. 43–64. This way of describing the episcopal ministry is problematic, to say the least, in that the same model is used to articulate the role of the laity in the life

In LG 24–25 the *munus docendi* (ministry of teaching) is described as "among the principal tasks of bishops." Bishops are "heralds of the faith," "teachers endowed with the authority of Christ." They are to make the faith bear fruit in the lives of the faithful and "vigilantly ward off errors that are threatening their flock" (LG 25). Reminiscent of the *Apostolic Tradition*, CD 12 describes the bishops' duty to show the faithful "the way divinely revealed for giving glory to God." The way of praising God is pointed out in the preaching of social justice. Bishops are to "take particular care to further the interests of the poor and the underprivileged to whom the Lord has sent them to preach the gospel" (CD 13). Already we note possibilities for the ministry of the deacon in assisting the bishop by encouraging the practice of biblical justice among the members of the local church.

Through the sacred ministry of the bishop, the people of God are sanctified (LG 26). The celebration of the eucharist is entrusted to the bishop's oversight, "by which the church continuously lives and grows." The sacramental life of the local church is directed by the bishop, "to whom has been entrusted the duty of presenting the worship of the Christian religion to the divine majesty, and of regulating it according to the commands of the Lord." Thus bishops are to exhort and instruct their people "so that in the liturgy, especially in the holy sacrifice of the mass, they fulfill their part with faith and devotion." "Deacons likewise have been ordained for the ministry," states CD 15, implying that they are to assist the bishop "as promoters and guardians of the whole liturgical life in the church which has been entrusted to them." It is their endeavor to make "the faithful acquire a deeper knowledge of the paschal mystery, and so live through the eucharist that they may form one closely-knit body united in the love of Christ." Under his "ministry of sanctification" (*munus sanctificandi*) the bishop serves the holiness of the local assembly entrusted to his care. The function of the deacon within as well as beyond the liturgy could perhaps assist the people, who have dispositions of a suitable heart and mind, to take a full, conscious, and active part in liturgical celebration.[50]

By counsel, persuasion, example, authority, and sacred power, the bishop governs the local church (LG 27). The pastoral authority of the bishop is not to be used for his personal gain, but is in service to the Gospel. Bishops are to remember "that the greater must become as the younger and the leader as one

---

and mission of the church. For a recent and succinct presentation of this issue, see Richard Gaillardetz, "Shifting Meanings in the Lay-Clergy Distinction," *Irish Theological Quarterly* 64 (1999): 115–39.

50. See Vatican Council II, *Sacrosanctum Concilium*, December 4, 1963, no. 11 and no. 14 (hereafter SC); in *Decrees* (ed. Tanner).

who serves" (see Lk 22, 26–27). Bishops have the right and duty "of directing everything that concerns the ordering of worship and the apostolate." Serving not as vicar of the pope, but as president of the people he governs, the bishop is not to "refuse to listen to his subjects whom he looks after ... and whom he exhorts cheerfully to cooperate with him." In exercising their pastoral function, bishops should be in their flock as "good shepherds who know their own sheep and whose sheep know them" (CD 16). They are to form their whole flock "into one family, conscious of their own duties," to live and work together "in a union of charity."

In exercising their episcopal governance, bishops are to be solicitous for the welfare of their flock:

They must be better prepared to give guidance for the welfare of the faithful according to the circumstances of each. Accordingly they must strive to acquire an accurate knowledge of their needs in the social conditions in which they live, using for this purpose the appropriate methods, especially those of social research. They must show themselves to be concerned for all no matter what their age, condition or nationality; no matter whether they are natives, immigrants or visitors. In exercising this pastoral care they must respect the place proper to their faithful in the affairs of the church, acknowledging also their duty and right to work actively for the building up of the mystical body of Christ.[51]

In this passage the Council has taken special care to point out the necessity of the bishop to be in tune with what is happening in the lives of his people. Already it is evident how the deacon could assist the bishop in his task, without taking on roles of a priestly or presidential nature. The necessity of the bishop to acquire knowledge of the needs and social conditions of his people provides an expansive field in which the charisms of the diaconate could be put to use.

Under the ministry of governance (*munus regendi*) the bishop is to use his authority to form the flock entrusted to him in ever-greater communion. Through the exercise of the episcopal charisms, members of the local assembly are brought to life, encouraged to take a more active role in worship and in the life and mission of the church. The pastoral authority of the bishop functions not to control the dispensation of charisms to the faithful—for they come from Christ through baptism and not from the episcopal office—but to bring them to life, to be exercised in harmony for the common mission of the church. As the concrete point of unity, it is under the bishop's charge that the activities of the church are ultimately coordinated. As president of the eucharistic assem-

---

51. CD 16, in *Decrees* (ed. Tanner), 2:927.

bly, it is the duty of the bishop to divide up the work of the church among the people of God according to charisms received in baptism and ordination.

In summary, the overall duty of the bishop is to promote unity among the people of God by safeguarding and promoting the fundamental Gospel principles in the life of the church. The bishop works to preserve the apostolic identity of the local church through his tasks of teaching the true faith, promoting right worship, and encouraging the practice of justice. It is his task to help all members make their own contribution, according to their various charisms, to the church's mission as a whole. The bishop is not the source of all activity in the church, but it is his duty to integrate the personal and baptismal gifts of the assembly into the life and mission of the church. As the sovereign high priest, the bishop functions as the center of unity and inspiration of the faithful. In the language of Ephesians, he is to equip the saints. In the language of the *Apostolic Tradition*, he is to help the local church praise and glorify God.

In order to build up the body of Christ, everyone is to fulfill his or her particular role in bringing the Gospel to life in the world. There is an inseparable connection between the church and her mission, between ecclesial *koinonia* (communion) and involvement in the world. "If there is no Church of God without its being missionary, there is no missionary church unless it is welded into the unity of the Body of Christ."[52] There cannot be one without the other. Thus, the bishop's task in safeguarding the apostolic faith, worship, and Gospel life also involves safeguarding and promoting *koinonia* so that the mission of the church (*diakonia*) might be accomplished. Baptism and eucharist, as the fundamental sacraments of unity, are also therefore the fundamental sacraments upon which the charisms of the ordained ministries stand. The work of the one ecclesiastical *ordo* is to promote an authentic baptismal and eucharistic life among the people of God, nothing more and nothing less. The bishop's ministry is truly a *diakonia*, where the Christological, pneumatological, and ecclesial principles are at play.

The Relationship between the Deacon and Ministerial Priests

In LG 29 the Council describes the ministry of the deacon in general terms: "For strengthened by sacramental grace, they are at the service of the people

---

52. Jean-Marie R. Tillard, *Chiesa di Chiese: L'ecclesiologia di communione* (Brescia: Queriniana, 1989), 39.

of God in the ministry of the liturgy, the word and charity, in communion with the bishops and his presbyterium." This passage is open to misunderstanding because it describes the ministry of the deacon in language very similar to that of the *tria munera* for the bishop. Careful examination of the phrase "in the ministry of the liturgy, the word and charity," reveals that the Council, faithful to the teaching of the *Apostolic Tradition,* did not attribute to the deacon the capacity to function *in persona Christi Capitis* (*in the person of Christ the Head*). The *relatio* written before the vote on LG 29 shows that the threefold service of liturgy, word, and charity is merely a general and brief way of representing the responsibilities of deacons.[53] The distinction must be maintained, however, between *diaconia liturgiae, verbi et caritatis* and the *munera santificandi, docendi,* and *regendi* that pertain to the office of the bishop. *Diaconia* is not an exact equivalent of *munus.* While the Council affirms later on in the article that deacons can be given the *cura animarum* (reinforcing the notion that deacons are indeed given an ecclesiastical ministry within the church), deacons are never said to act *in persona Christi Capitis.* The deacon indeed has a share in the mission of Christ, a share in the bishop's ministry that in the language of the Council is described in terms of the *tria munera,* but his share is not a participation in the headship of Christ. This distinction is crucial to maintain in the theology of the deacon. The language used by the Council to describe the ministry of the deacon in general cannot be used to support a theology of the deacon in which he is a participant in the ministerial priesthood of Christ, even to a lesser degree, by way of ordination.[54] This marks a change from the scholastic notion that the deacon participates in the priesthood of Christ without the "powers" necessary to perform certain priestly functions, a theology that was required by the failure to distinguish between *sacerdotium* and *ministerium* within the ecclesiastical ministry.[55]

The new language of the Second Vatican Council (or we might say, the more ancient language in the teaching of Vatican II) does not define the or-

53. Giuseppe Alberigo and Franca Magistretti (eds.), *Constitutionis Dogmaticae Lumen Gentium,* Synopsis Historica (Bologna: Istituto per le Scienze Religiose, 1975), 462: "Indicantur officia diaconorum in primis modo generali, brevi sed sententia, in triplici campo, scilicet 'in diaconia liturgiae, verbi et caritatis'; quod deinde magis specificatur per 'caritatis et administrationis.'"

54. Herve-Marie Legrand, "Le diaconat dans sa relation à la théologie de l'Église et des ministères: Reception et devenir du diaconat depuis Vatican II," in *Actes du Colloque Diaconat XXIe siècle* (Paris: Cerf, 1997), 13–41.

55. Hence, the *sacerdotium* involved matters related to the priesthood, but not strictly that of the priesthood. As such, the diaconate could have a share in the *sacerdotium* of Christ by way of his ordination, but only because *sacerdotium* was identical with the state of the sacramentally ordained, and the deacon was sacramentally ordained. See Vorgrimler, *Commentary,* 228.

dained ministry simply in the category of priesthood. It must now be recognized that, fundamentally, the ordained ministry is *diakonia*. Thus the deacon, who is named for the *diakonia*, can share in the mission of Christ without having a share in the ministerial priesthood. There is yet a fundamental unity among the three ministerial orders of bishop, priest, and deacon. The *sacerdotium* is a form of *ministerium*, but *ministerium* does not necessarily include the *sacerdotium*. The unity of the ecclesiastical ministry is found concretely in the office of the bishop, where the *sacerdotium* and *ministerium* are present in full. Presbyters and deacons have a limited share in the bishop's *sacerdotium* and *ministerium*, respectively participating in the ministry that the bishop has in different ways. They always exercise their respective offices in communion with him, never apart from him. As such, the deacons and presbyters have a relationship with one another by way of the bishop. Thus the Council was able to say that the deacon exercises his office "in communion with the bishop and his presbyters" (LG 29).

One must acknowledge that a small number of theologians today still adhere to the scholastic notion of the diaconate, but the limitations of this book do not allow for a complete rebuttal of those who adopt theological positions against the certain teaching of the Second Vatican Council.[56] This chapter only intends to lay out a developed theological understanding of the diaconate that is organically related to the teaching of the Council. One might simply refer, however, to the *Catechism of the Catholic Church* promulgated by Pope John Paul II, and the Apostolic Letter *Omnium in Mentem* of Pope Benedict XVI for the revision of the *Code of Canon Law*, to respond to those who either deny the sacramental character of the diaconate or who still insist upon relating it essentially to the ministerial priesthood.

It is interesting to note that both the original text of the *Code* of 1983 and the draft edition of the *Catechism* (originally composed in French) got the diaconate wrong precisely because they espoused the scholastic vision of the deacon. In canons 1008 and 1009 of the original text, a theological description of the entire ecclesiastical order was given using language that could certainly be applied to the bishop, and secondarily to the priest, but not to the deacon:

> Can. 1008: By divine institution some among the Christian faithful are constituted sacred ministers through the sacrament of orders by means of the indelible

---

56. For a good summary of the debate regarding the sacramental character of the diaconate, see the statement of the International Theological Commission, *From the Diakonia of Christ to the Diakonia of the Apostles* (Chicago: Hillenbrand Books, 2003), 54–55.

character with which they are marked; accordingly they are consecrated and deputed to shepherd the people of God, each in accord with his own grade of orders, by fulfilling in the person of Christ the Head the functions of teaching, sanctifying and governing.

> Can. 1009: §1. The orders are the episcopacy, the presbyterate, and the diaconate.

Taken together, canons 1008 and 1009 §1 explicitly connect the diaconate with the role of "fulfilling in the person of Christ the Head the functions of teaching, sanctifying and governing," language singularly associated with the ministerial priesthood.

This theological mistake has been corrected in the revision promulgated by Pope Benedict XVI.[57] Thus canon 1008 now reads: "By divine institution, some of the Christian faithful are marked with an indelible character and constituted as sacred ministers by the sacrament of holy orders. They are thus consecrated and deputed so that, each according to his own grade, they may serve the People of God by a new and specific title." And the revised canon 1009 now includes an extra third paragraph, which reads: "Those who are constituted in the order of the episcopate or the presbyterate receive the mission and capacity to act in the person of Christ the Head, whereas deacons are empowered to serve the people of God in the ministries of the liturgy, the word and charity." These combined revisions tether the *Code of Canon Law* more closely to the official Magisterial teaching of the Council on the diaconate found in LG 29. At once affirming the sacramental character of the diaconate, they also appropriately distinguish what the deacon and his service are not: neither priestly nor presidential.

Regarding the *Catechism*, it is worth noting that a deliberate effort was also taken on the part of the *Catechism* editors to correct inconsistent language involving the ordained ministry in the provisional edition. For example, the original French version and English first edition of the *Catechism* of 1994 made the following unsophisticated statement on the sacrament of holy orders at no. 875:

No one can bestow grace on himself; it must be given and offered. This fact presupposes ministers of grace, authorized and empowered by Christ. From him, they receive the mission and faculty ("the sacred power") to act *in persona Christi Capitis*. The ministry in which Christ's emissaries do and give by God's grace what they cannot do and give by their own powers, is called a "sacrament" by the Church's tradition. Indeed, the ministry of the Church is conferred by a special sacrament.

---

57. Pope Benedict XVI, *Omnium in Mentem*, Apostolic Letter, October 26, 2009; available at www.vatican.va.

This text, as it stood, was inconsistent with the teaching of LG 29 because no distinction was made concerning the deacon and his particular configuration to Christ in comparison to that of the priestly orders. Curiously, at no. 1554, the English first edition of the *Catechism* got the diaconate right and was precise about the distinction of the diaconate from the episcopacy and presbyterate.[58]

The second English edition of the *Catechism* of 1997 (which is a translation of the official Latin *editio typica*) revised no. 875 in the following manner:

... From him, bishops and priests receive the mission and faculty ("the sacred power") to act in persona Christi Capitis; deacons receive the strength to serve the people of God in the diaconia of the liturgy, word and charity, in communion with the bishop and his presbyterate....

The editors of the *Catechism* recognized the inaccuracy of the previous text and took extra care to distinguish the deacon from the other clergy, carefully avoiding language of *tria munera* (the threefold office of priest, prophet, and king) and *in persona Christi Capitis* for the diaconate. This specific change in the text brought the typical edition of the *Catechism* into conformity with the teaching of LG 29 on the deacon.

In order to safeguard the unique identity and function of the deacon, it is necessary to avoid confusing the diaconate with the ministerial priesthood. The influence of scholastic theology makes this task difficult at times, even many decades after the Second Vatican Council. As I now begin my final examination of the conciliar teaching on the ministry of the deacon in service to the people of God, I will be careful to note any indications in the conciliar teaching that might encourage one to view the diaconate in the perspective of the ministerial priesthood.

Having clarified the general description of the deacon's ministry, we are ready to proceed with an assessment of the list of possible functions for the deacon given in LG 29:

To the extent that he has been authorised by competent authority, he is to administer baptism solemnly, to reserve and distribute the eucharist, to assist at and bless marriages in the name of the church, to take viaticum to the dying, to read sacred

---

58. *Catechism of the Catholic Church* (Washington, D.C.: United States Catholic Conference, 1994), no. 1554: "Catholic doctrine, expressed in the liturgy, the Magisterium, and the constant practice of the Church, recognizes that there are two degrees of ministerial participation in the priesthood of Christ: the episcopacy and the presbyterate. The diaconate is intended to help and serve them. For this reason the term sacerdos in current usage denotes bishops and priests but not deacons."

scripture to the faithful, to instruct and exhort the people, to preside at the worship and prayer of the faithful, to administer sacramentals, and to preside at funeral services and burials. Dedicated to duties of charity and administration, deacons should bear in mind the admonition given by blessed Polycarp: "Merciful, sedulous, and walking in accordance with the truth of the Lord, who became the servant of all."

We note first of all a certain structure in the description of the deacon's ministry. Following the general sketch of the deacon's ministry in three general areas come the more specific categories of administrative and charitable duties.[59] Here the Council emphasizes its concern, citing the admonition of St. Polycarp that the deacon's ministry is to bear the Christological character of biblical *diakonia*.

In between the general and particular descriptions, ten tasks that are primarily liturgical are enumerated. These tasks were more or less allotted to the deacon in the course of history.[60] Notably absent is the ritual function of the deacon in the liturgy of the eucharist, the only real function that deacons had in the Latin West for over a thousand years.[61] This list is not to be considered definitive or complete. Given that the sphere of the deacon's ministry within the church was broadening beyond serving the eucharistic table, it was necessary to explain what relation his ministry would have to other sacraments as well as other very common aspects of parish ministry. One can imagine the priests (and faithful) saying to the bishops, "So, we are getting permanent deacons. Can they baptize? Can they officiate weddings? Funerals?" and so on. Hence, these liturgical functions are important examples that illustrate the phrase "for the care of souls" (*pro cura animarum*) in the next paragraph. The list thus leaves open the possibility of restricting or amplifying the specific duties of the deacon according to the concrete needs of the local church.[62] If

---

59. *Constitutionis Dogmaticae Lumen Gentium* (ed. Alberigo), 730: "quod deinde magis specificatur per <<caritatis et administrationis officia>>."

60. See ibid., 730–36. The most ancient function of distributing the eucharist is attested in the *Apologia* of Justin Martyr. Preaching (the 1917 *Code of Canon Law* [hereafter "CIC 1917"], c. 1342 §1) and baptism (CIC 1917, c. 741) are some of the more recent functions of the deacon. Officiating at matrimonial ceremonies and funeral rites derive directly from the desire of the Second Vatican Council itself.

61. In its desire to broaden the ministry of the deacon, the Council distanced itself from its own immediate experience of the deacon. Deacons rarely performed functions outside of the sanctuary for more than a millennium. See Edward Echlin, *The Deacon in the Church: Past and Future* (Staten Island: Alba House, 1971), 61–94.

62. The Council was evidently sensitive to the flexibility of the diaconate throughout history. This was no doubt due to the theological work on the diaconate that immediately preceded the Council. See Rahner, "On the Diaconate," 200–201: "It follows that whatever authentic basis we find for instituting the diaconate of the future in its distinctive form, it must be such that it does not in any sense depend

indeed these ten functions were all that deacons did, they would indeed look like "mini-priests."

While none of the functions listed strictly require the "powers" of the priesthood, all of them have something to do with helping overburdened priests in their pastoral work and building up communities where priests are not available. We see in the second paragraph of LG 29 the motive behind the Council's decision to reestablish a permanent diaconate: "Since these tasks, which are supremely necessary for the life of the church, can only with difficulty be carried out in many regions, according to the current discipline of the Latin church, the diaconate can for the future be restored as a proper and permanent grade of the hierarchy." Though LG is concerned primarily with the problems associated with the permanent diaconate under its dogmatic aspects, a pastoral motive is given for the restoration of the diaconate as a permanent grade.[63] In the mind of the Council, the deacon's ministry is most important in those areas where the above functions are carried out only with difficulty. The Council participants had in mind especially missionary territories, where a dearth of priests provides multiple occasions for the ministry of the deacon.[64]

One of the previous drafts of the text read that the ministry of the deacon would be effective in the future, "especially in the absence of priests" (*praesertim in absentia sacerdotis*).[65] Fortunately this phrase was removed, recognizing

---

upon the postulate that this concrete form of the diaconate as conceived of in the present must have been in existence all along and of necessity, and must continue to exist for all time. This means that the concrete situation of the Church is an essential element.... In seeking a theological basis for the future diaconate, therefore, we do not need to make it our aim to evolve any absolutely univocal and uniform type of deacon."

63. Much of the second paragraph of LG 29 concerns the process of reestablishing the diaconate, as well as the issue of celibacy. As these are issues primarily of discipline rather than fundamentals of a theology of the diaconate, I consider only the motives behind the restoration. For studies on the diaconate and celibacy, see the classic work by Wilhelm Schamoni, *Married Men as Ordained Deacons* (London: Burns and Oates, 1955).

64. Gérard Philips claims that many fathers hesitated to approve the reestablishment of the permanent diaconate, for they did not consider them necessary in their own countries where priests were not lacking. These were finally won over by the argument that some places may be more in need of the diaconate than others. See Philips, *La chiesa*, 333.

65. *Constitutionis Dogmaticae Lumen Gentium* (ed. Alberigo), 726. During the conciliar debate, Archbishop Mosquera said that bishops favored the restoration due to the shortage of priests: "Nemo est qui non videat quam opportune in schemate affirmetur necessitas diaconatum in futuro restituendi tamquam proprium ac permanentem gradum ecclesisticae hierarchiae, saltem ubi Ecclesia id postulet ad curam animarum. Rationes pastorales praesertim illud suadent, illis speciatim in locis ubi vel sacerdotes desunt, ut in missionibus," *Acta Synodalia Sacrosancti Concilii Oecumenici Vaticani II* (Rome: Typis Polyglottis Vaticanis, 1970–78) (hereafter AS), II.II, 623–24. Cardinal Barbieri suggested: "En

the possibility of the deacon's ministry even in the *presence* of priests.[66] The text as a whole, however, does not entirely avoid the image of the deacon as a stand-in for the priest. One cannot deny the fact that the decision of the Council fathers was influenced by their awareness of territories suffering from a lack of priests. That some important liturgical functions "can only with difficulty be carried out in many regions" was indeed a factor in the restoration of the permanent diaconate. This line of argument for the restoration of the permanent diaconate includes the Council's recognition that there are some ministries in the church today that do not necessarily involve the ministry of the priest, but are nonetheless appropriate for one in the ordained ministry. The deacon is recognized as one who, though not a priest, is beneficial to the life and mission of the church. The line of demarcation between the role of the priest and the ministry of the deacon has not been clearly drawn. Here we have the beginning of what would become the debate over what is proper to the ministry of the priest versus the deacon.

The deacon should not be seen today as a fill-in for the priest, but as one who is exercising charisms proper to his own order.[67] A diaconate will be doomed for confusion with the ministerial priesthood if it is based primarily upon what priests in a given area cannot accomplish, rather than what should be the deacon's ministry according to the charisms received in ordination. The unique ministry of the deacon therefore needs to be spelled out, especially *vis-à-vis* the priest. One helpful thing to remember is that LG 29 intends the ministry of the deacon—in the general areas of liturgy, word, and charity—to be more particularly specified in the duties of charity and administration. Here we have, in seminal form, what is commonly understood as the heart of what the diaconate is all about: the deacon's ministry is to be viewed in the perspective of charity. It is unfortunate that one has to literally "read between the lines"

---

cuanto a la creación del Diaconado en la Santa Iglesia, creo que esto viene a aportar una gran ayudar al Sacerdote en su labor apostólica. En efecto: el Diácono supliría en muchos casos a los Sacerdotes en su ministerio" (AS III.I, 547).

66. The reason given for the removal of the phrase was that transitional deacons already have functions to perform, even in the presence of priests. *Constitutionis Dogmaticae Lumen Gentium* (ed. Alberigo), 727–28: "De *officiis* diaconorum plures proposuerunt ut enumerarentur tanquam explenda <<*praesertim in absentia sacerdotis*>>. Quae tamen incisa non placuit. Etenim diaconi etiam praesentibus sacerdotibus varia officia in cura pastorali exercere possunt, v. g. quasi per modum probationis, antequam nempe ad sacerdotium promoveantur."

67. Deacons endanger their own identity when they are present for the parish celebrations of baptisms, funerals, and weddings only when they preside. Deacons should be encouraged to take their own place at these celebrations and not made to feel like a third wheel simply because the priest is accustomed to doing everything by himself.

to understand what the Council dogmatically intends. On the other hand, the historical context of the Council gives the fathers a legitimate excuse for not being clear about the specifics of the diaconal ministry. After all, the Council did not have the immediate experience of a functioning permanent diaconate from which to draw their theological reflection. In comparison to the concrete and immediate questions about the deacon's expanded liturgical functions, a certain amount of vagueness about "charity" and "administration" was in fact appropriate.

The Deacon in *Ad Gentes*

During the Council itself, a certain development did occur concerning the nature and ministry of the diaconate. Two years following the promulgation of LG, in the decree on missionary activity, *Ad Gentes*, the Council fathers addressed more specifically the circumstances of those areas where the functions in LG 29 could only be carried out with difficulty. Unlike LG 29, however, the liturgical duties of the deacon are given minimal attention in AG 16:

Where it seems opportune to episcopal conferences, the order of diaconate, as a permanent state of life, should be restored in accordance with the norms of the constitution of the church. It would be helpful to those men who are exercising what is in fact the ministry of a deacon—either by preaching the word of God as catechists, or by taking charge of scattered Christian communities in the name of the parish priest and the bishop, or by practising charity in social or charitable works—to be strengthened, and bound more closely to the altar, by the imposition of hands which has come down from the apostles, so that they may be able to carry out their ministry more effectively through the sacramental grace of the diaconate.[68]

The administrative and social works of the deacon are given emphasis in this passage, without any direct mention of liturgical tasks. Then again, it is recognized in this passage that ordination binds the candidate more closely to the altar, an obvious allusion to liturgical functions. Another extremely important difference, and not altogether unrelated to the difference in emphasis of the type of diaconal ministry described, is the underlying basis given for the restoration of the permanent diaconate in those territories where priests are not in abundance: the desire to have charisms and office united.

Karl Rahner was the prime theological architect for AG 16. While his theological argument for the restoration of the diaconate as a permanent grade did

---

68. *Decrees* (ed. Tanner), 2:1026.

not surface in the wording of LG 29, Rahner's thought was eventually accepted by the Council in this decree that was approved some two years after *Lumen Gentium*. Rahner's argument for the restoration of the permanent diaconate did not depend on a dearth of priests, but rather looked to the importance of conferring sacramental grace to those who are actually fulfilling the office for which the charisms are meant to assist: "We are not really concerned with introducing any new office, but only with the restoration of the sacramental conferring of an office that basically already exists though in an anonymous way ... when the office and the divine assurance of the grace necessary for fulfilling the office can be given in a sacramental manner ... they should be given in this way."[69] The genius of Rahner's argument rests on his understanding of ordination as a conferral of grace, not for the dignity of the person but for service to the church. Deacons are given the gifts of the Spirit to help them in their special ministry to the church. The church as a whole would benefit from the conferral of spiritual gifts upon those who are already performing what amounts to "diaconal work" in Rahner's estimation. The simple fact that lay people can be commissioned by a higher authority within the church to fulfill some of these same tasks (such as in the case of a catechist) does not nullify Rahner's argument. That there is an office (established already by church tradition), and that there is a rite for the sacramental conferral of the office, are all that is theologically necessary to ground the diaconate among the various ministries of the church. Where the benefit of charisms by way of ordination is possible, the charisms should be utilized.

Hence we see, in the two conciliar texts involving the reestablishment of the permanent diaconate in the Latin West, sketches of the ministry of the deacon and the motives for its restoration. We note that the varied ways of identifying concrete duties of the deacon are related to the different motives for restoration. While respecting the greater authority of the Dogmatic Constitution, the argument for restoration given in *Ad Gentes* is much more in harmony with the theology of the deacon that is described in the first two sentences of LG 29. If the reason of pastoral necessity (along the line of a lack of priests given in LG 29) is followed too closely, then the deacon risks being identified as a "mini-priest." Granted that where priests are lacking, the deacon's ministry could be appropriately expanded to shoulder the pastoral burden. But if the deacon's ministry is founded upon such an extra-ordinary situation, then it should be no surprise that he ends up appearing as an extra-ordinary minister.

---

69. Rahner, "The Theology for the Restoration of the Diaconate," 154.

Deacons do have a unique role to fulfill in communion with the bishop and priests, in service to the people of God. Moreover, one can rightly say that we have deacons *because* we have priests!

Both LG and AG are in agreement when it comes to describing the general function of the deacon in the church today. While *diakonia*, service, and charity apply to all in the ecclesiastical *ordo*, it was the desire of the Council that deacons be given the witness of charity as their special charge among the ordained ministers. It was the hope of the Council that the character of humble service would color the diaconate in such a way that deacons would be recognized as Christ's servants. The Council did not mandate particular functions. The Council only gave the goal to be achieved, providing the general, theological fundamentals from which structures for the diaconal ministry could develop.

Within the flexible nature of the diaconate is a framework of fundamental principles that serve to keep the diaconate from mutating into an entirely different kind of ministry. The fundamental theological structure of the deacon arises from his share "in the ministry of the bishop" (*in ministerio episcopi*). As the bishop is in service to the apostolic identity of his flock, so too is the deacon. We have seen that the ministry of the bishop, as articulated in *Lumen Gentium* and *Christus Dominus*, involves the perfection of *koinonia* as an integral part of preserving apostolicity. In communion with their bishop and the presbyterate, deacons serve the apostolic identity and *koinonia* of the local church in the three intimately united levels of living (charity), believing (word), and celebrating (liturgy).[70] Within this framework, the duties of charity and administration are to determine the deacon's duties more specifically. It is therefore evident that the deacon's sphere of ministry is not found entirely in the liturgical area (as it was for more than a thousand years in the Latin West), nor is it found entirely in the area of social work. The deacon, in some way yet to be determined, serves to bridge whatever distance may occur between liturgy around the altar and the praise and glory of God in daily life. The deacon therefore must have both liturgical functions and social functions in order to accomplish his ministry. To see more clearly how the deacon's ministry is in the perspective of charity, we must look beyond the conciliar texts themselves.

70. Borras, *La grâce du diaconat*, 29.

The Deacon in *Ad Pascendum*

Following the closure of the Second Vatican Council, Pope Paul VI issued several documents concerning the implementation of the permanent diaconate as outlined by the Council.[71] The final document, the Apostolic Letter *Ad Pascendum*, depicted the role of the deacon more fully than the conciliar texts:

Finally, Vatican Council II approved the wishes and requests that, where it would lead to the good of souls, the permanent diaconate should be restored as an intermediate order [*medius ordo*] between the higher grades of the ecclesiastical hierarchy and the rest of the people of God, being as it were a mediator [*interpres*] of the needs and desires of the Christian communities, an animator of the service or *diaconia* of the Church among the local Christian communities, and a sign or sacrament of Christ the Lord himself, who *came not to be served, but to serve.*[72]

Paul VI identifies the deacon as an intermediary between the higher grades of the church's hierarchy and the rest of the people of God. While one could interpret "intermediate order" as a step in a linear hierarchy, it is more likely here to have a different meaning. In the context of the ecclesiology of the Second Vatican Council, Paul VI's understanding of the intermediary nature of the deacon's order more than likely connotes *mediation*, bringing together more closely two entities, rather than *separation*. The deacon would not be a barrier, or buffer zone, between the higher clergy and the laity, but instead he would function more like a bridge or glue, binding everyone together more closely. This understanding is apparent in the following phrases, where the deacon's ministry is rooted in the needs of the people, as an animator of the church's *dia-*

---

71. *Sacrum Diaconatus Ordinem*, Apostolic Letter, June 18, 1967, in AAS 59 (1967): 697–704, implemented the recommendations of the Second Vatican Council by determining general norms governing the restoration of the permanent diaconate in the Latin church; *Pontificalis Romani Recognitio*, Apostolic Constitution, June 18, 1968, in AAS 60 (1968): 369–73, approved the new rite of conferring the episcopacy, presbyterate, and diaconate; *Ministeria Quaedam*, Apostolic Letter, August 15, 1972, in AAS 64 (1972): 529–34, suppressed the minor orders and declared that entry into the clerical state is joined with the diaconate—lectors and acolytes are no longer "ordained" but "installed"; and finally, *Ad Pascendum*, Apostolic Letter, August 15, 1972, in AAS 64 (1972): 534–40, which clarified the conditions for admission and ordination of candidates.

72. Author's translation. AAS 64 (1972): 536, "Concilium denique Vaticanum II optatis et precibus suffragatum est, ut Diaconatus permanens, ubi id animarum bono conduceret, instauraretur veluti medius ordo inter superiores ecclesiasticae hierarchiae gradus et reliquum populum Dei, quasi interpres necessitatum ac votorum christianarum communitatum, instimulator famulatus seu *diaconiae* Ecclesiae apud locales christianas communitates, signum vel sacramentum ipsius Christi Domini, qui *non venit ministrari, sed ministrare.*"

konia as a whole, and as a symbol of Christ the servant. Fulfilling these tasks, the deacon brings about a greater communion among the people of God, rather than being an additional rank-figure in the structure of power and authority between the bishop and priests on the one hand, and the laity on the other.

Not only does the deacon function as a bridge between the laity and the higher clergy, but he also has as the object of his ministry the unity among the laity themselves in their concern for the needs of one another. The pope states later on, "By word and example they [deacons] should work so that all the faithful in imitation of Christ, may place themselves at the constant service of their brothers and sisters." *Koinonia* through charitable service is at the heart of the deacon's ministry. The notion of the deacon as an intermediary in this service perhaps opens a new door in our search for a more precise, clear, and accurate description of the unique ministry of the deacon *vis-à-vis* the bishop, presbyterate, and laity.

Paul VI's desire to utilize deacons for the encouragement of the people of God to submit their personal gifts and talents in service to the good of all is continued in the recent documents on the permanent diaconate from the Congregation of Catholic Education and the Congregation for the Clergy. Drawing on Paul VI's *Ad Pascendum*, the *Basic Norms for the Formation of Permanent Deacons* gives a brief theological outline of the deacon's ministry: "As a participation in the one ecclesiastical ministry, he is a specific sacramental sign, in the Church, of Christ the servant. His role is to 'express the needs and desires of the Christian communities' and to be 'a driving force for service, or *diakonia*,' which is an essential part of the mission of the Church."[73] Here Paul VI's description of the function of the deacon as a mediator between the higher clergy and the laity is continued. The deacon's intermediary role operates, in some way, to express the needs and desires of the people who are the object of the bishop's and priests' ministry, as well as to be a driving force for service among all the people of God. A similar passage is found in the *Directory for the Ministry and Life of Permanent Deacons.*[74]

73. Congregation for Catholic Education, *Basic Norms for the Formation of Permanent Deacons* (Vatican City: Libreria Editrice Vaticana, 1998), no. 5 (24–25).

74. Congregation for the Clergy, *Directory for the Ministry and Life of Permanent Deacons* (Vatican City: Libreria Editrice Vaticana, 1998), no. 37 (101): "In virtue of the Sacrament of Orders, deacons, in communion with the bishop and the diocesan presbyterate, participate in the same pastoral functions, but exercise them differently in serving and assisting the bishop and his priests. As this participation is brought about by the sacrament, they serve God's people in the name of Christ. For this reason, they exercise it in humility and charity.... Their authority, therefore, exercised in hierarchical communion with the bishop and his priests, and required by the same unity of consecration and mission, is a

The articulation of the deacon as an intermediary incorporates the Christological, pneumatological, and ecclesial elements of biblical *diakonia*. The ecclesial character of the deacon's role as an intermediary among the people of God is found in his service to unity (expressing the needs and desires of the Christian community) and in keeping watch over the apostolic identity of the service of charity among the people of God. Deacons equip the saints and build up the body of Christ for the praise and glory of God in this way. From the perspective of the pneumatological character of *diakonia*, the deacon is able to perform the function of an intermediary by way of the charisms received in the gift of the Spirit at his ordination. Serving God's people in the name of Christ, deacons are to exercise their authority in humility and charity, thereby conforming their ministry according to the Christological character of biblical *diakonia*.

Conclusion

I began this chapter with important questions derived from my analysis of biblical *diakonia*. The first question, in light of the specific Hellenistic context of *diakonia*, concerned the higher authority from which the deacon receives his mandate or commission. In the ordination of a deacon, the candidate receives a share in the mission of Christ by way of the gift of the Spirit. Thus, it is from God that the deacon receives his charge. The deacon does not, however, receive this charge independent from the church. Only through the church's mediation does a candidate receive the Spirit and charisms necessary for the fulfillment of his functions. The mediation process, known as "ordination," is effectively expressed through the participation of the people, the bishop's imposition of hands, and the prayer of ordination spoken aloud by the bishop and prayed fervently in the hearts of the assembly. While the deacon does indeed receive a noble charge from heaven, it is not for his honor but for the good of the church. By way of ordination the candidate is received into the order of the diaconate, as a member of the one ecclesiastical *ordo*, and is given the sacramental graces necessary for the fulfillment of his office. Thus the deacon serves the people of God in communion with the bishop and his presbyters.

The second question concerned the exact nature of the deacon's ministry. This question was complicated by the fact that prior to the Second Vatican

---

service of charity which seeks to help and foster all members of a particular Church, so that they may participate, in a spirit of communion and according to their proper charisms, in the life and mission of the Church."

Council, there was very little living experience of the ministry of the deacon beyond the liturgy. In a very real sense, it had been forgotten. In the attempt to "remember" the deacon at the Second Vatican Council, we saw how important the *Apostolic Tradition* was for the Council in clarifying the nature and ministry of the deacon within the one ecclesiastical *ordo*. The diaconate, as an ordained ministry, is a gift of God to the church. The deacon has a share in the apostolic office of preserving the authentic identity of the *ekklesia*. The community of believers is assisted by the ordained ministers to praise and glorify God. God is praised and glorified in the preservation of the authentic teaching of the apostles, the worship of God, and charitable life. The charisms given to the deacon at ordination distinguish him from the other clergy, as well as the laity. These charisms, however, are in addition to and not in place of the baptismal charism he shares in common with the rest of the people of God. The diaconal charisms help the deacon bring to life the charisms given to the people of God in their baptism. Calling forth the gifts of the baptized is a ministry that he has in common with the bishop, and by extension, with the presbyterate, but in a distinct way—he is not a presiding priest.

The ministry of the deacon complements the ministry of the bishop. We have seen the authorities in the church, following the theological and pastoral outlines drawn by the Council, continue to shape the ministry of the deacon in terms of service as an intermediary. In his direct service to the higher clergy and to the laity, the deacon is to work at fostering a greater *koinonia* by encouraging everyone to submit his or her particular charisms to the good of all. Like the bishop, the deacon is to animate, inspire, and coordinate the charisms of the people for the fulfillment of the mission entrusted to the church as a whole: to witness God's plan of salvation for all. The deacon also expresses the needs and desires of the community to the bishop, to the priests, and to the church at large. Serving to unite the head and body more firmly together, the deacon has a unique position among the people of God. Precisely because he is not the head (or represents the bishop as the presbyters do) and at the same time is a member of the ecclesiastical *ordo*, the deacon is able to function as an intermediary between the two. His function as an intermediary is not therefore a barrier but a bridge to unite the various members of the body of Christ.

In summary, the deacon assists the people of God to strengthen the bonds of unity and charity, keeping a vigilant watch over the charisms given for the benefit of all. Christ the servant is made visible to the people of God and to the world in the icon that is the deacon.

The ministry of the deacon is indeed a *diakonia* in the biblical sense. Conformed to the figure of Christ the servant through the outpouring of the Holy Spirit, the deacon is a concrete symbol and animator of Christian service. The deacon is a living reminder of the self-emptying service Christ rendered in his obedience to the Father's will of salvation for all. The deacon requires the gifts of the Spirit to fulfill his tasks. It is a commission that he cannot take for himself, but requires the prayer and invocation of the church. The noble charge of the deacon received in ordination empowers him to build up the church for the praise and glory of God. Modeled upon the example of Christ, the deacon serves not his own will but the will of God. In his expressions of care and concern for those in need, the deacon motivates the entire body of Christ to continue walking in the way of the Lord Jesus.

Any notion of the deacon that would distinguish him too much from priests and bishops risks violating the unity of the sacrament of order. Likewise, to conceive the gift of the Spirit at the ordination of a deacon as independent or separate from baptism would involve the creation of a false division within the people of God. As I conclude this chapter and begin my effort to further our understanding of the unique position and function of the deacon among the people of God, I must recognize and respect the tension that rightfully exists between the deacon and the higher clergy as well as between the ordained deacon and the baptized and confirmed faithful. Whatever my conclusions might be, we must respect these tensions, tensions that prominently come to the fore when considering the nature and function of the deacon in the Latin rite.

The following chapters will explore the intermediary role that the deacon can play and has played in the history of the church. Only after understanding the sociology of intermediary roles, the history of the deacon's social functions, and the related value of the deacon's liturgical ministry as an icon or symbol of communion will we be prepared to understand fully the diaconate as it is called to function in the church today. The dialogical relationship of the deacon *vis-à-vis* the bishop and his presbyterate, and *vis-à-vis* the rest of the people of God, will be my focus as I explore the administrative dimension of the deacon's ministry in the next chapter and following. More specifically, we recall that the deacon is called to express the needs and desires of the Christian community. How this might be accomplished concretely will be our ultimate concern. I will focus my attention upon the use of power and authority within the church. The way members of the body of Christ relate to one another in terms of power is not only an issue of the Gospel, but also of sociology. This human dimension of the church will therefore be explored to help us understand the particular charisms of diaconal ministry.

PART 2

The Diaconate as *medius ordo*

CHAPTER 3

Social Mediation

"Ministry," "service," and "charity" are words commonly used to describe diaconal ministry, for indeed they are at the heart of it. They do not, however, refer to diaconal ministry alone, and consequently fail to satisfy our search for a more precise description of the diaconate. On the one hand, "ministry" (unlike priestly-presidency for the presbyter) is too broad and too vague a term to capture succinctly the unique charism of the diaconate. On the other hand, to reduce the deacon fundamentally to a charitable worker is too restrictive; inadequately accounting for many other functions the deacon has fulfilled and continues to fulfill in the church. Can we be more exact about the charism of the diaconate than "ministry," "service," or "charity"? Is there something more fundamental about deacons that makes them ideal candidates for the necessary and noble role of directing and promoting works of charity among the people of God?

My investigation of the Second Vatican Council's teaching on the deacon has shown that the ministry of the deacon is described in biblical terms as *diakonia*, a service that flows from the gift of the Spirit for the building up of the church. It is to be exercised in conformity to the humble example of Jesus. *Diakonia*, as stated in chapter 1, means more than just humble service—it is the fulfillment of a mandate by a "go-between," and is indeed a particular kind of service in the Christian context. *Diakonia* as an activity is not, however, ministry that is unique to the deacon: it describes the ministry of the bishop, presbyters, and the church as a whole. In fact, the Council's description of the deacon as being ordained "not to the priesthood, but to the ministry," emphasizes this point of commonality among the one ministerial *ordo* of the ordained ministers. It grounds the deacon's ministry in the service of communion. In preserving the apostolic identity of the community through correct teaching, right worship, and just living, the deacon shares in the ministry held by the bishop. For this reason, the deacon's unique character within the one ministerial *ordo* is not found in biblical *diakonia*, though it is essentially rooted in it. Nor can the deacon's uniqueness be found in the qualifier "not to the priesthood." This helps to say what the deacon is not; the role of priestly-presidency that is attributed to the bishop and his priests, which serves as the underlying basis for all the functions they perform in service to the church, is *excluded* from the deacon's purview. The deacon is not ordained to act in the person of Christ the Head; instead, he is ordained "to the ministry." But if priestly-presidency is at the core of the ministry of the bishop and his presbyterate, what is the corresponding substance of the diaconate?

Pope Paul VI's description of the diaconate as an "intermediate order" between the sacerdotal orders and the Christian faithful provides a possible way forward in my effort to describe more clearly the unique role of the deacon within the church. This practical application of the theology of the deacon as received from scripture, tradition, and the Magisterium does not require the characterization of the diaconate as an intermediate sacramental reality between the baptized and ordained faithful, as the International Theological Commission warned against.[1] The theological specificity of the deacon lies in his unique character from the sacrament of holy orders as a nonpriestly minister in service to the apostolic communion of the church. Nor does Paul VI's articulation of the diaconate as an "intermediate order" require any notion of further separation of the priestly orders from the laity, as if the diaconate were a wedge in between the two. In fact, as we shall soon see, the role of the deacon in the church is just the opposite.

An intermediary is someone through whom two other parties communicate.[2] The presence of an intermediate subject makes real dialogue possible between parties who are not in direct communication with one another. The concept of the diaconate as an intermediate order leads us to consider the deacon's service in terms of support for dialogue among the people of God.

1. International Theological Commission, *From the Diakonia*, 104: "It would be a theological error to identify the diaconate as 'medius ordo' with a kind of intermediate (sacramental?) reality between the baptized and the ordained faithful. The fact that the diaconate belongs to the sacrament of Holy Orders is sure doctrine.... It is true that it belongs to the deacon to accomplish some sort of task of mediation, but it would not be theologically correct to make that task into the expression of the diaconate's theological nature or its specifying note.... These theological clarifications do not imply a total rejection of all mediating function on the part of the deacon. The notion is based on the witnesses of ecclesial tradition."

2. *New Webster's Dictionary and Thesaurus of the English Language* (Danbury, Conn.: Lexicon Publications, 1993), 504.

Dialogical structures ensure the proper distribution of knowledge of, and responsibility for, the life and mission of the church among all her members. Such ministry ultimately promotes greater communion, as the unity of the local church depends upon fruitful dialogue between her members. If, indeed, the deacon is a part of the dialogical structure of the church, then this reality will be theologically significant in our search for a more fundamental *raison d'être* of the deacon.

The theoretical framework for an intermediary role of the deacon has already been laid out. In part 1 of this book, I was careful to point out that in theological terms the deacon is *other* than the bishop and his priests, and *other* than the laity. While distinctly *other*, the deacon is nonetheless directly related to both the clergy of a higher grade (by virtue of ordination) and the laity (by virtue of not sharing in the presidency of the assembly). The deacon therefore stands not only in the unique position as *other*, but is also *among* the people of God. From this dual perspective, the nature of the diaconate allows the deacon to serve as an intermediary, whether in the specific dialogue between shepherd and flock, or generally among the people of God as a whole. Thus, I have already established the likelihood that the deacon's central role could be that of an intermediary. My objective in part 2, therefore, is to ascertain how the diaconate functions concretely as an intermediate order among the people of God.

What is a "social intermediary"? Before I answer this question, a word is in order about my methodology. I will elucidate the social context of the deacon among the people of God by drawing from the insights of the social sciences. For example, the nonritual roles of the deacon that involve the "expression of needs and desires of the community" pertain to the social need for the mediation of power and authority. Another topic studied by sociologists is social cohesion, which relates very much to the deacon's duties in promoting charitable works among the people of God. In this manner, sociology will help my theological investigation. But I do not intend to replace theology with sociology.

Sociology and theology are sciences that have distinct objects and methodologies. The science that studies God is theology; the science that studies human groups is sociology. The sociologist is not concerned with the individual's personal relationship with God, but with a religion's implications for a social group.[3] The theologian is interested in human persons and society, but

---

3. Joseph H. Fichter, *A Sociologist Looks at Religion*, Theology and Life Series 23 (Wilmington, Del.: Michael Glazier, 1988), 11: "Sociology of religion is a secular science dealing with a sacred subject, but the focus of this science is on the people who worship God and not on the God who is worshipped. The science that studies God is theology. The science that studies human groups is sociology. We are

only as they relate to God of faith. The intent of bringing sociological insights into this theological investigation is not to sociologically construct the diaconate, but to interpret sociologically the historical role of the deacon for the sake of better theological understanding. I have selected scholars from the field of sociology who are respected by their peers and whose insights can contribute an assessment of the deacon's role that is compatible with the Christian faith (adjustments being made, if necessary). My synthesis will link the social reality of the diaconate with the theological foundation upon which it stands.

Social Structures of Mediation

Let us return to the question: what is a social intermediary, particularly in the ecclesial context? An intermediary is a figure through whom other parties communicate. This simple definition concerns itself very little with either the nature of the dialogue or the participants. It can apply to something as solemn as the communication of divine revelation, or to something as mundane as a student passing a note for someone else across the aisle during class. The following analysis of the deacon as a social intermediary among the people of God requires a more complex understanding of the social dimension of the church. The nature of social intermediaries, and the particular aims they serve, will reveal certain characteristics important to the concrete data of the nonritual ministry of the deacon.

The nature and purpose of "intermediate structures" can be gleaned from an investigation of terms that are both theologically and sociologically significant. Some terms concern the hierarchical relationship that exists between the bishop and his people, and other terms concern the horizontal relationship that exists among the people of God, and between the church and the larger society. I will address the latter in a moment; for now, I will examine the principles concerning the nature and role of intermediate institutions in the exercise of power and authority by the bishop and his priests.

---

not concerned here with the individual's personal relationship with God. The religious believer may be studied by psychologists, and often is, but it is the religious group that comes under the scrutiny of the social scientist. In making these distinctions between theology and sociology, between the divine being and human beings, and between psychology and sociology, we recognize that religion can be studied from many different perspectives."

Social Mediation of the Power and Authority of the Ministerial Priesthood

Any group of human beings generates structures of power and authority: to be human involves rights and the exercise of those rights.[4] Power and authority are central to societies like the state. For the church the center of gravity is not authority, but the enduring life of Christ in the power of the Spirit.[5] Power and authority in the church are therefore not only anthropological realities, they are also spiritual realities. This distinction alters the manner in which power and authority are conferred and exercised in the church, but it does not alter the anthropological requirements that lie behind them: such as the need for the mediation of power and authority.

To understand the social importance of dialogue and mediating agents in the exercise of power, and to appreciate the role of an intermediate figure, we must have an adequate familiarity with some key social concepts. Here are some summary definitions: *power, authority, legitimacy,* and *legitimation* all concern the process of decisionmaking in every human organization, including the church. The distinction between power and authority is not always adequately understood. Power essentially concerns the *ability* to act, whereas authority generally concerns the *right* to act. *Legitimacy* refers to the objective validation of authority, and *legitimation* to the subjective reception and efficacy of that authority. *Institutions* are the patterned ways of acting in the social world, such that certain individuals are expected to perform defined roles within the community. *Intermediate structures* are mediating institutions that spread societal resources (such as power, knowledge, and material resources) throughout the social body. In bringing the needs and desires of the people to the governing authority, these mediating institutions socially distribute the resources of power and knowledge. Intermediate institutions also bridge the gap between the needs of individuals and the resources that are available in the community at large, tying individuals together more closely with social bonds.

---

4. John O'Grady, "Authority and Power: Issues for the Contemporary Church," *Louvain Studies* 10 (1984): 129.

5. John L. McKenzie, *Authority in the Church* (New York: Sheed and Ward, 1966), 22.

Power

A classic definition of power in society comes from a foundational scholar of sociology, Max Weber: "Power is the probability that one actor in a social relationship will be in a position to carry out his own will despite resistance."[6] Other sociologists have described power as "the ability to get somebody else to do what you want him to do through your control over energetic processes of interest to him."[7] Both of these definitions concern the *ability* of an individual to act. But such definitions of power seem to have more to do with the philosophy of Nietzsche than the Gospel. Power rooted in the ability to dominate another does not resemble the Christological character of biblical *diakonia*; hence, definitions of this sort are not helpful for this particular context without further qualifications. Drawing upon the works of sociologists, Karl Rahner defined power in terms that can be applied to more than just the mighty of this world. Rahner sees power as "a certain self-assertion and resistance proper to a given being and hence as its innate possibility of acting spontaneously, without the previous consent of another, to interfere with and change the actual constitution of that other."[8] As with the sociologist, Rahner defines power in terms of ability, but one that is grounded in "being." The orders of power correspond to the various orders of "being" that make up the multiple realities of the world. As such, "all beings, simply because they exist—in themselves and in contrast to others—inevitably have power in a certain sense and to a certain degree."[9]

The philosopher Hannah Arendt, taking a different tack, argues for a distinction between power and violence (i.e., force used against another): "Power corresponds to the human ability not just to act but to act in concert."[10] Arendt's definition is promising for Christian theology in that the *ability*, to

6. Max Weber, *The Theory of Social and Economic Organisation* (New York: Oxford University Press, 1947), 152.

7. Richard N. Adams, *Energy and Structure: A Theory of Social Power* (Austin: University of Texas Press, 1975), 121.

8. Karl Rahner, "Theology of Power," in *Theological Investigations*, vol. 4: *More Recent Writings*, trans. Kevin Smyth (Baltimore, Md.: Helicon Press, 1966), 391.

9. Rahner, "Theology of Power," 391–92.

10. Hannah Arendt, *On Violence* (New York: Harcourt, Brace and World, 1970), 44: "Power is never the property of an individual; it belongs to a group and remains in existence only so long as the group keeps together. When we say of somebody that he is 'in power' we actually refer to his being empowered by a certain number of people to act in their name. The moment the group, from which the power originated to begin with (*potestas in populo*, without a people or group there is no power), disappears, 'his power' also vanishes."

which power refers, is not rooted in domination. "Acting in concert" is the key element of her definition, connecting the harmonious activity of the community with the exercise of true power. In contrast to the sociological schools that see power as making one's own will prevail even against opposition, Arendt rejects the notion that force or violence is the culmination of power. The origin of true power, for Arendt, lies in the decision to act jointly and together. Thus, the community figures prominently in her conception of power.

The importance Arendt gives to the community in her definition has a certain affinity with Catholic theology: power or ability (which we can recognize as a charism in the church) has more to do with the community acting together, rather than domination for personal gain. Power in this sense, even though possessed by individuals, "belongs" to the entire community. This is similar to Paul's teaching that the gifts of the Spirit are for the common good of the church, not for personal benefit. Arendt's definition of power as the ability "to act in concert," shows that true power is exercised with the community in mind, even if that community is secular in nature. It is only logical for her to deduce that if members of a social group generate power, and act together for a common purpose, then some sort of assent by the members is essential for the existence of power. Arendt's definition therefore connects the exercise of power with the need for communication or dialogue among the members of the community.

The difficulty in applying Arendt's definition to the church lies in her claim that the collective members of the community are the source of power. Greater nuance is necessary. While it may be true that the collective members are the source of all power in other human organizations, they are not so for the church. The Spirit is the giver of all spiritual gifts (i.e., powers), even though the church has a role in the transmission of charisms to individuals. "If the priest and the bishop fulfill their office duly, they do it not in virtue of a grant of power from a superior ecclesiastical office, but in virtue of the Holy Spirit who is given them."[11] In the case of ordination, the church designates members for offices that require a special outpouring of the Spirit. Thus the discernment of the community for offices in the church is an indispensable part of the process of the conferral of some powers. Fundamentally, however, it is the Spirit who gives the necessary gifts for office, and these gifts, once given, cannot be taken away by the will of the people.[12] Nor, in the case of baptism, is the Spirit lim-

---

11. McKenzie, *Authority in the Church*, 100: "There may be ultimately no better statement of the difference between the authority in the Church and secular authority than this."

12. See Herbert Vorgrimler, *Sacramental Theology*, trans. Linda M. Maloney (Collegeville, Minn.:

ited by the will of the community. The church does not select which charisms will be given to one and not to another: God makes this decision alone.[13] For the society of the church, the fundamental source of power is none other than God.

Arendt's emphasis of the community in her conception of power does have valid applications for the understanding of the exercise of charisms in the church. Stressing its positive aspects, Arendt's definition of power as "the human ability to act in concert" is far closer to the Christian context than the definitions provided by some sociologists. She understands power not merely as the potential to force one's will, but as relationship, as something that binds people together. We see here an affirmation of the principle that charism, office and community go together.

Authority

If power is the *ability* to act, authority stands for the *right* to act. Authority is "the right and power to command and be obeyed, or to do something," or "someone whose knowledge and opinions command respect and belief."[14] Authority can be vested in persons or in an office.[15] Authority can stand for institutionalized or formalized power. It is power aggregated to social structures and directed to specific ends.[16] For a specific reason, a person may, according to a set standard, influence the thought, opinion, or behavior of another. Influence is an important word in our definition of authority, for it takes into account the rights and the dignity of the other. Authority is the accepted right for one to influence another, not the mere strength to do so.

Liturgical Press, 1992), 241: "On the one hand, this does not imply a 'democratizating' of the Church in principle, but on the other hand a much greater cooperation on the part of the church communities in the appointment of their ministers is theologically legitimate and practically possible." What is most important to keep in mind here is that ordained ministry only makes sense in relation to the community of faith.

13. The fact that the Spirit is not limited to working only within the visible realities of the church and her sacraments is explicitly recognized in the eucharistic prayers of the liturgy today. In praying to God for those who have died, the church prays not only for those who were baptized, but also for "all who were pleasing to you at their passing from this life" (Eucharistic Prayer III).

14. *New Webster's Dictionary*, 64.

15. Arendt, *On Violence*, 45: "It can be vested in persons—there is such a thing as personal authority, as, for instance, in the relation between parent and child, between teacher and pupil—or it can be vested in an office, as, for instance, in the Roman senate (*auctoritatis in senatu*) or in the hierarchical offices of the Church (a priest can grant valid absolution even though he is drunk)."

16. David N. Power, "The Basis for Official Ministry in the Church," *Jurist* 41 (1981): 329.

Various models of authority have existed within the church, based upon different structures for the conferral of rights.[17] An autocratic or *absolute authority* admits of no limitations. The divine right of kings, for example, allowed no limitations or interference in the right of the king to govern as he saw fit. The signing of the Magna Carta in 1215 by King John eroded the divine right of the monarch in England. Legal authority replaced absolute authority, as rulers in England began a process that would eventually establish laws and bodies of legislators. As individual rights came under the protection of the law, autocratic and absolute authority became increasingly limited.

Learned authority, the right to influence people based upon the expertise of the person with intelligence and education, is another form of authority. When society turns to the authority of experts, it continues the practice of wise counsel, allowing the education of the expert to influence decisions made. Similar to learned authority is the familiar *charismatic authority* based on the quality of the person. There is a certain air of popularity about charismatic leaders. Those with gifts that transcend the experience of most other members of society often arise.[18] Max Weber adopts the notion of "charisma" from the vocabulary of early Christianity and defines it as a certain quality of an individual personality, by virtue of which that person is set apart from ordinary people and treated as a leader.[19] Charismatic figures are movers and shakers, who revolutionize commonly accepted notions and structures. Captivated by their personal powers of persuasion, the community often confers upon them the right to influence their thoughts, opinions, and behavior. Such authority can be helpful or destructive to society, depending upon the nature of the charismatic person and the ends for which they use their God-given and socially accepted capacity. Charismatic authority in itself is neither good nor bad, but the exercise of such authority can be.

Social Institutions for Power and Authority

Weber has shown that charismatic authority can transform into a more structured or institutionalized form of authority within a given community. Weber's

17. The various models presented in the following two paragraphs are drawn from O'Grady, "Authority and Power," 124–26.

18. Martin Hengel, *The Charismatic Leader and His Followers* (New York: Crossroad, 1981).

19. Shmuel Eisenstadt (ed.), *Max Weber on Charisma and Institution Building* (Chicago: University of Chicago Press, 1968), 48.

concept of the "routinization of charisma" stresses the dual nature of "charisma." On the one hand, charisma tends toward innovation and is the "greatest revolutionary force."[20] On the other hand, the endurance of the innovation is dependent upon the charisma stabilizing itself in some manner. "Routinization" is necessary in order for the innovation resulting from the outpouring of charisma to survive. As a social figure, Jesus could be described as someone who held charismatic authority, as could also the apostles, most especially Paul.[21] However, the "revolution" begun by their preaching of the Gospel did not end with their departure from the scene. A cult of personality does not adequately describe, in sociological terms, how the innovation that is the church has continued down through the centuries. Nor does personal "charisma" adequately explain the nature of authority within the church today.

"Routinization" is the process by which the once-personal charisma of the leader is transferred to a permanent social structure. Once "routinized," charisma is no longer said to be personal—it is inherent in something more objective. One is still justified in speaking of charisma because there remains an extraordinary quality, not accessible to everyone, but it survives as a structured element that legitimates the authority of the successors of the charismatic hero.[22] It is then that charisma has been routinized as the charisma of office. Charisma becomes disassociated from a particular individual and becomes an objective, transferable reality. It may be transmitted from one bearer to another, for example, through the ritual laying on of hands.[23] Although the change into a permanent structure significantly transforms charisma's mode of operation, it remains a very important element of the social structure.

Theologically, much more could be said about the formation of the episcopal office. My point here is that in sociological terms the "charismatic" authority of Jesus and his earliest disciples is the origin of the episcopal office. When charisma is routinized and becomes a permanent structure, then its essence and mode of operation are significantly transformed, but it still remains a very important element of the social structure. The bishop's authority is not due to his personal charisma, but to the office he holds. The rights associated with

---

20. Max Weber, *Economy and Society*, ed. Günther Roth and Claus Wittich (New York: Bedminster Press, 1968), 1:243–44.

21. Their powers are not regarded as accessible to everyone, but are viewed as stemming from divine origins. See Christopher Rowland, *Christian Origins: An Account of the Setting and Character of the Most Important Messianic Sect of Judaism* (London: SPCK, 1985), 266–71.

22. Weber, *Economy and Society*, 3:1135 and 1146–47.

23. Eisenstadt, *Max Weber on Charisma*, 57.

the office of bishop are dependent, however, on the authority of Jesus and the early leaders of the church.[24] Routinization of charisma accounts for charismatic authority seeking stabilization in a permanent structure. The structured relationship that exists today between the bishop and his flock developed from the teaching and example of Jesus and the apostles within a given social milieu. The social context was, and remains, an influence upon the structures of power and authority within the church.

Examples from Church History

In this effort to understand the nature of a social mediator, I have uncovered some insights that pertain to the genesis, alteration, manifestation, and purpose of institutions for power and authority. It is important to note, however, that the diaconate is a social structure produced not just by social forces, but also by grace. Our faith compels us to hold that God has created the church, and it is under the Spirit's inspiration that she is guided in her continuing development. This fundamental belief in the origin of the church does not, however, contradict the statement that the church as a human structure entails human production.[25]

There is a relationship between belief, social structures, and social setting.[26] The dialectic between faith and social context not only accounts for

24. Margaret Y. MacDonald, *The Pauline Churches: A Socio-Historical Study of Institutionalization in the Pauline and Deutero-Pauline Writings*, Society for New Testament Studies Monograph Series 60 (Cambridge: Cambridge University Press, 1988), 60: "Although it is impossible to speak of fixed offices in the Pauline communities, the formalization or institutionalization of roles is progressing rapidly. The fluidity of these roles is related to the 'open' level of institutionalization in the church; leadership patterns are free to develop in different ways in different communities. The existence of authority structures can be detected in Paul's dealings with the Jerusalem church, his fellow worker and his communities. Moreover, leadership in Paul's communities may be related not only to Spirit possession, but also to social status. A dependence/independence relationship between Paul and his congregations is visible in Paul's father-type leadership; he allows for his children to remain dependent on him while at the same time calling for self-sufficiency. With the death of Paul, it can be expected that the Pauline communities' need for independence will become more crucial and further institutionalization will be required to deal with the problems of leadership. Already, however, Paul's legitimation of leadership patterns contributes to the stabilizing of roles by guiding their development in a certain direction."

25. An analogy could be made here with the inspiration of the scriptures and the human individuals who wrote them.

26. MacDonald, *The Pauline Churches*, 60: "The leadership structures of Paul's communities are not shaped in a straightforward manner by his theology; the relationship between the structures and the ideas is dialectical. Similarly, Paul is at home in a particular social setting; once again, the relationship between the individual and the social world is dialectical. A purely charismatic ministry and

the shape of the authority structures as they emerged in the early church, but also for the numerous alterations in the administrative structure of the church down through the centuries. While faith has maintained the episcopacy as a production of the theological and structural core of authority in the Roman Catholic church, the shape of that office in the Roman church has not always been the same. It is not necessary to posit a change in faith to account for these alterations; instead we may suggest a change in the social world.

Church governance has functioned by means of a variety of structures in the course of history. At various times, it has adopted the features of the feudal state, the absolute monarchical state, and the corporation.[27] There was a progression in the centralization of authority from the Peace of Constantine until the Second Vatican Council. In the primitive church, the problems of administration that come with large organizations, and the competition of state and society, had yet to be faced. The bishop did not rule autocratically, but in a collegial fashion with his presbyterate. Though the bishop and his presbyterate held real authority, decisions were made in close proximity to the local church, which at the time was largely autonomous and self-sufficient.

The rapid growth of the church at the time of Constantine's conversion brought profound changes to ecclesial life. To be able to cope with the state on a more equal footing, the church had to develop an organizational structure beyond the local level. No longer would a bishop with his presbyters and people decide policy at home; policy would be decided by bishops in councils far from home. The intimate bond between the bishop and his people loosened. The leader who used to be considered wedded to his church could now be transferred. Two other great moments led to increasing centralization. The Gregorian reform wrested away from the nobility the power over the church they had acquired under Charlemagne. From the viewpoint of power distribution in the church, the most significant feature of the Gregorian reform was the inauguration of a policy of Roman centralization. The Roman pontiff alone could transfer, depose or reinstate bishops, make laws for the whole church, divide and unite dioceses. The twelfth and thirteenth centuries saw the progression of papal authority to directly appoint new bishops. If the pope was

concept of authority based exclusively on Spirit-endowment presents an unrealistic picture of the human society of the Apostle."

27. The following description of the history of the administrative structures of the church is drawn from John E. Lynch, "Power in the Church: an Historico-critical Survey," in *Power in the Church*, ed. James H. Provost and Knut Walf, Concilium 197/3 (Edinburgh: T. and T. Clark, 1988), 13–22, except where other citations are made.

becoming an absolute monarch in the Western church, the bishop was becoming an autocrat in the diocese. The revival of Roman law in the twelfth century fostered the notion of absolutism. The clergy were not his cooperators but his subjects. When the bishop went on a visitation, he did so as a judge rather than a shepherd. Canonists referred to a pastor "governing" his parish instead of "serving" or caring for the people. From top to bottom the church had evolved into an almost military structure of governance.

The First Vatican Council, which defined papal infallibility and power, confirmed and also qualified the policy of Roman centralization that had been in effect since the time of Gregorian reform. By contrast, the Second Vatican Council—by elucidating the role, rights, and responsibilities of every bishop—provided, in principle, a reversal of this centralizing trend. Instead of a monarchical structure, the church is seen to be a hierarchical communion with the pope at its head. All ecclesial jurisdiction is essentially episcopal (LG 22); it has the same source as orders, namely episcopal ordination (LG 21). The 1983 *Code of Canon Law* has canonized conciliar teaching, more or less. The diocesan bishop has all the ordinary, proper, and immediate power required for carrying out his pastoral office (c. 381). He can dispense from the universal law in disciplinary matters, except for certain reserved cases. The bishop is to use his authority in a spirit of co-responsibility, consulting with the presbyteral council, the diocesan pastoral council, and the finance council.[28]

This succinct review of the history of the shape of power and authority in the church brings to light the changing structures of governance that have accompanied changing social worlds of different epochs. We could say that the social dialect modified the practice of episcopal authority according to the changing social realities. In the beginning, the bishop and his presbyterate made decisions in the midst of the community. (We shall soon see the deacon as an essential figure in that structure of governance.) As the church grew in numbers, and as the center of gravity shifted from within the local church

28. Despite all of these theoretical and legal developments in the church, of course, there are still disagreements and tensions on precise policies of centralization versus decentralization, both on the global and local levels in the church. Observers sometimes note that, instead of seeing the pope as king over a church conceived as an earthly kingdom, the early twenty-first century has a new paradigm of centralization: the international corporation or NGO. We may see the pope as the Steve Jobs of our global religious brand, a powerful and ideally charismatic leader providing visionary leadership and continually working to tailor the church's message and services to meet the needs of people today. By analogy, the bishops become regional managers, individual churches become local "franchises," and the faithful become customers. There are both insights and serious distortions in this new "centralization" analogy.

more toward the pope, the practice of consultation was not as necessary as it had been before. Insofar as the people accepted church authorities as monarchical figures, there was less social need for the bishop to consult his "subjects." Well into the twenty-first century, however, the institution of monarchy is less and less a part of our social consciousness. Instead, our social context pulls the structure of authority in a very different direction—toward a greater participation by the people in the decisionmaking process.[29]

Legitimacy and Legitimation

Weber's concept of the routinization of charisma shows why the office of bishop commands a certain amount of respect and authority from an anthropological perspective. *Legitimacy*, as I intend it here, refers to the objective validity of authority: the office of bishop in itself is an objectively valid form of authority in the church. *Legitimation*, on the other hand, concerns the subjective acceptance by the community of one's exercise of episcopal authority. The social context determines to a certain extent what the people consider acceptable. The phrase "moral authority" captures in essence what is meant by legitimacy. (By way of a military analogy, one may hold the rank of an officer, and thereby have inherent rights and responsibilities. Whether or not troops under the command of an officer actually respect the officer is another matter. Officers are trained to earn their troops' respect by leadership based on "moral authority.")

Most of the literature in sociology deals with civil societies where power comes directly from the people. As noted above, power in the church does not follow the secular model in which the people create leaders; rather, the power of leadership comes directly from God. As such, disputes today within the church are not usually made over the existence of authority, but its exercise.[30]

---

29. Malcolm C. Goldsmith, "Power, Authority and Conflict," in *Sociology, Theology and Conflict*, ed. Denys E. H. Whiteley and Roderick Martin (Oxford: Basil Blackwell, 1969), 54–55.

30. Patrick Granfield, "Legitimation and Bureaucratisation of Ecclesial Power," in *Power in the Church*, ed. James H. Provost and Knut Walf, Concilium 197/3 (Edinburgh: T. and T. Clark, 1988), 86: "By legitimacy in the ecclesial context, I mean that power which is established in accord with the law, divine and positive. Legitimacy refers to the possession of ecclesial power. It is de jure or objective authority. One has it or one does not: it is a factual either/or. The authority of duly appointed and ordained Pope and bishops, as long as they remain in the faith, is legitimate; it is power that has its source in God (Rom. 13:1) and shares in the authority of Christ through the Holy Spirit. By legitimation, I mean the acceptance of the exercise of authority by the members of the Church. Do the faithful find ecclesial authority credible, have confidence in it, and follow its directions? Legitimation, as a justification of the exercise of authority, refers to de facto or subjective reception and efficacy of authority. It is a matter of degree, more or less present. Therefore we speak of a crisis of legitimation in the Church

Church authority is effectively legitimate, but it still has to be subjectively appropriated by the faithful. Failure to accept the exercise of authority may not affect its essential core, but it certainly renders it less efficacious. A vital, believing community needs members who have confidence in their God-given authorities and are willing to support them.

It is necessary that those in authority must act (and be seen to act) in harmony with the norms that are valued in that particular society.[31] Because the church is a voluntary society, there is an even greater need for legitimation. A high level of legitimation is accorded to the institutions of the church when the faithful approve of their authority's actions and consider them credible and authentic. Confidence in church authority is a fragile entity and is easier to lose than restore. Legitimation is a fluctuating measure of consensus; it has ebbed and flowed throughout the history of the church. "Legitimate power is socially accepted power, power which feels bound to the objectives, standards and traditions of the social system and tries to act in a way that will be in line with the maintenance and welfare of the whole."[32]

The standards, norms, and values of contemporary social contexts have increasingly veered toward greater democratization. Individuals desire and expect to have their voices heard by those making decisions for them. What we can see from the sociological perspective is that the effective exercise of authority demands a healthy dialogue between the bishop and his people. Consultation serves to make the bishop's own authority more credible in the eyes of the people, thus reducing tension and anxiety—forces that can tear social bonds apart.

Intermediate Structures

The effective exercise of power and authority in the church depends upon institutions. In their coauthored document, *To Empower People*, Peter L. Berger and Richard John Neuhaus articulated two conflicting desires plaguing society: (1) the continuing desire for the services provided by the modern welfare state, and (2) a growing resentment of "big" government and bureaucracy.[33] A

rather than a crisis of legitimacy.... Legitimation is a response to authority; it is complete when the goals of the member and the goals of the institution coincide."

31. See Franz-Xaver Kaufmann, "The Sociology of Knowledge and the Problem of Authority," *Journal of Ecumenical Studies* 19 (1982): 18–31.

32. Wigand Siebel, "The Exercise of Power in Today's Church," in *Power in the Church*, ed. James H. Provost and Knut Walf, Concilium 197/3 (Edinburgh: T. and T. Clark, 1988), 40.

33. Peter Berger and Richard Neuhaus, *To Empower People: The Role of Mediating Structures in Public*

firmly rooted division between private and public life is the source of conflict, and has brought about many unwanted social consequences. The individual, they claim, has a hard time seeing himself as part of the larger society, and the larger social structures suffer from a lack of value and meaning. "For the individual in modern society, life is an ongoing migration between these two spheres, public and private."[34]

Optimistically, Berger and Neuhaus pointed out that many individuals have bridged this division successfully because they have access to institutions that mediate between the two spheres. "Such institutions have a private face, giving private life a measure of stability, and they have a public face, transferring meaning and value to the megastructures."[35] These mediating institutions prevent the isolation of the individual, as well as the threat of alienation of the public order. In other words, mediating structures allow an individual to become more personally involved in a society. Without institutionally reliable processes of mediation, they assert, the political order becomes detached from the values and realities of individual life. Deprived of its moral foundation, the political order is "delegitimated," requiring coercion rather than consent. As it is so crucial to the stabilization of governing authority, such mediation cannot be sporadic and occasional; it must be institutionalized in structures.[36] Mediating institutions, standing between the individual in his or her private life and the large institutions of public life, are necessary for socialization: they bring the individual into the social world, and the social world into the individual. Through these institutions, the values and desires of the individual shape the social world, and the social world more effectively shapes the individual.

Berger and Neuhaus's concept of mediating structures in the realm of the state has implications for our consideration of the diaconate as an intermediate institution. Mediating structures in the context of the church could allow for greater participation of the laity in the life of the church if these structures were to express the needs and desires of the faithful. Taking part in decisions

---

Policy (Washington, D.C.: American Enterprise Institute, 1977). Republished in *To Empower People: From State to Civil Society*, ed. Michael Novak, 2nd ed. (Washington, D.C.: AEI Press, 1996), 157–208.

34. Ibid., 159.

35. Ibid.

36. Ibid., 164: "The theme is *empowerment*. One of the most debilitating results of modernization is a feeling of powerlessness in the face of institutions controlled by those whom we do not know and whose values we often do not share.... The mediating structures under discussion here are the principal expressions of the real values and the real needs of people in our society.... The paradigm of mediating structures aims at empowering poor people to do the things that the more affluent can already do, aims at spreading the power around a bit more."

made by the bishop in such manner, the individual would become more personally involved in the larger social structure that is the church. In addition, greater value and meaning would be given to the exercise of the bishop's office, thereby legitimating his role. Intermediate structures are not therefore added barriers between the bishop and his people, as one might erroneously think. They are channels of communication that influence the bishop in his decision-making and the people in their acceptance of the bishop's exercise of authority. If a mediating structure were to hinder the relationship in any way, it would cease to be a true mediating structure.[37]

The goal of such mediation cannot be, of course, simply the involvement of more and more of the lay faithful in the sometimes internecine debates of church politics. As Pope Francis has repeatedly stressed, the church must not be "self-referential" but instead extend its concern to "the peripheries" of a modern society awash in unprecedented affluence but also social fragmentation.[38] At the heart of what Francis calls a "throwaway culture," particularly in the United States, is a "radical individualism" that was expertly described in the classic sociological study *Habits of the Heart*, from a team of researchers headed by Robert Bellah.[39] American "rugged individualism" encourages a work ethic of "pull yourself up by your bootstraps," providing little impetus for one to be concerned about the misfortunes of others. The cultural ties that make individuals aware of their belonging to one another are shredded by this ideol-

37. In the twentieth anniversary edition of their publication, Berger and Neuhaus caution against misappropriation of the phrase "mediating structure." "Mediation is as mediation does," they remind us. In their original publication, they offered some broad categories of mediating structures such as voluntary associations, church, and neighborhood. "To be sure, some grass-roots organizations and local communities might indeed be mediating structures. But they might not be, either being invasions of people's life worlds by agents from the outside, in which case they are simply branches of mega-institutions, or being enclaves of private meanings and lifestyles with no relation to the larger society." Taken from Peter L. Berger and Richard J. Neuhaus, "Peter Berger and Richard John Neuhaus Respond," in *To Empower People*, 149. These cautions are appropriate for mediating structures in the church. It is not simply good enough to have pastoral councils, synods, or a permanent diaconate program, but to have these institutions function properly.

38. Pope Francis, *Evangelii Gaudium*, Apostolic Exhortation, November 24, 2013; official English translation: *The Joy of the Gospel* (Vatican City: Libreria Editrice Vaticana, 2013), par. 20.

39. Pope Francis, *Laudato Si'*, Encyclical Letter, May 24, 2015, par. 16. Robert N. Bellah, Richard Madsen, William Sullivan, Ann Swidler, and Steve Tipton, *Habits of the Heart: Individualism and Commitment in American Life: Updated Edition with a New Introduction* (Los Angeles: University of California Press, 1985–96), 47. See also Jean Bethke Elshtain, *Democracy on Trial* (New York: Basic Books, 1995), and Donald L. Gelpi, "Conversion: Beyond the Impasses of Individualism," in *Beyond Individualism: Toward a Retrieval of Moral Discourse in America*, ed. Donald Gelpi (Notre Dame, Ind.: University of Notre Dame Press, 1989).

ogy, "freeing" the individual to pursue his or her own self-interest. In short, a utilitarian individualist would hold that society as a whole would be better off if everyone was left alone to pursue their own private good.

It is no wonder that a society dominated by utilitarian individualism will have trouble with traditional institutions, like marriage, that require sacrifice for the good of others. The exercise of responsibility, that is, active concern for others, must be added to the list of actions dependent upon institutions: "responsibility is something we exercise as individuals but within and on behalf of institutions."[40] The problem at hand, in Bellah and his colleagues' view, is to consider how individuals can really make a difference in the institutions that have such an impact on our lives. Active and informed participation can enhance our lives and counter the anxiety we experience when we focus too exclusively on the quest for purely private satisfactions. Indeed, finding the institutional forms to make this participation possible is a necessary condition for solving problems associated with social cohesion.

The problem with our institutions is that they are (in the phrase of Princeton sociologist Robert Wuthnow) "porous," due to an increasing preference for commitments that are more short-term and "loose."[41] "Porous" describes the character of those institutions which have social boundaries that permit people, goods, information, and other resources to flow across them with relative ease.[42] This means that people drift in and out of volunteer organizations, including those associated with the church, but never develop lasting informal ties. Wuthnow observes: "Under today's more porous conditions, those who have traditionally been disadvantaged, such as minorities, the poor, new immigrants, and the elderly, are still likely to suffer the most, but they are more likely to slip through the cracks as individuals rather than as entire classes of people."[43] Po-

40. Robert N. Bellah, Richard Madsen, William Sullivan, Ann Swidler, and Steve Tipton, *The Good Society* (New York: Vintage Books, 1991), 13.

41. Robert Wuthnow, *Loose Connections: Joining Together in America's Fragmented Communities* (Cambridge, Mass.: Harvard University Press, 1998), 77: "Evidence points to a decline in organizational memberships and an increase in individual volunteering.... Individual volunteering appears to be a more attractive way of being connected to one's community.... Volunteering can be a more transient, short-term activity than belonging to fraternal orders, service clubs, and other membership organizations that reward loyalty and long-term commitment. A volunteer can spend an evening a week on an activity for a few months as time permits, rather than having to make a long-term commitment to support an organization. Although volunteers speak of making friends with fellow volunteers, evidence also suggests that volunteering is less likely to be a source of the deep, enduring relationships on which people can depend for assistance than is participation in churches, neighborhood gatherings, or bowling leagues."

42. Ibid., 59.

43. Ibid., 75: "Besides allowing more people to slip through the cracks, porousness makes it harder

rous institutions do not hold individuals tightly together, and as a consequence, they leak. People fall through the cracks, and deep, enduring relationships are not readily engendered among members of society. What seems necessary today more than ever are healthy, less porous institutions that provide the requisite social conditions for sustained involvement. Traditional institutions, such as the church, should not adapt to the changing social environment to appease the desire for more loose connections, but just the opposite.[44]

The church, as an institution that engenders long-term commitment and abiding concern for others, would help plug the leaks and fill the cracks of our porous society if the people of God were to practice what they preach. Intermediate institutions within the church could be structured to provide the necessary institutional needs for the individual members of the church to put into practice their concern and responsibility for others. The deacon could be a figure empowering believers to go beyond a consumerist mentality in relation to the church, and instead to live out the church's mission of service towards the needy and vulnerable.

Summary

In my effort to define more precisely the meaning of "social intermediary," I have explored the meanings of power, authority, legitimacy, legitimation, institution, and mediating structures. I have sociologically defined power as the ability to influence the thinking and behavior of the community, and authority as the right to exercise that power. Furthermore, power and authority are validated in objective terms by office (the routinization of charism), and subjective terms in their proper exercise (legitimation). Moreover, the changing social context can account for the modifications of social structures in the church down through the ages. Institutions, those patterned social arrangements that make for more efficient social living, are also the very means by which major

---

for their needs to be met through the established sources of voluntary assistance. Community organizations sometimes find it more difficult to recruit members or to enlist them in programs that require regular commitment over long periods of time."

44. Ibid., 82. Although he effectively brings to light the acute social problems associated with loose connections and porous institutions, Wuthnow seems to backtrack in his conclusion when he claims that it is "uncertain" whether these newer models will work. He even goes so far as to suggest that perhaps a desire for a more tightly bound society "may reflect a yearning for a world that no longer exists." The challenge, he writes, "is to recognize that people do need to band together, but in more strategic ways, more loosely, and in a wider variety of networks." Wuthnow appears to have accepted defeat with these statements.

decisions are made, power and authority are legitimated, and concern for one another is socially reinforced. Mediating structures (institutions that stand in between the individual and the larger societal structures) are necessary for the individual to bridge the cultural gap between private and public life. Preaching solidarity is not enough; it must be stabilized in institutions such as these.

Within the context of the above realities, I define a "social intermediary" as the following: *an institution in which roles have been entrusted (and therefore knowledge, power, and authority to perform these roles) to facilitate the distribution of power, authority, and resources throughout the social body.* I would now like to apply this definition to the diaconate as an *intermediate order* among the people of God. Two possible branches of mediation arise. (1) The deacon may serve as an intermediary between the bishop and the laity, and (2) the deacon may serve as an intermediary between individuals in need and the people of God as a whole. If indeed the deacon is an intermediary figure, then we expect to see his ministry involve one or both of the following: the communication of knowledge about those in need to the community at large, and the communication of ideas between the people and the bishop. Such activity would benefit the community as a whole. There would be greater participation by all in the life and mission of the church according to their proper powers and authority. Enhanced personal engagement in the life and ministry of the church would forge the bonds of communion ever more tightly, counteracting the trend of the larger society toward individualism.

I have succinctly articulated the sociological background for our investigation of the diaconate as an intermediate order, but for the sake of clarity I have resisted the temptation to appropriate this material immediately into theological form. What is still necessary is to consider the deacon not only as a social intermediary, but a social intermediary *among the people of God.* I have, to a certain extent, made some connections between sociology and theology. For example, in my discussion of power and authority, I concentrated on the office of the bishop and the rights of the laity; in the discussion on legitimacy and legitimation, I focused once again on the figure of the bishop. But what is needed now is to show power, authority, and legitimacy from the perspective of the Second Vatican Council. Furthermore, the social phenomenon of individualism will be compared against the backdrop of the social teaching of the church, choosing a representative sample of texts to avoid a lengthy presentation. In this manner, I hope to make a theological appropriation of the sociological insights presented above, and point out the significance of the deacon as an intermediary among the people of God.

CHAPTER 4

Social Mediation and the
People of God

Taking the insights gleaned from the preceding analysis of the need for social mediation, I will now view them in light of church teaching, integrating them appropriately into a theological framework. Nature and grace are not fundamentally opposed to one another. Hence, it should not be surprising that we will find great agreement between what has been presented above sociologically, and what will be presented below theologically. A foundational text comes from LG 8, which reveals how the Council fathers understood the relationship between the social structure of the church and her divine nature:

Christ, the one mediator, set up his holy church here on earth as a visible structure, a community of faith, hope and love; and he sustains it unceasingly and through it he pours out grace and truth on everyone. This society, however, equipped with hierarchical structures, and the mystical body of Christ, a visible assembly and a spiritual community, an earthly church and a church enriched with heavenly gifts, must not be considered as two things, but as forming one complex reality comprising a human and a divine element. It is therefore by no mean analogy that it is likened to the mystery of the incarnate Word. For just as the assumed nature serves the divine Word as a living instrument of salvation inseparably joined with him, in a similar way the social structure of the church serves the Spirit of Christ who vivifies the church towards the growth of the body (see Eph 4, 16).[1]

In the "complex reality" of the church, priority is given to the supernatural dimension of the church. Her human dimension is in service to the divine. The thrust of this passage, however, does not emphasize a difference between divine and human elements; it emphasizes their unity in the church. The church is

---

1. *Decrees* (ed. Tanner), 2:854.

not composed of two separate things: it is "one complex reality" composed of two elements. Instrumentally related to the Spirit, social structures are part of the very constitution of the church. The diaconate as an intermediate structure should not be considered simply as a concession to sociological needs, but as an instrument of the Spirit for the growth of the church in service to the Gospel.

Power and Authority in the New Testament

The preceding evaluation of the social significance of intermediate structures required the consideration of power and authority. Power (as ability) and authority (as the right to exercise that ability) are spread throughout the social body in various degrees. The difference in power and authority among the individuals of a society engenders a need for mediating structures, structures that "spread power around a bit more." Having purified my working definition of power from the notion of domination, I turned to a definition of power that is communally oriented. The power I wish to consider in this chapter is not the kind that culminates in violence, but which is found in the community "acting in concert." With this kind of power and authority in the background, I painted a social portrait of intermediate institutions, suggestive of the deacon in terms of mediating the power and authority of the bishop *vis-à-vis* the laity, and mediating the power and authority of the church *vis-à-vis* the poor.

Power and authority are anthropological realities that influence the social structure of the church. A theological evaluation of power and authority among the people of God, with special reference to the deacon, begins with scripture. The study of *diakonia* in the New Testament in part 1 exposited a threefold nuance of that term: as a gift from the Spirit (pneumatological), ecclesiastical ministry is for the building up of the church (ecclesial), and not for the honor of the individual (Christological). The anthropological realities of power and authority are also nuanced in the Christian context, such that power and authority have as their object the benefit of the church, not domination.

ἐξουσία and δύναμις

The two words in the New Testament that concern us most are ἐξουσία (*exousia*) and δύναμις (*dunamis*). The Greek words deriving from the stem δυνα- have the same basic meaning: "being able" or "capacity."[2] Its use in classical

---

2. Walter Grundmann, "δύναμαι/δύναμις," in TDNT 2:284.

Greek implies the concept of cosmic power, which fashions the world and operates in it, inwardly holding it together.[3] It can stand for the various forms of power: physical, moral, spiritual, or intellectual. The Old Testament concept of power is distinct from that of the Hellenistic cosmic powers of the universe, because YHWH is a personal God who acts in history on his own power. It is through the power of YHWH that Israel is delivered from human and natural forces at the Red Sea. In the Old Testament it is not bare force (power in terms of nature) that is key, but the will that determines the use of power.[4] Where the idea of God is personal, religious life focuses on entering into and sustaining a living relationship with the Godhead, not the control of forces of nature. Obedience to the divine will and the use of prayer to influence the will of God are the hallmarks of religions based on a personal God.[5]

The Greek word *exousia* is somewhat ambiguous. It also denotes "ability," like *dunamis*, but refers more to external freedom rather than intrinsic ability.[6] It is the possibility granted by a higher authority, and therefore the right to do something or the right over something.[7] It concerns the power of decision. Thus it is not always possible to distinguish between authority and power, between *exousia* and *dunamis*. The derived meanings of *exousia* are "authoritative position," "office," "office-bearers," or "rulers." In the Greek version of the Old Testament, the Septuagint (LXX), *exousia* means right, authority, permission or freedom, often concerning a right or permission given by God.[8] Thus, *exousia* presupposes a divine commission and authorization.

The Authority of Jesus

The word *exousia* denotes Christ's divinely given power and authority to act. Jesus is exalted to be "the Christ" and "Lord" in the kingdom of God (Acts 2:36). He has the authority to forgive sins (Mk 2:10). When the scribes ask about the power to forgive (*dunatai*), Jesus responds using *exousia*, which comprises both the right and the power to effect forgiveness. There is also reference to his "authority" to expel demons (Mk 3:15, 6:7; Lk 10:19). "In this respect the use of *exousia* for the power which decides, and for authority based

3. Ibid., 287.
4. Ibid., 291.
5. Ibid., 294.
6. Wendelin Foerster, "ἔξεστιν/ἐξουσία," in TDNT 3:562.
7. Ibid.
8. Ibid., 564.

on a commissioning force, agrees with the actual mode of exorcism by a word of command."⁹ Furthermore, the word *exousia* is used to describe the impression made by Jesus teaching: "What is this? A new teaching—with authority! He commands even the unclean spirits, and they obey him" (Mk 1:27). Luke renders it this way: "They were all amazed and kept saying to one another, 'What kind of utterance is this? For with authority and power he commands the unclean spirits, and out they come!'" (Lk 4:36). The Sanhedrin ask, "By what authority are you doing these things? Who gave you this authority to do them?" (Mk 11:28). Both Matthew and Luke record the same incident (Mt 21:25, Lk 20:2) and although we do not find an explicit answer, there is no doubt that the authority of Jesus is from God.

The Authority of the Disciples

In the New Testament, no office, no authority, and no service performed in the community stands without the cross. In the church all power and authority are fundamentally the power and authority of Christ. At the end of the Gospel of Matthew, the Eleven are given a share in the authority of Jesus, and he commissions them to make disciples of all nations (Mt 28:18–20). The commissioning of disciples is repeated in Mark 6:7 and in Luke: "He summoned the twelve and gave them power [*dunamin*] and authority [*exousian*] over all demons and to cure diseases, and he sent them out to proclaim the kingdom of God and to heal" (9:1). Apostles share in the authority of Jesus to heal, to teach, and to cast out demons. Luke includes an instance of seventy other disciples, and he uses both authority and power to describe their commission (Lk 10:19). In the Gospel of Matthew, in two instances Jesus implies that his followers have the power to forgive sins, to "bind and loose" (Mt 18:19). Peter, as the leader of the disciples, has the keys to the kingdom of heaven and thus can "bind and loose" (Mt 16:19).

In the prologue of John's Gospel, we find the word *exousia* used to describe what Jesus gives to those who believe in him: "But to those who did accept him he gave power [*exousian*] to become children of God" (Jn 1:12). Otherwise, the Gospel emphasizes that Jesus is the sole figure of authority and power in the community of believers, the shepherd of his one flock (Jn 10:11–18). Qualifying the image of the shepherd-ruler from the Old Testament, Jesus presented himself as the Good Shepherd who lays down his life for his sheep: "This is why the Father loves me, because I lay down my life in order to take it up again.

9. Ibid., 569.

No one takes it from me, but I lay it down on my own. I have power [*exousian*] to lay it down, and power [*exousian*] to take it up again. This command I have received from my Father" (Jn 10:17–18).[10] Jesus's authority is revealed in his freedom to lay down his own life; it is not so much power over others but freedom from coercion. In his authority to lay down his life and to take it up again, Jesus has the freedom to love his sheep. Authority in the Johannine concept is never separate from the service of love.

Although the Gospel of John never mentions Jesus commissioning others with power and authority over evil spirits, the epilogue (chapter 21) includes a passage where Jesus invites Peter to become the shepherd of his flock.[11] In the dialogue between Peter and the resurrected Jesus, there is Peter's reparation for the threefold denial at Annas's house. Jesus is about to leave his sheep, so he entrusts his flock to Peter. He "first insists on the Johannine criterion of love, and then makes Peter a shepherd—but the sheep remain Jesus.'"[12] The authority of Peter is therefore rooted in love. As a matter of fact, Peter is to manifest the love of the Good Shepherd by laying down his own life for Jesus's sheep. From the Johannine conception, we can consider power as the intrinsic ability to love, and authority as the freedom to exercise that love. Pastoral authority, as in the image of Peter in the epilogue, has its basis in the pastoral authority of the Good Shepherd. Sharing in the authority of Jesus ultimately means sharing in his salvific love for others.

Authority and power in the New Testament therefore presuppose responsible use. Authority is to be at the service of love in the Christian community. John makes the connection between self-emptying (*kenosis*) and authority in the image of the Good Shepherd. In the experience of the church, the danger has been to evaluate power and authority simply in worldly terms.[13] Those

---

10. Raymond Brown, *The Gospel According to John (i–xii)*, Anchor Bible 29 (London: Geoffrey Chapman, 1971), 392: "The figure of the true shepherd of the flock who leads the sheep out to pasture reminds us of the symbolic description of Joshua (who bears the same Hebrew name as Jesus) in Num xxvii 16–17: 'Appoint a man over the congregation [LXX *synagoge*] ... who shall lead them out and bring them in, that the congregation of the Lord may not be like sheep without a shepherd.'"

11. O'Grady, "Authority and Power," 135. Raymond Brown, *The Gospel and Epistles of John: A Concise Commentary* (Collegeville, Minn.: Liturgical Press, 1988), 100: "Plausibly the Fourth Gospel once ended with c. 20. The supplementary c. 21 shows Johannine characteristics (e.g., Nathanael, Cana, beloved disciple), and so it probably represents another collection of early appearance stories which the final redactor found in the tradition and added to the work of the evangelist."

12. Brown, *The Gospel and Epistles of John*, 103.

13. McKenzie, *Authority in the Church*, 32: "One can conceive of two dangers to the unity and integrity of the Church: anarchy and the secularization of power. Of the two, Jesus spoke very little about the danger of anarchy; he spoke frequently and earnestly about the danger of the secularization of power.

who hold pastoral authority can either misuse it for their personal desires, or use it for the good of the church. Domination is one way to exercise authority, but love is the Christian way. As we turn our attention to the consideration of the power and authority vested in the bishop and the laity, it is important that we keep before our eyes the ultimate objective—charity.

The Relationship between Bishop and Laity in the Perspective of Vatican II

Echoes of the New Testament understanding of power and authority, and their social characteristics described earlier, are found in the teachings of the Second Vatican Council. If power concerns the capacity to influence the thinking and behavior of a human community, then "power" in the church concerns the ability to bring about, influence, and sustain her life and mission.[14] Charisms are what make everyone, from the newly baptized to the bishop, capable of actions that pertain to the spread of the Gospel. Thus charisms are, in a very real sense, "power."

We recall from chapter 1 that the relationship between the ordained ministers and the laity is expressed in the link between baptism and eucharist. Although the laity have not been ordained to fulfill an ecclesiastical office, they nonetheless have their own place in the eucharistic assembly by virtue of their baptism. Relying heavily on New Testament sources, the Council fathers declared that every one of the faithful has the right and duty to exercise their charisms "in the Church and in the world for the good of humanity and for the building up of the Church."[15] Charisms are not limited to a select few in the church. Everyone has their own particular "gift" of power to be used for the benefit of the church's life and mission. This power includes the skills, talents,

---

If the Church remains organized about her true center, which is Christian love infused by the indwelling Spirit, the Church can never collapse into anarchy. But if she turns into an authoritarian structure, Christian love is inhibited, and the authoritarian structure can itself become the occasion of anarchy."

14. Power, "Basis," 329.

15. *Apostolicam Actuositatem*, no. 3, in *Decrees* (ed. Tanner), 2:983: "The holy Spirit, who works the sanctification of God's people through ministry and sacrament, also gives special gifts to the faithful (See 1 Cor 12,7), 'apportioning to each one individually as he wills' (1 Cor 12, 11).... Through receiving these gifts of grace, however unspectacular, every one of the faithful has the right and duty to exercise them in the church and in the world for the good of humanity and for the building up of the church. They do this in the freedom of the Spirit who 'blows where he wills' (Jn 3,8) and, at the same time, in communion with the fellowship in Christ, especially with his pastors, whose part it is to judge about their true nature and ordered use, not indeed so as to extinguish the Spirit but in order to test everything and to hold on to what is good (see 1 Th 5, 12, 19, 21)."

expertise, or whatever may allow someone to contribute to the single purpose for which the church exists: the communion of all humanity with God and one another. The laity are "empowered" by baptism to take their place in the eucharistic assembly, and the clergy are "empowered" by ordination to fulfill the offices given them. With these charisms come authority, the right to utilize them in the life and mission of the church. The sacramental distribution of power and authority throughout the people of God gives every member the right to participate in the life and mission of the church according to their own charism.

The origin of these powers is the Spirit, and anyone born of the Spirit has a freedom like the wind blowing "where it wills."[16] The bishop, however, has the power and authority, charism and office, to judge their nature and order their use for their harmonious exercise. The ecclesiastical ministry of the bishop is directed to assist the fulfillment of roles that pertain to the laity. The conferral of authority and power (office and charisms) takes place at ordination for the benefit of the whole people of God, not for the personal gain of the bishop. The bishop is not the channel through whom the various charisms are given to the people of God, but he is their principle of unity. In coordinating all other ministries and services, the bishop exercises decisionmaking power for their harmonious and fruitful exercise.

It is the whole church, in all its members, that continues and extends the mission of Jesus Christ, not just the ecclesiastical ministries. Consequently, Vatican II has given a prominent place to the themes of co-responsibility, co-operation, and participation by the people of God in the life and mission of the church. The interrelationship between the ecclesiastical orders and the laity flows from the ecclesiology sanctioned by Vatican II; the church as the people of God. The first draft of LG was originally structured according to three key dimensions of the church in the following sequence: the mystery of the church, its hierarchical organization, and then the people of God. During the Council the schema was restructured and rewritten. The final text reprioritized the different dimensions of the church: Chapter I on the mystery of the church, Chapter II on the people of God, Chapter III on the hierarchy, Chapter IV on the laity, Chapter V on the universal call to holiness, and Chapter VI on religious. This restructuring shifted emphasis from the hierarchy as distinct from the people of God, to the fact "that all—hierarchy and lay persons—are equally members of the one people."[17]

---

16. Jn 3:8.

17. Gérard Philips, "History of the Constitution," in *Commentary on the Documents of Vatican II*, ed. Herbert Vorgrimler (New York: Herder and Herder, 1966–69), 1:127–28.

We recall from chapter 2 that the ecclesiastical ministry is entrusted to bishops, in whom the apostolic tradition is "manifested and safeguarded" (LG 20). With priests and deacons as their helpers, bishops receive charge of the community, "presiding in the place of God over the flock, whose shepherds they are, as teachers of doctrine, priests of sacred worship and ministers of government." Among their principal tasks, bishops are "heralds of the faith," and "teachers endowed with the authority of Christ" (LG 25). They are to "take particular care to further the interests of the poor and the underprivileged to whom the Lord has sent them to preach the gospel" (CD 13). Bishops are to exhort and instruct their people "so that in the liturgy, especially in the holy sacrifice of the mass, they fulfil their part with faith and devotion" (CD 15). By counsel, persuasion, example, authority, and sacred power, the bishop governs the local church (LG 27). Bishops have the right and duty "of directing everything that concerns the ordering of worship and the apostolate." The authority and power of the episcopacy is ordered to the active participation of all the people of God, in spreading the Gospel of salvation.

The ministry of the bishop, however, is not a matter of giving orders down a chain of command. Though the Council desired to firmly establish the dignity, power, and authority of the episcopacy, it equally emphasized the promotion of laity in the life and mission of the church. Thus we read the Council's call to bishops to be among their flock as "good shepherds who know their own sheep and whose sheep know them" (CD 16). Bishops, the Council writes, are to

strive to acquire an accurate knowledge of their [the laity's] needs in the social conditions in which they live, using for this purpose the appropriate methods.... They must show themselves to be concerned for all no matter what their age, condition or nationality; no matter whether they are natives, immigrants or visitors. In exercising this pastoral care they must respect the place proper to their faithful in the affairs of the church, acknowledging also their duty and right to work actively for the building up of the mystical body of Christ.[18]

In order to fulfill their ministry, bishops must acquire knowledge of the people whom they serve. Sociologists observe that knowledge is socially distributed: "No individual internalizes the totality of what is objectivated as reality in his society."[19] Hence, the bishop must utilize institutions that mediate knowledge of the various sectors in the life of the church. These "mediating

18. CD 16, in *Decrees* (ed. Tanner), 2:927.

19. Peter L. Berger and Thomas Luckmann, *The Social Construction of Reality: A Treatise in the Sociology of Knowledge* (New York: Anchor Books, 1967), 134.

structures," as Berger and Neuhaus argued, are necessary to stabilize the individual's personal connection to the larger church. Here we see a function for the diaconate as an intermediate structure between the bishop and the laity, if we assume that the deacon's role-specific knowledge concerns the needs and desires of the laity.

Bishops are not only to be concerned about the needs of the laity, but they are also charged to "show themselves" to be so concerned. The bishop is not simply an administrator; he is a shepherd. In his service to the communion of the church, the bishop is a concrete expression of the love of Christ for his bride the church. The bishop is to appear concerned for the people he serves, not simply for the sociological motive of legitimation, but to fulfill his task as a *diakonos* or ambassador of Christ. The intermediate role of the deacon could include representing the bishop in his care and concern for the people of God. This intermediary function by the deacon is essentially different from other intermediate structures that exist in the church between the bishop and the people, such as councils and synods. As a unique representative of the bishop, the deacon could mediate his care and concern for the individual members of his flock in a personal manner.

Intermediate structures are necessary for the laity to participate in the decisions that concern the life and mission of the church. The Second Vatican Council, following this thinking, encouraged the use of institutions set up by the church for the laity to freely make their opinions known to the pastors, especially in matters that they are competent.

They [laity] should make known to these pastors their needs and desires with that freedom and confidence which befits children of God and sisters and brothers in Christ. In accordance with the knowledge, competence or authority that they possess, they have the right and indeed sometimes the duty to make known their opinion on matters which concern the good of the church. If possible this should be done through the institutions set up for this purpose by the Church; and it should always be done with respect for the truth, with courage and with prudence, and in a spirit of reverence and love towards those who by reason of their sacred office represent Christ.... [Bishops] should willingly make use of their prudent counsel.... With a father's love they should pay careful attention in Christ to the projects, the requests and the desires put forward by the laity.[20]

The image of the church presented here is not that of a linear hierarchy, but one of family. As brothers and sisters in Christ, the laity are encouraged to speak

20. LG 37, in *Decrees* (ed. Tanner), 2:879.

up to their brothers who are bishops on matters that concern the good of the church. It is more than a right; it is an obligation for the laity to be actively engaged in the affairs of the church.

The Council does not hold out a right for the laity to have a democratic vote, only the right of the laity to share responsibility in decisionmaking. This certainly cuts against the democratic grain of our culture, although it must be said that even our "representative democracy" makes very few decisions by direct vote. I may also suggest that the making of a choice is not always the most important question; usually, it is not even the most influential or powerful, but only one element of the whole decisionmaking process. Decisionmaking is a complex process, whether made by an individual, a small group, or a large community. It occurs in stages, all of which entail the exercise of influence and power but only one of which is the making of a choice. Increasing the avenues of participation by the laity in the stages of decisionmaking in the church would be one way for more people to share responsibility for her life and mission.[21]

Shared decisionmaking is not an issue of ensuring an equal amount of power among everyone, but having as many as possible productively contribute to decisions made for the good of the church. Pastors of parishes, for example, know well that major decisions require a long process of consultation and input, and that by the time it has reached their desk for a final decision, often the right decision should have already been made clear. The pastor serves to guarantee that a proper process of decisionmaking was followed. Thus, whenever the laity are given the chance to offer their informed, expert, and authoritative opinion or solution, the bishop and the church benefit.[22] In order to realize the fruitful collaboration of the laity with the pastoral authorities, the necessary relative information must also be shared with them. The exercise of power and authority, understood as communal and not simply possessed by individuals, necessitates intermediate structures to distribute the requisite knowledge for participation. The practice of shared responsibility can do much to alleviate crises of legitimation by increasing the number of channels through which a wider number of individuals would be involved in the decisionmaking process.[23]

21. Robert T. Kennedy, "Shared Responsibility in Ecclesial Decision-Making," *Studia Canonica* 14 (1980): 9.

22. Gerard Wackenheim, "Ecclesiology and Sociology," in *The Church as Institution*, ed. Gregory Baum and Andrew Greeley, Concilium 91 (New York: Herder and Herder, 1974), 39.

23. Granfield, "Legitimation," 90.

The ideal situation would have the bishop meet with the entire assembly every time a major issue concerning the life and mission of the church arose. This is a theoretical ideal, as it would involve participation by everyone. This is also only an ideal, as the concrete circumstances of life do not allow for it, even in the smallest of communities. But institutions do allow for greater mediated participation because they are patterned ways of getting things done in an efficient manner. Major decisions are made within and on behalf of institutions in the church, just as they are in society. The church must rely on institutions for shared responsibility in decisionmaking, and one of these institutions could very well be the diaconate.

The Council fathers of Vatican II envisioned an ideal situation, where the bishop and laity formed a "familiar relationship" through shared responsibility. This kind of exercise of pastoral authority would strengthen in the laity a sense of their own responsibility, fire their enthusiasm, and would more easily join them to the work of the pastors. The pastors, on their part, would make "clearer and more suitable decisions both in spiritual and in temporal affairs," helping the whole church to carry out its mission more effectively.[24] The ministry of the bishop, therefore, is not simply a matter of issuing administrative orders, but also of showing his personal care and concern by listening to his flock. The laity have a right and duty to speak up to their brothers who are pastors, and the pastors have an obligation to hear them. Authority, declared the Council, does not only reside in the ordained but among the laity as well. Thus through the gifts of power and authority, charism and office, members of the entire eucharistic assembly are encouraged to take a more active role in worship and in the life and mission of the church. The pastoral authority of the bishop functions not to control the dispensation of charisms to the faithful, but to bring them to life. As president of the eucharistic assembly, the bishop alone is the concrete point of unity. It is his responsibility to ensure the proper exercise of charisms received in the sacraments of baptism and ordination in the mission of the church. In order to concretely manifest the pneumatological, Christological, and ecclesial characteristics of the apostolic office, the bishop must

24. LG 37, in *Decrees* (ed. Tanner), 2:880: "From this familiar relationship between laity and pastors many advantages for the church can be expected: for in this way there is strengthened in the laity a sense of their own responsibility, their enthusiasm is fired, and the strengths of the laity are more easily joined to the work of the pastors. The pastors, for their part, helped by the experience of the laity, are able to make clearer and more suitable decisions both in spiritual and in temporal affairs. In this way the whole church, strengthened by all its members, is able more effectively to carry out its mission for the life of the world."

therefore utilize intermediary structures for the proper exercise of his power and authority.

Christian Solidarity

Though the phenomenon of "utilitarian individualism" in modern society is sociologically related to the competitive environment introduced by the industrialization of Western society, its theological origins are more pervasive and much more ancient. The Bible explains the general human condition from the point of view of faith and hope in God. The story of the Fall in Genesis 3 gives an explanation for the fragmentation of society: disobedience rooted in the lack of trust in God.[25] Following the account of the Fall, Genesis 4–11 depict the fracturing of human society as a direct result of our fractured relationship with God. Every kind of relationship was disrupted by humiliation, domination, subordination, conflict, suffering, and struggle; whether among animals, between nature and mankind, among human beings, between God and mankind, between God and animals, and even within the individual as expressed in shame.[26] Cut off from God and cut off from others in society, human beings take up defensive positions that generate divisions. We can therefore speak of individualism as a social sin, the erosion of relationships that allow us to live as God intended. It is a consequence of a deep-rooted suspicion that the good of others, or the common good, is opposed to the good of the individual. Competition instead of cooperation creates a world of "everyone for himself."

God has sought to overcome sin and its consequences through the establishment of covenants, divine interventions in history to recreate community. The Old Covenant established through Moses dominates the last four books of the Pentateuch, and recurs in the historical books. The Covenant imposes upon Israel the responsibility of recognizing YHWH alone as God, and of keeping his commandments. Participation in the Covenant places one in relationship to God and the people of the Covenant, and through these relationships the Israelite is blessed. The choice of Israel is an election to responsibility

---

25. In his commentary on Gn 3, Claus Westermann, *Genesis 1–11. A Commentary*, trans. John J. Scullion (London: SPCK, 1984), 276, describes the passage of the Fall as revealing truths about the human condition as experienced, not as historical accounts: "This narrative explains human existence in its essential elements as something which came about in primeval time, and indeed the created state in contrast to the state of humanity limited by death, suffering and sin. It is a misunderstanding of the narrative as a whole to explain it as a succession of historical or quasi-historical incidents."

26. Terrence E. Fretheim, "Genesis," in *The New Interpreter's Bible: A Commentary in Twelve Volumes* (Nashville, Tenn.: Abingdon Press, 1994), 1:362–63.

and obligation, not favoritism. For Christians, the culmination of this Covenant is found in the New Covenant established in the blood of Jesus Christ, from which the community of disciples, the New Israel, the body of Christ, the church is born. By the will of God and command of the Gospel, the invitation to share in the kingdom is to be proclaimed to all peoples without exception (Mt 28:19). To share in the blessings of the New Covenant means to share in the benefits that result from communion with God and the church.[27]

As participants in the New Covenant, Christians are obliged (and graced) to love God and neighbor. To love God is to love our neighbor. In feeding the hungry, welcoming the stranger, clothing the naked, caring for the sick, and visiting the imprisoned, God himself is loved (Mt 25:31–46). Furthermore, the unity of the body of Christ found in the gift of the Spirit overcomes the many divisions that exist in the world. Once baptized into the death and resurrection of Jesus, we are a new creation; old divisions no longer apply. God shows no partiality, and so there is no distinction whatsoever: "For all of you who were baptized into Christ have clothed yourselves with Christ. There is neither Jew nor Greek, there is neither slave nor free person, there is not male and female; for you are all one in Christ Jesus" (Gal 3:27–28). The Apostle James reminds us that distinctions between poverty and wealth have no purpose in the assembly of the faithful. The rich will not fare any better than the poor in the life to come, so it makes no sense to allow such distinctions to divide the church now (Jam 2:1–13). Peace, reconciliation, and solidarity are among the most important gifts that the church has to offer a divided world.

The motive of faith drives the people of God to promote and develop the exercise of concern and responsibility for others in society. Catholic social teaching has stressed the virtue of solidarity as one of its key principles since its beginning in the nineteenth century with Pope Leo XIII's *Rerum Novarum*. Leo sought to interpret the ills of liberal capitalism and its counterpart, collectivism, in light of this faith-based motivation.[28] Liberal capitalism stressed individualism so much that it dehumanized people, exalting individual choice and interests over our common humanity and responsibility for others. And

27. The description of Covenant theology in the Old Testament in this paragraph is taken from the section "Israel-God's Covenanted People" in John L. McKenzie, "Aspects of Old Testament Thought," in NJBC, 1284–1315; and Delbert R. Hillers, *Covenant: The History of a Biblical Idea* (Baltimore, Md.: Johns Hopkins University Press, 1969). The acclaimed Old Testament theologian, Walter Brueggemann, published a work that confronts the issues of faithfulness, responsibility, and justice from a biblical perspective. See his *The Covenanted Self: Explorations in Law and Covenant*, ed. Patrick D. Miller (Minneapolis, Minn.: Fortress Press, 1999).

28. Pope Leo XIII, *Rerum Novarum*, Encyclical Letter, May 15, 1891; available at www.vatican.va.

if excessive individualism dehumanized people, collectivism tended to deper-
sonalize by completely subordinating individuals to the collective will as represented by communist (or fascist) governments.[29]

Building upon the criticism of liberal capitalism and socialism in *Rerum
Novarum*, Pope Pius XI's *Quadragesimo Anno* made more explicit the principles of Christian solidarity. Pius XI addressed the rights and dignity of workers,
encouraging an outlook of shared responsibilities between laborers, owners,
and managers, rather than a competitive and conflicting social reality.[30] Pope
John XXIII, in *Mater et Magistra* and *Pacem in Terris*, broadened the concept
of solidarity from within nations to the practice of solidarity among nations.[31]
The Second Vatican Council in *Gaudium et Spes* articulated the church's union
with those who suffer the hardships of a harsh social world.[32] Pope Paul VI's
Populorum Progressio emphasized the spirit of solidarity needed for integral
human development.[33]

In *Laborem Exercens* Pope John Paul II acknowledged the importance of
the historical movements that had promoted worker solidarity.[34] Finally, in
Sollicitudo Rei Socialis, John Paul II called special attention to the deeper aspi-
rations within the human heart that inspire the "virtue" of solidarity:

The exercise of solidarity *within each society* is valid when its members recognize
one another as persons. Those who are more influential, because they have a greater
share of goods and common services, should feel *responsible* for the weaker and be
ready to share with them all they possess....

Solidarity helps us to see the "other"—whether a *person, people, or nation*—not just
as some kind of instrument, with a work capacity and physical strength to be ex-
ploited at low cost and then discarded when no longer useful, but as our "neighbor,"
a "helper" (cf. *Gen.* 2:18–20), to be made a sharer, on a par with ourselves, in the

---

29. Matthew Lamb, "Solidarity," in *The New Dictionary of Catholic Social Thought*, ed. Judith Dwyer
(Collegeville, Minn.: Liturgical Press, 1994), 908.

30. Pope Pius XI, *Quadragesimo Anno*, Encyclical Letter, May 15, 1931, in AAS 23 (1931): 177–228.

31. Pope John XXIII, *Mater et Magistra*, Encyclical Letter, May 15, 1961, in AAS 53 (1961): 401–64;
Pacem in Terris, Encyclical Letter, April 11, 1963, in AAS 55 (1963): 257–304.

32. GS 1. The opening words of the Pastoral Constitution state it well: "The joys and hopes, the
sorrows and anxieties of people today, especially of the poor and those afflicted, are also the joys and
hopes, sorrows and anxieties of Christ's disciples. Indeed, there is nothing truly human which does not
resonate in their hearts." *Decrees* (ed. Tanner), 2:1069.

33. Pope Paul VI, *Populorum Progressio*, Encyclical Letter, March 26, 1967, in AAS 59 (1967):
257–99.

34. Pope John Paul II, *Laborem Exercens*, Encyclical Letter, September 14, 1981, in AAS 73 (1981):
577–647.

banquet of life to which all are equally invited by God. Hence the importance of reawakening the *religious awareness* of individuals and peoples.[35]

Solidarity is not just a vague feeling of compassion, but a firm and persevering determination to commit oneself to the common good. It springs from the recognition by the individual, even those who are materially rich, of their need for community. Through the practice of solidarity, the social world becomes less cold and mechanical, more warm and human. In this perspective, solidarity is both a human and a Gospel imperative.

The concept of solidarity is not far from the virtue of charity. Expanding the motive for the practice of solidarity, John Paul II pointed out the specifically Christian impetus for social concern. The neighbor is "not only a human being with his or her own rights and a fundamental equality with everyone else, but becomes the *living image* of God and Father, redeemed by the blood of Jesus Christ and placed under the permanent action of the Holy Spirit."[36] The virtue of solidarity allows the individual to see others as they fundamentally are: not simply as workers or managers, consumers or providers, but as persons. As a way of life, solidarity binds the individual to others in enduring relationships. For Christians, solidarity is not one option among others, but is a fundamental requirement of the New Covenant. Love for God means recognizing the "living image of God" in others, especially those who are in need. The practice or "virtue" of solidarity therefore leads one to greater conversion into the Gospel way of life.

On the hundredth anniversary of *Rerum Novarum*, John Paul II promulgated the social encyclical *Centesimus Annus*, in part to address the contemporary situation of a vibrant, free capitalist economy in the West and the collapse of

35. Pope John Paul II, *Sollicitudo Rei Socialis*, Encyclical Letter, December 30, 1987, in AAS 80 (1988): 513–86; official English translation: *The Social Concern of the Church* (Washington, D.C.: United States Catholic Conference, 1988), no. 39 (75–76).

36. Pope John Paul II, *Sollicitudo Rei Socialis*, par. 40 (78–79): "Solidarity is undoubtedly a Christian virtue.... One's neighbor is then not only a human being with his or her own rights and a fundamental equality with everyone else, but becomes the living image of God and Father, redeemed by the blood of Jesus Christ and placed under the permanent action of the Holy Spirit. One's neighbor must therefore be loved, even if an enemy, with the same love with which the Lord loves him or her; and for that person's sake one must be ready for sacrifice, even the ultimate one: to lay down one's life for the brethren.... Beyond human and natural bonds, already so close and strong, there is discerned in the light of faith a new model of the unity of the Human race, which must ultimately inspire our solidarity. The supreme model of unity, which is a reflection of the intimate life of God, one God in three Persons, is what we Christians mean by the word 'communion.' This specifically Christian communion, jealously preserved, extended and enriched with the Lord's help, is the soul of the Church's vocation to be a 'sacrament.'"

communism in the East. Toward the end of the document, the pontiff advocates a recommitment to solidarity in order to combat the social problems of the day.[37] Writing as the shepherd of the universal church, the pope claims that the "individualistic mentality" menacing the development of human society is not simply an American phenomenon, but is "widespread." To overcome this pervasive mentality, teaches the pontiff, the individual needs to be introduced into a network of relationships, thereby making society more "personalized." Adequate structures to strengthen the social fabric for the process of "personalization" are needed. The transformation of an "impersonal mass" into a personalized society, however, is not simply a matter of changing structures, but fundamentally requires the conversion of hearts.

In *Evangelium Vitae* John Paul II addressed contemporary issues that touch upon the failure to accept others in society as persons.[38] The specific issues of abortion, euthanasia, and capital punishment, the pope contended, are a result of the breakdown of a genuinely human coexistence and the disintegration of the state. The breakdown of social bonds encourages and allows for the notion of unwarranted absolute autonomy of the individual: "If the promotion of the self is understood in terms of absolute autonomy, people inevitably reach the point of rejecting one another. Everyone else is considered an enemy from whom one has to defend oneself."[39] The spiritual and social consequences of the individualistic mentality impel the church, from a motive of faith, to preach more loudly and practice more consistently the Gospel of life. The church, as symbol and reality of the kingdom, should express the confidence of the Christian faith that the true good of society is not opposed to the true good of the individual, even when this entails the greatest sacrifice the individual can make. In order to translate the faith of the individual into a more personalized society, the church must provide the means necessary for the people of God to exercise the virtue of solidarity.

Following upon the legacy of John Paul II, Pope Benedict XVI issued two encyclical letters applying the social doctrine of the church to the practical aspects of modern life: *Deus Caritas Est* and *Caritas in Veritate*. He wrote: "Love of neighbour is a path that leads to the encounter with God, and that closing

37. Pope John Paul II, *Centesimus Annus*, Encyclical Letter, May 1, 1991; official English translation: *On the Hundredth Anniversary of Rerum Novarum* (Washington, D.C.: United States Catholic Conference, 1991), par. 49 (96).

38. Pope John Paul II, *Evangelium Vitae*, Encyclical Letter, March 25, 1995, in AAS 87 (1995): 401–522; English translation: "The Gospel of Life," *Origins* 24 (1995): 689–725.

39. Pope John Paul II, *Evangelium Vitae*, par. 20.

our eyes to our neighbour also blinds us to God."[40] "Love—caritas—is an extraordinary force which leads people to opt for courageous and generous engagement in the field of justice and peace."[41] "Charity is at the heart of the church's social doctrine," it "is the principle not only of micro-relationships (with friends, with family members or within small groups) but also of macro-relationships (social, economic and political ones)."[42]

And in *Laudato Si'*, Pope Francis made a passionate call for a united effort to address the social implications of environmental concerns and to attend to "human ecology."[43] Authentic human development must be given priority, recognizing the unique place of human beings in all creation, who are made in the image and likeness of God. "Authentic human development has a moral character. It presumes full respect for the human person, but it must also be concerned for the world around us."[44]

Among these social encyclicals, one would do well to include consideration of Pope Francis's apostolic exhortation, *Evangelii Gaudium*, in which he described the social dimension of evangelization in light of the "signs of the times." Evangelization and social progress go hand in hand; our efforts at evangelization must include the application of Gospel values to the social conditions people encounter in daily life.[45]

Thus, institutions that facilitate concrete acts of charity by the people of God serve not only the material needs of the poor, but also the unity of the church and the well-being of the entire human society. Empowered with the grace of the New Covenant, the people of God are sent out to the world to heal divisions and overcome alienation of every sort. When the church fulfills her obligation "to love one another," it is then that her unity with God is made manifest. In uniting the people of God to those in need, intermediate structures manifest the church's love for God, allow for deeper conversion and communion, and preserve the apostolic identity of the local assembly. Such could be the role of the diaconate as an "intermediate order."

40. Pope Benedict XVI, *Deus Caritas Est*, Encyclical Letter, December 25, 2005, par. 16; official English translation: *God Is Love* (Vatican City: Libreria Editrice Vaticana, 2006), 20.

41. Pope Benedict XVI, *Caritas in Veritate*, Encyclical Letter, June 29, 2005, par. 1; available at www.vatican.va.

42. Ibid., par. 2.

43. Pope Francis, *Laudato Si'*, par. 6 (quoting *Centesimus Annus*, par. 38).

44. Ibid., par. 5.

45. Pope Francis, *Evangelii Gaudium*, par. 51.

Conclusion

The role of an intermediary figure between the bishop and the people, and between the people of God and the individual in need, is consistent with the theological foundations of the ministry of the deacon. The ecclesiastical ministry, flowing from the gift of the Spirit, is conformed to the example of Christ the selfless servant, and oriented toward the active participation of the faithful in the life and mission of the church. Perhaps the greatest challenge for pastoral authorities in the church today is the empowerment and encouragement of the laity to assume their rightful role, to engage their particular charisms fruitfully in the life and mission of the church.[46] Ordained to the ministry of the bishop, the deacon's ministry is to assist him in providing the necessary structures for the exercise of the baptismal charisms of the laity. Because the diaconate does not share in the *sacerdotium* of the bishop, the deacon stands in a unique position to meet some of these structural needs. The role of a social intermediary can help us to understand the type of "assistance" the deacon renders the bishop, and the type of "service" the deacon renders to the people.

The diaconate order could be socially structured to mediate the power and authority of the bishop and his priests, but only if the deacon were to enjoy immediate contact with the pastoral authority and the people. To serve as an intermediary in this capacity, the deacon must have (in some manner) the ear of the bishop. The deacon must also have regular contact with the laity, such that their needs and desires would be well known to the deacon. We can describe the role of the deacon as intermediary in sociological language: he would facilitate the distribution of knowledge, serve to legitimate the bishop's exercise of authority, and manifest the right of competent laity to influence decisions concerning the good of the church. Furthermore, if the role of the diaconate were so structured as to entail the direction and promotion of works of charity, the deacon could bridge the gap between a private, individualized faith and an active, social concern for others in need. As an intermediate institution, the diaconate would mediate the "powers" (the abilities of time, talent, and treasure) and "authority" (the expertise and right to participation) of the laity. Lives lived in active solidarity cement the ties that bind individual Christians to one another and to the world that they are called to serve. The cultural pressures that encourage individualism and alienation today could be opposed by such a mediating function of the deacon.

46. John Coriden, "The Permanent Diaconate/Meaning of Ministry," *Origins* 7, no. 4 (1978): 655.

The ultimate work of the church—to form human society into true communion with God and one another—can only be accomplished through the personal participation of individuals. An external power or authority cannot coerce the individual's choice for the Christian life, today less than ever. Though the choice to "love one another" is made within the recesses of the heart of the individual, it is not made without the assistance of institutions. The community of the church, with its social structures in service to the Spirit, provides the necessary social and theological environment for the individual to exercise his or her choice for the Christian way of life.[47] If the diaconate were structured, as described above, to mediate the relationships between bishop and flock, or between the people of God and individuals in need, the deacon would not simply serve to bring about greater social cohesion, but greater personal conversion. The performance of diaconal ministry would not only manifest the unity of the church, but would also manifest her love.

In our endeavor to delineate the nature and purpose of a social intermediary in the church, we have uncovered a relationship between social structure and the life and mission of the church. The diaconate as an intermediate order among the people of God touches upon the constitution of the church, her very nature and purpose. Such a description of a social intermediary in the context of the church will help our examination of evidence for diaconal ministry in the concrete, which we will turn to in the next chapter. The following are some key points, drawn from my evaluation of the social intermediary, to note in my investigation of the deacon's concrete, nonritual ministry:

1. The diaconate is an institution with an ordered, "typified" way of accomplishing certain tasks within the church. The roles entrusted to the diaconate relate to specific sectors in the life of the church in which the deacon is the "expert." The deacon as specialist implies a greater amount of knowledge than most about the ministry entrusted to him by the church.

2. The diaconate as an intermediate institution implies a twofold orientation of the deacon's ministry. If the deacon were to mediate the power

---

47. The necessity for institutions (and therefore the church) in the life of faith pertains to the old dictum used by the Second Vatican Council, "extra ecclesiam nulla salus." In using this expression, the Council explicitly directs itself to Catholics and limits its validity to those who know the necessity of the church for salvation. The expression serves to exhort the members of the church to be faithful. With regard to non-Christians, the Council said that they are ordered in diverse ways to the people of God. See the document published by the International Theological Commission, *Christianity and the World of Religions*, trans. in *Origins* 27 (1997): 150–66, esp. 159–60.

and authority of the bishop, then the ministry of the deacon would involve regular contact with the bishop as well as the people. The deacon would have knowledge about the bishop's concerns for the church, as well as the needs and desires of the laity.

3. If the deacon were to mediate between the individual members of the church and those in need, then the deacon would be knowledgeable of the needs of the "poor" in the community. The deacon would also know the gifts and talents of the members of the church, seeking to utilize them as best as possible in accomplishing the work of the church. In order to gain this specialized knowledge, the ministry of the deacon would place him in regular contact with the people of God and the poor among them.

4. In light of the social dialectic of knowledge, we can expect to find changing forms of diaconal ministry throughout history. All institutions within the church are exposed to the influence of societal forces. Changing forms of the diaconate, however, must be evaluated in light of the theological foundations upon which the deacon stands. The deacon is ordained not to the priesthood, but to assist the bishop and his priest in service to the people. Models of the diaconate that are more than or less than this should be treated with skepticism.

PART 3

The Witness of History

CHAPTER 5

Precedents for
the Deacon as Social
Intermediary

The Second Vatican Council taught that deacons are ordained to serve the people of God and empowered by sacramental grace to fulfill the tasks entrusted
to them. In specifying these tasks, Paul VI described the diaconate as an intermediate order that would express the needs and desires of the Christian faithful to the bishop, and that connects the people of God (including the bishop)
to those in need. My investigation of the social nature of the church demonstrated that her life and mission does indeed require intermediate structures
among the people of God. But is this a new understanding of the diaconate,
crafted by the Council and Paul VI, without roots in the history of the deacon?

To answer this concern, in this chapter I will examine texts that describe
the deacon as a social intermediary among the people of God. This will show
a historical connection between diaconal charisms and mediating functions
in the exercise of the diaconate. I will not review every function that has ever
been entrusted to the deacon throughout history; I will only demonstrate that
the deacon has functioned as a social intermediary, and bring that evidence
to light. I shall observe two types of intermediation: (1) between the bishop
and the laity, and (2) between the people of God and those on the margins of
society. In other words, I shall pay attention to the sectors of the church that
have been entrusted to the deacon's expertise, and the structured manner in
which deacons mediate the power, authority, love, and solidarity of the people
of God.

The diversity of roles held by the deacon in the Latin West makes it difficult for theologians to grasp the essential character of the diaconate. As the

circumstances and needs of the church changed, so did the flexible office of the deacon.[1] The deacon's roles were a social "incarnation" of different theological understandings of the church, either as organic and collegial or as linear-hierarchical (in which the deacon serves the priest and the priest serves the bishop).[2] For example, the degree of participation in the administration of the church by deacons was wide-ranging: from the merely cultic and transitional figure prevalent in the medieval and modern periods, to the example of the powerful archdeacon throughout the Middle Ages, whose authority at times rivaled that of presbyters. History does not provide a linear development of the diaconal office. Consequently, to structure my analysis of diaconal ministry simply in terms of historical progression would not be beneficial.

Instead, my analysis of texts that concern the role of the deacon as a social intermediary will comprise two general categories. First, I shall explore in this chapter the functions of deacons as they appear at their apex in what I shall call the "Golden Age" of the diaconate. In the pre-Nicene church, deacons were significant ecclesiastical ministers. In this period, there were deacons who worked immediately with the bishop in the administration of church affairs, as well as those who administered regional areas of the bishop's responsibility, areas that were known as deaconries. There is even evidence that some deacons occasionally assisted the bishop without the supervision of presbyters at small country churches and other sacred sites. The ecclesial context of the deacon in this era is notably collegial and organic. In my search for a clearer understanding of the deacon and his appropriate roles following the Second Vatican Council, the diaconate of the Golden Age is very appealing because in this period the utilization of diaconal charisms occurred in a context that was similar to the vision of church and ministry found in the teachings of Vatican II.

Second, I shall explore in the next chapter the functions of what came to be known as the archdeacon. The office of archdeacon began at least by the

---

1. See Gula, "A Theology of the Diaconate—Part One," 634.

2. Berger and Luckmann, *The Social Construction of Reality*, 79, offers the following methodological insight: "The analysis of roles is of particular importance to the sociology of knowledge because it reveals the mediations between the macroscopic universes of meaning objectivated in a society and the ways by which these universes are subjectively real to individuals." One could therefore study the roles of the diaconate as a method for reconstructing the image of the church held in the minds of individuals in various social contexts. My study of diaconal roles in this thesis, however, is to argue that the deacon has had the role of social intermediary in history. Awareness of the interplay between ecclesial context and diaconal functions will help us critically evaluate the roles of the diaconate today. An underlying theme of this book is to delineate how diaconal functions could help the church achieve the ecclesial context she is seeking following the Second Vatican Council.

middle of the fourth century and was greatly influenced by processes at work in the following centuries. In the model of the archdeacon, the nonliturgical roles of all the deacons of a "diocese" were given to a single, very influential figure, one who did much more than *assist* the bishop in the governance of the diocese. The medieval-canonical model of the archdeacon is too important to leave unconsidered, even if the ecclesial context associated with this model of the diaconate is not altogether appealing. But observing the problems associated with the model of archdeacon will preserve us from being doomed to repeat a historical form that failed to thrive.

I will not, in the present chapter, immediately connect the historical roles described in these early sources to the role of deacons today. Readers may wonder, for instance, what the implications may be for present-day practices of these findings, such as the immediate relationship between deacons and bishops (rather than the subordination of deacons under priests), or the responsibility of deacons in the Golden Age for church administration. I will wait until the end of chapter 6 and chapters 8 and 9 to connect the findings of these historical investigations to the present day, keeping in mind as well the biblical and theological foundations laid in the previous chapters. For the time being, it is best to examine the historical record in the light of the sociological categories I have already explored. Let us begin, then, with texts that describe the role of the deacon as a social intermediary during the Golden Age, beginning with his intermediary ministry between bishop and laity.

The Deacon as Intermediary between Bishop and Laity

The years spanning from roughly the death of Clement I of Rome to the Council of Nicaea (100–325 A.D.) have been called the "Golden Age" of the diaconate.[3] As the diaconate developed in this period, deacons flourished in num-

---

3. The changing structures of ministry during this period make it difficult to pinpoint precise moments in the diaconate's rise and fall. It is generally agreed that the fourth century was a period of radical transition for the diaconate. See Echlin, *The Deacon in the Church*, 28. Echlin calls the "Golden Age" of the diaconate the time period from Ignatius of Antioch to the Council of Nicaea. "The seeds of diaconal decline were already planted with the rise of sacerdotalism in the third century and the restrictive legislation of the early fourth century. A confusion of roles between deacons and 'priests' and a struggle for identity continued into the Middle Ages. Gradually the diaconate receded in importance until the diaconal order became merely a preliminary and ceremonial step to the sacralized priesthood" (61). Though the decline of the diaconate had its roots in the third century, Barnett claims that it continued to flourish long after, even up to the beginning of the seventh century. See James M.

bers and influence, especially in comparison with the centuries that followed. This flourishing was rooted in the role of the deacon as a social intermediary in the church.

Chapter 1 illustrated the rather sketchy New Testament witness of the "office of deacon," providing very few hints of what might have comprised the ministry of the "deacon" in that era. Some *diakonoi* were associated with the *episkopoi* in the New Testament, appearing subordinate to them; they perhaps assisted the *episkopoi* in the administration of the Christian communities, but nothing is known with certainty. The texts we find in the Golden Age, however, reveal with greater clarity the role of the deacon within the church. In assisting the bishop in the leadership of the church, deacons administrated the church's property and extended the bishop's pastoral care to the sick and poor. These were functions important to the exercise of the bishop's ministry and for the life and mission of the church. The deacon of the Golden Age enjoyed a direct relationship with the bishop, and he worked in communion with him and his presbyterate in fulfilling a ministry that was highly esteemed.

Western Texts of the Apostolic Age

The Church Order known as the *Apostolic Tradition* of Hippolytus is the primary text referenced in the following investigation of diaconal ministry in the pre-Nicene Western church. In the span of time between the compositions of the New Testament and the AT, there is not a lot of direct information about diaconal ministry. Texts from the intervening Apostolic Age, however, witness the ecclesial context of the diaconate on the eve of the Golden Age. The few texts from the Apostolic Age (both in the West and East) that concern the diaconate reveal the development of the diaconate within a collegial and organically structured church.

There is general consensus today that first- and second-century Roman Christianity was widely diverse, both ethnically and theologically, heavily influenced by a strong Jewish component that was predominantly Greek-speaking, and drew its membership almost exclusively from the non-elite classes of the city.[4] The two Western texts that we shall examine from the Apostolic Age were

---

Barnett, *The Diaconate: A Full and Equal Order*, rev. ed. (Valley Forge, Penn.: Trinity Press International, 1979–95), 43.

4. Carolyn Osiek, *The Shepherd of Hermas*, ed. Helmut Koester, Hermeneia (Minneapolis, Minn.: Fortress Press, 1999), 20–21. The Christian community at Rome was not only one of the largest, but also highly representative of the various currents of thought, tradition, and practice of the whole

written by Romans in this cultural milieu. Clement I of Rome wrote a letter to the church at Corinth at the end of the first century, from which we have a snapshot of how at least one influential man of this age conceived the church. The *Shepherd of Hermas* provides a passing glance at the diaconate through the critical eye of a Roman at the beginning of the second century. These two documents support the idea that the ministerial order was still as yet in transition, and that concern for one another within the community of the church was a ministry highly regarded.

Clement I of Rome

The flourishing development of the diaconate in the Golden Age can be attributed, in part, to the ecclesial environment of the pre-Nicene church. The letter of Clement I to the Corinthians evidences the ideal of a collegially structured and unified church. Clement, who is traditionally considered the third successor of Peter as bishop of Rome, wrote his letter in the name and authority of the Roman community.[5] Written around the year 96 A.D., the letter appeared following the persecution under Domitian.[6] It is the earliest piece of Christian literature outside the New Testament for which the name and date of the author are historically attested.[7] Clement uses language that is remi-

---

Christian church. Rome was at this period a strong center of Jewish life and learning. The Latinization of Roman Christianity was only completed by the mid-third century. See George LaPiana, "The Roman Church at the End of the Second Century," *Harvard Theological Review* 18 (1925): 201–77; Carolyn Osiek, "The Early Second Century through the Eyes of Hermas: Continuity and Change," *Biblical Theology Bulletin* 20 (1990): 116–22; Harry J. Leon, *The Jews of Ancient Rome*, rev. ed. (Peabody, Mass.: Hendrickson, 1994), 35–38.

5. John Fuellenbach, *Ecclesiastical Office and the Primacy of Rome: An Evaluation of Recent Theological Discussion of First Clement*, ed. Johannes Quasten, The Catholic University of America Studies in Antiquity 20 (Washington, D.C.: The Catholic University of America Press, 1980), 5. The actual office that Clement held in Rome is much disputed. Some hold that Clement was indeed the fourth bishop of Rome; see Quasten, *Patrology*, 1:42; *The Apostolic Fathers: Clement, Ignatius, and Polycarp*, ed. and trans. Joseph Lightfoot, 2nd ed. (Peabody, Mass.: Hendrickson, 1989), 1.1:67–69; and Jurgens, *The Faith of the Early Fathers*, 1:6. Others hold him to be "a leading presbyter among others," who may have functioned as a "foreign Secretary" of the Roman church. For this view see Staniforth, *Early Christian Writings*, 17–20, and Leslie W. Barnard, *Studies in The Apostolic Fathers and Their Background* (Oxford: Basil Blackwell, 1966), 9. In a similar vein, John A. Robinson, *Re-dating the New Testament* (London: SCM Press, 1976), 328–33, presents the possibility that Clement wrote the letter in the early 70s A.D. as a "correspondent" or secretary of the Roman presbyterate, and then twenty-five years later became the bishop of Rome.

6. Staniforth, *Early Christian Writings*, 17.

7. Quasten, *Patrology*, 1:43.

niscent of the late Pauline corpus, revealing a ministerial structure still in transition. The leaders in the church at Corinth are called *episkopoi* and *diakonoi* in some passages (e.g., chap. 42, nos. 4–5), and in others, simply *presbyteroi* (e.g., chap. 44, no. 5). The church in this time period evidently had a church order that was early in its development. While there is very little evidence regarding the diaconal ministry in the letter, it does indicate the ecclesial context that existed when the diaconate entered the Golden Age.

Within a generation after the death of Paul, there were renewed factions creating a disturbance at Corinth concerning the church's ministry. The letter of Clement is evidence of discord within the early church over the exercise of power and authority.[8] Whether it concerned legitimacy or legitimation is not clear, but it appears only a very small minority of the community remained loyal to the presbyter-bishops.[9] The letter of Clement, nonetheless, reveals a certain structure of the church at Corinth, and more significantly, the kind of church order the author thought it should be. The letter attempts to reconcile the various factions by calling for unity with the presbyter-bishops and deacons, teaching that there is a given order in the church that must be followed.

Clement uses various analogies to explain this order: the civil order, a military organization, and a human body. In the civil world, subordination of rank and distinction of office are the necessary conditions of life. This hierarchal structure is especially true of the military, where obedience is greatly prized.[10] Even in this analogy, Clement stresses not the superiority of leaders, but the need for each rank to do their part. But that sense of the part as necessary to the whole is emphasized even more organically by the body analogy. Clement echoes Paul's letter to the Corinthians by writing: "Let us take our body as an example. The head without the feet is nothing; so likewise the feet without the head are nothing: even the smallest limbs of our body are necessary and useful for the whole body: but all the members conspire and unite in subjection, that the whole body may be saved."[11] This interdependence of the members within the church suggests a more collegial and not linear-hierarchal ordering, although some hierarchy (the head) remains. The diversity of roles and of relationships is seen as a harmonic strength. Weakness sets in when the order is

8. Schweizer proposes that behind the dispute may have been the defenders of an older and freer order who opposed the consolidation of the institutional church. Schweizer, *Church Order in the New Testament*, 146.

9. Quasten, *Patrology*, 1:43.

10. Lightfoot, *Apostolic Fathers*, 1.2:290.

11. Ibid., 1.2:291.

violated, when one attempts to exist without the other. A "disorder" of this sort is thus detrimental to the whole body.

Clement gave concrete examples of what it means to live and function as a member of a body. In chapter 38 he writes:

So in our case let the whole body be saved in Christ Jesus, and let each man be subject unto his neighbour, according as also he was appointed with his special grace. Let not the strong neglect the weak; and let the weak respect the strong. Let the rich minister aid to the poor; and let the poor give thanks to God, because He hath given him one through whom his wants may be supplied. Let the wise display his wisdom, not in words, but in good works.[12]

With these words Clement drew upon the motive of faith to argue for a social life in which individuals are concerned and involved with the needs of others. Respect for the diversity of roles within the community parallels a sense of community and of belonging to one another.

The *Shepherd of Hermas* ·

At the start of the Golden Age, the *Shepherd of Hermas* refers to the ministry of deacons in an indirect manner. Although numbered among the Apostolic Fathers, the *Shepherd* belongs in reality to the apocryphal apocalypses, a book of revelations that were granted to Hermas in Rome by the agency of two heavenly figures.[13] In the third vision of its original section (ca. 96 A.D.), an aged lady employs the symbol of a tower under construction and points out the destiny of Christianity.[14] As every stone not suitable for the masonry of the tower is rejected, so every sinner who does not do penance shall be excluded from the church. "Now listen about the stones that go into the building. Those that are square and white and fit into their joints are the apostles and overseers and teachers and deacons who proceed mindful of the dignity of God, who have governed and taught and served the elect of God in holiness and dignity."[15]

Like Clement's body analogy, this "building" analogy carries echoes of the

---

12. Lightfoot, *Apostolic Fathers*, 1.2:291.

13. Berthold Altaner, *Patrology*, trans. Hilda Graef (Freiburg: Herder and Herder, 1958), 84.

14. A recent study on the *Shepherd* claims that there is little doubt that the geographical origin of *Hermas* is central Italy, and most likely Rome. The date of the writing is much more complex. The best assignment of the date is an expanded duration of time beginning from the very last years of the first century stretching through most of the first half of the second century. See Osiek, *Shepherd*, 18–20.

15. Vision 3.5.1; translation from Osiek, *Shepherd*, 66.

New Testament.[16] Members involved in the ministry of the church, who performed their appropriate tasks with reverence and holiness, are compared to
the neatly fitting stones of the tower. It is obvious that the function of overseeing is applied to the bishops, teaching to the teachers, and "giving service" to
the deacons. The deacons and the service they provided occupied an integral
place in the building up of the church, alongside apostles, bishops, and teachers. The inclusion of apostles and teachers with bishops and deacons, on the
other hand, shows that the church was still in the early stages of transition into
a well-defined and ordered leadership.[17]

A description of the kind of service rendered by the deacon is given in the
second part of the book (ca. 140 A.D.). The role of deacons in social welfare
and administration of church finances is firmly attested, although only, as in a
photographic negative, by a condemnation of those who failed to fulfill their
office and function in the community due to greed. The author speaks of *diakonoi* "who minister badly and despoil the living of widows and orphans, and
made profit for themselves off the ministry entrusted to them to do."[18] The
care of the weak and the poor was a special concern of the church in this era,
and the second part of Hermas's *Shepherd* is direct evidence that deacons had
responsibility in providing charity to the less fortunate through the administration of the church's material wealth.[19] What was only implied or indirectly
seen in 1 Timothy 3 concerning the administrative functions of deacons is now
clearly indicated. Those who held the office of deacon performed these particular functions within the community of the church.

Eastern Texts of the Apostolic Age

Though my primary concern is the diaconate of the Latin West, the examination of certain texts from the East is helpful for understanding the theological
and historical context of the Church Order of Rome. We should not presume
that the early Roman practice originated and developed apart from the influences of other practices that are geographically different. I will therefore examine the letters of Ignatius of Antioch and Polycarp of Smyrna. My examination
of Eastern Apostolic Age texts shall begin, however, with the *Didache*, the only
known Church Order to predate the Church Order of the West.

16. 1 Pt 2:5.
17. Osiek, *Shepherd*, 71.
18. Parable 9.26.2; translation from Osiek, *Shepherd*, 242.
19. Osiek, *Shepherd*, 249.

The *Didache*

The *Didache*, or *The Teaching of the Twelve Apostles*, is considered the most important patristic find of the latter half of the nineteenth century.[20] It is the oldest source of ecclesiastical law which we possess.[21] The *Didache*, in its sections on church order, seems to suppose a small town or rural community in Syria.[22] Scholarly estimates of its date range from before the end of the first century, to a date at the turn of the century, and to a date as late as 150.[23] As the *Didache* does not show a distinct threefold ministry of bishops, priests, and deacons, it most likely represents apostolic or subapostolic thought.

The *Didache* reflects a church order in transition from a less structured ministry in the early church of apostles, prophets, and teachers (as seen in the Pauline letters) to one of bishops, presbyters, and deacons.[24] The *Didache* attests to the existence of functioning prophets and teachers. *Episkopoi* and *diakonoi* are mentioned in the plural throughout the document, while *presbyteroi* are never mentioned.[25] Chapter 15 reveals that a plurality of ordering existed until the end of the first century, and perhaps into the beginning of the second: "Accordingly, elect for yourselves bishops and deacons, men who are an honor to the Lord, of gentle disposition, not attached to money, honest and well-tried; for they, too, render you the sacred service of the prophets and teachers. Do not, then, despise them; after all, they are your dignitaries together with the prophets and teachers."[26] The requirement that deacons should be "not attached to money" may reflect the tradition of assigning financial responsibility to them. There is the implication that prophets and teachers already held a respected position within the community. Bishops and deacons, on the other hand, were beginning to replace them in a transition from itinerant and charismatic to settled and indigenous leadership, especially insofar as the ministry of the former is described as being identical to that of the latter.[27]

20. James Kleist, "The Didache," ed. Johannes Quasten, Ancient Christian Writers (hereafter ACW) 6 (Westminster, Md.: Newman, 1948), 3.

21. Quasten, *Patrology*, 1:30.

22. Kleist, "The Didache," 4; Quasten, *Patrology*, 1:37; Henry Bettenson (ed. and trans.), *The Early Christian Fathers* (New York: Oxford University Press, 1969), 6.

23. Kleist, "The Didache," 4; Schweizer, *Church Order*, 139; Quasten, *Patrology*, 1:37.

24. Bettenson, *The Early Christian Fathers*, 7.

25. Quasten, *Patrology*, 1:33.

26. Translation from Kleist, "The Didache," 24.

27. J. Robert Wright, "The Emergence of the Diaconate," *Liturgy* 2 (1982): 21.

Ignatius of Antioch

In the letters of Ignatius of Antioch, bishop and martyr, we have evidence of a developed church order. "Of all fathers of the Church, early or late, no one is more incisive or more persistent in advocating the claims of the threefold ministry to allegiance than Ignatius."[28] While on his journey from Syria to Rome, where he was thrown to wild beasts, Ignatius wrote seven letters that are generally dated to the beginning of the second century, for his martyrdom occurred sometime during the reign of Trajan (98–117 A.D.).[29] For the first time, these letters depict vividly the clearly distinguishable orders of bishops, presbyters, and deacons. Unlike the pastoral letters in the New Testament and the letter of Clement, bishops and presbyters are distinct, and the terms are never used synonymously. The bishop emerges as the president of the presbyterate, the form of which is usually signified today by the term "mono-episcopate." The listing of bishop first, presbyters second, and deacons third is maintained throughout his letters.[30]

The kind of office held by the bishop was not that of a monarch ruling over the church, but rather that of a president of the community and of the presbyteral council.[31] Ignatius enforced this order almost solely as a security for doctrinal purity. For him the unity of the body was a guarantee of the unity of faith. The threefold ministry was the husk, the shell, which protected the precious kernel that is the truth.[32]

In the preface of his letter to the Philadelphians, deacons as well as bishops and presbyters are described as having been "appointed according to the mind of Jesus Christ, whom after His own will He confirmed and established by His Holy Spirit."[33] Ignatius, like Clement, posits the authentic origin of the threefold ministry in Jesus Christ, with a noted emphasis on the pneumatological element underlining the legitimacy of the deacon's establishment. In the letter to the Magnesians, Ignatius gives the clergy titles of a graded sort, where "the bishop is godly [*axiotheos*], the presbyters worthy [*axioi*] and the deacon [a] fellow-servant [*sundoulos*]."[34] Ignatius also makes use of analogy to describe

---

28. Lightfoot, *Apostolic Fathers*, 2.1:39.
29. Quasten, *Patrology*, 1:63.
30. Wright, "The Emergence of the Diaconate," 20.
31. Barnett, *The Diaconate*, 49.
32. Lightfoot, *Apostolic Fathers*, 2.1:40.
33. Ibid., 2.2:563.
34. Magnesians, no. 2; Wright, "The Emergence of the Diaconate," 20.

the relationships between those in orders and the rest of the church. In his letter to the Trallians (3) he writes: "In like manner let all men respect the deacons as Jesus Christ, even as they should respect the bishop as being a type of the Father and the presbyters as the council of God and as the college of Apostles. Apart from these there is not even the name of a church."[35]

The analogy of the bishop as the Father, presbyters as the council of God and the college of apostles, and deacons as Jesus Christ is most common in his works.[36] What must be kept in mind, however, is that analogies are not direct descriptions. Ignatius is not addressing questions of our day about the threefold order of the church, or the place and function of the diaconate in the community. He is arguing for unity with the ministerial leadership for the sake of preserving the true faith. The idea that office holders in the church (primarily the bishop) are responsible for preserving the faith is nothing new; we have seen this conception before already in the New Testament. What is surprising, however, is his statement that without the threefold ministry "there is not even the name of a church." The members of the clergy, therefore, are a guarantee of the presence of the church. Deacons, as constituting the clergy with the bishop and presbyters, occupy a vital office within the structured order of the church.

Ignatius's analogy incorporates a structure of order that is collegial. There is not a linear relationship from deacon to presbyter to bishop. Yet the bishop is seen as the superior authority, in communion with his college of presbyters and his fellow workers, the deacons. Furthermore, there is a particular and special relationship depicted between the bishop and his deacons, where the bishop is a type of God the Father and the deacon of Jesus Christ. The fact that Ignatius associates the deacons with Jesus Christ cannot be taken as evidence favoring their superiority over the presbyters. Ignatius also employs other analogies where the bishop is Jesus Christ (Mag. 3, Eph. 3), and in one place, the presbyterate is Jesus Christ's "law" to which the deacon must submit (Mag. 2). Though deacons are to be respected as Jesus Christ and are "entrusted with the *diakonia* of Jesus" (Mag. 6), it would not be true to state without qualification that "for Ignatius the deacon, and only the deacon, is the antitype [*sic*] or representative of Jesus Christ."[37]

The fullest statement on the diaconate by Ignatius is found in his letter

35. Translation in Lightfoot, *Apostolic Fathers*, 2.2:555.

36. Wright, "The Emergence of the Diaconate," 20. See also Ignatius's letter to the *Magnesians*, no. 6.

37. Wright, "The Emergence of the Diaconate," 21. The deacon is the *tupos* of the "antitype" Jesus Christ. Wright has evidently confused the terms.

to the Trallians (2). Ignatius writes: "And those likewise who are deacons of the mysteries of Jesus Christ must please all men in all ways. For they are not deacons of meats and drinks but servants of the Church of God. It is right therefore that they should beware of blame as of fire."[38] The concern of Ignatius that deacons be upright and respectable men is reminiscent of 1 Timothy 3. The reference to the "mysteries of Jesus Christ" may imply liturgical functions for the deacons, but this is disputed.[39] This passage at the very least is a development from the duties given to the Seven in Acts 6. Ignatius rejects any notion of their function as merely waiting on tables, and points out that the deacons are "servants of the Church of God." In many passages Ignatius calls the deacons his "fellow-servants" (*sundouloi*), and one time he notes that diaconal functions include serving as a messenger between distant churches.[40] Still, in other places Ignatius alludes to some sort of function that involved the ministry of the word of God. In Philadelphians 11 he writes: "But as touching Philo the deacon from Cilicia, a man of good report, who now also ministereth to me in the word of God."[41]

In the letters of Ignatius, we are presented with a well-developed threefold structure of ministry, beyond what we had seen in earlier or contemporary writers, in which deacons have an integral place. Their importance is attested in his consideration of them as types of Jesus Christ, wherein the deacons have been entrusted with his *diakonia*. Deacons were considered confirmed and established by the Holy Spirit of Christ, justifying their existence within the threefold order. It is directly attested that their functions go beyond that of charitable service to the poor: they include service to the bishop in the liturgy and the ministry of the word, as well as the administrative roles of messenger and helper. In this early period of the church's history we already see evidence of a well-structured and distinct diaconate with a plurality of functions, some liturgical and others administrative and social. For Ignatius deacons played a significant role in maintaining the purity of the church's faith.

---

38. Lightfoot, *Apostolic Fathers*, 2.2:555.

39. Barnett, *The Diaconate*, 49, argues quite well that the reference to "mystery" here does not refer to sacred rites, but to the "secret knowledge of God's plan revealed in the Gospel." On the other hand, others see a connection with 1 Tm 3:9, 1 Cor 4:1, and 1 Cor 13:2, implying a liturgical function. See Wright, "The Emergence of the Diaconate," 21.

40. *Magnesians*, no. 2, *Philadelphians*, no. 4, *Smyrneans*, no. 12, *Philadelphians*, no. 10.

41. Lightfoot, *Apostolic Fathers*, 2.2:566.

Polycarp of Smyrna

After the martyrdom of Ignatius (ca. 110 A.D.) Polycarp of Smyrna sent a copy of the letters of Ignatius to the church at Philippi, along with a communication in his own hand, known today as his letter to the Philippians. Textual variations and evidence apart from the letter show that it is really two letters that Polycarp wrote to the Philippians, at different times, which were copied out at an early date onto the same papyrus roll and thus merged into one letter. The first, consisting of chapters 13 and 14, was the short cover letter sent by Polycarp with the letters of Ignatius, asking for reliable information regarding Ignatius's death, thus dating the letter shortly after 110. Chapters 1–12 were written twenty years later.[42]

In this "second" letter (ca. 130 A.D.) Polycarp makes no mention of a bishop at Philippi, but he does speak of obedience due to presbyters and deacons, setting forth qualifications for presbyters and deacons, reminiscent of 1 Timothy 3.[43] "In like manner deacons should be blameless in the presence of His righteousness, as deacons of God and Christ and not of men; not calumniators, not double-tongued, not lovers of money, temperate in all things, compassionate, diligent, walking according to the truth of the Lord who became a minister (deacon) of all."[44] In this passage we have a direct correlation of the "diaconate" of Christ and that of the church office. Polycarp emphasizes the idea that the deacons are not simply servants of men, but have a service to perform in relation to God and Christ. This document indicates the existence of a diaconate in the middle of the second century at Philippi, where the service of the deacon is in communion with the other clergy for the service of God and church.

Summary of the Apostolic Age

By the end of the Apostolic Age the leadership of the church had clearly passed from apostles, prophets, and teachers found in the primitive church to the threefold order of bishops, presbyters, and deacons. The functions of the earlier charismatic leaders were not dropped, but continued through the charisma of the orders. Deacons, in particular, continued to perform works of service for

42. See Quasten, *Patrology*, 1:77–80.

43. *Philippians*, no. 5. It is possible that a council of presbyters governed the Christian community of Philippi. See Quasten, *Patrology*, 1:80.

44. *Philippians*, no. 5, as translated in Lightfoot, *Apostolic Fathers*, 2.2:473.

the poor. They performed the *diakonia* of Christ, holding functions that were increasingly not to be interchanged with those of the other orders.[45]

The diaconate was being formed and defined more and more while the threefold order of ministry was taking shape as a whole. A single bishop presiding over the college of presbyters and the church, with his deacons at his side, was a common structure by the middle of the second century. The deacon was always considered in close connection to the bishop, while the deacon held an office that was in service to God and the church as a whole. It would not be accurate to picture the deacon as an office independent from the bishop and presbyters. Nor would it be accurate, at this point in the church's development, to see a linear hierarchy of the deacons serving the priests, who in turn serve the bishop. The texts of the subapostolic period, rather, suggest a collegial and organic structure where each member serves the good of all. The form of the threefold ministry, therefore, does not replace the ministry that the entire church holds. The threefold order serves to build up the church by helping all the members fulfill their own ministry for the expansion of the heavenly kingdom. The understanding of the diaconate during this era, then, is an office with origins in the mind and example of Christ, confirmed and established by the Holy Spirit. It occupied a unique place within the structure of the church, and began to develop particular functions for the service to God and the church in cooperation with the bishop and presbyters.

The Church Order of the Roman West

The Church Orders of the early church testify, over a span of two to three centuries, to a special relationship between the deacon and the bishop. These various collections or documents from the first centuries of the church profess to be teachings handed down from the apostles about Christian doctrine, worship, and ecclesiastical order.[46] Comprised mostly during the third and fourth centuries, these collections are closely related to each other: some of the later ones are essentially reworkings of the earlier ones. Their authors did not merely intend to preserve the traditions they received, but to adapt them to new circumstances in their communities.[47] These are important ancient texts; although they must be used cautiously, they do witness to the institutions and

---

45. Gregory Dix, *The Shape of the Liturgy* (Westminster: Dacre Press, 1945), 112.

46. Norbert Brox, "Church Orders," in *Sacramentum Mundi: An Encyclopedia of Theology*, ed. Karl Rahner et al. (London: Burns and Oates, 1968), 1:373.

47. Studer, "Liturgical Documents of the First Four Centuries," 201.

discipline that flourished in the church in previous centuries.[48] Fortunately for this study, the functions of the deacon are fleshed out in greater detail in the Church Orders than in the New Testament. They also indicate a growing complexity in the organization of the church. My investigation of the deacon as a social intermediary in history will therefore continue with a consideration of an important document for the history of the diaconate in the Roman West.

We have already encountered the Church Order known as the *Apostolic Tradition* of Hippolytus in our examination of the roots of the Second Vatican Council's doctrine on the diaconate in LG 29. The AT was written originally in Greek (ca. 215 A.D.), and provides a rudimentary "sacramentary" with sets of rules and forms for the ordination and functions of the various ranks of the hierarchy.[49] More than likely, it reflects the forms and rites already traditional and customs already long established, perhaps as early as the second half of the second century.[50]

Caution must be taken in utilizing the AT as a source that attests specifically to third-century Roman practice. Although the whole section on the diaconate has generally been accepted by scholars as original, some have suggested that the AT was retouched by fourth-century hands in order to bring it into line with then-current doctrine and practice.[51] One scholar claims that "the denial to the deacon of a share in the *sacerdotium*, 'priesthood,' as well as a place in the 'counsel of the clergy,' belongs more to the fourth-century understanding of the ministry than it does to the second and third centuries."[52] Simply because the understanding of the diaconate in the AT is more common in the fourth century than the third, however, is not enough of a basis to reject it as original.[53] Whether or not the AT reflects third- or fourth-century

48. Reference to other historical sources helps us determine the degree to which the Church Orders of both East and West represent actual practice rather than the ideal. Where uniformity exists among the various Church Orders of time and place, there is a greater likelihood that fact rather than desire is being expressed.

49. Quasten, *Patrologia*, 2:180–81.

50. Ronald C. D. Jasper and Geoffrey J. Cuming, *Prayers of the Eucharist: Early and Reformed*, 2nd ed. (New York: Oxford University Press, 1980), 21.

51. Paul F. Bradshaw, *Ordination Rites of the Ancient Churches of East and West* (New York: Pueblo, 1990), 3.

52. Paul F. Bradshaw, "Ordination," in *Essays on Hippolytus*, ed. Geoffrey J. Cuming, Grove Liturgical Study 15 (Nottingham: Grove Books, 1978), 36. Bradshaw finds it difficult to accept only one author insofar as the document is full of repetitions. He cautiously uses the word "conjectures" to state his belief that the majority of the passage concerning deacons reflects a growth by stages throughout the fourth century "as successive redactors sought to clarify the relationship between the three orders, a subject of intense debate at that period" (ibid.).

53. See Douglas Powell, "Ordo Presbyterii," *Journal of Theological Studies* 26 (1975): 308–11.

thought, it still indicates the Roman tradition and practice of the diaconate in the Golden Age.

The diaconal ordination ritual in the AT expresses the deacon's direct relationship to the bishop, in so far as the bishop alone lays hands on the candidate for the diaconate. The commentary on the ordination rite gives the following reason why the bishop alone lays on hands:

> In the ordination of a deacon, the bishop alone shall lay on hands, because he is not being ordained to the priesthood, but to the service of the bishop, to do what is ordered by him. For he does not share in the counsel of the clergy, but administers and informs the bishop of what is fitting; he does not receive the common spirit of seniority in which the presbyters share, but that which is entrusted to him under the bishop's authority. For this reason the bishop alone shall ordain a deacon; but on a presbyter the presbyters alone shall lay hands, because of the common and like spirit of their order.[54]

That the deacon is directly under the authority of the bishop, and not the presbyterate, is clear enough in this passage. Deacons are to do that which the bishop entrusts to them. The author of the AT appears to envisage the diaconate as co-ordinate to the presbyter and directly subordinate to the episcopacy.

FIGURE 5.1

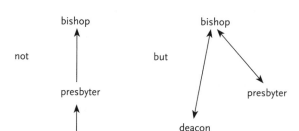

---

54. AT, no. 8; in *Hippolytus* (trans. Cuming), 13.

Although this way of conceiving the structure of the ordained ministry was not maintained through the Middle Ages, it helps us to understand why the relationship between deacons and presbyters has never been clearly defined.[55]

The deacons are charged to administer that which the bishop orders them to do, and to inform the bishop of what is fitting ("curas agens et indicans episcopo quae oportet"). The deacon is therefore concerned with matters for which the bishop has responsibility. The AT describes the diaconal ministry as including administrative responsibilities over the property of the community.[56] Here we have direct evidence, though given in a general manner, of the deacon as a mediator of the bishop's power and authority. The deacon does not simply assist the person of the bishop—he assists the bishop in the performance of the bishop's ministry. The deacon is a source of knowledge for the bishop. These functions to which the AT refers presuppose that the diaconate was an institution with established expectations, patterned modes of acting, and role-specific knowledge, by which the bishop was able to make appropriate pastoral decisions. The bishop was expected (in another institutional role) to assign tasks and make decisions, based upon knowledge mediated through the institution of the diaconate. Whatever services the church expected from the bishop, therefore, were in general a matter of concern also for the deacon.

The sort of knowledge the community expected their deacons to have is found in the concrete examples of what constitutes the deacon's nonliturgical ministry given later in the AT. First, the deacons, in collaboration with the subdeacons, are to keep the bishop informed about the sick in the community: "Each deacon, with the subdeacons, shall attend on the bishop. They shall inform him of those who are ill, so that, if he pleases, he may visit them. For a sick man is greatly comforted when the high-priest remembers him" (AT 34).[57] This passage presupposes that the deacons knew the sick of the community and were responsible for seeing to the welfare of the sick in the bishop's

55. A Gallican document that was perhaps written ca. 490 A.D. testifies to the direct subordination of deacons to presbyters. *Statuta ecclesia antiqua*, c. 57 (37), in *Corpus Christianorum. Series Latina* (Turnhout: Brépols, 1953–) (hereafter CCSL), 148:175: "Diaconus ita se presbyteri ut episcopi ministrum nouerit."

56. Both Dix and Botte have this understanding of "curas agens." Dix, *Apostolic Tradition*, 15: "He is not the fellow-counsellor of the [whole] clergy but to take charge <of property>." Botte, *La Tradition*, 25: "En effet il ne fait pas partie du conseil du clergé, mais il administre et il signale à l'évêque ce qui est nécessaire."

57. Translation from Cuming, *Hippolytus*, 27. Botte, *La Tradition*, 80: "Diaconus uero unusquisque cum subdiac<o>nibus ad episcopum obseruent. Suggeretur etiam illi qui infirmantur, ut, si placuerit episcopo, uisitet eos. Ualde enim oblectatur infirmus cum memor eius fuerit princeps sacerdotum."

name.[58] This passage also presupposes a congregation still small enough to enable the bishop to visit the sick personally, but large enough to require the assistance of deacons and to make the bishop's visit a great event to the sick individual.[59] Through the ministry of deacons, the bishop's service to the sick and needy of the community found its ordinary expression.

The AT also described the structured manner in which the deacons met with their bishop:

The deacons and priests [presbyteri] shall assemble daily at the place which the bishop appoints for them. Let the deacons not fail to assemble at all times, unless illness hinders them. When all have assembled, let them teach those who are in the church, and in this way, when they have prayed, let each one go to the work which falls to him.[60]

According to Easton, the clergy received their assignments for their duties of the day at these daily congregations.[61] Beginning each day with a gathering of the clergy, deacons fulfilled their ordination mandate to serve the church in the ministry of the bishop. It does not seem likely, however, that the church of the third century was merely spontaneous and informal. Certainly patterns had already been formulated so that the responsibilities normally given to the deacons would not have been entirely new to them every day.

The numerical limitation of the deacons in a given church was perhaps one reason why their absence was so noticeable. Though the number of presbyters increased as needed, the Roman church continued to limit the number of deacons to seven in accord with the Seven of Acts 6. The first record we have of the tradition that holds Acts 6 as the establishment of the office of deacon is from the *Adversus Haereses* of Irenaeus of Lyons (ca. 185 A.D.). He writes: "The Nicolatians are the followers of that Nicolas who was one of the seven first ordained to the diaconate by the apostles."[62] He later continues: "And still further, Stephen, who was chosen the first deacon by the apostles, and who, of

58. This role is attested as early as the *Shepherd of Hermas* as a prime example.

59. *The Apostolic Tradition of Hippolytus*, trans. Burton S. Easton (Ann Arbor, Mich.: Cushing-Malloy, 1924–62), 102.

60. AT 39; Cuming, *Hippolytus*, 28. Botte, *La Tradition*, 86: "Diaconi autem et presbyteri congregentur quotidie in locum quem episcopus praecipiet eis. Et diaconi quidem ne negligant congregari in tempore omni, nisi infirmitas impediat eos. Cum congregati sunt omnes, doceant illos qui sunt in ecclesia, et hoc modo cum oraverint, unusquisque eat ad opera quae competunt ei."

61. Easton, *The Apostolic Tradition*, 60.

62. In *The Ante-Nicene Fathers: Translations of the Writings of the Fathers Down to A.D. 325*, ed. Alexander Roberts and James Donaldson (Grand Rapids, Mich.: Eerdmans, 1951–57), 1:352 (hereafter ANF).

all men, was the first to follow the footsteps of the martyrdom of the Lord."[63] Irenaeus thus is the first written witness to a tradition that the Seven of Acts 6 were the first deacons.[64] Further, Eusebius records a letter of Cornelius, bishop of Rome, to Fabius of the church of the Antiochenes saying that there are in Rome "forty-six presbyters, seven deacons, seven sub-deacons, forty-two acolytes, fifty-two exorcists, readers, and janitors, and over fifteen hundred widows and persons in distress."[65] Thus it is apparent that for the Roman church, and all other cities that maintained the tradition of seven deacons, the importance of deacons increased as the church grew in size. Perhaps the introduction of subdeacons can be associated with this social factor.[66]

Finally, the AT alludes to another ministry of deacons when it discusses the responsibility of caring for the cemeteries: "No man may be heavily charged for burying a man in the cemeteries; it is the property of all the poor. But the fee of the workman and the price of the tiles shall be paid to him who digs. The bishop shall provide for those who are in that place and look after it, so that there may be no heavy charge for those who come to those places."[67] Dix comments that this passage hints at the mismanagement of "the cemetery" which was under the care of the deacon Callistus at the time the AT was written.[68] In his *Refutation of All Heresies*, Hippolytus wrote: "And after Victor's death, Zephyrinus, having had Callistus as a fellow-worker in the management

63. ANF 1:434.

64. As noted in chapter 1, above, Lécuyer allows for exceptions to the tradition begun by Irenaeus, including John Chrysostom. See Lécuyer, "Les diacres dans le nouveau testament," 24–25.

65. Eusebius Pamphili, *The Church History of Eusebius*, trans. Arthur C. McGiffert, in *A Selected Library of the Nicene and Post-Nicene Fathers of the Christian Church*, ed. Philip Schaff (Grand Rapids, Mich.: Eerdmans, 1952–56), Second Series, 1:288 (hereafter NPNF-I for First Series, NPNF-II for Second Series). In addition to Rome, the major cities of Milan and Carthage held the number of deacons to seven. See Schamoni, *Married Men*, 21. The local council of Neocaesarea (320 A.D.) ruled that only seven deacons be appointed in any city, regardless of its size. See NPNF-II 14:86. This limitation was not universal in the West, nor did it last. The Synod of Toledo (597 A.D.) decreed that "according to the *canones*" there should be employed in a church one priest and one deacon. See Schamoni, *Married Men*, 25–26.

66. Mention of the subdeacon in the Syrian *Didascalia* (first half of the third century) provides evidence that the subdiaconate had become widespread if not universal by the middle of the third century. See Barnett, *Diaconate*, 87. For an analysis of the changing status of the subdiaconal order, see Roger E. Reynolds, "The Subdiaconate as a Sacred and Superior Order," in *Clerics in the Early Middle Ages. Hierarchy and Image*, Variorum Collected Studies Series cs669 (Brookfield: Ashgate, 1999), 4:1–46.

67. AT 40; Cuming, *Hippolytus*, 28–29; Botte, *La Tradition*, 86: "Ne gravetur homo ad sepeliendum hominem in coemeteriis: res enim est omnis pauperis. Sed detur merces operarii ei qui effodit et pretium laterum. Qui sunt in loco illo et qui curam habent, episcopus nutriat eos ut nemo gravetur ex eis qui veniunt ad haec loca."

68. Dix, *The Treatise on the Apostolic Tradition of St. Hippolytus of Rome*, xxxvi.

of his clergy, paid him respect to his own damage; and transferring this person from Antium, appointed him over the cemetery."[69] Although the AT does not specifically mention deacons as having care of cemeteries, the administration of the cemetery was a specific duty for the deacon Callistus.

The importance of the bishop's concern for tfhe care of the cemetery is better understood in light of the social context of Rome in the third century. Christians of this time period experienced great persecution. The bodies of many martyrs were laid to rest in the cemetery to which the AT refers. That it was considered part of the bishop's ministry, with a deacon given the responsibility of the care of the cemetery, says something about the value these sacred sites had for the church. The practice of entrusting cemeteries to the care of a deacon was not unique to the third century. The deacon Severus was active in its administration nearly a hundred years after Callistus, under Pope Marcellinus.[70] The care of the cemetery was also closely connected to the development of the structures for pastoral supervision in the Roman church.[71] The care and concern expressed for the dead through the ministry of deacons symbolically witnessed not only the Gospel hope of resurrection, but also the dignity of human life in a "culture of death."

It has been claimed that the AT's description of the charism of the diaconate in the negative (i.e., the deacon is *not* ordained to the *sacerdotium*, does *not* share in the counsel of the presbyters, and does not share in the "common spirit of seniority") contains "an attack on deacons under cover of an outline of their duties, and a corresponding exaltation of presbyters."[72] The notorious disdain that Hippolytus had for the deacon Callistus (who later became pope) perhaps colored his view of the diaconate.[73] While the AT did indeed reflect an effort to re-

69. Hippolytus, *The Refutation of All Heresies* (*Philosophumena*), in ANF 5:130.

70. Wright, "The Emergence of the Diaconate," 22.

71. F. Murphy, "Catacombs," in *New Catholic Encyclopedia*, ed. Catholic University of America Editorial Staff (Palatine, Ill.: Jack Heraty and Associates, 1981), 3:97: "In the 3rd century Christian places of burial came under the ownership of the local community. The cemetery of Callistus on the Via Appia had been confided to the charge of the Deacon Callistus (later pope) by Pope Zephyrinus (199–217); and under Pope Fabian (236–250) the seven (regionary) deacons had control of the cemeteries attached to the churches of their regions. In the 4th century, they came under the charge of the priests attached to the title churches, each of which had its own cemetery along the nearest consular road outside the city."

72. Dix, *The Shape of the Liturgy*, xxxv.

73. Edward Echlin, "The Deacon's Golden Age," *Worship* 45 (1971): 37; Fulbert Cayre, *Manual of Patrology and History of Theology*, trans. H. Howitt (Paris: Desclee, 1935), 1:223. See Hippolytus, *The Refutation of All Heresies* (*Philosophumena*), bk. ix, chap. 7, where Callistus is described as responsible for the cemetery in Rome and the bishop's personal assistant.

strain the power and prestige of the diaconate, it also provided an example of the type of ministry proper to deacons in its day. Hence, other scholars argue that the AT is a credible witness to a tradition of the deacon as a minister ordained to the service of the bishop's ministry.[74] The deacon's office was clearly understood as a means of assisting the bishop to accomplish his episcopal ministry.

The Didascalia Apostolorum *of the East*

The AT reveals the deacon as a kind of social intermediary among the Christian faithful in the pre-Nicene Western church. Other documents from the pre-Nicene Eastern church only serve to confirm the intermediate nature of the diaconate's role in the church. The Church Order known as the *Didascalia Apostolorum* (the *Catholic Teaching of the Twelve Apostles and Holy Disciples of our Saviour*, hereafter "DA") depicts the deacon as closely associated with the bishop and very much involved with the communication of knowledge, resources, and power throughout the social body of the church.

The degree to which the AT represents the actual thought and practice of its time period can be ascertained to a certain extent by looking to another Church Order of roughly the same time period. DA was composed in the first part of the third century for a community in northern Syria heavily influenced by Jewish culture.[75] Unlike the social context of the AT in the large, imperial city of Rome, the church described in the DA is a much smaller community. The DA is addressed to the church as a whole, not primarily to the clergy, implying a general notion of the spiritual competence and responsibility of the members of the church.[76] This itself expresses the DA's sense of the Holy Spirit as the source of life and as "the characteristic possession and mark of Christians, both collectively and individually."[77] Thus the DA exhibits the nature of the church community as organic and collegial.

The author of the DA depicts a Syriac diaconate similar to the Roman diaconate described in the AT. The deacon is a minister ordained to serve the church through ministerial assistance to the bishop; the DA provides explicit references concerning the deacon's everyday ministry. The social context of the

74. Botte, *La Tradition*, xiv: "Sans doute a-t-il précisé certains points, de sa propre autorité. Mais, dans l'ensemble, on est en droit de penser que la *Tradition* représente bien la discipline romaine au début du IIIe siècle."

75. Quasten, *Patrology*, 2:147.

76. James V. Bartlet, *Church Life and Church-Order during the First Four Centuries* (Oxford: Oxford University Press, 1943), 154.

77. Ibid.

Syrian community does not demand a complex organizational system like the Roman daily congregation, and perhaps as a result the author of the DA has in mind a very close relationship between the deacons and their bishop. The bishop is to appoint "workers of righteousness" as helpers and co-operators.[78] With language reminiscent of Ignatius of Antioch, the author writes:

> Let the bishops and the deacons, then, be of one mind; and do you shepherd the people diligently with one accord. For you ought both to be one body, father and son; for you are in the likeness of the lordship. And let the deacon make known all things to the bishop, even as Christ to His Father. But what things he can, let the deacon order, and all the rest let the bishop judge. Yet let the deacon be the hearing of the bishop, and his mouth and his heart and his soul; for when you are both of one mind, through your agreement there will be peace in the Church.[79]

The deacons and the bishop are to be unified ("of one mind") a point made stronger later in the document, when the bishop and the deacon are considered as "one soul dwelling in two bodies."[80] Although such unanimity presupposes regular and close contact between the deacon and the bishop, it would be false to suppose that the deacon never did anything beyond the bishop's immediate sphere. This passage also expresses the desire for deacons to do all that they can on their own, leaving the more important matters to the judgement of the bishop. Functioning in this way, both proximately and remotely to the bishop, the deacon appears as the primary intermediary between the bishop and the people: the deacon is the very "hearing," "mouth," "heart," and "soul" of the bishop. Through the deacon acting as a social intermediary, the pastoral ministry of the bishop is extended beyond the immediate presence of the bishop to individuals on the margins of the community.

Later on in the text, the role of the deacon in mediating between the bishop and the people is put forthrightly:

---

78. DA, no. 16; in *The Liturgical Portions of the Didascalia*, ed. and trans. Sebastian P. Brock and Michael Vasey, Liturgical Study 29 (Bramcote: Grove Books, 1982), 22: "For this reason, O bishop, appoint for yourself workers of righteousness as helpers who can co-operate with you, for salvation. Of those who are pleasing to you out of all the people, you should choose and appoint as deacons: a man for the performance of most things that are necessary, but a woman for the ministry of women."

79. DA, no. 11; in *Didascalia Apostolorum: The Syriac Version Translated and Accompanied by the Verona Latin Fragments*, trans. Richard H. Connolly (Oxford: Clarendon Press, 1929), 109.

80. DA, no. 16; Connolly, *Didascalia*, 148: "And let him labour and toil in every place whither he is sent to minister or to speak of some matter to anyone. For it behooves each one to know his office and to be diligent in executing it. And be you (bishop and deacon) of one counsel and of one purpose, and one soul dwelling in two bodies."

But let them [the people] have very free access to the deacons, and not be troubling the head all the time: they can make known what they require through the servants, that is, through the deacons. For neither can anyone approach the Lord God Almighty except through Christ. Everything, then, that they want to do, they should make known to the bishop through the deacons, and then do it. For formerly in the temple of the sanctuary nothing was offered or done without the priest.[81]

Although the community was quite small, deacons were still important as social intermediaries so that individuals of the community could have at least mediate access to the head of their community at all times. Furthermore, the DA expresses the right of the people to speak their mind and to take up initiatives on their own. The language used for this point is strikingly similar to that of the conciliar documents of Vatican II addressed previously in this book. Thus it is through the deacons that the needs and desires of the Christian faithful are expressed to the bishop.

Concrete examples of the intermediate nature of the deacon's ministry are also given in the DA. The bishop in the DA is both immediately accessible to his flock and mediately accessible through the assistance of deacons:

Therefore, present your offerings to the bishop, either you yourselves, or through the deacons; and when he has received them, he will distribute them justly. For the bishop is well acquainted with those who are in distress, and he dispenses and gives to each what is appropriate; in this way one person will not receive several times over on the same day or in the same week, while another does not receive even a small amount. For whomsoever the priest and steward of God knows to be in great distress, to him does he do good, as it is required of him.[82]

It is important to point out that access to the bishop is not limited to the channels that are the deacons. The deacons are not a barrier between the bishop and his flock, but are additional avenues of mediation to bind the bishop and the people more closely together. The deacon assists the bishop and the people when immediate and direct contact cannot take place between them.

Concern is also stated explicitly in this passage over the just distribution of the offerings, implying the necessity and expectation of the bishop to be aware of those who are suffering. It was primarily the bishop's responsibility to administer the care and concern of the community for those in need. Sociologically, this would require institutions that mediate knowledge of the needs of the people and structure the distribution of offerings in a fair manner. The

---

81. DA, no. 9; Brock, *The Liturgical Portions*, 12.
82. DA, no. 9; Brock, *The Liturgical Portions*, 11.

diaconate appears as an intermediate institution by which the bishop received information concerning the needs of the people, and made decisions concerning the just distribution of the community's resources.

The DA exhibits further evidence of the deacon as a social intermediary when deacons are expressly charged to assist the bishop in the pastoral care of the sick: "It is required of you deacons that you visit all who are in need, and inform the bishop of those who are in distress; and you shall be his soul and his mind; and in all things you should take trouble, and be obedient to him."[83] This expectation for the deacon is repeated again: "And let the deacons go in to those in distress, and let them visit each person and provide him with what he needs."[84] If the deacons served faithfully in these matters, their ministry would not only manifest the love and concern of the Good Shepherd in heaven but also legitimate the bishop's exercise of authority in overseeing the distribution of the community's wealth. It can be safely assumed that because deacons were immediately involved with the care of those in dire circumstances, they also communicated the necessary information to the community as a whole so that the church could better respond to the needs of individuals.

Evidence for the ministry of hospitality as a diaconal ministry can also be found in the DA. Although the context for such ministry is liturgical, it nonetheless reveals a function that is not strictly ritualistic. Pastoral hospitality was significant enough for the author of the DA to go into detail as to how visitors were to be screened and welcomed into the assembly for prayer:

As for the deacons, let one always stand by the offerings of the eucharist; and let another stand outside the door and observe those who enter. But afterwards, when you offer the oblation, let them serve together in the church. . . . But if a brother or sister should come from another congregation, let the deacon enquire of her and find out whether she is married, or again, whether she is a widow who is a believer, and whether she is a daughter of the church, or possibly belongs to one of the heresies; and then let him conduct her to the appropriate place.[85]

Two concerns are expressed in this passage over the deacons' role in "guarding" the doors to the assembly. First, there is a concern over maintaining the purity of the congregation. As extensions of the bishop, deacons maintained a strict observance of those who joined in the eucharistic assembly. They were expected to screen out those who did not belong to the community.

83. Ibid.
84. DA, no. 18; Brock, *The Liturgical Portions*, 24.
85. DA, no. 12; Brock, *The Liturgical Portions*, 16.

Second, this passage expresses the need to welcome members of the assembly and visitors from other congregations so that they might take their rightful places in the assembly. The deacon's ministry of hospitality described in the passage touches directly upon the internal ordering and cohesion of the assembly.[86] The ministry of the deacons involved manifesting and safeguarding the communion of the assembly, enforcing the ecclesial structures that maintained individuals as members of the assembly.

The DA also suggests that the deacons were involved in the administration of justice and reconciliation between individuals of the community: "First, then, let your adjudications take place on Mondays so that if by chance anyone should contest your verdict, you may have time until Sunday to settle the matter and make peace between those who are at odds, and can reconcile them on the Sunday. The presbyters and the deacons should be continuously present with the bishops in all judgments."[87] Although no explicit reason is given for the presence of presbyters and deacons at the court of judgement and reconciliation of the bishop, it is only reasonable to suggest that the deacons were more than spectators. It is of great concern to the author of the DA that the bishop provide a just and reasonable resolution to the internal problems that arise within the community. Deacons could have assisted the bishop in making a "prudent and diligent inquiry."[88]

Comparing the Apostolic Tradition
and the *Didascalia Apostolorum*

In conclusion, the DA confirms much of the testimony of the AT concerning the close relationship between the bishop and the deacon in the pastoral governance of the local church. As recorded in the DA, deacons act as channels of communication between the bishop and his people. They visit all who are

86. Jean P. Audet, *Structures of Christian Priesthood: A Study of Home, Marriage, and Celibacy in the Pastoral Service of the Church*, trans. Rosemary Sheed (New York: MacMillan, 1968), 62: "Nor can we doubt that this pastoral welcome was one of the most important functions in the service of the *ekklesia*, for it was effectively this which actually re-formed the *ekklesia* every time it assembled to hear the word, or renew the 'Lord's Supper,' or both. Thus it was in large measure upon the quality of the pastoral welcome within the assembly that its whole internal order and cohesion directly depended. Similarly, at every gathering, it was primarily the pastoral welcome which, in the concrete, re-created the bonds of Christian brotherhood around the word and the eucharist. At the beginning, therefore, it was that welcome which made the 'communion' of the *ekklesia*; without it, it would not have been long before everything else ground to a helpless halt."

87. DA, no. 11; Brock, *The Liturgical Portions*, 13–14.

88. DA, no. 11; Connolly, *Didascalia*, 112 and 115.

in need and inform the bishop of those who are in distress. The bishop relied upon his deacons to keep him in touch with the community over which he presided. Good pastoral decisions necessitated such communication between the deacon and the bishop. The deacons were the normal avenues for individuals to meet with their pastor. Although we do not have direct evidence of how the deacon's ministry was directed by the bishop, it is safe to presume that the deacon had immediate access to the bishop regularly. Perhaps the smallness of the community (in comparison to Rome) did not necessitate anything resembling the daily congregation. Deacons had regular access to the bishop, and the people had free access to the deacons. The diaconal ministry thus expressed the care and concern of the bishop to the people in need, and provided the bishop with the requisite knowledge to make sound pastoral decisions.

While the AT called the deacon a minister ordained for the bishop's service, the DA calls the deacon the bishop's hearing, mouth, heart, and soul. The deacon shares in the ministry of the bishop, concerned with maintaining familiarity of the bishop with the needs, conditions, and desires of the people. The deacon is also busy with the distribution of the assembly's offerings of charity to those in need, under the supervision of the bishop. The DA suggests, however, a greater sense of the deacon's independence. The deacon is to handle some things on his own, and only with the greater matters should he bother the bishop. We are therefore justified in claiming that at the apex of the Golden Age of the diaconate, deacons were directly under the bishop, worked in communion with the presbyters, and mediated the power and authority of the bishop. They also mediated the resources of the assembly with those in need and were expected to provide hospitality to visitors. The AT describes the administration of the cemetery as the pastoral responsibility of the bishop, one in which deacons shared at this time. The DA suggests that deacons played a role, along with the presbyters, in the administration of justice and reconciliation. The AT and the DA corroborate each other's claims concerning the concrete ministry of the deacon as minister of charity.

There are discrepancies, however. While the AT sharply distinguishes between the presbyters and the deacons (*non ad sacerdotium, sed ad ministerium*), the DA is not so clear. Often, both the deacons and the presbyters are spoken of together with little to distinguish them other than their titles. In comparing the two the AT emphasizes the status of the presbyter while the DA seems to favor the status of the deacon. Nonetheless, neither Church Order subordinates the deacon to the presbyter. It is clear in both documents that the deacon is subordinate only to the bishop.

Another discrepancy concerns the number of deacons. Although the AT does not mention the limitation of deacons to the number seven, it implies this limitation in the concern over the deacon's absence in the daily congregation. Independent historical evidence shows that the number of deacons was limited to seven in Rome in the third century, as well as other major cities in the West. The DA, however, strongly advocates the opposite tendency: "And let there be deacons in proportion to the number of the congregation of the people of the church, so that they may be able to know everyone and relieve everyone individually; so that, for the aged women who are infirm, and the brethren and sisters who are ill, for everyone they may provide the appropriate ministry."[89] It is the community's needs, not a symbolic figure, which determines the number of deacons.

The DA mentions the subdeacon only once in passing, thus downplaying the significance of this office in the community. The fact that bishops were free to ordain as many deacons as necessary suggests why such little attention was given to the subdeacon in the DA. They were hardly more than the servants of the deacons and even inferior to the lector.[90] What is most important to recognize in this passage, however, is that the institution of the diaconate is tied directly to the needs of the people.

Thus, the DA seems to corroborate my findings from the AT, insofar as the deacon appears as a social intermediary. The deacons were ordained for service in close proximity to the bishop, making them perfect candidates to mediate the power and authority of the bishop. The bishop and community relied upon them to know who was in need, and to bring the concerns of the community to the leadership of the community. Involved with works of charity and hospitality, the deacon served the preservation and the practice of communion among the Christian faithful. This model of the diaconate as the bishop's assistant is exemplified in the later Church Orders of the East, and in the altered form of the medieval archdeacon that I will treat in the following chapter.

The Deacon as Intermediary between the Church and Those on the Margins

The sources encountered so far from the East and West directly support my thesis that the deacon has served the church as an intermediate institution

---

89. DA, no. 16; Brock, *The Liturgical Portions*, 23.
90. Connolly, *Didascalia*, xli–xlii.

between the bishop and his flock. The following sources provide explicit evidence that the diaconate was also an intermediate institution for those on the margins of the community.

The Epistle to James

The *Epistle of Clement to James*, an introduction to the *Homilies* in the *Pseudo-Clementines*, describes the duties of the deacon as follows:

> Moreover let the deacons of the church, going about with intelligence, be as eyes to the bishop, carefully inquiring into the doings of each member of the church, ascertaining who is about to sin, in order that, being arrested with admonition by the president, he may happily not accomplish sin. Let them check the disorderly, that they may not desist from assembling to hear the discourses, so that they may be able to counteract by the word of truth those anxieties that fall upon the heart from every side, by means of worldly casualties and evil communications; for if they long remain fallow, they become fuel for the fire. And let them learn who are suffering under bodily disease, and let them bring them to the notice of the multitude who do not know of them, that they may visit them, and supply their wants according to the judgment of the president. Yea, though they do this without his knowledge, they do nothing amiss. These things, then, and things like these, let the deacons attend to.[91]

It is evident that the *Epistle* reflects the growing tendency of the deacon to do more things on his own. It explicitly states that the deacon does nothing wrong by acting without the knowledge of the "president" of the community, but this is not to say that deacons operate independently of the "president." Expanding upon the DA's analogy that the deacon is the bishop's ear, mouth, heart, and soul, the *Epistle* also refers to the deacon as the bishop's "eyes."[92] The deacon plays an important role as a primary channel of information for the president of the community. The deacon's service as the eyes of the bishop is intended for the good of the individuals of the community, although the

91. *Epistle of Clement to James*, in ANF 8:220. This letter was ostensibly written by Clement of Rome to James of Jerusalem, along with another supposedly written by the Apostle Peter to James, in order to give the *Homilies* credibility. The dating and source of the *Pseudo-Clementines* are very much disputed. Probably dating from 313–25 A.D. in their present form, they were based on an earlier work written in the early decades of the third century in Syria. See Quasten, *Patrology*, 1:60–62.

92. This analogy is also mentioned in the late-fourth-century Eastern Church Order, *The Apostolic Constitutions*, in ANF 7:416: "And let the deacon refer all things to the bishop, as Christ does to His Father ... let the deacon be the bishop's ear, eye, and mouth, and heart and soul." The analogy of the deacon as the bishop's eye will be taken up by the medieval canonists to describe the office of archdeacon.

description given here of the deacon as a busybody is contrary to our modern sensitivities for privacy.

Most intriguing is the *Epistle*'s explicit description of the form of the deacon's intermediate character: the deacon is a bridge between the poor and the community at large. Whereas the emphasis had been placed upon the deacon bringing the needs of the poor to the bishop, here the deacon is to motivate and challenge the community to satisfy the needs of the poor. The role of the bishop is not totally neglected, for he continues to fulfill the responsibility of determining what is necessary. The bishop must be advised as to the needs of the people and be made aware of the charisms available within the community to satisfy these needs. Deacons are clearly described here as servants of the church, and not merely personal attendants of the bishop. The deacon serves to animate the faithful to fulfill their Gospel obligation, working to bind the church more closely in solidarity with those in need.

Apostolic Church Order

Another document of the pre-Nicene church that testifies to the role of the deacon as animator of the faithful is the *Apostolic Church Order* or *Ecclesiastical Canons of the Holy Apostles* (hereafter "ACO"), which goes back to the third and fourth centuries and reflects conditions in Syria or Egypt.[93] It is evident that the ACO enjoyed a wide reputation throughout the East, for Latin, Syriac, Coptic, Arabic, and Ethiopic translations were made from the original Greek text.[94] A section of these thirty canons, 15–29, concerns ecclesiastical organization. Canons 20 and 21 deal with the duties of the deacon. In these canons deacons are charged to encourage those who are well off to contribute what they are able. The deacons are to compel the rich to help the poor because the Lord had warned about failing to feed the hungry: "The deacons shall compel those having possessions to lay [them] up for good works, in consideration of the words of our teacher: 'Ye saw me hungry, and did not feed me.'"[95] Thus, the ministry of the deacon is directly related to bringing about greater concern for the needs of others in the community, bridging the gap between those who have resources and those who are in need of them.

---

93. Studer, "Liturgical Documents," 204.

94. Ibid.

95. Adolf von Harnack, *Sources of the Apostolic Canons*, trans. John Owen (London: F. Norgate and Co., 1895), 22.

Other Western Evidence of Diaconal Ministry in the Pre-Nicene Church

Turning our attention back to the West, it is important to bring to light some other witnesses to the "shape" of the diaconate in the Golden Age. From the writings of a North African bishop, some canons of local councils or synods, and other historical writings, a clearer picture of the deacon comes into focus. In all instances what is to be noted is that the deacons were very much involved with administration, and that they assisted the bishop in his responsibility of pastoral governance of the local church. There is no evidence from this time period that deacons were in direct service to presbyters.

Cyprian of Carthage

Nearly thirty years after the death of Tertullian and roughly a year before the Decian persecution broke out, St. Cyprian was elected bishop of Carthage (ca. 248 A.D.).[96] Cyprian is unique within the first centuries of Christianity in the emphasis he places on the structures and institutions through which the concrete church is recognizable. In his conception the church is a corporate body in which every member has an honorable function.[97] Divinely appointed bishops, without whom there could be no church, govern the body of Christ.[98]

Due to the Decian persecution, Cyprian fled from Carthage, relying on the clergy to carry out necessary administrative functions. Through his many letters to the clergy at Carthage from his place of concealment, Cyprian controlled, warned, directed, and maintained "his episcopal superintendence in his absence, in all matters connected with the well-being of the Church."[99] In these letters, we see how Cyprian relied on his deacons and presbyters to mediate information to him concerning the needs of the local church.[100] Cyprian's letter attests that deacons were intermediaries, through whom the concerns of the people were brought to the bishop.

Likewise, Cyprian used deacons to administer pastoral care on his behalf. In this manner the deacons functioned in communion with the bishop and

96. Quasten, *Patrology*, 2:341.
97. A. Cleveland Coxe, "Introductory Notice to Cyprian," in ANF 5:263.
98. Epistles LVII, no. 3, in ANF 5:353; LXIV, no. 3, in ANF 5:366.
99. Coxe, "Introductory Notice to Cyprian," in ANF 5:265.
100. Epistle XII, no. 1, in ANF 5:293.

collegially with the presbyters: "I request that you [presbyters and deacons] will diligently take care of the widows, and of the sick, and of all the poor. Moreover, you may supply the expenses for strangers, if any should be indigent, from my own portion, which I have left with Rogatianus, our fellow-presbyter."[101] The deacons shared a prominent role with the presbyters in the administration of the finances of the church at Carthage. There is no description of the differences between the presbyters' and deacons' functions. They apparently were equally "competent" to perform administrative functions. Cyprian did not consider deacons as "servants of presbyters"; rather, the deacons ministered with them under the supervision of the bishop.

The extreme conditions of Cyprian's exile made for a unique set of circumstances, in which the deacons fulfilled the needs of the church in a manner suitable to them, namely through their administrative assistance. Cyprian was able to maintain leadership as bishop, even if from a distance, through the presence of his presbyters and deacons in Carthage. The deacons were, practically speaking, administratively necessary. Here we have an example of how flexible the functions of church office were regarded; they could be adapted to meet the needs the church was called to serve.[102]

As important as they were, Cyprian also found it necessary to remind the deacons of their proper place:

But deacons ought to remember that the Lord chose apostles, that is, bishops and overseers; while apostles appointed for themselves deacons after the ascent of the Lord into heaven, as ministers of their episcopacy and of the Church. But if we may dare anything against God who makes bishops, deacons may also dare against us by whom they are made; and therefore it behooves the deacon of whom you write to repent of his audacity, and to acknowledge the honour of the priest, and to satisfy the bishop set over him with full humility.[103]

Here we have Cyprian's articulation of the kind of relationship that exists between a bishop and his deacons. Following Irenaeus's interpretation of Acts 6, Cyprian argues that the episcopal order is a higher order because "the Lord chose apostles, that is, bishops," while the apostles "appointed" deacons. Deacons are "made" by the bishops, who alone are the direct successors of the

---

101. Epistle XXXV in ANF 5:314.

102. Gula, "Theology of the Diaconate—Part One," 629.

103. Epistle LXIV, no. 3, in ANF 5:366. The deacon was to "acknowledge the honour of the priest," that is, the bishop, as "sacerdos" for Cyprian refers to the bishop. "Epistula 3, Cyprianus Rogatiano Fatri S." CCSL 3b:14–15: "Et ideo oportet diaconum de quo scribis agere audaciae suae paenitentiam et honorem sacerdotis agnoscere et episcopo praeposito suo plena humilitate satisfacere."

apostles. The diaconate for Cyprian is therefore something of a subordinate ministry, but nonetheless an order worthy of respect. Cyprian must have been incredibly proud of his own deacons at the moment of his death. In the account of his martyrdom on September 14, 258, the classic fidelity of deacons to their bishop is portrayed, for they are said to have stepped forth to stand beside him at the last.[104]

During the same year of Cyprian's martyrdom, the bishop of Rome and four of his deacons were arrested as they were officiating in the catacombs on August 6, and four days later the principal deacon of that city, St. Lawrence, met a similar fate.

Left alone by the pope's martyrdom, [Laurence] was summoned to hand over his treasures. He asked for three days' grace and used them to distribute all the wealth in his charge to the poor of Rome. He then presented to the prefect a crowd of cripples and poor persons, saying: "This is the Church's treasure, these poor, who are rich in their faith"; upon which the enraged prefect condemned Laurence to be tortured on a white-hot grid-iron.[105]

Through the heroic ministry of deacons, the church's care for the poor and weak did not slacken, even during the most tortuous times of persecutions. The prominence gained by deacons because of their responsibility for the church's material wealth was, however, quickly becoming a source of tension with the presbyters.

The church had an organized structure for the assistance of those in need among the community. Certainly not all of the charitable works were performed through the ministry of the deacon. The institution of the family also worked to alleviate the needs of family members by means of "natural obligations." But when the family could not take care of their own, or when a family structure was not present (as in the case of widows and orphans), then the larger family of the church (liturgically expressed in baptism and eucharist) would provide assistance as part of the practice of *koinonia*. The bishop, as head of the local church, is the point of concentration for this authority and obligation to take care of those in need. The diaconate assisted the bishop in his care and concern for the members of the church as an intermediate institution.[106]

---

104. Wright, "The Emergence of the Diaconate," 67.

105. Michel Riquet, *Christian Charity in Action*, trans. P. Hepburne-Scott, Twentieth Century Encyclopedia of Catholicism 105 (New York: Hawthorne Books, 1961), 55–56.

106. Charles Munier, *L'Église dans l'Empire Romain* (*IIe–IIIe*): *IIIe partie Église et Cité*, Histoire du

Regional Deacons

The persecution of Christians did not squash the spirit of charity that motivated works of charity among the members of the church at Rome. In fact, the church's mission to the poor appears to have thrived through the ministry of deacons during this time period. Pope Fabian found it necessary to create administrative districts in his city in order to properly fulfill the church's mission. The *Liber Pontificalis* credits Fabian (236–50 A.D.) with the division of the city of Rome into seven regions, each in the charge of one of the seven deacons of Rome.[107] This assertion is supported by the account given by Eusebius mentioned previously.[108] These "episcopal deacons" were responsible for temporal administration and for the implementation of the *frumentatio*, or relief of the poor. This charitable work had become so burdensome that the organization of regional districts for deacons was necessary. The institution of regional deacons must not be confused with the establishment of *diaconiae*, distribution centers that were monastic in character and endowed by popes and lay people of later centuries.[109]

Deacons in Outlying Areas

During the Golden Age not all the deacons served as the bishop's principal or chief deacon (as in the examples of Callistus and Lawrence) or as one of the regional deacons. Evidence from early local councils supports the notion that deacons were also assigned to chapel communities not under the immediate direction of the bishop. Some scholars connect this to the expansion of the

---

Droit et des Institutions de l'Église en Occident, tome II, vol. 3, ed. Gabriel Le Bras and Jean Gaudemet (Paris: Editions Cujas, 1979), 95.

107. Riquet, *Christian Charity*, 54. The deacons were entrusted with the administration of the material possessions of the church, accumulated from the offerings of the people. These duties gave them considerable influence, greater even than that of the presbyters.

108. Eusebius, *Church History*, 288.

109. Roger E. Reynolds, "Clerics in the Early Middle Ages: Hierarchies and Functions," in *Clerics in the Early Middle Ages: Hierarchy and Image*, Variorum Collected Studies Series cs669 (Brookfield: Ashgate, 1999), I, 12: "By the time of Pope Hadrian I there were some eighteen or nineteen *diaconiae* in the city of Rome, buildings in which foodstuffs were kept and distributed to the poor. Scattered very unevenly throughout the city, they were usually connected to a church, called a *diaconia*, and were administered either by laymen or monks, who might live in a *monasteria diaconiae*. The overseer of the *diaconia* was called the *pater* or *dispensator diaconiae*. From 731 A.D., some of these *diaconiae* were used as stational churches, in which case the *pater diaconiae* would meet and reverence the pope on his arrival at the station." See also Collins, *Diakonia*, 66–69.

church from larger towns into the countryside, when a presbyter or deacon was sent to a rural assembly.[110] One author claims that the deacons were "precursor and pioneer of the priest in filial churches."[111] While the deacon's office may have given him the prestige to be in charge of the local community, his lack of requisite ordination for certain liturgical functions would make him an unlikely candidate as a "parish pastor" for a long period of time.[112]

Nonetheless, there is evidence that leads to the conclusion that deacons did exercise leadership in at least some rural congregations in the third and fourth centuries. The Council of Elvira took place in Spain between 300 and 306 A.D. Canon 77 of this council refers to deacons in charge of people: "If a deacon, ruling a people without a bishop or presbyter, has baptized some of them, the bishop must bring them to perfection of it through his blessing."[113] The Council of Arles in 314 A.D. declared in canon 15: "Concerning deacons, whom we have known to offer in many places: it is determined that this must never happen."[114] Deacons were only one solution for the church's expansion into the countryside, a solution that was not common; nor would it last for very long.

The expansion of diaconal ministry into "parishes," as they would later be called, removed the deacon from an immediate relationship with bishop. If deacons were serving with a presbyter, it is very doubtful that the deacons would have regularly met with their bishop. The same was true when deacons served without presbyters, as the canon from the Council of Elvira indicates. Examples of deacons with a charge for the pastoral care of a "parish church" quickly died out in the history of the church, as this kind of ministry was to be restricted more and more to members of the order of presbyter.[115]

110. Alfred W. W. Dale, *The Synod of Elvira and Christian Life in the Fourth Century* (London: Macmillan Press, 1882), 70.

111. Schamoni, *Married Men*, 32. This opinion of Schamoni is not shared by many. The presence of presbyters and *chorepiscopoi* during this same time period would argue against seeing the deacon as precursor to the presbyter-pastor.

112. Barnett, *The Diaconate*, 77.

113. Jurgens, *The Faith of the Early Fathers*, 1:257; Joseph Mansi (ed.), *Sacrorum Conciliorum Novae et Amplissima Collectio* (Florence: 1758–98), 2:18: "Si quis diaconus regens plebem, sine episcopo, vel presbytero aliquos baptizaverit, episcopus eos per benedictionem perficere debebit."

114. Jurgens, *The Faith of the Early Fathers*, 1:273; *Sacrorum Conciliorum* (ed. Mansi), 473: "De diaconibus quos cognovimus multis locis offerre, placuit minime fieri debere."

115. It is to be pointed out, however, that the legal possibility of a deacon "having a parish" only ended with the promulgation of the CIC 1917. The canonical structure that allowed the "deacon" this possibility had more to do with the benefice of the church than its pastoral care. See T. Lincoln Bouscaren, "Canon 453," *Canon Law Digest* 1 (1934): 246: "Although before the Code a deacon might

Conclusion

The nature of the pre-Nicene church fostered the development of the diaconate so that deacons collegially served the church as a whole with presbyters and the bishop. The most ancient records reveal the diaconate to be a well-functioning and firmly established ecclesiastical ministry. Taking the structure of the diaconate for granted, and reflecting the long-held traditions of their respective communities, the Church Orders give evidence of the kinds of ministry deacons actually exercised. There were a variety of diaconal functions that satisfied basic organizational needs of individual church communities. Ancient deacons assisted their bishops in the nonliturgical aspects of community life, often in a personal manner. As extensions of the bishop, deacons were intimately involved in day-to-day efforts of pastoral governance over the flock. There is solid evidence that deacons expressed the needs and desires of the faithful to the bishop, and that they exhibited the care and concern of the bishop to those in need. In the Golden Age of the diaconate, we have the prime example of the deacon serving as a social intermediary among the people of God.

There are not, at this point, widespread examples of deacons serving presbyters beyond the liturgy.[116] This is a very important distinction to make between the pre-Nicene and post-Nicene church. The unity of the ecclesiastical *ordo* was manifested in the collegial manner in which the deacons fulfilled their functions in communion with the bishop and his presbyters. This collegial manner of the exercise of charisms allowed the deacons to wield a great amount of influence in decisions made by the higher clergy. Three different types of deacons are attested in the Golden Age: (1) the chief deacon, (2) the regional deacon, and (3) the deacon of an outlying church or sacred site.

The churches of the pre-Constantine era were relatively small. In most places a single bishop presided over the church and could administer its needs with the assistance of the deacons and the counsel of the presbyterate. However, the situation was soon to change with the rapid growth of the church in the next century, signaled by the adoption of Constantine's policy of toleration and

---

lawfully have a parish, that general capacity is not a vested right, as it does not depend upon any past fact. But if a deacon before the Code had actually received a parish, he would have the vested right; and in that case, the Code (c. 453), under the general norm expressed in cc. 4 and 10, would not take that right away." CIC 1917, c. 453 §1: "Ut quis in parochum valide assumatur, debet esse in sacro presbyteratus ordine constitutus."

116. The evidence of deacons serving with presbyters in outlying areas only indicates that deacons served with presbyters, not necessarily "under" them.

the resulting delegation of more and more duties to the presbyters. The three forms of the diaconate in the Golden Age will virtually collapse into only one form by the time of the Middle Ages, as far as the nonritual diaconal ministry is concerned. I will examine the reasons for this decline in the next chapter.

The only surviving form of the diaconate as a social institution of mediation will be that of the archdeacon, whose title appears for the first time in the late fourth century. In the next chapter I shall also explore in-depth this model of the diaconate because of its importance in the history of the diaconate. My task is to determine the relationship between the medieval archdeacon and the diaconate of the Golden Age. Is the medieval-canonical archdeacon a legitimate development or corruption of the diaconate?

CHAPTER 6

The Transformation and Decline of the Diaconate

When the Second Vatican Council sought to renew the permanent diaconate in the Latin West, it drew its inspiration from the biblical and patristic eras of the deacon. This was a contrast with the then-dominant theology of the diaconate, which was grounded in the high medieval period when the diaconate had become merely a transitional stage on the path to the priesthood. I have already examined the biblical witness (chapter 1) and what scholars have called the Golden Age of the diaconate, 100–325 A.D. (chapter 5). We saw how the deacon functioned in the Golden Age as a social intermediary, giving historical examples of what I described in chapter 3 on social mediation. The deacon functioned as a social intermediary between two pairs: the bishop and the laity, and the people of God (including the bishop) and those on the margins. This chapter focuses on the question of the deacon's ministry as a social intermediary during the rise of the archdeacon and the long decline of the permanent diaconate between the Golden Age and the High Middle Ages.

The symbolic end-date of the Golden Age is usually given as Council of Nicaea (325 A.D.), but the council itself was only partly to blame for the changes in the diaconate. Following the conversion of Constantine to Christianity in 312 A.D., he issued the Edict of Milan (313 A.D.), which was an imperial policy of religious toleration. While Christianity had not yet become the official religion of the Roman Empire, the emperor did provide some support, and radical changes took place in the church's ministry throughout the rest of the fourth century. The legalization of the church greatly affected the number of members in the church, and much of the church property confiscated during the persecutions was restored. The social structures of the church had to adapt to the new social pressures, and the church increasingly looked to the imperial state as its model for organization.

The change of the diaconate in this era can only be understood in relation to changes in the episcopate and presbyterate. All three orders together underwent a marked transformation. During the fourth century, social circumstances favored the rise of presbyters to function more like bishops, thereby beginning a process that would end with the eclipse of the importance of those deacons who were not fortunate enough to hold the office of archdeacon.[1] The realignment of ordination charisms and ministerial functions during the early Middle Ages would devastate the diaconate until its renewal at the Second Vatican Council. In examining this history, we will see the factors that led to the decline of the true deacon, which we will then apply in subsequent chapters to the question of how to avoid a similar decline in the renewed diaconate.

The Subordination of Deacons to Presbyters

The deacon entered the fourth century with considerable importance and prestige in the church. Deacons served not only as assistants of the bishops but also represented them on occasion at church councils. Frequently, deacons were elected bishops because of their administrative capabilities and expertise.[2] The practice of the *cursus honorum* (the requirement of progressing successively from lower ecclesiastical grades to the higher) had not taken hold.

1. Dix, *The Shape of the Liturgy*, 34: "It is in the fourth century, when the peace of the church and the immense growth of numbers had made it impossible for bishops in most places still to act as the only ministers of all sacraments to their churches, that we find the real change taking place in the functions of the presbyter. He becomes the permanent liturgical minister of a separate congregation, to whom he normally supplies most of those 'liturgies' of sacraments and teaching for which the pre-Nicene church had habitually looked to the bishop."

2. Other examples of this phenomenon continued into the Middle Ages. Felix, a deacon of the Roman church, was appointed to succeed Liberius as bishop of Rome in 355. In 449 Leo the Great sent Hilary the deacon as his legate to the Council of Ephesus; Hilary subsequently succeeded Leo as bishop. Gregory the Great, who as a deacon had been sent by Pelagius II of Rome as his emissary to the imperial court in Constantinople, returned to Rome and was elected bishop in 590. As late as the eleventh century, Hildebrand was the archdeacon of Rome when he was sent as ambassador of the church of Rome to the emperor, and he subsequently became the bishop of Rome. It is an interesting historical anomaly that he sat on the papal throne for more than two months prior to his becoming a bishop, for a month as a deacon and then as a priest. He was elected and enthroned as pope while still in deacon's orders on April 22, 1073, ordained a priest on May 22, and bishop on June 29. See Joseph Lécuyer, *What Is a Priest?*, trans. Lancelot Sheppard (New York: Hawthorne Books, 1959), 64–65, and Allan J. MacDonald, *Hildebrand: A Life of Gregory VII* (London: Methuen, 1932), 58, 89, 92, 95.

The deacon Athanasius was perhaps the most notable example of the fourth century. He played a leading role in the first Ecumenical Council in Nicaea in 325 A.D. Theodoret tells us that although a very young man, Athanasius was "the principal deacon" of Alexandria and attended the Council of Nicaea in the retinue of its bishop, Alexander.[3] Athanasius succeeded Alexander shortly after the close of the Council.

It is in the first Ecumenical Council that we see the formal turning point of the diaconate from development into decline. Evidently, problems with deacons became so widespread that it was necessary for the universal council to address them (alongside its dominant concerns like the Arian heresy). For the first time, deacons were officially subordinated to the presbyters in a canon that was binding for the whole church, East and West:

It has come to the attention of this holy and great synod that in some places and cities deacons give communion to presbyters, although neither canon nor custom allow this, namely that those who have no authority to offer should give the body of Christ to those who do offer. Moreover it has become known that some of the deacons now receive the eucharist even before the bishops. All these practices must be suppressed. Deacons must remain within their own limits, knowing that they are the ministers of the bishop and subordinate to the presbyters. Let them receive the eucharist according to their order after the presbyters from the hands of the bishop and presbyters, for such an arrangement is contrary to the canon and to rank. If anyone refuses to comply even after these decrees, he is to be suspended from the diaconate.[4]

With this canon, deacons would remain forever subordinate to the presbyters, in terms of the "grade" of their order. This canon did not, however, refer to the deacons as ministers of the presbyters. They were still viewed as ministers of the bishop. Once more, there is no condemnation here of the administrative functions of the deacon, only the transgression of liturgical customs. Deacons are not ordained to "offer" the sacrifice. The deacon is a minister of the bishop, and is subordinate to the presbyter who can offer the sacrifice. The Council of Nicaea brought to the universal level the distinction between deacons and presbyters found earlier in the Roman *Apostolic Tradition*.

This official "downgrading" of the deacon, however, was the beginning of the erosion of the deacon's influence in the governance of the diocese. The presbyter's office took on more and more functions that had been reserved

3. Theodoret, *Ecclesiastical History*, in NPNF-II 3:60–61.
4. C. 18; trans. in *Decrees* (ed. Tanner), 1:14–15.

to the episcopate, and the deacon's office was simultaneously minimized.[5] The rise of the presbyterate is one of the major reasons for the termination of the diaconal model prevalent in the Golden Age. During the Golden Age of the deacon, the Roman presbyters were collegially structured, enjoying the status of the primary counselors of the bishop. They joined in the laying on of hands at the oblation and ordination of other presbyters. By the end of the second half of the fourth century, however, presbyters began assuming offices of leadership in rural communities, presiding over the assemblies and fulfilling liturgical functions that had been associated with the bishops. With the delegation of the bishop's liturgical functions to the presbyter, and the latter's assumption of the bishop's pastoral role, the bishop's church was acquiring characteristics of what would later be called a "diocese." Although the bishop continued his role in his own cathedral, he was also head of the churches of the city and the surrounding communities, which were becoming "parishes."[6]

As presbyters assumed the place of bishops in local congregations, their identity was drastically altered. They were more and more identified as "priests." The *Apostolic Tradition*, as well as Tertullian, had already referred to them as participating in the priesthood of Christ, but it was not until the latter half of the fourth century that the association of priesthood with the presbyterate was universal.[7] The priesthood, which had originally belonged to the whole church with the bishop as "high priest," was now increasingly associated with the bishop and presbyters. As the bishop absorbed the corporate and collegial governmental authority of the presbyterate, the presbyter in return was entrusted with some of the bishop's liturgical functions.[8] In the fifth century

---

5. Roger E. Reynolds, "An Early Medieval Tract on the Diaconate," in *Clerical Orders in the Early Middle Ages: Duties and Ordination*, Variorum Collected Studies Series cs670 (Brookfield: Ashgate, 1999), vii, 97. See also Ferdinand Prat, "Les prétentions des diacres romains au quatrième siècle," *Recherches de Science Religieuse* 3 (1912): 463–75.

6. In the West, there seems to have been a quicker delegation of powers from bishop to presbyter without the intermediary chorbishops (bishops who had charge of smaller communities under the authority of a primary bishop) than in the East. See Jean Gaudemet, "Les chorévêques," in *L'Église dans L'Empire Romain (IVe–Ve siècles)*, Histoire du Droit et des Instituions de l'Église en Occident, tome III, ed. Gabriel Le Bras (Paris: Sirey, 1990), 374–75; and "Chorepiscopus," in *The Oxford Dictionary of the Christian Church*, ed. Frank L. Cross and Elizabeth Livingston, 3rd ed. (New York: Oxford University Press, 1997), 331.

7. Tertullian, *On Baptism*, no. 17, in ANF 3:677: "Unless bishops, or priests, or deacons, be on the spot, *other* disciples are called *i.e. to the work.*" Dix, *Shape of the Liturgy*, 34; Gregory Dix, "Ministry in the Early Church c. a.d. 90–410," in *The Apostolic Ministry: Essays on the History and Doctrine of Episcopacy*, ed. Kenneth E. Kirk (London: Hodder and Stoughton, 1946), 282.

8. Dix, *Shape of the Liturgy*, 34.

the word *presbyter* became synonymous with *priest* even though officially presbyters were still regarded as "priests of the second order."

In becoming similar to bishops as "pastors" of "local parishes," the shape of the presbyterate could not remain the same as before. Previously they were mainly a council of advisors who worked together in a single community; now they were individuals who acted alone in separate parishes. Formerly they had few liturgical duties; now their duties were primarily liturgical. And whereas before their authority had come partly from being accepted by their fellow presbyters and approved by the people, now it was seen as coming entirely from the bishop. Like the deacons, presbyters were becoming regarded as extensions of the bishop's ministry.

The decline of the diaconate, however, cannot simply be blamed on the rise of the presbyterate. To some extent the deacons brought their decline on themselves by tending to abuse their authority, to the consternation of the bishops who appointed them. Ambrosiaster, in the time of Pope Damasus (366–84 A.D.), was moved to write "On the Boastfulness of the Roman Deacons" because the deacons in Rome attempted to take precedence over the presbyters.[9] One scholar suggests that Ambrosiaster's treatise was occasioned by the attempts of certain Roman deacons to assert themselves even against Pope Damasus.[10] Toward the first part of the fifth century, Jerome likewise wrote a letter that revealed how upset he was over what he considered the arrogance of the Roman deacons:

But you will say, how comes it then that at Rome a presbyter is only ordained on the recommendation of a deacon? To which I reply as follows. Why do you bring forward a custom which exists in one city only? Why do you oppose to the laws of the Church a paltry exception which has given rise to arrogance and pride? ... Their fewness makes deacons persons of consequence while presbyters are less thought of owing to their great numbers. But even in the Church of Rome the deacons stand while the presbyters seat themselves, although bad habits have by degrees so far crept in that I have seen a deacon, in the absence of the bishop, seat himself among the presbyters, and at social gatherings give his blessing to them.[11]

9. Ambrosiaster, "De jactantia romanarum levitarum," *Patrologia Cursus Completus, Series Latina* (hereafter PL), ed. J.-P. Migne (Paris: 1841–55), 35:2301–3. This tract was *Quaestio* 101 of his *Quaestiones Veteris et Novi Testamenti.*

10. Pratt, "Les Prétentions des Diacres Romains," 473–74. See also Berhard Domagalski, "Römische Diakone im 4. Jahrhundert," in *Der Diakon: Wiederentdeckung und Erneuerung seines Dienstes,* ed. Josef Plöger and Herman Weber (Freiburg: Herder, 1981), 46–47.

11. Jerome, "Letter to Evangelus," trans. W. Fremantle, in NPNF-II 6:289.

Jerome was concerned about showing that presbyters and bishops were the same, and so it is no surprise that he was upset when the deacons did not treat the presbyters with due respect.[12] Jerome thought that deacons were not only subordinate to presbyters, but that they were also to serve those of the same "rank" as the bishop.

Evidently, Jerome was not alone in his opinion that deacons are ordained to serve the presbyters. Haughty deacons and the alteration of the presbyteral ministry led to a new structure of the deacon's relationship to the presbyter. While Nicaea had insisted that the deacon was subordinate to the presbyter and minister of the bishop, fifth-century canonical legislation identified the deacon as a minister of the presbyter. Hearkening back to the AT, the Gallican *Statuta Ecclesiae antiqua* (ca. 490 A.D.) lays down the norms for diaconal ordination, norms which would influence later ordination rites.[13] "When a deacon is ordained, let the bishop alone, who blesses him, place his hands above his head, because he is consecrated not for the priesthood but for the ministry."[14] There is present in this canon a slight alteration of the parallel passage found in the AT. The deacon is no longer ordained "to the ministry of the bishop," but simply "to the ministry." As is evident from below, the SEA envisions the diaconate as an institution of service to both the bishop and the presbyter. In canon 57 the following explicit description of the diaconal office is given: "Thus the deacon shall have recognized he is the presbyter's as well

12. Jerome goes on to write: "Of the names presbyter and bishop the first denotes age, the second rank. In writing both to Titus and Timothy the apostle speaks of the ordination of bishops and of deacons, but says not a word of the ordination of presbyters; for the fact is that the word bishops includes presbyters also" (ibid.).

13. Hereafter SEA. Perhaps written by Gennadius of Marseilles, it contains a collection of disciplinary and ordination canons composed towards the end of the fifth century. The author seems to have wanted to correct current usage by invoking an earlier tradition. For this reason, there are many similarities between the SEA and the AT. This document is important because it is a source for ordination rituals from the eighth century onwards. See Puglisi, *Epistemological Principles*, 129; Bradshaw, *Ordination Rites*, 14–15; and Roger E. Reynolds, "The Ordination of Clerics in the Middle Ages," in *Clerical Orders in the Early Middle Ages: Duties and Ordination*, Variorum Collected Studies Series cs670 (Brookfield: Ashgate, 1999), XI, 2; and Roger E. Reynolds, "The Portrait of the Ecclesiastical Officers in the *Raganaldus Sacramentary* and its Liturgico-Canonical Significance," in *Clerics in the Early Middle Ages: Hierarchy and Image*, Variorum Collected Studies Series cs669 (Brookfield: Ashgate, 1999), VII, 437.

14. C. 92, in *Sources of Catholic Dogma* (thirtieth edition of *Enchiridion Symbolorum*), ed. Heinrich Denzinger, trans. Roy Deferrari (St. Louis, Mo.: Herder, 1957) (hereafter Denz.), no. 63. Charles Munier and Bernard Botte (eds.), *Les Statuta ecclesiae antiqua: edition, études critiques*, Bibliothèque de l'Institut de Droit canonique de l'Université de Strasbourg 5 (Paris: Presses Universitaires de France, 1960), reprinted as "Statuta ecclesiae antiqva" in *Concilia Galliae. A. 314 – A. 506*, CCSL 148.

as the bishop's minister."[15] No longer would the West envision the diaconate as parallel to the presbyteral order; they would be envisioned in a relationship of linear subordination. The consequences of such an understanding of the diaconate would remove the majority of deacons from their close association with the bishop and realign them to the presbyters instead.[16]

Sacralization of the Ministry

By the end of the fifth century the subordination of the deacons to the presbyters was universal in the West, save the figure of the archdeacon. The deacon was more and more at the service of presbyters in parish churches rather than of immediate assistance to the bishop at the level of the diocese. This decline in status was further cemented by the sacralization of the ministry, together with its requirement of celibacy for all clergy (including deacons). At the core of the sacralization of the ministry was the reorientation of the ministry around the specifically priestly action of consecrating the bread and wine into the body and blood of Christ. The power over the body of Christ in the eucharist, than which nothing could be considered of greater dignity, thus became the heart of the Christian ministry.[17] Deacons had always had liturgical functions, but in the process of sacralization of the ministry the liturgy became more and more the sphere of the diaconate. Between the early period of the Church Orders and the later part of the patristic era, the center of gravity for diaconal functions shifted dramatically from assistance in community life to engagement predominantly in liturgical ministry, where the deacon was subordinate, if not ultimately superfluous.

15. Munier and Botte, *Les Statuta ecclesiae antiqua*, 175: "Diaconus ita se presbyteri, ut episcopi ministrum nouerit."

16. The final Eastern Church Order to derive from the AT, the so-called *Testament of Our Lord*, was probably written in Syria during the fifth century (see Bradshaw, *Ordination Rites*, 4). Like the SEA, the *Testament* also shows a shift in the conceptualization of the deacon as ordained to "the ministry of the bishop." It states: "[The deacon] is ordained not to the priesthood but to the ministry of attending to the bishop and the Church." Grant Sperry-White (ed.), *The Testamentum Domini: A Test for Students, with Introduction, Translation, and Notes*, Grove Liturgical Study 66 (Bramcote: Grove Books Limited, 1991), 43.

17. Cooke, *Ministry to Word*, 556. Cooke cites a phrase from Gregory VII's twenty-first epistle: "Et, quod maximum est in Christiana religione ... proprio ore corpus et sanguinem Domini conficere."

Levitical Typology and the Requirement
of Continence/Celibacy

In the fourth century, there was a particular emphasis regarding Christian ministers in terms of temple and cult. It is in this time period that the language of the Jewish Temple would be used to describe the ministers of the New Covenant. With the destruction of the Temple in 70 A.D., and the disappearance of pagan mysteries and priesthoods, there was no longer any danger of confusing Christian ceremonies with those of the pagans. Thus, Christian bishops became "high priests," presbyters became "priests," and the deacons "Levites."[18]

Ambrose of Milan (ca. 333–97 A.D.) makes an extended reference to the deacon as Levitical in his work *On the Ministerial Offices*, insisting that the deacon refrain from conjugal intercourse: "But ye know that the ministerial office must be kept pure and unspotted and must not be defiled by conjugal intercourse; ye know this, I say, who have received the gifts of the sacred ministry, with pure bodies, and unspoilt modesty, and without ever having enjoyed conjugal intercourse.... Learn then, Priest and Levite, what it means to wash thy clothes."[19] The cultic association of the deacon with the office of the Levites in the Old Testament also brought with it the expectation, in the West, of the deacon to practice continence in relation to his functions at the altar.[20]

As sacerdotalism increased the gulf between the clergy and the laity (*ordo et plebs*), the deacons tended to move further and further away from the world of the laity. The deacons began to be seen "primarily as those who handled holy things and who dealt with the realm of the sacred," which required celibacy.[21] The Council of Elvira in Spain (300–306 A.D.) declared in canon 33: "It is decided that marriage be altogether prohibited to bishops, priests, and

18. "Letter to Evangelus," 289: "In fact as if to tell us that the traditions handed down by the apostles were taken by them from the old testament, bishops, presbyters and deacons occupy in the church the same positions as those which were occupied by Aaron, his sons, and the Levites in the temple."

19. *De Officiis Ministrorum*, in NPNF-II 10:41.

20. The concept of the deacon being prefigured in the Old Testament Levite does not fully account for the practice of perpetual continence for the deacon. It merely establishes the deacon as a cultic figure, for which in the Jewish mindset only periodic continence was required. Some argue that the development of "daily Mass" figures into the transformation of the requirement of continence for ritual actions into mandatory celibacy. For an extensive discussion of the cultic correlation with the obligation of continence and celibacy for the deacon, see Ernst Dassman, "Diakonat und Zölibat," in *Der Diakon: Wiederentdeckung und Erneuerung seines Dienstes*, ed. Josef Plöger and Hermann Weber (Freiburg: Herder, 1981), 57–67.

21. Nowell, *The Ministry of Service*, 33.

deacons, or to all clerics placed in the ministry, and that they keep away from their wives and not beget children; whoever does this shall be deprived of the honor of the clerical office."[22] The Council of Nicaea, in canon 3, forbade the clergy, including the deacon, to "live with a woman" if they had been unmarried when ordained.[23] Over time, the requirement of continence developed into an absolute requirement that all the clergy be celibate. The final stage of the enforcement of celibacy for the clergy in the West came with the First and Second Lateran Councils of 1123 and 1139, which declared clerical marriage invalid instead of only illicit.[24] Mandatory celibacy, along with the decrease in importance of the diaconate's functions, kept the diaconate from remaining a permanent and lifelong order.[25] What point was there for a man to commit himself to lifelong celibacy in order to remain at a "lower" grade that had little influence on the life of the church?

The *cursus honorum*

Another important factor in the decline of the diaconate comes from the development of the practice of the *cursus honorum* (literally, "course" or "progression of honors"). The transformation represented by the *cursus* stands in marked contrast to the organic and collegial structure of the church in the early patristic era. Prior to the fourth century the deacon assisted the bishop, but the deacon also directly served the church as a whole. The deacon was not primarily an assistant to the person of the bishop, but to his ministry. Clement I was clear in his description of the importance of every member in the church. All the orders were related to one another in service to the church as a whole. But by the end of the fourth century, the church's structure was beginning to take on a different configuration. The organic and collegial structure eventually gave way to a vertical and hierarchically oriented structure.[26]

Before the fourth century, deacons were frequently ordained *per saltum*

---

22. Denz., no. 25; *Sacrorum Conciliorum* (ed. Mansi), 2:11: "Placuit in totum prohiberi episcopis, presbyteris, & diaconibus, vel omnibus clericis positis in ministerio, abstinere se a conjugibus suis, & non generare filios: quicumque vero fecerit, ab honore clericatus exterminetur."

23. *Decrees* (ed. Tanner), 1:7.

24. For the historical progression of the requirement of continence and celibacy for the major orders, see Borras and Pottier, *La grâce du diaconat*, 63–68.

25. Ibid., 63.

26. For a complete study of the birth of the hierarchy, see Alexandre Faivre, *Naissance d'un hiérarchie: Les premières étapes du cursus clerical* (Paris: Beauchesne, 1977).

as bishops (i.e., without having been ordained to the order of presbyter).[27] During the fourth century, it became the standard practice that one had to pass through the successive grades, from lower to higher, without skipping any "stage"—deacon to priest to bishop.[28] With the practice of the *cursus per gradum*, orders gradually came to be regarded by and large as rungs on the clerical ladder through which one had to attain the "full ministry" of the priesthood. Christian community life was thus hierarchically ordered from top to bottom, from bishop down to laity, as seen in Augustine's *De civitate Dei* and Dionysius's *Hierarchia ekklesiastike*.[29] The consequence of the *cursus* was that the diaconate simply became, for most men, a step to the priesthood. While the diaconate was assured a stable place in the hierarchy (for no cleric could become a priest without first becoming a deacon), the discipline of the *cursus* also gutted the diaconal order of "permanent deacons."

By the fifth century, the deacon became more an expert of the liturgy than an expert on charitable works. At Rome, deacons were functioning as cantors for the elaborate Gradual between the reading and the Gospel.[30] Pope Gregory the Great complained at the synod of Rome (595 A.D.) that deacons were no longer looking after the poor but were chanting psalms instead.[31] He attempted to bring back charitable works as the proper service of deacons by transferring the function of cantoring to singers, but to no avail.[32] The trans-

---

27. The practice of *per saltum* ordinations of archdeacons to the episcopacy continued until the end of the first millennium, but was increasingly rare after the fourth century. The first Roman deacon called to the papal throne to be ordained a presbyter prior to the episcopate was the archdeacon Hildebrand in 1073. See Borras and Pottier, *La grâce du diaconat*, 48, and Michel Andrieu, "La carrière ecclésiastique des papes et les documents liturgiques du moyen âge," *Revue des sciences religieuses* 23 (1947): 90–120.

28. Barnett, *The Diaconate*, 105: "It is true that the idea of *cursus honorum* grew up in the fourth century, and many, perhaps most, probably did go through the succession of grades. But it appears to have been a long time before the rule became binding." Certainly by the eleventh century, with the example of the archdeacon Hildebrand, the practice of the *cursus* was in effect.

29. Cooke, *Ministry*, 557, gives a good description of the hierarchical ordering of the church as seen in these texts.

30. Edward R. Hardy, "Deacons in History and Practice," in *The Diaconate Now*, ed. Richard T. Nolan (Washington, D.C.: Corpus Books, 1968), 21.

31. Walter Croce, "From the History of the Diaconate," in *Foundations of the Renewal of the Diaconate*, trans. William F. Schmitz (Washington, D.C.: United States Conference of Catholic Bishops, 2003), 83: "The melodies of the Easter 'Exultet' have preserved for us right down to this very day an example of that vocal art, which was cherished with such love and joy by the deacons of those earlier days."

32. *Sacrorum Conciliorum* (ed. Mansi), 9:1226: "In sancta Romana ecclesia, cui divina dispensatio praeesse me voluit, dudum consuetudo est valde reprehensibilis exorta, ut quidam ad sacri altaris

formation of the deacon's expertise from charitable works to liturgical chanting sharply curtailed the intermediate character of the diaconate.

The Leonine Sacramentary

The transformation of the deacon from a social intermediary into a temporary, cultic figure is reflected in the ordination prayers of the Middle Ages. The Leonine Sacramentary (hereafter "LS"), an incomplete seventh-century book preserved at Verona, is the oldest known text containing the classical Roman ordination prayers.[33] The formularies of ordination go back probably to the middle of the fifth century, and St. Leo the Great is most likely the author.[34] The LS has the prayers for the ordination of bishops, deacons, and presbyters, in that order.[35] This early medieval ordination prayer reveals an image of the deacon different from that found in the AT.[36] In the LS, the mystery of the

---

ministerium cantores eligantur, & in diaconatus ordine constituti modulationi vocis inserviant, quos ad praedicationis officium eleemosynarumque studium vacare congruebat. Unde sit plerumque, ut ad sacrum ministerium dum blanda vox quaeritur, quaeri congrua vita negligatur, & cantor minister Deum moribus stimulet, cum populum vocibus delectat. Qua in re praesenti decreto constituo, ut in hac sede sacri altaris ministri cantare non debeant, solumque evangelicae lectionis officium inter missarum solennia exolvant; psalmos vero ac reliquas lectiones censeo per subdiaconos, vel, si necessitas (a) fuerit, per minores ordines exhiberi. Si quis autem contra hoc decretum meum venire tentaverit, anathema sit. Et omnes responderunt: Anathema sit."

33. Miguel S. Gros, "Les plus anciennes formules romaines de benediction des diacres," *Ecclesia Orans* 5 (1988): 45; and Bradshaw, *Ordination Rites*, 14: "The next evidence occurs in the eighth century. The Gelasian Sacramentary, the more-or-less Gallican book known as the *Missale Francorum*, and various eighth-century adaptations of the Gelasian contain these same prayers.... The manner of performing the rites is described in some of the *Ordines Romani*, or ceremonial handbooks, of this period, which in some cases include the text of the ordination prayers as well. The oldest of these, *Ordo* XXXIV, apparently dates from the middle of the eighth century." For the development of the liturgical books see Cyrille Vogel, *Medieval Liturgy: An Introduction to the Sources*, ed. and trans. William Storey and Niels Rasmussen (Washington, D.C.: Pastoral Press, 1986), 38–46; and Eric Palazzo, *A History of Liturgical Books from the Beginning to the Thirteenth Century*, trans. Madeleine Beaumont (Collegeville, Minn.: Liturgical Press, 1998), 173–236.

34. Puglisi, *Epistemological Principles*, 86.

35. Gros, "Les plus anciennes formules," 46: "On ne voit pas bien la raison pour laquelle le compilateur du sacramentaire a placé la bénédiction des diacres entre la consécration des évêque-prêtre-diacre tel que nous le trouvons dans la «Tradition Apostolique» et dans le sacramentaire Grégorien, ou encore l'ordre inverse. Peut-être est-ce une erreur du compilateur, mais en tout cas ce déplacement nous démontre que le rituel de bénédiction des diacres a eu une existence indépendante des autres rituels avant d'être inséré dans le sacramentaire *Veronense*."

36. Bradshaw, *Ordination Rites*, 217: "Assist us, we beseech you, almighty God, giver of honors, distributor of orders, and bestower of offices; who, abiding in yourself, make all things new, and order everything by your Word, Power, and Wisdom, Jesus Christ, your Son our Lord—by everlasting

church is understood as a spiritual temple. It refers explicitly to the Levitical typology, considering the deacon's competence in terms of service at the altar. It is noteworthy that the institution of the Seven in Acts is not recalled in this prayer.[37] The blessing prayer of the LS asks that the ordinand be faithful in his ministry, including the observance of purity and chastity. These virtues describe what should be the life of the deacon, who is to receive a particular dignity associated with the mysteries of the altar; the emphasis falls upon the requisite personal holiness rather than the need for requisite pastoral attitudes, understood in terms of service to the people of God.[38] Finally, the prayer also introduces the idea, more than likely not present in the original AT, that the diaconal ministry is a provisional office—a simple stage in the *cursus* for higher grades. Thus the LS reveals the sacralized and subordinate form of the diaconate that would later be confirmed by the Council of Trent.[39]

---

providence you prepare and apportion to each particular time what is appropriate—whose body, your Church, you permit to grow and spread, diversified by a variety of heavenly graces and knit together in the distinction of its members, united through the wondrous law of the whole structure for the increase of your temple, establishing the service of sacred office in three ranks of ministers to do duty in your name, the sons of Levi having been chosen first, that by remaining in faithful vigilance over the mystical workings of your house, they might obtain by a perpetual apportionment an inheritance of everlasting blessing. Look favorably also on these your servants, we beseech you, Lord, whom we humbly dedicate to serve in your sanctuaries in the office of deacon. And although indeed being men we are ignorant of divine thought and highest reason, we judge their life as best we can; but things unknown to us do not slip by you, Lord, things hidden do not escape you. You are the witness of sins, you are the discerner of minds, you are able truly to bring heavenly judgment on them or else grant to the unworthy what we ask. Send upon them, Lord, we beseech you, the Holy Spirit, by whom, faithfully accomplishing the work of ministry, they may be strengthened with the gift of your sevenfold grace. May the pattern of every virtue abound in them: discreet authority, unfailing modesty, purity of innocence, and the observance of spiritual discipline. May your commandments be reflected in their conduct, so that by the example of their chastity they may win the imitation of the holy people, and displaying the testimony of a good conscience, may persevere strong and stable in Christ, and by fitting advancements from a lower rank may be worthy through your grace to take up higher things." PL 55:114–15: "sacri muneris servitutem trinis gradibus ministrorum nomini tuo militare constituens, electis ab initio Levi filiis, qui mysticis operationibus domus tuae fidelibus excubiis permanentes.... In moribus eorum praecepta tua fulgeant, ut suae castitatis exemplo imitationem sanctae plebis acquirant, et bonum conscientiae testimonium praeferentes, in Christo firmi et stabiles perseverent, dignisque successibus de inferiori gradu per gratiam tuam capere potiora mereantur."

37. Association with the Seven of Acts will follow shortly, with the *Missale Francorum*: "and by [your] indulgence [being] more pure, he may become worthy of the rank of those whom your apostles, at the direction of the Holy Spirit, chose in sevenfold number, with blessed Stephen as their chief and leader." Bradshaw, *Ordination Rites*, 226.

38. Franco Brovelli, "Ordine e ministeri," in *I Sacramenti: teologia e storia della celebrazione*, ed. Brovelli, 4th ed., Anàmnesis 3/1 (Genova: Marietti, 1995), 265.

39. During the debate at the Council of Trent on the reform of the ordained ministry, the

Summary

The diaconate was once a permanent order in the service of the whole church, which functioned collegially with the other two orders. Following the fourth century, it atrophied to an obligatory stage for the cleric as he ascended to a higher order. The sacralization of the ordained ministry in the third and fourth centuries radically changed the role of the deacon. Deacons lost their "expertise" as those who knew the needs of the sick and poor in the community. While the presbyterate acquired additional roles, the deacon was reduced to playing a part on the fringe of the liturgy. The threefold collegial ministry of the pre-Nicene church, where the presbyters and deacons were in direct relation to the bishop, transformed into a linear hierarchy in which the deacon was directly related to the priest-presbyter. By the time of the Reformation, virtually every deacon in the West fulfilled only cultic roles of service to presbyters in the liturgy. Thus we observe the birth of what will later be known as the "transitional diaconate," a form of the diaconate that exists even today.[40] Evidence of the deacon as a social intermediary is, consequently, very much reduced during the Middle Ages. The specific figure of the archdeacon, however, is another story.

---

intervention of a bishop at the Council reveals that there were even some in the fifteenth century who understood the deacon to be an intermediary: "I desire the function of the subdeacon and deacon, diligently collected from the writings of the fathers and decrees of the councils, to be restored and put to use, especially the functions of deacons. The Church has always used their services, not only in ministering at the altar, but in baptism, in care of hospitals, of widows, and of suffering persons. Finally, all the needs and concerns of the people are mediated to the bishop by deacons." *Concilium Tridentinum: Diariorum, actorum, epistolarum, tractatum, nova collectio*, Societas Goerresiana (Frieburg: Herder, 1965), 589; translated in Echlin, *The Deacon in the Church*, 98. The Council, however, continued to view the diaconate as a stepping stone to the priesthood, as seen in c. 2 of the "Canons on the sacrament of order," Session 23, in *Decrees* (ed. Tanner), 2:743.

40. CIC, c. 1050. Borras and Pottier, *La grâce du diaconat*, 93–95, argue that the continued practice of ordaining transitional deacons for the priesthood prevents the reception of the diaconate as a complementary mode of participation in the ecclesiastical *ordo*.

The Medieval Archdeacon

The title "archdeacon" appears for the first time in the fourth century.[41] The archdeacon was not necessarily the senior deacon, for his designation was left to the free choice of the bishop.[42] Neither did the term archdeacon originally denote the one in charge of the other deacons, but the single individual who was the "bishop's deacon": "So long as other deacons still had charge of their diaconal regions, the archdeacon remained *primus inter pares*; but in the course of time, when the other deacons ceased to have any administrative duties, and the archdeacon acquired ever greater and greater power in the diocese—including ordinary jurisdiction over other deacons—the parity vanished."[43] The designation of an archdeacon attests that by the fourth century only one deacon was the bishop's personal assistant, not all the deacons. Thus we see the original and immediate relationship between the deacon and the bishop persist into the later patristic era and the Middle Ages in the office of the archdeacon. He was the close assistant and "eye" of the bishop.[44]

The archdeacon was a person of confidence whom the bishop often took on travels and sent as his representative to councils or on other important and delicate missions.[45] Pope Leo the Great, who had been the archdeacon of Rome, noted that the archdeacon's authority included disposing of all cases in the ecclesiastical administration.[46] The archdeacon, as an auxiliary

41. Alain Amanieu, "Archidiacre," in *Dictionnaire de Droit Canonique contenant tous les termes du droit canonique avec un Sommaire de l'Histoire et des Institutions et de l'état actuel de la discipline*, ed. Raoul Naz (Paris: Librairie Letouzey et Ané, 1935), 1:949. Barnett, *Diaconate*, 218, writes: "The first reference to the office is that of Optatus, bishop of Milevis, writing c. 365." Cf. *De Schismate Donatistarum* [Against the Donatists] in PL 11:916: "cum correptionem archidiaconi Caeciliani ferre non posset."

42. Gaudemet, *L'Église dans l'Empire Romain (IV*-V* siècles)*, 373. Gaudemet notes that sometimes the college of deacons elected one of their own.

43. John Bligh, "Deacons in the Latin West Since the Fourth Century," *Theology* 58 (1955): 423. Beyond the regional deacons, during the Middle Ages there were also "simple deacons (called *diaconi forenses*) who served the priests in liturgical services in diverse churches." See Reynolds, "Clerics in the Early Middle Ages," 5.

44. The Pseudo-Clementine letter to James, previously considered in this book, is cited by Innocent III (1198–1216) to describe the role of the archdeacon. See Aemilius Friedberg (ed.), *Corpus Iuris Canonici. Editio Lipsiensis secunda post Aemilii Ludouici Richteri curas ad librorum manu scriptorum et editionis romanae fidem recognouit et adnotatione critica instruxit Aemilius Friedberg, Pars Secunda: Decretalium Collectiones* (Graz: Akademische Druck, 1879–1955), 151.

45. Pratt, "Les Prétentions," 472.

46. Joseph W. Pokusa, *A Canonical-Historical Study of the Diaconate in the Western Church*, The Catholic University of America Canon Law Studies 495 (Washington, D.C.: The Catholic University of America Press, 1979), 112–13.

of the bishop, eventually adopted all the trappings of the modern-day vicar general.[47]

The broad range of archdiaconal duties demanded a knowledgeable person with administrative expertise. The duties performed by archdeacons varied from diocese to diocese and depended at first upon how much authority and independence was granted to them by their individual bishops.[48] These duties could include the supervision of widows, orphans, and travelers; hence, the connection between charitable works and diaconal charisms was continued to some degree.[49] Charitable work in and among the people, however, was probably not an everyday affair for the archdeacon as it was for the ancient deacons of Rome. The archdeacon was consumed with responsibilities further up the administrative ladder. The shift from ministry that entailed regular contact with the people to a more bureaucratic exercise of authority is exemplified in the fact that the archdeacon often managed the church's affairs during the vacancies of the episcopal see. This was only natural as he had been the one primarily involved in the administration of the church while the bishop was still in power.[50] Nonetheless, the power of the archdeacon before the seventh century was not as expansive as it would be in the following centuries. The archdeacon was not yet an indispensable structure for the bishop in his governance, especially concerning the governance of the other clergy.[51]

In the eighth century, however, the power and authority of the archdeacon grew as he became considered more and more the "vicar" of the bishop. The *Ordo Romanus I* described the archdeacon of Rome as the *vicarius* of the pope, "and as such his administrative and jurisdictional powers were wide."[52] The

47. Borras and Pottier, *La grâce du diaconat*, 56, notes that the office of vicar general was created to replace the functions of the archdeacon.

48. Gaudemet, *L'Église dans l'Empire*, 374.

49. The archdeacon was not, however, the only institutional way of providing for the poor. The SEA reveals that this was an appropriate function of the archpresbyter. See SEA, c. 7, in CCSL 148:167.

50. Amanieu, "Archidiacre," 953–56, lists seven major archdiaconal duties at the beginning of the seventh century: (1) governance of the clergy, (2) representation of the bishop at councils, (3) special aid to the bishop in the governance of the diocese, (4) exercise of the office of judge, (5) management of the wealth of a deceased cleric, (6) execution of ecclesiastical property, and (7) participation in the care of a diocese without a bishop, along with the archpresbyter and *primicerius* (these three figures made up the *servantes locum sanctae Sedis* which governed the affairs of the church *sede vacante* or when the bishop was impeded).

51. Amanieu, "Archidiacre," 956.

52. Reynolds, "Clerics in the Early Middle Ages," I, 8. others For an explanation of the historical setting of the Roman *ordines*, see Cassian Folsom, "The Liturgical Books of the Roman Rite," in *Handbook for Liturgical Studies* (ed. Chupungco), 1:291–92.

archdeacon was the true vicar of the bishop, the first person in the episcopal family, to whom all other clergy were subject.[53] The promotion of ecclesiastical discipline was an extensive area of the archdeacon's responsibility. The Pseudo-Isidorian book *Epistula ad Leudefreudum*, composed in Spain somewhere between the late seventh and early ninth centuries, attests to the archdeacon's authority over the lower clergy: "He [the archdeacon] settles quarrels among those in parishes; visits parishes as the bishop's representative; reports to the bishop about diocesan basilicas needing repairs, the ornaments and goods of parochial basilicas, and regarding ecclesiastical liberties; notifies the bishop regarding the misdeeds of canons; notifies presbyters of fast days; and announces fast and feast days publicly in the church."[54] The archdeacon, therefore, took his own place in the linear hierarchy that developed after the Golden Age of the diaconate. His office elevated him above the other members of his own order. By this point in time the archdeacon was not simply the "bishop's deacon," he was also the "chief deacon" in charge of the other deacons.

The formation of the junior clergy had long since been entrusted to the archdeacon, who trained them in what Optatus of Mileve called the *diaconium*.[55] The archdeacon scrutinized their observance of canonical discipline and expertise in their duties. His role at ordination ceremonies symbolically expressed his authority over their training:

93. When a subdeacon is ordained, since he does not receive the imposition of hands, let him receive from the hand of the bishop the empty paten and the empty chalice, and from the hand of the archdeacon let him receive the ewer with the basin and towel.

94. When an acolyte is ordained, let him be taught by the bishop how he ought to conduct himself in his office, but from the archdeacon let him receive a candlestick with a candle, so that he may know that he is responsible for lighting the lamps of the church; let him also receive an empty cruet for the presentation of the wine in the eucharist of the blood of Christ....

97. When a doorkeeper is ordained, after he has been instructed by the archdeacon how he ought to act in the house of God, when he is presented by the archdeacon let the bishop hand him the keys of the church from the altar.[56]

53. Amanieu, "Archdiacre," 959.
54. Reynolds, "Clerics in the Early Middle Ages," I, 19.
55. Amanieu, "Archidiacre," 951.
56. SEA, cc. 93, 94, 97; translation from Bradshaw, *Ordination Rites*, 222.

In Rome this symbolic role was extended even to the ceremonial testimony that a deacon was worthy to be ordained a presbyter.[57]

By the eighth century, the archdeacon's authority over the clergy at times even included authority over the archpresbyter. By the eighth and ninth centuries, the archpresbyter in urban areas was primarily concerned with the oversight of the liturgical practices of other priest-presbyters in the cathedral and parochial churches; in rural settings, the archpresbyter had somewhat greater jurisdictional power but even this was always less than that of the archdeacon.[58] Even though the archpresbyter was immediately responsible for subordinate clerics in rural areas, "the archdeacon was an intermediary in those matters which involved the cognizance of the bishop."[59] In the performance of his duties, the archdeacon served as the eyes of the bishop, helping the leader of the church become aware of the community's needs. If circumstances focused the bishop's vigilance more narrowly upon the clergy, no less did the archdeacon keep the bishop informed without being overwhelmed. There is no denying the incredible power and authority of the archdeacon himself; without doubt, he was in practice superior to the presbyters. The historical instances of archdeacons "promoted" to the presbyterate in order to render them ineligible for the office of archdeacon exemplify both the power held by archdeacons, and the fact that the office was still associated with diaconal charisms.[60]

The archdeacon held an office superior to that of the presbyter—even the archpresbyter—because it was understood that the archdeacon was the bishop's vicar. Only upon the death of the bishop of Rome did the archdeacon take second place to the archpresbyter, as the archdeacon's vicarious powers ceased with the death of the bishop.[61] With further developments of the archdeacon as vicar of the bishop, the role of the archdeacon was more and more disengaged from the original setting of the deacon in the Golden Age. The archdea-

---

57. Prat, "Les Prétentions," 471. *Ordo Romanus XXXIV*, 11: "If he wishes to consecrate him as a presbyter, the archdeacon takes hold of him and leads him outside the chancel barrier, removes his dalmatic from him, and then vests him in a chasuble and leads him back to the bishop" (quoted in Bradshaw, *Ordination Rites*, 220).

58. Reynolds, "Clerics in the Early Middle Ages," I, 29.

59. Pokusa, *A Canonical-Historical Study*, 118.

60. Hardy, "Deacons in History and Practice," 21, gives the examples of Leo the Great and Gregory the Great who intervened on behalf of archdeacons in other dioceses, preventing the bishops from "promoting" their archdeacons to the priesthood in an attempt to "degrade" them. Amanieu, "Archidiacre," 596, claims that when Pope Gregory ruled that the deacon-made-presbyter was to retain the office of archdeacon, it was the first recorded instance of an archdeacon not of the diaconal order.

61. Amanieu, "Archidiacre," 958.

con would soon cease to be the head of the body of deacons and become more like an ecclesiastical magistrate, subordinate to the bishop but acting rather independently from him.[62] The archdeacon had accumulated so much power and so many functions that new offices were created to shoulder some of the archdeacon's burdensome responsibilities.[63]

A factor that diminished the power of the office of archdeacon was the creation of multiple archdeacons within the diocese. In some countries large dioceses were divided into distinct "archdeaconries."[64] Originally, the territory of the archdeacon was the same as the territory of the bishop, and as such his authority and jurisdiction were diocese-wide. With the creation of the archdeaconries came the multiplication of archdeacons and the division of power within the diocese. These figures were no longer simply "vicars" of the bishop, but were more like "prelates" of their territories within the diocese. The archdeaconries developed, in fact, from the remains of the structures left by the chorbishops (fully ordained bishops, but only for a rural area and with limited jurisdiction under a local ordinary).[65]

The rural archdeacons lost immediate association with the bishop, reducing their intermediate character. The more the archdeacons became magistrates independent of immediate association with the bishop, the less there was a rationale for an actual deacon to hold the office of archdeacon. The division of the diocese into archdeaconries in the ninth century thus coincides

---

62. Anthony Bevilacqua, *Procedure in the Ecclesiastical Courts of the Church of England with Its Historical Antecedents in the Roman and Decretal Law* (Rome: Pontificia Universitas Gregoriana, 1956), 15–16, notes the great variety of cases which came before English ecclesistaical tribunals. He indicates that "the Court of the Archdeacon became a court distinct from the diocesan tribunal soon after the Norman Conquest (1066)" (21). Unless there was a specific diocesan restriction, the "Court of the Archdeacon could be the court of first instance in all ordinary ecclesiastical causes" (22).

63. Reynolds, "Clerics in the Early Middle Ages," I, 8, lists several ecclesiastical officials, some of the most noteworthy being the following: the *primicerius* acted as master of ceremonies and judge, and aided the pope in discussions of councils, and might be the envoy of the pope to distant lands; the *primicerius* replaced an archdeacon or archpresbyter when they were absent. The *secundicerius* assisted the *primicerius* and pope in receiving oaths, and acted in financial and property matters, as well as acting as envoy and notary. The *defensores* served as ambassadors or envoys. There were seven regional *notaries* of Rome. The *primicerius notarium* was one of the chief senior officials who handled most of the daily business of the Roman church.

64. Joseph W. Pokusa, "The Diaconate: A History of Law Following Practice," *Jurist* 45 (1985): 111.

65. Amanieu, "Archidiacre," 963. "Chorbishop" was a term used to identify those who, though fully ordained, could exercise only limited powers as a bishop in a rural area. Chorbishops prevented the excessive multiplication of bishoprics. The Council of Laodicea (357 A.D.) declared that priests representing the diocesan bishop should replace the chorbishops. See "Chorepiscopus" in Joseph F. Kelly, *The Concise Dictionary of Early Christianity* (Collegeville, Minn.: Liturgical Press, 1992), 31.

with the practice of appointing presbyters to the office of archdeacon.[66] As archdeacons were assigned distinct territorial subdivisions of the diocese, they gradually ceased to be simple vicars of the bishop and claimed as their own various jurisdictional rights within their own territories.[67]

The transformed ninth-century office of archdeacon departed radically from what was originally the theological core of the diaconate. The unique diaconal character suited for the mediation of power and authority of the bishop no longer found a supportive structure for its exercise in the office of archdeacon. The office of archdeacon itself became a structure of general oversight over a distinct territory. It became too much like the office of the bishop or his presbyters in the exercise of *episkopé*: the role of the archdeacon was now more oversight than mediation, more presidential than auxiliary. Thus, the office of archdeacon slipped quite naturally into the hands of the presbyters. Dividing the one office of the archdeacon into multiple archdeaconries, furthermore, deprived the bishop of a single vicar for the whole diocese. This role would be supplied by the creation of a new office, the vicar general, which required ordination to the presbyterate.[68] By the time of the Council of Trent, the presbyterate had fully absorbed what had been the ministry of (a few select) deacons. It was even commonplace to find the very title of archdeacon given to a presbyter in the twelfth century.[69] Beyond the twelfth century and until the Second Vatican Council, there are only rare and unusual instances of permanent deacons serving the church even as archdeacons.

Famous Deacons from the Middle Ages to the Nineteenth Century

While the permanence and importance that had once been associated with the diaconate had all but vanished, there were remarkable diaconal figures that kept the historic reality of the diaconate from dying out completely. It is noteworthy that in the churches of the East deacons still functioned on a

---

66. Amanieu, "Archidiacre," 962.

67. Ibid., 965.

68. See Session 23 of the Council of Trent, cc. 2–6; Session 24, c. 20; and Session 25, c. 3.

69. Pokusa, *A Canonical-Historical Study*, 233: "The period from Isidore of Seville through Gratian witnessed widespread establishment of an archdiaconate very different from that of the bishop's single archdeacon in the patristic era. This evolved archdiaconate, basically non-liturgical in its responsibilities, was no longer necessarily associated with the diaconal order. The title of the evolving office nevertheless remained the archdiaconate."

permanent basis, although their ministry was primarily liturgical.[70] From the eighth century Alcuin provides an example of a diaconal figure who was of great importance for his administrative service. Born of a noble family near York, England, in 730 A.D., he was ordained a deacon forty years later. A scholar who was also thoroughly grounded in the management of political affairs, he was a career cleric who "never went beyond the diaconate" in the court of Charlemagne. He was the emperor's most distinguished adviser and rekindled the light of classical and biblical learning in the Frankish kingdom. He retired as Abbot of Tours in 796 A.D., and died there on May 19, 804, as a deacon.[71]

In the thirteenth century the Franciscan friar Thomas of Celano, a contemporary of the "Seraphic Saint," wrote the earliest biography of Francis of Assisi by command of Pope Gregory IX in 1228.[72] In describing the eucharist on Christmas Eve (1223) at Greccio, when Francis had a crèche prepared and thus inaugurated the custom of putting nativity scenes in the churches at Christmas, Francis is mentioned as a deacon: "The saint of God was clothed with the vestments of a deacon, for he was a deacon, and he sang the holy Gospel in a sonorous voice.... Then he preached to the people standing about."[73] It is known that Francis often preached throughout the countryside, although repeatedly interrupting his activity to retreat to solitary hermitage.[74] After living a life of humble service and poverty, this much beloved deacon-Saint died at S. Maria degli Angeli (Portiuncula) near Assisi, and was buried on October 4, 1226.[75] Whether or not he truly was a deacon, the humble way of St. Francis provides a concrete example of how the deacon continues Christ's presence in the world.

The Cardinal Deacon Francesco Piccolomini had administered the Diocese of Siena for forty years as a deacon before his election to the papacy in 1503, after which he took the name Pius III.[76] The Cardinal Deacon Reginald

70. See Georges Florovsky, "The Problem of Diaconate in the Orthodox Church," in *The Diaconate Now*, ed. Richard T. Nolan (Washington, D.C.: Corpus Books, 1968), 81–98.

71. Luitpold Wallach, "Alcuin," in *New Catholic Encyclopedia*, 1:279.

72. Anonymous, "Thomas of Celano," in *Oxford Dictionary of the Christian Church*, ed. Frank L. Cross and Elizabeth A. Livingston, 3rd ed. (New York: Oxford University Press, 1997), 1617.

73. Thomas of Celano, *The First Life of St. Francis*, no. 30 (86), trans. in Marion A. Habig, *St. Francis of Assisi: Writings and Early Biographies: English Omnibus of the Sources for the Life of St. Francis* (Chicago: Franciscan Herald Press, 1972), 301. Lothar Hardick, "Francis of Assisi, St.," in *New Catholic Encyclopedia*, 6:29.

74. Hardick, "Francis of Assisi," 29.

75. Ibid.

76. D. R. Campbell, "Pius III, Pope," in *New Catholic Encyclopedia*, 11:394–95. Cardinal Deacon Piccolomini's father was Nanno Todeschini, and his mother, Laodinica Piccolomini, was the sister of

Pole, one of three papal legates that opened the Council of Trent, was only later ordained presbyter on the eve of his consecration to the episcopate.[77]

There were rare individuals after the Council of Trent who held the office of deacon for a great part of their lives. These deacons, however, were primarily political in form. Ercole Consalvi (1757–1824) was an Italian statesman who entered the papal service and was eventually created a cardinal and made Secretary of State by Pius VII in 1800.[78] Having never "advanced" beyond the diaconate, Cardinal Consalvi's ministry was lifelong diplomatic service. His main achievement was the Concordate of 1801 with France, which made possible the reconstruction of the Catholic church after the French Revolution.[79] Giacomo Antonelli (1806–76), the cardinal secretary of state for Pius IX, was ordained to the diaconate in 1840, never proceeding beyond it.[80] Having arranged the safe flight of the pope to Gaeta, Cardinal Antonelli became the virtual temporal ruler of Rome down to 1870, being nicknamed the "Red Pope."[81] With the end of the Papal States in 1870, there was no longer any need for these diaconal cardinals, the last of them dying early in the pontificate of Leo XIII.[82] Under a ruling made by St. John XXIII and subsequently confirmed by St. John Paul II, all cardinals, whatever their rank, are to be ordained bishops unless granted a personal dispensation by the pope.[83] Thus today even the rare form of the diaconate, known as the papal deacon, exists no longer.

Pope Pius II (Enea Silvio Piccolomini). Pius II conferred upon his nephew the use of the Piccolomini surname. Barnett confuses the two Piccolomini popes in his book. See Barnett, *The Diaconate*, 84–85 and 252.

77. William Schenk, *Reginald Pole: Cardinal of England* (New York: Longmans, Green and Company, 1950), 111, and Hardy, "Deacons in History and Practice," 26. For more on the life of Reginald Cardinal Pole, see also Frederick G. Lee's *Reginald Pole, Cardinal Archbishop of Canterbury: An Historical Sketch with an Introductory Prologue and Practical Epilogue* (New York: G. P. Putnam's Sons, 1888).

78. Anonymous, "Consalvi, Ercole," in *The Oxford Dictionary of the Christian Church*, ed. Frank L. Cross and Elizabeth A. Livingston, 3rd ed. (New York: Oxford University Press, 1997), 401.

79. Guillaume De Bertier de Sauvigny, "Consalvi, Ercole," in *New Catholic Encyclopedia*, 4:191–92.

80. Cross and Livingston, "Consalvi," 79.

81. Roger Aubert, "Antonelli, Giacomo," in *New Catholic Encyclopedia*, 1:641–42.

82. Hardy, "Deacons in History and Practice," 34.

83. CIC, c. 351 §1: "Those promoted as cardinals are men freely selected by the Roman Pontiff, who are at least in the order of the presbyterate and are especially outstanding for their doctrine, morals, piety and prudence in action; those, however, who are not yet bishops must receive episcopal consecration."

Theological Evaluation of the
Medieval Archdeacon

The deacons of the Middle Ages who served as "regular" deacons in the parishes (who were neither the bishop's personal assistant nor had duties at the diocesan level) were, however, quite different from their predecessors.[84] While we are not absolutely clear about the ministry of these parish-deacons, all the evidence leads scholars to conclude that they were primarily cultic functionaries in the Middle Ages.[85] Evidence of the *monasteria diaconiae* in Rome suggests that presbyters and religious orders took over what had been a key function of the diaconate in the church: care for the poor.

By the Middle Ages, deacons were no longer expected to be knowledgeable about the poor and others in need. Thus, it is unlikely that within the social world of the medieval church these "regular" deacons would have been the patterned means through whom authority and power were mediated. Other structures of mediation between the church and the marginalized members of the community arose to fulfill what the diaconate did not or could not accomplish any longer.

On the other hand, the archdeacon was in some ways closer to the original character of the diaconate than the parish-deacons in the Middle Ages. Though the archdeacon was more administrator than social worker, he was still the bishop's eyes and hands. As we have seen, however, the role of the archdeacon by the ninth century was also beginning to be absorbed slowly by others, primarily presbyters. The reasons for this transformation may have more to do with the archdeacon assuming roles more suitable to the presbyteral charism, rather than the presbyter taking over truly diaconal roles. As the presbyterate broke up to fulfill the needs of outlying communities away from the bishop,

---

84. That there were thousands of deacons in the medieval period is attested in the obituaries and necrologies of that time period. See Reynolds, "An Early Medieval Tract," VII, 98n8.

85. Whether deacons mediated the power and authority of the presbyter in the parish is an important question. Evidence suggests that they did not. A late-ninth-century tract devoted solely to the diaconate, *Collectio Dacheriana, Vat. Reg. Lat. 845,* never mentions duties of the deacon outside the sanctuary. This suggests that these roles, if any, were of little significance to the community. See Reynolds, "An Early Medieval Tract," VII, 97–98: "From Isidore of Seville through Amalarius of Metz and Rabanus Maurus, most tracts on sacred orders describe the deacon simply as one among the many steps in the ecclesiastical cursus leading to the higher sacerdotal grades and rehearse his origins and functions in terms of the well-worn texts of late patristic antiquity. The deacon remains an important order in the ecclesiastical hierarchy, but his duties are primarily liturgical, and he is clearly subordinated to the *sacerdotes*, whose assistant he is" (98).

but still under his authority, the archdeacon, as the bishop's personal assistant, exercised a certain superior jurisdiction, in the practical order, over individual presbyters. Even the archpresbyter was under the archdeacon in the chain-of-command that existed outside the liturgy. Thus the archdeacon became an intermediate institution between the bishop and the clergy, including the individual members of the presbyterate, rather than the bishop and the laity or the poor.

With this development we see the exercise of *episkopé* by the archdeacon, and not simply the assistance of the bishop's exercise of authority. But this later form of the office of archdeacon was diaconal in title only. The eucharistic assembly already had charisms, other than the bishop, that pertained to the presidential oversight of the community—the charisms associated with presbyteral ordination. Having little connection anymore with the charisms of the diaconate, the archdeacon in the twelfth century and afterwards was typically an office for presbyters. Consequently, this late-medieval model of the archdeacon has little to do with our understanding of the diaconate today.

In Gradu Inferiori and Diaconal Subordination

But there is one aspect of the powerful medieval archdeacon that is still relevant; the history of his exercise of power forces us to reexamine the meaning of the teaching found in LG 29, that the deacon is *in gradu inferiori*. Before the Second Vatican Council, some theologians surmised that the only kind of jurisdiction for the deacon is that which is subordinate to the presbyters.[86] But other theologians refute the idea that the deacons must "always" be subordinate to presbyters in the practical order. Herve Legrand, drawing from the history of the archdeacon, remarks: "Admittedly, the deacons are to be placed after the priests, but they are servants only of the bishop, who can entrust some functions to them in which they have authority over priests."[87] Legrand is keen to safeguard the complementary and parallel structures of the diaconate and presbyterate. The relationship between the members of the two orders can

---

86. Augustinus Kerkvoorde, "The Theology of the Diaconate," in *Foundations for the Renewal of the Diaconate*, trans. William F. Schmitz (Washington, D.C.: United States Catholic Conference, 1993), 132: "It appears evident to us that the jurisdiction of the deacon must always be subordinated to that of the bishop and even of the priest. In the past, some deacons exercised an inordinate jurisdiction (the archdeacon, the cardinal-deacon) that overshadowed that of the priests and even some bishops. This is illogical. The fact, however, that the jurisdiction of the deacon has been reduced to practically zero makes no sense either."

87. Legrand, "Le diaconat," 35.

only be determined on the practical level by considering the specific functions entrusted to them by the bishop. In some instances, it could very well be that a presbyter would "depend" on a deacon because of the nature of the deacon's given role.[88]

In his theological reflection on the Second Vatican Council's teaching on the diaconate, Karl Rahner also rejects the deacon's subordination to the presbyter in an absolute sense. With regard to the celebration of the sacraments, the priest is definitely distinct and superior to the deacon. This does not imply, however, "that the diaconate is simply a 'lower' degree from every point of view. When we think of the ministry on behalf of the poor, and of many other tasks which belong primarily to the deacon, it is no longer easy to perceive how the diaconate could be designated in this connection as a lower degree."[89] Rahner's analysis of the relationship between the presbyterate and diaconate is noteworthy in that he does not rely upon the historical figure of the archdeacon. Roles that pertain to the mediation of power and authority among the people of God fit rather well in Rahner's vision of the diaconate: these roles are a field in which the deacon could have his own sphere of competence, alongside and independent of the presbyterate.

The Second Vatican Council in LG entrusted "duties of charity and administration" to the diaconate. With respect to their duties of charity at the diocesan level, deacons could be "superior" to an individual presbyter in terms of power, authority, and jurisdiction. The deacon assigned to this sort of ministry at the parish level, however, would necessarily fall under the direct authority of the pastor-presbyter. Nevertheless, it is safe to claim that the diaconate is not subordinate to the presbyterate in the same way that it is always subordinate to the bishop.

How bishops use deacons in the administration of the diocese should be carefully considered, for the duties entrusted to deacons are to be in conformity to the charisms they have received in ordination. That there are limits to what a bishop can entrust to a deacon has been made clear: a deacon cannot preside at the eucharistic offering, nor can he preside as shepherd over a portion of the bishop's flock. Deacons are not the shepherds. They are assistants (and much needed ones) to those who have the responsibility of shepherding. Just exactly where administrative assistance of the bishop's *episkopé* crosses

88. Ibid., 37. See also Borras and Pottier, *La grâce du diaconat*, 56.
89. Karl Rahner, "The Teaching of the Second Vatican Council on the Diaconate," in *Foundations for the Renewal of the Diaconate*, trans. David Bourke (Washington, D.C.: United States Conference of Catholic Bishops, 2003), 190.

over into the exercise of governance in the sense of a shepherd is not always clear. At what point do administrative duties involve the exercise of presbyteral rather than diaconal charisms under the authority of the bishop?

Looking back at the history from our vantage point today, there are two points at which the office of the medieval archdeacon seems to have gone beyond its diaconal character. First, the bishop and his presbyters alone constitute a single presbyterate. Deacons as a class or as individuals, including the bishop's deacon, do not share in this collegial governance of the diocese. This is an important theological distinction to maintain. As I argued in chapter 1, the unique character and dignity of the diaconal order depends upon this distinction. The use of the archdeacon as a mediator between the bishop and his presbyterate contradicts my understanding of the diaconate as shaped by the Church Orders from the Golden Age of the diaconate. The relationship between the bishop and his priests is inherently presbyteral. To insert a deacon in between the bishop and his presbyterate would insert the deacon into the presbyterate itself. Where there is need for mediation between bishop and presbyterate, a presbyteral structure best fulfills this role, not a deacon.[90] Direct governance of the presbyterate itself is therefore a function beyond the deacon's ordination mandate. It is no wonder that the archdeacon, thus conceived, became a role for presbyters and not deacons.

Second, the governance of the diocese by the deacon as the bishop's vicar, whether the bishop is present or absent from the diocese, is another contradiction. Before the seventh century, administrative oversight of the presbyters was not a normal responsibility for deacons, including the archdeacon. Role conflict and ambiguity only intensified as the diaconate was consolidated into the single figure of the archdeacon. Only the presbyterate, with the bishop as its head, has the charge of governance of the entire diocese. While deacons can assist this ministry, they do not provide it themselves. The duties of administration that involve the governance of the presbyterate or the diocese as a whole are proper to the bishop and his presbyterate, but not to the diaconate. The medieval archdeacon, insofar as he exercised this kind of authority, should not serve as a model for the diaconate today.

90. The presbyteral council, which is mandated by the CIC for every diocese, is a prime example of an intermediate institution between the presbyterate and the bishop. CIC, c. 495 §1: "A presbyteral council is to be established in each diocese, that is, a body of priests who are to be like a senate of the bishop, representing the presbyterate; this council is to aid the bishop in the governance of the diocese according to the norm of law, in order that the pastoral welfare of the portion of the people of God entrusted to him may be promoted as effectively as possible."

However, there are other administrative duties that do not pertain to the full or direct exercise of governance over the presbyterate or the entire diocese. Insofar as the archdeacon served as the bishop's representative in matters that pertain to diaconal ordination charisms, he was a proper model for the contemporary diaconate. The office of the archdeacon was a parallel structure to that of the presbyterate, serving the bishop directly and without subordination to the presbyters. This structure allowed the archdeacon access to the bishop to mediate the needs of those for whom the bishop and deacon were ordained.

Conclusion

My investigation of historical precedents for the deacon as a social intermediary among the people of God has led to many positive results. The deacons were very important to the life of the church in the third and fourth century. As chief liaisons, they had constant contact with the laity and the bishop; the deacon was responsible for the care of the sick, feeding the poor, burial of the dead, the extension of hospitality, and the administration of temporalities. In performing these tasks, deacons were essential in the bishop's exercise of pastoral care for his flock. The deacon was also important in animating the faithful to fulfill their obligations to those in need. It was the deacon's role to build up the community of the faithful by reminding them of their obligation to serve. They were not only effective agents of communion, but also visible, everyday reminders of the Gospel command to love one another.

As the sphere of liturgy came to have a primary position in the deacon's ministry, the part of ministry that was not cultic was delegated to second place. The sacralization of the ministry, with the disciplines of celibacy and the *cursus honorum*, consequently deprived the diaconate of its original vigor. Though it had been important for the life and mission of the church, the diaconate was virtually removed from the social structure of the church except for the figure of the archdeacon. During this era of the diaconate, the social function of the deacon as a mediator of power and authority among the people of God was not expressly recognized or practiced. The archdeacon himself accumulated so much power and authority that he could no longer be said to function as a social intermediary in our sense of the word. Though he was nominally the spokesman for the poor and all others under him, including the other clergy, he was not much different sociologically from the bishop.

But even the history of the archdeacon supports my thesis that the deacon is, at root, a social intermediary among the people of God. There is a direct correlation between the disengagement from an authentic, intermediate social function of the office of archdeacon and its termination. History shows that the diaconate was vital to the life and mission of the church when it served as an intermediate institution among the people of God in the Golden Age. This is an important lesson from history for the restructuring of the diaconate for today, as we make a second attempt to incorporate the diaconate into a larger church structure that includes parishes and dioceses. But the essential social role of the deacon does not mean that his liturgical role is not also important. In the next chapter, I will fill in the complete role of the deacon by connecting his social intermediation to his symbolic role in the liturgy of the eucharist and among the people of God.

PART 4

The Deacon Today

CHAPTER 7

The Deacon in the Liturgy

An Epiphany of Service

In the Golden Age of the diaconate, prior to the Council of Nicaea (325 A.D.), the deacon could accurately be described as a steward of Christ's mercy. The diaconate served the communion of the church by mediating power, authority, knowledge, care, and concern; the deacon bound the bishop more closely to his people and united the people of God in solidarity with those in need. As the church grew, and the diaconate's duties became solely focused on the liturgy, this activity of mercy waned, and so too did the number of permanent deacons and their importance to the people of God. Hence, the renewal of the diaconate following the Second Vatican Council justly embraces the restoration of nonritual functions for the deacon. Deacons will thrive if they serve as a structure of mercy for the church, an institution that I have been calling throughout this book a "social intermediary" between the bishop and his people, and the bishop and the poor.

And yet, the Council also affirmed and even enlarged the deacon's liturgical ministry. Was this a mistake, a concession to the desire for deacons to be "mini-priests," that hampers their unique ministries as social intermediaries? Part of the answer is to recall that the liturgy is not some isolated "spiritual" activity cut off from the life of the people of God. The basic principle governing liturgical ministry is enunciated in the constitution of the Second Vatican Council, *Sacrosanctum Concilium*, when it affirms the liturgy as an act of the whole church, in which all actively participate, each according to one's order or

This chapter is derived from a paper delivered at a plenary session of the National Association of Diaconate Directors Convention, April 22, 2015; published in *Josephinum Diaconal Review* (Fall 2015): 3–23.

office in the church.[1] Awareness of the communal context of Christian worship is necessary for a proper examination of the ritual functions of the deacon. The fathers of the Second Vatican Council taught that the deacon's liturgical service is an important complement to his other ministries. In LG 29 the Council fathers deemed *diaconia liturgiae* to be one of the fundamental components of the ministry of deacons. When the fathers reiterated their understanding of the deacon in AG 16, they used a theologically packed statement that associates the diaconal service of administration and social works with service at the altar: through ordination the deacon is "strengthened, and bound more closely to the altar."[2] This is why the deacon joins the priests and bishops in reverencing the altar with a kiss at the beginning and end of Mass. Diaconal ordination confers spiritual charisms that pertain to the service of the people of God both within the liturgy and outside it.

For the purposes of this chapter, I will leave aside most of the "new" liturgical roles for deacons—such as baptisms, weddings, and funerals—so as to focus on the one constant in the history of the diaconate in the liturgy: the eucharist. Certainly the other roles bear analysis; as I stated in chapter 2, they are not an exhaustive list, nor an irreformable one that could not be amended to better suit the needs of the church or avoid role confusion with priests. Hence, I will examine more of these activities in chapters 8–9. While those duties are not foundational to the theology of the deacon, as I have argued, the presence of the deacon in the eucharistic liturgy can be said to be basic to the specific form of ordained ministry that is the diaconate.

It is in the eucharistic liturgy that the church and the roles of her members are most especially made clear, for "the preeminent manifestation of the Church is present in the full, active participation of all God's holy people in these liturgical celebrations, especially the same eucharist, in a single prayer, at one altar at which the bishop presides, surrounded by his college of presbyters and by his ministers."[3] In the eucharist the eschatological reality of the church is made manifest. The Mass is the liturgical anticipation of that banquet

---

1. Vatican Council II, *Sacrosanctum Concilium*, December 4, 1963, no. 26, in *Decrees* (ed. Tanner), 2:826.

2. AG 16: "Per impositionem manuum inde ab apostolis traditam corroborari et altari arctius coniungi, ut ministerium suum per gratiam sacramentalem diaconatus efficacius expleant," trans. in *Decrees* (ed. Tanner), 2:1026.

3. *Sacrosanctum Concilium*, no. 41, as quoted in Congregation for Divine Worship and the Discipline of the Sacraments, *Ceremonial of Bishops. Revised by Decree of the Second Vatican Ecumenical Council and Published by Authority of Pope John Paul II. Prepared by the International Commission on English in the Liturgy* (Collegeville, Minn.: Liturgical Press, 1989), no. 11 (20).

which is still to come with the return of Christ, who is the head of the historical church and the slain Lamb in heaven.[4] The roles of the deacon in the
Mass therefore can rightly be taken as the paradigmatic, ritual expression of
the ministry of the deacon.

This chapter will show how the deacon's ministry in the symbolic order
relates to his ministry of service as a steward of Christ's mercy. Previously, it
has been demonstrated that the deacon serves as a unique minister of communion and solidarity in the practical order.[5] I have accomplished this through
both sociological and historical investigations, together with the theological.
The deacon's liturgical functions, far from being separate from their social role,
add a key dimension to their ministry as a bridge between the bishop and the
people. To understand this fully, I will ask the reader to consider some rather
technical insights gleaned from experts in the human sciences, specifically the
cultural anthropology of symbols, once again in service to theological understanding.[6] In this chapter, I seek to understand what the deacon's ritual actions "say" and "do" to the community that celebrates the eucharist.

We will see that symbolism of the diaconate, while exemplified in the
Mass, is not limited to the performance of ritualized roles: as a sacramentally ordained minister, the deacon is not only a periodic liturgical symbol but
an enduring symbol of Christ's love and mercy in the world. Thus the aim of
this chapter is to examine the symbolic presence of the deacon in the liturgy
and among the people of God, and argue that the deacon-symbol bridges the
distance between the altar and Christian life like no other symbol. To put it
simply, the deacon in the liturgy is an epiphany of service.

4. Johann Auer and Joseph Ratzinger, *A General Doctrine of the Sacraments and the Mystery of
the Eucharist*, vol. 6: *Dogmatic Theology*, ed. Hugh Riley, trans. Erasmo Leiva-Merikakis (Washington,
D.C.: The Catholic University of America Press, 1995), 349–450.

5. See also W. Shawn McKnight, "The Uniqueness of the Deacon," in *The Character of the Deacon:
Spiritual and Pastoral Foundations*, ed. James Keating (Mahwah, N.J.: Paulist Press, 2017), 61–84.

6. R. Kevin Seasoltz, "Anthropology and Liturgical Theology," in *Liturgy and Human Passage*,
ed. David Power and Louis Maldonado, Concilium 112 (New York: Seabury Press, 1979), 7–8: "As a
science, anthropology is generally separated into two main branches: physical anthropology which
is concerned with certain aspects of human biology, especially the study of human evolution; and
cultural anthropology which is concerned with social behavior, beliefs, and languages, as well as the
shared ways in which people act, think, and make things. Although physical anthropology may affect
other areas of theological investigation, it has little or no effect on sacramental or liturgical theology.
The insights of the cultural anthropologists, however, are often quite useful to the liturgist or sacramental theologian."

Anthropological Antecedents
of the Deacon's Ritual Roles

Cultural anthropologists regard ritual as a type of social language that is perfor-
mative. At root, human ritual involves: (1) nonverbal actions that (2) "say" and
"do" things. Not only does ritual provide an explanation for how things are, it
also has great power of action. Through ritual, one season changes into another; a boy becomes a man, a girl becomes a woman, a young couple becomes a
family, and ill persons become healthy.[7]

In his book on Christian liturgy, the influential scholar Fr. Louis Bouyer
recognized the importance of what he called "anthropological antecedents"
in the study of our Christian rites. He wrote: "With the help of the modern
sciences that deal with man, we intend to examine what might be described as
the anthropological antecedents to Christianity. From this study, the human
character of Christianity should emerge with a clarity that would otherwise
be hardly suspected."[8] Fr. Bouyer's point is related to the sacramental principle, *gratia supponit naturam* (grace builds on nature); grace elevates nature
but does not replace it. Consequently, one must recognize that the liturgical
rites of the church are not simply given to us from on high, but "emerge out
of popular consciousness formed by a symbiosis of Gospel and world."[9] The
field of liturgy today acknowledges that there are anthropological roots in all of
the Catholic liturgical rites. Our examination of the ritual roles of the deacon
as an epiphany of service will likewise be aided by the work of anthropologists
and sociologists who have explored the connections between ritual activity
and social life.

7. J. Christopher Crocker, "Ritual and the Development of Social Structure: Liminality and Inversion," in *The Roots of Ritual*, ed. James D. Shaugnessy (Grand Rapids, Mich.: Eerdmans, 1973), 49–50.

8. Louis Bouyer, *Rite and Man: Natural Sacredness and Christian Liturgy*, trans. M. Joseph Costelloe, University of Notre Dame Liturgical Studies 7 (Notre Dame, Ind.: University of Notre Dame
Press, 1963), 2. For a recent argument for the general use of anthropology in theology, see Andrea Grillo, *Teologia Fondamentale e Liturgia: Il rapporto tra immediatezza e mediazione nella riflessione teologica*,
ed. R. Cecolin, A. N. Terrin, and F. Trolese, Caro Salutis Cardo Studi 10 (Padova: Edizioni Messaggero
Padova, 1995), esp. 227–36.

9. Aidan Kavanagh, "Life-Cycle Events, Civil Ritual and the Christian," in *Liturgy and Human
Passage*, ed. David Power and Louis Maldonado, Concilium 112 (New York: Seabury Press, 1979), 15.

Ritual and Social Life

The late Mary Douglas elucidated the social significance of ritual in many of her works. She found that social cohesion and concern for others are reinforced by ritual. Where strong social bonds are found in human societies, there tends to be abundant ritual activity. Conversely, the more individualism is present, the less ritual activity is to be found. Hence, the more ritually engaged a society or group, the less likely there is to be an individualistic approach to religion and social obligations. Douglas bemoaned the decline among members of industrialized societies in their ability to read nonverbal signs, that is, for ritual to have an effect upon them. She claimed that the flight "away from ritual" was induced by an emphasis upon the subjective "inner experience," driving our modern, developed societies further along the path of individualism. And she used the example of the penitential practice of abstaining from meat on Fridays by the immigrant Irish in London to showcase her point.[10]

Affirming Douglas's basic point, noted American sociologist Robert Bellah once argued in *America* magazine that U.S. society should make a deliberate return to ritualism.[11] Bellah believes that the cultural roots for American individualism are found in what he termed the "Protestant cultural code" and its consequent resistance to ritual. "The Reformers," he stated, "fearing idolatry and magic, attacked the doctrine of transubstantiation and other Catholic practices. Afraid of the idea of the sacred in the world, they, in effect, pushed God out of the world into radical transcendence."[12] He claims that this attitude culminates in a Gnostic approach to the Christian faith, "where accepting Jesus Christ as one's personal Lord and savior becomes almost the whole of

10. Mary Douglas, *Natural Symbols: Explorations in Cosmology*, rev. ed. (London: Routledge, 1973–96), 36: "The Bog Irishman in his faithfulness to the rule of Friday abstinence is undeniably like the primitive ritualist. Magical rules have always an expressive function. Whatever other functions they perform, disciplinary, anxiety-reducing, or sanctioning of moral codes, they have first and foremost a symbolic function. The official symbolism of Friday abstinence was originally personal mortification, a small weekly celebration of the annual celebration of Good Friday. Thus it pointed directly to Calvary and Redemption. It could hardly have a more central load of meaning for Christian worship. In reporting that it has become empty and meaningless, what is meant is that its symbols are no longer seen to point in that direction or anywhere in particular." The effects of these ritual markers being relaxed are carefully analyzed in Maria C. Morrow, *Sin in the Sixties: Catholics and Confession 1955–1975* (Washington, D.C.: The Catholic University of America Press, 2016).

11. Robert N. Bellah, "Religion and the Shape of National Culture," *America* 181, no. 3 (August 7, 1999): 9–14.

12. Ibid., 11.

piety."[13] Consequently, when the sacredness of the individual is not balanced by concern for the common good, one finds a religious environment within which greater individualism is encouraged rather than discouraged.[14]

The works of Douglas and Bellah affirm that ritual can be a powerful tool for the promotion of solidarity, communion, and mercy among members of society. Douglas articulated the importance of ritual as a nonverbal language code of condensed symbols that reinforces one's place in society. Ritual and its powerfully symbolic mechanism, according to Bellah, are indispensable means for the promotion of concern for others. These social-anthropological anteced-ents of ritual give us greater reason to appreciate the ritual role of the deacon as a steward of Christ's mercy in the Catholic Mass.

Merely teaching about social justice is not enough; nor is simply providing social structures for the practice of charity. Human nature requires ritual ex-pression for there to be communion among the people of God. As much as we may wish to focus the energy and resources of the diaconate upon charitable works, the anthropological need to communicate and reinforce symbolically the Gospel's vision of communion and social justice must also be taken into account. Such communion is always first and foremost a gift from God, but it is also always only partially realized in the concrete community of the church. The next section of this chapter will therefore explore Victor Turner's under-standing of the internal mechanism of the ritual process in order to ascertain more precisely *how* ritual influences social dynamics. Turner's theory provides the means by which we can describe how the deacon-symbol is at the service of communion and mercy, both within the liturgy and outside it.

Victor Turner and *communitas*

Victor Turner, a convert to Catholicism early in his career, wrote extensive-ly on ritual and its function in society. Turner's unique contribution was his

---

13. Ibid., 12.

14. Bellah does not seek the elimination of individualism entirely, but rather to reconnect it to the public realm. See Robert N. Bellah et al., *Habits of the Heart: Individualism and Commitment in American Life* (Los Angeles: University of California Press, 1996), 247–48: "Religious individualism is, in many ways, appropriate in our kind of society. It is no more going to go away than is secular individualism.... It would seem that a vital and enduring religious individualism can only survive in a renewed relationship with established religious bodies. Such a renewed relationship would require changes on both sides. Churches and sects would have to learn that they can sustain more autonomy than they had thought, and religious individualists would have to learn that solitude without commu-nity is merely loneliness."

"processual" theory of society as always in flux, always becoming without ever fully realizing its potential.[15] Contrary to the school in which he was trained, Turner's research and reflection led him to see society as a continuous dynamic process rather than a timeless entity.[16] This processual view of society prevents its reduction to merely structural forms. For Turner, society consists of two mutually interdependent and interactive poles that he called "structure" and "anti-structure."

Structure

By "structure," Turner meant a more or less distinctive arrangement of mutually dependent institutions and the institutional organization of social positions that they imply.[17] Social structures define who a person is: they could be anything from job descriptions, signs of rank, or bureaucratic organizational charts, to formal operational logic, rubrics, and legal codes like canon law.[18] Social structures apportion power, authority, wealth, and knowledge throughout a given social body, although not in an equal or egalitarian manner. Structure is the framework on which society hangs.

Structure is positive and necessary for life because it organizes society to meet material needs.[19] Social structures benefit human society by providing an orderly social world, with a recognized system of responsibility and control, and prescribed ways of acting toward one another. Structures such as speed limits, stop lights, and the police allow travelers to drive with a sufficient sense of safety, even though we may at times chafe at such constraints. Indeed, how close do you feel to the police officer as a person when he pulls you over with sirens and lights glaring? Or the IRS agent who comes calling about your past tax returns?

15. Victor Turner, *Dramas, Fields, and Metaphors: Symbolic Action in Human Society* (Ithaca, N.Y.: Cornell University Press, 1996), 24 and 43–45.

16. Mary Collins, "Ritual Symbols and the Ritual Process: The Work of Victor W. Turner," *Worship* 50 (1976): 341. Victor Turner, *Revelation and Divination in Ndembu Ritual* (Ithaca, N.Y.: Cornell University Press, 1975), 86: "I employed a method of analysis derived essentially from Durkheim and Radcliffe-Brown.... But this method did not enable me to handle the complexity, assymetry, and antinomy which characterize real social processes, of which ritual performances may be said to constitute phases or stages."

17. Turner, *Dramas, Fields, and Metaphors*, 272.

18. Urban Holmes, "Liminality and Liturgy," *Worship* 47 (1973): 389.

19. Victor Turner, "Variations on a Theme of Liminality," in *Secular Ritual*, ed. Sally F. Moore and Barbara G. Meyerhoff (Assen: Van Gorcum and Co., 1977), 46–47, as cited in Bobby C. Alexander, *Victor Turner Revisited: Ritual as Social Change*, ed. Susan Thistlethwaite, American Academy of Religion Academy Series 74 (Atlanta: Scholars Press, 1991), 35.

Differentiation among social statuses and roles, as well as the norms and conventions that enforce these differences, create feelings of "alienation," "distance," "inequality," and "exploitation."[20] Turner equated social structures with the propensity for individualism and isolation among members of society. Differences in power and authority, as well as wealth and knowledge, are normally "structured" and divide individuals from one another. "Structure," he wrote, "is all that holds people apart, defines their differences, and constrains their actions."[21] This separation of people according to their social status can become opposition and a reason for struggle between persons and groups.[22]

This inborn weakness of structure prevents society from ever attaining a final resting state; society, therefore, remains always in process. While structure provides a framework by which society is able to get along in day-to-day affairs, it is not the matrix from which community originates. Something else must account for the community dimension of society, something that blunts the sharp effects of structure. Society is more than a system of rules; it is or should be a community of persons. Although Turner accepts the necessity of established institutions for society, he also recognizes that social structures have their limitations: social structures alone do not explain what makes a society a community.

Anti-Structure

Turner gives the name "anti-structure" to the opposite dialectical pole of structure, the fundamental component of human community that tempers the isolating forces of "structure." Anti-structure is the generic human bond without which there could be no society.[23] It represents the basic human need to relate to other human beings personally and not simply through formal, structured relationships. As structure tends to generate conflict, anti-structure builds social cohesion; it makes society into a community of persons. Turner uses the terms *communitas* and "liminality" to represent the two aspects of anti-structure.[24] *Communitas* has to do with the feeling we have when relating to or bonding with one or more individuals, person to person, whereas liminali-

---

20. Turner, *Dramas, Fields, and Metaphors*, 272.

21. Ibid., 47.

22. Victor Turner, *The Ritual Process: Structure and Anti-Structure* (New York: Aldine De Gruyter, 1969–95), 126.

23. Ibid., 97.

24. Turner, *Dramas, Fields, and Metaphors*, 202.

ty is "the state of being in-between successive participations in social milieux dominated by social structural considerations." These "in-between" times and spaces that break up our lives are often when and where we experience *communitas*, like the breaks between sessions at a professional conference when the participants get to know each other.[25] Importantly, ritual is just such a liminal domain.

Turner makes use of the Latin term *communitas* rather than the English term "community" in order to distinguish *communitas* as a modality of social relationships from "a geographical area of common living."[26] *Communitas* is not structure with its signs reversed, minuses instead of plusses (as in the case of matter and antimatter), but rather the *font and source* of all structures and, at the same time, their critique.[27] It emerges where the rough edges of social structure are not.[28] *Communitas* is society experienced or perceived as a relatively undifferentiated communion of equal individuals.[29] *Communitas* provides more direct, person-to-person ways of knowing and experiencing relationships, absent the encumbrances of social status. As a response to the "existential deprivation" caused by social differentiation, *communitas* represents "the desire for total, unmediated relationships between person and person ... in the very act of realizing their commonness," as well as the recognition of individuals "as equal in terms of shared humanity."[30]

Communitas can take place *en masse*, among the 400,000 people at Woodstock, an August 1969 festival of music "for peace" and "free love." Woodstock, named for the closest town in New York state, came at a time when young people had pent up frustration with the social establishment (especially the Vietnam War). Woodstock was designed to be a unique experience for people, primarily young people of the counter-cultural generation, to relate to each other person to person, contrary to the social boundaries then in force. The burden of structure (the social encumbrances and demands of the late 1960s) created a need for a *communitas* experience.

---

25. Ibid., 52: "What I call liminality ... whether formal or unformalized, is not precisely the same as *communitas*, for it is a sphere or domain of action or thought rather than a social modality. Indeed, liminality may imply solitude rather than society, the voluntary or involuntary withdrawal of an individual from a social-structural matrix. It may imply alienation from rather than more authentic participation in social existence."

26. Ibid., 201.

27. Ibid., 202.

28. Turner, *The Ritual Process*, 126.

29. Ibid., 96.

30. Turner, *Dramas, Fields, and Metaphors*, 272; Turner, *The Ritual Process*, 177.

But *communitas* can come in simpler ways as well. In the modern work-place, if structure is the team meeting or the one-on-one with a boss, *communitas* can happen in the liminal spaces of the company picnic or (especially) the happy hour after work. At the local bar, where the blue collar laborer and the white collar executive sit down together and have a beer, nobody is higher or lower. We are reminded that our coworkers are just human beings, not social statuses.

From Turner's point of view, *communitas* is a real human need, as is social structure. But *communitas* stands in continuous tension with social structure.[31] As structure and *communitas* are in dialectical opposition, they are equal modalities of human society.[32] The modalities of structure and anti-structure together "constitute the human condition, as regards man's relations with his fellow man."[33] *Communitas* provides social cohesion, a sense of duty to one another in society; structure, on the other hand, provides the needed organization and institutions necessary for common life. At Woodstock, the reason this *communitas* experience could only occur over a short span of four days was because, eventually, the regular business of life had to get done. In temporarily setting aside social structures, something as simple as taking out the trash became an enormous problem.

As a basic human need, *communitas* thus presents an ever-present challenge to social structures. The need for directness, to relate to other human beings as human beings, forces *communitas* to erupt whenever structure has a stranglehold over people in society. And in Turner's theory, the unresolved tension between the material necessity for social structures and their inborn inadequacy for complete social unity generates the social need for ritual. "Liminality," that other dimension of anti-structure, is the domain (ritual or otherwise) in which individuals are freed up from the constraints of structure in order to experience *communitas*.

Symbols of *communitas*

Turner held that the pure experience of *communitas* in the liminal moment of ritual could not last for long. By its nature, liminal *communitas* is spontaneous, immediate, and momentary. For it to be sustained for any length of time, even a few days, some kind of organization is necessary. Woodstock, for instance,

---

31. Turner, *Dramas, Fields, and Metaphors*, 274; Turner, *The Ritual Process*, 127.
32. Turner, *The Ritual Process*, 203.
33. Ibid., 130.

was not simply a bunch of young people hanging out; it was a music festival, and there still had to be performers on stage to set the tone and give the gathering purpose. Many experiences of *communitas* revolve around playing games, whether a group of friends playing or a large crowd watching a college football game, and these games can have rules from the simplest (tag) to the highly complex (football). But they share the feature that the participants or the fans enter as equals and share an experience in common with the other participants, while some participants, such as the musicians at Woodstock or the coach of the football team, may be called upon to a different experience of leading.

All of this prepares us to see that the Catholic Mass, although highly structured and led by ministers, can be a *communitas* experience for most parishioners. We all gather in a common space, with social status left at the door, and people more often than not sit side-by-side with people they might not otherwise encounter in their everyday lives. The ritual of the Mass brings people together in ways that they do not normally experience in the regular, workaday world. While the priest and deacon should not see themselves as rockstars on a stage, the ritual actions they perform do give a tone and purpose to the gathering among the people. One hopes that this sociality spills over into personal interaction, say at coffee and donuts afterwards. But the foundation is the Mass itself.

Turner calls these "institutionalized modalities of *communitas*." While spontaneous *communitas* is by nature concrete, immediate, personal, direct, and down-to-earth, a special characteristic of *communitas* is its power to encode itself in special symbol systems.[34] Operating on the symbolic level, ritual is able to evoke *communitas* by stripping away the definitions of the self found in our day-to-day structured existence, and by uncovering the more fundamental symbols of the meaning of human life.[35] These symbols, which always engage us first as feeling, are far more powerful than intellectual discourse about *communitas* alone. Why, for instance, pass around a greeting card for everyone in the office to write something they could just say aloud (e.g., congratulations)? The physical card, and the ritual of passing it around and writing on it, are a ritual that requires more thought and effort.

Turner therefore finds agreement with Douglas and Bellah in holding that teaching and preaching are not enough to instill a sense of the generic human

34. Ibid., *The Ritual Process*, 129.
35. Holmes, "Liminality and Liturgy," 390.

bond in society; the experience of *communitas* is dependent upon symbolic action. I shall explore, therefore, Turner's understanding of the relationship between symbols of *communitas* and individualism, and the attributes of symbolic figures of *communitas*, to help elucidate the deacon's liturgical roles as epiphanies of service.

Symbols of *communitas* and individualism

Symbols of *communitas*, which arise out of the matrix of liminal moments of existential *communitas*, can counteract the forces of individualism and alienation in society. The great importance Turner gives to the symbols of *communitas* for social life cannot be underscored enough. While spontaneous *communitas* is passing, changes that become incorporated into the social structures as a result of the experience of *communitas* are a different matter. On these occasions, the residue of the *communitas* experience carries over into structured society by altering it in some way. The concept of institutionalizing the experience of *communitas* allows one to picture more vividly the interrelation between *communitas* and structure. When Turner speaks of a certain unity in the tension that exists between the poles of structure and anti-structure, he is referring to those instances when a greater appreciation for *communitas* has actually altered the patterned ways of doing things in every day society. *Communitas* has the power to change the way we think and act with regard to our fellow man and woman in our regular lives.

It is not surprising that Turner found the heart of Christian worship to be in its *communitas* moments. As a corporate, institutional attempt to achieve the experience or reality of communion, Christian worship is distinctly and critically different from the world of structure surrounding it. The dynamic exchange that occurs with symbols of *communitas* is a key element in the process of creating a more communion-oriented assembly of ritual participants.

The power of ritual is this: the orchestration of sensory experience in symbol effectively embeds allied values into people's consciousness, endowing the moral with sensory power and the sensory with moral power.[36] Symbols of *communitas* are like units of "memory," wherein a group's values and

---

36. Victor Turner, *The Forest of Symbols: Aspects of Ndembu Ritual* (Ithaca, N.Y.: Cornell University Press, 1967), 30. The ritual symbol, "with its social excitement and directly physiological stimuli ... effects an interchange of qualities between its poles of meaning. Norms and values, on the one hand, become saturated with emotion, while the gross and basic emotions become ennobled through contact with social values."

deeply-held beliefs are stored.[37] The symbol, as the fundamental unit of ritual, is the necessary mechanism that periodically converts what is socially obligatory into what is personally desirable.[38] Ritual provides tangible and compelling personal experiences of the rightness and naturalness of the group's social moral values. Symbols make *communitas* values "the stuff of one's own experience of the world."[39]

Ritual, therefore, plays an important role in the process of social change. It binds the two societal forces of structure and *communitas* together. The effect of this mating is the incorporation of *communitas* values into the society's everyday structure.[40] Social structure itself, therefore, is not necessarily an impediment for ritual. But structures contrary to *communitas* limit the experience of spontaneous *communitas* in everyday life, and hence limit the effectiveness of ritual to induce and experience of *communitas*. Symbols of *communitas* operate in ritual to restructure society according to the more universal principles, but not to negate structures altogether.

Attributes of symbols of *communitas*

Symbols of *communitas* share many of the attributes of *communitas* itself. Turner described the figure who symbolizes *communitas* in the following way: "he is a stranger, a mediator, [who] acts for the whole community ... represents peace as against feud, and is unaligned with any specific political segment."[41] The symbolic figure of *communitas* mediates between the high and low, the powerful and weak, the rich and the poor. He is a reminder of the basic human bond and our fundamental commonness. Turner described St. Francis of Assisi, who marked himself with the symbolism of poverty, as a liminal figure who represented the religious values of *communitas* (in relation to both the structured church and the surrounding secular society). We know that Francis's idea of poverty, associated with *communitas,* was so extreme as to cause immense difficulties for his developing religious order. But the poverty of Francis, even in its institutionalized form as a rule for his order, was potent. Turner notes

37. Victor Turner, "Passages, Margins, and Poverty: Religious Symbols of *Communitas.* Part One," *Worship* 46 (1972): 399 and 409.

38. Turner, *The Forest of Symbols,* 46. See 90: The symbol is "the smallest unit of ritual which still retains the specific properties of ritual behavior."

39. Catherine Bell, *Ritual: Perspectives and Dimensions* (New York: Oxford University Press, 1999), 41.

40. Ibid.

41. Turner, *The Ritual Process,* 120.

that liminality often draws on poverty for its repertoire of symbols, particularly for its symbols of social relationship.[42]

Poverty's cousin, humility, also represents *communitas*. This is most clearly evident in the rituals of status elevation and reversal. In rituals of status elevation, such as at a coronation (or ordination), the subject is conveyed irreversibly from a lower to a higher position in an institutionalized system of positions, and he or she "learns" the importance of remaining rooted in *communitas* through a form of ritualized humiliation. For instance, in the rite of ordination the new priests prostrate themselves on the ground during the Litany of Saints. In some coronation rights, the new king or queen must kneel in order to be crowned. This humbling of the candidate has the long-term effect of pointing out to the candidate the social dimension of the office about to be received: it reminds them that the new position is not for themselves as much as it is for the common good.

Similarly, the rituals of status reversal have the same effect, but are tied to cyclical events that remind those in authority of the ultimate primacy of *communitas* over structure.[43] Think here of the medieval Feast of Fools. Or when young children, in a light moment of playfulness, are given the unusual opportunity to boss their parents around. Children love that kind of play. "He has thrown down the rulers from their thrones but lifted up the lowly."[44]

Hence, institutionalized *communitas* refers to *structures that are in fact at the service of communitas*: they employ structure to engender the possibility of relating to others more directly or intimately. The symbolic figures of *communitas* eschew the use of raw power and authority, and instead use the tools of persuasion and suggestion to instigate positive social change. Their exercise of whatever power they may have is marked by a humility that deflects any concerns of authoritarianism.

Turner advocates reinterpreting the symbols used in Christian worship using this perspective. No longer should we simply identify the way in which Christian symbols reflect or express the existing structure, but rather identify the way in which they point to and recreate the experience of *communitas*, as well as critique the existing social order.[45] Following the suggestion of Turner,

42. Ibid., 146.
43. Ibid., 166–203.
44. Lk 1:52.
45. Turner, "Passages, Margins, and Poverty," 494: "The vain task of trying to find out in what precise way certain symbols found in the ritual, poetry, or iconography of a given society 'reflect' or 'express' its social or political structure can then be abandoned. Symbols may well reflect not structure but anti-structure, and not only 'reflect' it but contribute to *creating* it."

we wish to ponder how the symbolic function of the deacon is oriented toward the support of *communitas* (or theologically, communion) among the people of God.

The Deacon as Symbol of *communitas*

According to the *National Directory for the Formation, Ministry and Life of Permanent Deacons in the United States*, deacons have a "special role to promote communion and to counter the strong emphasis on individualism prevalent in the United States."[46] The deacon does this by linking together the individual and diverse segments of the community of believers. Thus, the deacon functions in the church to combat excessive individualism, not only in his day-to-day roles, but also in the periodic moments of liturgy. In identifying the deacon as a symbol of *communitas* in the Mass, we can see, in a nuanced way, how the ritual function of the deacon is in service to the communion of the church.

From Anthropological *communitas* to Theological Communion

The anthropological principle of *communitas* is not precisely the theological principle of communion. The foundation of Turner's theory of community is what he called the "basic human bond." To assert that the true origin of human community is God, or better yet, the love that is God, one can make the transition from Turner's anthropology to Christian theology. In such a theological perspective, Turner's concept of *communitas* is valuable in describing the natural basis (the anthropological antecedent) for the supernatural communion of the people of God. Turner's theory lends itself to an understanding of the church as communion that is both dynamic and appreciative of her structures.

The Book of Acts, for example, offers an idealized description of the early church as a community immersed in *communitas* values: "All who believed were together and had all things in common; they would sell their property and possessions and divide them among all according to each one's need."[47]

---

46. United States Conference of Catholic Bishops, *National Directory for the Formation, Ministry, and Life of Permanent Deacons in the United States* (Washington, D.C.: United States Conference of Catholic Bishops, 2005), no. 57 (31).

47. Acts 2:44–45. See Luke Timothy Johnson, *The Acts of the Apostles*, Sacra Pagina 5, ed. Daniel Harrington (Collegeville, Minn.: Liturgical Press, 1992), 61: "Luke's portrait of this first community is obviously idealized. Not that the first believers could not have been intense in their unity and joy;

The parallels between this description of the early church and Turner's description of liminality and *communitas* are not difficult to see. This biblical passage, however, reveals a more than merely human bond at work in the lives and experiences of the first Christians. Their theological bond is referred to as *koinonia*, in English, communion.

After the new Christians received the Holy Spirit, they could not go back to their old way of living. Their joy in the new life they had received meant that they felt moved by the Spirit to form an intense community of believers. Prayer and "the breaking of bread" were part of the routine, liminal moments which reinforced the spiritual fellowship of the church. They held all things in common and enjoyed intimate fellowship in their homes. The Spirit inspired many of them to great acts of generosity: "There was not a needy person among them, for as many as owned lands or houses sold them and brought the proceeds of what was sold. They laid it at the apostles' feet, and it was distributed to each as any had need."[48] The social divisions present in the outside secular world did not seem to matter, for the first Christians appear to have lived as a single, large family. This particular passage from Acts reminds the church of successive generations how the church should ideally be experienced—more community than institution. Indeed, the scriptures, as a form of ideological *communitas*, have spurred on many a reform movement and religious order to purge acquired habits and structures that have inhibited the true life and mission of the church.

As communion involves more than the human bond of *communitas*, the origin of Christian communion has to be located in the love of God. This love, we are told in the scriptures, is the origin and fundamental principle of the love Christians have for one another. "If someone who has worldly means sees a brother in need and refuses him compassion, how can the love of God remain in him? Children, let us love not in word or speech but in deed and truth."[49] Love is the central, binding force of Christian community. St. Paul encourages the members of the church at Colossae to put on "compassion, kindness, humility, meekness, and patience. Bear with one another and, if anyone has a complaint against another, forgive each other; just as the Lord has forgiven you, so you also must forgive. Above all, clothe yourselves with love, which binds everything together in perfect harmony."[50]

---

they probably were.... But the description is idealized in the literary sense, especially in his use of the language associated in Hellenistic philosophy with the *topos* on friendship, when he characterizes the community as having *koinonia*, and holding all their possessions in common (*panta koina*)."

48. Acts 4:34–35.

49. 1 Jn 3:17–18.

50. Col 3:12–14.

The *communitas* of the church, born from the experience of God's first love, empowers the church to proclaim the good news of communion with God and his people. This Gospel both supports and challenges Christians in their everyday life. Today, the church continues to be what Turner called a "normative *communitas*" over and against the various secular structures: the church is both a sign and reality of the kingdom of God that is yet to come, where the false distinctions between men and women, rich and poor, slaves and masters, Jews and Greeks, no longer hold people apart.[51] In the covenant established in the death and resurrection of Jesus, all worldly structures lose their significance before the all-powerful love of the Father. All people are one in Christ Jesus, regardless of the divisions that exist in society along racial, economic, and gender-specific lines.

The Deacon's Symbolic Orientation

The unity of the liturgical assembly is given prominent attention in the *General Instruction of the Roman Missal* (hereafter "GIRM") when it describes the people of God as the subject of liturgical action: "The celebration of Mass, as the action of Christ and the People of God arrayed hierarchically, is the center of the whole Christian life for the Church both universal and local, as well as for each of the faithful individually."[52] The communion of the liturgical assembly, which John Paul II described as "the pre-eminent place of unity," is not only expressed but also regenerated in the action of the eucharist.[53] To experience the renewal of communion, however, requires the avoidance of individualism or division: the practice of charity goes hand in hand with the offering of the eucharist.

The ritual of the eucharist thus responds to excessive individualism and structural divisions experienced in our day-to-day world. In this sacramental memorial, the individual steps out of the socially structured world and into a liminal period of sacrificial abandonment to the good. In this liminal moment, we wrestle with the memory of Christ and the stirrings of the Spirit in our hearts. The corporate community of the church and the individual are made vulnerable and are challenged to make advancements in the journey toward

51. See Gal 4:26–28 and Col 3:11.

52. Congregation for Divine Worship and Discipline of the Sacraments, *General Instruction of the Roman Missal*, third typical edition, no. 16, in *The Liturgy Documents: A Parish Resource*, 4th ed. (Chicago: Liturgy Training Publications, 2004), 40.

53. Pope John Paul II, *Dies Domini*, Apostolic Letter, May 31, 1998, par. 36; available at www.vatican.va.

greater communion with God and each other. The ritual transgression of social structures in the eucharist displays the order of justice with its implications for society.

The Ritual Role of the Deacon in the Mass

Participation in the eucharist continues the transformation and empowerment of the celebrants so that they may return to life with deeper understanding, renewed strength, and invigorated hope. Authentic eucharistic worship is therefore eminently related to the practice of social justice.[54] Deacons, by their presence at the celebration and by the tasks they accomplish in accord with their charism, serve the authentic worship of the church. Deacons unite the service of the table of the Word to the tables of eucharist and charity in their ritual ministry. They are the ministers of the threshold, the ones who assist the assembly to enter the profundity of the mystery being celebrated and thereafter to go back to the world to which the assembly is sent.[55]

As one intimately involved in the life and charitable work of the community, the deacon should be well qualified to model the compassion and service of Christ, to voice the needs of the community to the assembly itself, and to call the assembly to active, full participation in the mission of the church. The GIRM describes the deacon in general terms as a servant of the assembly, assisting the bishop or priest and the laity.[56] Consequently, the deacon's function in the Mass is not limited to the descriptions provided in the GIRM. For example, the *Ceremonial of Bishops* mentions the appropriateness of the deacon as a master of ceremonies, though the GIRM does not.[57] Our concern,

54. See R. Kevin Seasoltz, "Justice and the Eucharist," in *Living Bread, Saving Cup: Readings on the Eucharist*, ed. R. Kevin Seasoltz (Collegeville, Minn.: Liturgical Press, 1982–87), 322. Christopher Kiesling critiques the liturgical reform following the Second Vatican Council from the perspective of social justice in his article, "Liturgy and Social Justice," *Worship* 51 (1977): 351–61. Unfortunately, Kiesling gives no attention to the liturgical role of the deacon. See also William Shawn McKnight, "Ritual and the Call to Service: How the Eucharist Promotes the Practice of Social Justice," *Newman Review* 2 (2001): 79–96.

55. Olivier Windels, "Le ministère diaconal en liturgie," *Nouvelle revue théologique* 119, no. 3 (1977): 397–404.

56. Congregation for Divine Worship and the Discipline of the Sacraments, *General Instruction of the Roman Missal*, no. 94.

57. Congregation for Divine Worship and the Discipline of the Sacraments, *Ceremonial of Bishops*, no. 36 (26): "Within a celebration a master of ceremonies who is an ordained deacon may wear a dalmatic and the other diaconal vestments." It is worthy of note that only members of the order of deacons may wear their proper vestments for the eucharistic liturgy when serving as masters of

however, is to consider certain key roles of the deacon that are most directly related to the observance of *communitas* values and the experience of spiritual communion in the Mass.

There are seven duties that are ordinarily the deacon's and which favor the understanding of the deacon as a symbol of *communitas*: (1) the proclamation of the Gospel; (2) the announcement of the general intercessions; (3) the preparation of the gifts; (4) the elevation of the chalice; (5) the invitation to offer the sign of peace; (6) the distribution of the eucharist; and finally, (7) the dismissal.

The proclamation of the Gospel

In the ordination rite of the deacon, as the bishop hands the newly ordained deacon the Gospel book, the bishop says to the deacon: "Receive the Gospel of Christ, whose herald you have become. Believe what you read, teach what you believe, and practice what you teach."[58] It is the privilege of the deacon to proclaim the Gospel in the liturgy.[59] In the West the delivery of the Gospel was the deacon's duty from the earliest of times.[60] St. Jerome (ca. 420 A.D.) mentions deacons reading the Gospel, implying that it was a customary function for deacons at that time.[61]

In the proclamation of the Gospel, the assembly hears the story of God's love for us in the gift of the Son. Special significance is given to the reading of the Gospel in several ways: the special blessing the deacon receives from the priest or bishop, which manifests his mandate to preach the Gospel; the use

ceremonies. Presbyters (or a bishop, as in the case of the master of ceremonies of the current pope) do not wear stoles when serving as masters of ceremonies. This restriction visually testifies that the service of a master of ceremonies is proper to the charism of the diaconate only and not to the other orders.

58. Congregation for Divine Worship and Discipline of the Sacraments, *Rites of Ordination of a Bishop, of Priests, and of Deacons*, second typical edition, no. 238 (Washington, D.C.: United States Conference of Catholic Bishops, 2003), 162.

59. Congregation for Divine Worship and the Discipline of the Sacraments, *General Instruction of the Roman Missal*, no. 94; United States Conference of Catholic Bishops, *National Directory*, no. 35.

60. Josef A. Jungmann, *The Mass of the Roman Rite: Its Origins and Development (Missarum Sollemnia)*, trans. Francis A. Brunner and revised by Charles K. Riepe (London: Burns and Oates, 1951–61), 284.

61. Jerome, "Letter to Sabinianus," in NPNF-II 6:292: "and to remove all suspicion, you used to be for ever reading Christ's gospel as if you were a deacon indeed." The Syrian *Apostolic Constitutions* (ca. 380 A.D.) attests deacons reading the Gospel in the liturgy of the eucharist. See W. Jardine Grisbrooke, *The Liturgical Portions of the Apostolic Constitutions: A Text for Students*, Grove Liturgical Study 61 (Bramcote: Grove Books Limited, 1990), 15: "Afterwards let our Acts be read, and the Epistles of Paul our fellow-worker, which he sent to the Churches under the direction of the Holy Spirit; and after that let a presbyter or a deacon read the Gospels" (II, 57, 7).

of a special Gospel book, which contains Christ's words; the reservation of its proclamation to the deacon; the utilization of special signs that surround its proclamation, such as the greeting by the deacon, the blessing, and procession with candles and incense; and finally, the assembly's standing throughout the proclamation, a sign of their respect and active reception of the word. The proclamation of the Gospel is treated with special reverence because the Gospel tells the story of Jesus's life, the culmination of all that came before and the source of all that follows in the history of salvation: they are the most sacred form of "ideological *communitas*" that the church possesses.

The greatest personal honor given to the deacon as minister of the Gospel is the formal preaching of the homily at Mass.[62] The *National Directory* states: "In his preaching and teaching, the deacon articulates the needs and hopes of the people he has experienced, thereby animating, motivating, and facilitating a commitment among the lay faithful to an evangelical service in the world."[63] In this statement is found one of the most developed articulations of the role of the deacon in our day. The vision of the deacon's role in the church and wider community presented here is noteworthy for how it matches the sacramental character of the diaconate with the contemporary needs we experience in the United States. In this perspective we can see more clearly how the deacon's ministry of the Word is an epiphany of service.

The general intercessions

The general intercessions are one form of response to the word proclaimed, received, and pondered. Following the introduction by the priest, "it is the deacon himself who normally announces the intentions of the Prayer of the Faithful, from the ambo" (GIRM 177). The GIRM describes the general intercessions as the people "exercising the office of their baptismal priesthood" (GIRM 69), interceding for all humanity in that petitions are offered for the church, for civil authorities, for those oppressed by various needs, for all people, and for the salvation of the world (GIRM 70). After the announcement of each intention by the deacon, the assembly prays a common invocation, which is in the form of a supplication usually addressed to Christ. The general intercessions thus manifest the corporate, priestly nature of the church and broaden the vision of the local assembly, moving them beyond their own immediate

---

62. Congregation for Divine Worship and the Discipline of the Sacraments, *General Instruction of the Roman Missal*, no. 66 (35).

63. United States Conference of Catholic Bishops, *National Directory*, no. 58 (31).

problems, worries, and needs, and causes them to consider the needs of others.

It is significant that the deacon has a role in this liminal moment of the liturgy between the proclamation of the Word and the offering of the eucharist. At this time, the hearts, minds, and voices of the laity are brought into active participation in the liturgy on behalf of the needs of the wider human community. In some of the earlier traditions, the general intercessions of the assembly ended with the sign of peace. This sequence appropriately associated the communion of the assembly and their mission of care and concern for those beyond the community.

It is most fitting that the deacon, who is a social intermediary, be given the privilege to announce the intentions of the assembly. In doing so, the deacon directly confronts our tendency toward individualism. The liturgy of the Word is not completed, however, by simply instilling concern for others in the minds and hearts of the faithful. The eucharistic passage toward greater communion continues in the presentation and preparation of the gifts. The flow of the Mass moves from the concern for others expressed in our prayer of the general intercessions, to the action of taking up a collection and the presentation of the other gifts for the eucharistic offering.

Presentation and preparation of the gifts

The rites of presentation and preparation of the gifts concern the procession of gifts from and by the people, and their preparation by the deacon. The procession manifests the laity's charity and their own participation in the eucharist offered at the altar by the priest-officiant. The GIRM states succinctly the procedure and purpose of the rite of presentation: "It is praiseworthy for the bread and wine to be presented by the faithful. They are then accepted at an appropriate place by the priest or the deacon and carried to the altar.... It is well also that money or other gifts for the poor or for the Church, brought by the faithful or collected in the church, should be received."[64] The essential nucleus of this part of the liturgy is the deposition on the altar of the bread and wine that will become the body and blood of Christ. "The preparation of the altar and gifts corresponds to the Lord's 'taking' of bread and wine at the Last Supper."[65] The procession of bread and wine by the laity has its own special

---

64. Congregation for Divine Worship and the Discipline of the Sacraments, *General Instruction of the Roman Missal*, no. 73 (52).

65. Michael Witczak, "The Sacramentary of Paul VI," in *Handbook for Liturgical Studies* (ed. Chupungco), 3:151.

meaning of self-offering, but it also symbolizes in the larger context the duties of fraternal charity.[66] The practice of taking up a collection for the poor during the eucharistic ceremony, and then uniting it with the procession of material elements for the eucharistic offering, maintains a ritual connection between eucharistic worship and fraternal charity. As we recall, St. Paul stressed the importance of fraternal charity as the context of the eucharist in his first letter to the Corinthian church. The procession of gifts manifests the sharing of the whole assembly in the eucharist, as well as the sharing of their gifts received from God with those in need.[67]

The significance of deacons assisting with the reception and preparation of the bread and wine is seen in its fullness only in relation to their role in the distribution of Communion back to the people later in the Mass. The deacon is intimately involved in the process of the *sacrum commercium*, where the holy exchange takes place "in the procession with the gifts to the altar, followed by the prayer over them, and their return to the people in communion."[68] The deacon is an assistant here to both the priest-officiant and the laity. Using Turner's language, the deacon's function is a ceremonial reflection of his position in the church. As the deacon mediates the flow of information, materials, power, and knowledge outside of the liminal domain of the Mass, so he mediates, assists and arranges the flow and distribution that occurs between the people and the altar. In this the deacon assists the engagement of the laity's charisms in the action of the eucharist, affirming the fundamental unity of the assembly, and he assists social action for those in need.

66. Dix, *The Shape of the Liturgy*, 118: "In the primitive rite this self-offering was expressed by *action* in the offertory, simply by the silent setting of the church's offerings by the church's servants (the deacons) upon the altar, which in the early symbolism was itself thought of as representing Christ."

67. Jungmann, *The Mass*, 316: "The evolution must have been such that the offerings which had always been made for the needs of the Church and the poor were gradually drawn more closely into the liturgical pattern. The tie-in with the eucharistic celebration was all the easier since it had been customary to think of every gift to the Church and the poor as a gift to God, or even to designate it as an offering, an oblation. Thus, such gifts of Christian charity were joined to the offering of the Eucharist. It was, then, but a step to connect the offering made by the faithful with the ritual preparation of the gifts for the eucharistic sacrifice—a step which would be taken naturally in an age which was liturgically alive. Thus we find in almost all the liturgies since the fourth century an offering (in some form or other) of gifts directed towards the Eucharist. As a passing custom it was practically universal in the Church."

68. Ralph Keifer, "Preparation of the Altar and the Gifts or Offertory?," *Worship* 48 (1974): 599.

The elevation of the chalice

The most exalted assistance the deacon provides at the altar is the sacrificial gesture of elevating the chalice at the end of the eucharistic prayer. Unlike the showing of the eucharistic species to the faithful at other times, which the priest or bishop does by himself, the sacrificial gesture lifting up the consecrated bread and wine represents our giving back to God the Father the Son he gave us. Originally, the deacon assisted at this apex of the eucharistic liturgy out of physical necessity. The *Ordo Romanus I* of the early Middle Ages describes the sacrificial gestures of offering in the following way: "the bishop elevates the consecrated bread and with it touches the heavy chalice that the archdeacon at his side likewise elevates by its handles; the two celebrants retain this posture until the Amen of the congregation has died away."[69] The proximity of the deacon to the priest, both within and outside the liturgy, necessarily entails a close cooperation between the two. As the deacon assists the priest in the sacrificial gesture that accompanies the doxology of the eucharistic prayer, so he helps the one who has the responsibility of presidency over the charisms of the people of God outside the liturgy. The deacon assists the head of the community in making sure that the charisms of the people of God are fully utilized and are offered by them sacrificially for the service of the Gospel.

The sign of peace

Following the Lord's Prayer and the prayer for peace in the embolism, it is the deacon who invites the assembly to exchange the sign of peace (GIRM 181). In the Roman tradition, the sign of peace takes place after the eucharistic prayer as a seal of the sacrificial offering rather than preparing for it. This was probably not always the case for the West, for St. Justin Martyr and the *Apostolic Tradition* attributed to Hippolytus mention the sign of peace at the beginning of the eucharistic liturgy, and St. Cyprian connects the peace with the gifts carried to the altar.[70] In 416 A.D. Pope Innocent I wrote to the bishop of Gubbio,

69. *Ordo Romanus* I, nos. 89–90, in Michel Andrieu, *Les "Ordines Romani" du haut moyen âge* (Louvain: Spicilegium sacrum Lovaniense, 1931), 2:96. Referenced in Robert Cabié in *The Church at Prayer*, ed. Aimé G. Martimort, vol. 2: *The Eucharist*, trans. Matthew J. O'Connell (Collegeville, Minn.: Liturgical Press, 1986), 106.

70. Cabié, *The Eucharist*, 115. St. Justin Martyr and the *Apostolic Tradition of St. Hippolytus*, however, only mention the kiss of peace in connection with initiation or ordination. Cabié notes with interest "that the kiss of peace was exchanged before communion in Churches in which the preparation of the gifts involved a procession of the faithful to the sanctuary."

insisting that the only proper moment for the sign of peace was after the eucharistic prayer, the sign serving as the prayer's completion.[71] Ever since, the sign of peace has followed the eucharistic prayer and preceded Communion in the Roman liturgy.[72] The sign of peace, coming as it does after the prayer and before the Communion rite, signifies that God's loving action in the Paschal sacrifice is the source of the assembly's peace. The ritual gesture of the sign of peace thus declares peace and communion to be the fruit of the eucharist, and not simply the result of the participants' desire, effort, or willpower.

The sign of peace is also a sign of the individual's dedication to living the charity it signifies: it is a ritual rejection of the individualistic lifestyle. It also checks the tendency to perceive the reception of Communion that follows in an individualistic manner. After calling upon "Our Father" in the Lord's Prayer, participants encounter one another directly in the sign of peace. In this moment there is a breakdown of social restraints that Turner associated with the experience of *communitas*. The normal structures of society are altered, as the people are personally present to those around them in a direct and immediate fashion. They "are nakedly sisters and brothers before God, stripped of all roles and distinctions and pretenses and impediments, free of all baggage that we normally carry."[73] If this recognition of one another is genuine, the symbol's efficaciousness will not only alter but will create the reality it signifies. "That experience is meant to be a fresh glimpse—being stung to a new awareness—of other people: seeing other people with one's kingdom glasses and with a profound reverence, simply as sisters and brothers under God in the Spirit through Christ."[74] Thus, the sign of peace is an important stage along the ritual path to communion in the eucharist.

The deacon's role in the sign of peace is very simple. The deacon gives a straightforward, verbal invitation to the assembly to engage in the ritual act. What is significant is that the church has given this role *ordinarily* to the order of deacons. It is true that the deacon is generally the one who addresses the movement and posture of the assembly anyway, but the invitation to the sign of peace is much more significant than inviting the people to stand or be seat-

71. Innocent I, *Epistola* 25, cap. 1 (PL 20:553).

72. Domenic E. Serra, "The Greeting of Peace in the Revised Sacramentary: A New Pastoral Option," in *Liturgy for the New Millennium: A Commentary on the Revised Sacramentary. Essays in Honor of Anscar J. Chupungco, O.S.B.*, ed. Mark Francis and Keith Pecklers (Collegeville, Minn.: Liturgical Press, 2000), 102.

73. Robert W. Hovda, "Pastoral Guidelines," in *It Is Your Own Mystery: A Guide to the Communion Rite*, ed. Melissa Kay (Washington, D.C.: Liturgical Conference, 1977), 19.

74. Ibid., 20.

ed. At this ritual moment, the deacon more directly facilitates the assembly's entry into the mystery of fraternal communion during the eucharistic passage. The process leading to communion with God is never separate from progress in communion on the horizontal level.

Distribution of Communion

The ritual passage to communion culminates in the assembly's reception of Communion. The sign of peace, the breaking of bread, and the distribution of Communion can be seen as a single, sacramental action, different moments in the expression of one reality. And the deacon has an important role at each stage. The gift presented by the laity, arranged by the deacon and blessed by the priest-officiant is now returned to the laity as the gift of God. Consequently, the principal action of the Communion rite is the procession of the assembly to the altar: unlike the entrance procession, which involves the presider and the ministers of the celebration, and the procession at the preparation of the gifts, which involves representatives of the community, this procession involves all those who will participate in Communion. They are members of the body of Christ receiving the body of Christ.[75]

The act of receiving Communion is an intimate gesture of receiving the Lord. Communion binds the communicants to one another and to God in fellowship by eating and drinking, actions that are anthropologically significant. Eating and drinking in the context of a meal pertain to more than the satiation of hunger and thirst. The consumption of nourishment takes on a social reality when received and shared with other people. Fellowship distinguishes a meal from a casual grouping of people eating and drinking at the same time, as one would at a fast-food bar at an airport. Communion ritually manifests the fellowship of those who share the same meal that is the eucharist.

The role of the deacon in this normative experience of *communitas* is important for my thesis. The deacon assists the priest-officiant in preparing and distributing the sanctified elements. Furthermore, there is a special relationship between the deacon and the cup: the deacon distributes "the Eucharist to the faithful, especially under the species of wine" (GIRM 94). Not only does the deacon distribute Communion to the assembly, but also to those who are absent from the eucharistic gathering because of illness: "As an ordinary minister of Holy Communion, the deacon distributes the Body of Christ to the

75. Witczak, "The Sacramentary of Paul VI," 166.

faithful during the celebration of the Mass and, outside of it, administers Viaticum to the sick."[76] In giving Communion to the home-bound, the deacon ritually communicates the love and concern of the assembly to those who are marginalized by their illness. The deacon thus extends the sacramental communion of the assembly even to those physically separate from it. The deacon's ritual role in preparing and distributing the eucharist symbolically manifests the communion of the church, even serving as a bridge to overcome certain obstacles that prevent the participation of some of the faithful.

Dismissal

Finally, it is the deacon who gives the last word at Mass to the people, dismissing the assembly back into the world from which they came. Back to the same world, yes, but with the assembly changed by their experience of communion with God and one another, and with a sense of being "missioned." While it is the function of the priest or bishop to give the final blessing, it is the role of the deacon to give the command to the people to live out the mysteries they have received. The deacon has been given new formulae, at the behest of Pope Benedict XVI, to make this more explicit ("Go and announce the Gospel of the Lord"; and "Go in peace, glorifying the Lord by your life").[77] Having moved further along the path of conversion, the people are now empowered to manifest the mercy of God in their daily life. They are sent forth to carry the Word made flesh into the world. The deacon, in distinction to the priest, is *the* personal symbolic figure who manifests the bridge between worship at the altar and the worship of moral life. Having a foot in the sanctuary and in the public square, deacons are unique in their ability to manifest the comprehensive character of true Christian worship.

Conclusion: The Deacon Is a Symbol of *Communitas*

My consideration of diaconal roles in the Mass suggests that the deacon is a symbol of *communitas*. Their liturgical roles induce a symbiotic interpenetration of individual and society, warding off sentiments and notions of excessive utilitarian individualism. As with other authentic Christian symbols, in vary-

---

76. Congregation for the Clergy, *Directory*, no. 32 (98).

77. Pope Benedict XVI, *Sacramentum Caritatis*, Post-Synodal Apostolic Exhortation, February 22, 2007, par. 51; available at www.vatican.va.

ing degrees, they effectively communicate the overarching Christian cosmology within which the individual believer is bonded to the church. Symbols, including the symbolic role of the deacon in the Mass, are a necessary part of the internalization process that we call conversion, for they influence the transformation of the whole person. Christian conversion is about adopting a whole new way of living in relation to God and others, not just accepting concepts or doctrinal definitions. This is why preaching and teaching the concept of communion is not enough. Entry into the kingdom of God requires a transformed heart, emptied of all selfish desires and motivations, and overflowing with love for others.

The image of Christ the servant evokes the fundamental attitude that all Christians are called to have in the world. All of the church's symbols of *communitas* refer in some way to Christ the servant, challenging and invigorating her members to change themselves and transform the world into an authentic human community of love. These symbols affirm the rightness and naturalness of the church's communion values. Through the dynamic exchange of symbols of *communitas* in the Mass, the communion lived and preached by Jesus Christ becomes the personal desire of the members in the body of Christ.

The deacon is thus an important figure in the church's symbolic ratification of her own identity as the people of the New Covenant. But deacons are not the only operative symbols of *communitas* in the ritual passage to communion. Nor do deacons have a monopoly on the service they provide in the Mass. In their absence, others can fulfill the concrete services deacons render in the liturgy, but only in a strictly practical sense. The symbolism of the diaconate belongs only to the members of the order and to no others.

The gift of diaconal spirit makes them symbolic figures of Christ the servant and empowers them to perform certain functions reserved to them within the life of the church. The ritual functions of the deacon in the Mass bring into focus the communion already present in the church. Insofar as the deacon serves the entire assembly's active participation in the eucharistic action, the fundamental unity of the church rooted in baptism is brought to the surface and experienced. Insofar as the deacon assists the assembly's active concern for the needs of others, the deacon is a sign of the church's solidarity with the poor. In these ways the deacon is a sign of the kingdom in the life and mission of the church.

The same ritual functions of the deacon also challenge the assembly where communion and solidarity are lacking. In communities where access to the decisionmaking process is sharply curtailed, the deacon's ritual roles would challenge the propriety of such behavior. By engaging the charisms of the assembly (as evident in the general intercessions, preparation of the gifts, sign of peace, and Communion) deacons guide individuals into the corporate action of the eucharist. The deacon's assistance to the assembly counters any tendency of the Mass to become an offering of just the priest-officiant and not that of the whole assembly. In serving as a symbol of *communitas*, the deacon's ritual role challenges the attitudes and behaviors of the assembly that are contrary to the eschatological values of the kingdom.

As herald of the Gospel, announcer of the intentions, assistant at the presentation and preparation of the gifts, instigator of the sign of peace, distributor of the eucharist, and the one who missions the assembly, the deacon is ordained to symbolize Christ the servant to the assembly in a way that no one else can. Only the deacon is ritually deputed to fulfill these functions as a deacon. Because he has been specially graced to symbolize Christ the servant, both within the liturgical assembly and in the church's everyday structure, the deacon creatively regenerates communion among the people of God. The very person of the deacon is a permanent sign that points to the fundamental ground of the church's communion—the love who is God—and animates the people of God to respond with active charity toward one another. Thus, the church's practice of entrusting to the figure of the deacon these functions associated with social mediation and *communitas* symbolism is respectful of the anthropological dimension of the church as well as her theological purpose. To fulfill their mission of transforming the world into the kingdom, the people of God need a structure such as the diaconate and the symbolism of the deacon to bridge the distance between the altar and their social life. For these reasons the deacon is, especially in the liturgy, an epiphany of service.

CHAPTER 8

Evaluating the Structure of Diaconal Ministry Today

Having explored the role of the deacon through its biblical, historical, and anthropological roots, I am now ready to articulate a clear role for the deacon in keeping with the restoration of the diaconate as a stable order among the people of God as called for by the Second Vatican Council. In essence, I have confirmed the teaching of Pope Paul VI following the Council: the diaconate is an intermediate order that should accomplish three ends: express the needs and desires of the Christian faithful, serve as a driving force for service among the people of God, and symbolize Christ the servant. I have expressed these first two elements using the sociological concept of a "social intermediary" and the third role using the anthropological concept of a symbol of *communitas* (or, theologically speaking, Communion). This role is a true *diakonia*, the service of a "go-between" commissioned by God to unite more closely the people of God and to draw them into relations that are truly human and filled with divine charity. They place the deacon in a unique position to answer Pope Francis's call to be ministers of mercy.

This role specificity, we have seen, was not fully fleshed out by the Second Vatican Council, but it does build upon the foundation of the Council's teaching. It taught that deacons, strengthened by sacramental grace, serve the church by fulfilling the tasks entrusted to them. In chapter 2, I noted that the concrete tasks of the diaconate were left largely undetermined by the Council. The Council did not even wish to bind the church of future generations to its own specific listing of liturgical functions that it deemed possible for the diaconate. The Council did, however, lay the foundation from which the specific tasks of diaconal ministry were to develop. In LG 29, the Council used the general categories of *liturgy, word,* and *charity* to describe the ministry of deacons, linking diaconal ministry with that of bishops and presbyters. With greater specificity, LG 29 states that "duties of charity and administration" constitute the domain of diaconal ministry. The Council again highlighted the deacon's service of charity and administration in AG 16. In other words, the Council gave only a general sketch of diaconal ministry and left the responsibility of filling in the details to future competent authorities. It did firmly establish the service of charity as the fundamental logic of the diaconate.

The study of intermediate social structures in chapter 3 found that Paul VI's threefold vision for the diaconate, if properly implemented, could benefit the life and mission of the church. As an intermediate institution, the diaconate could assist the participation of the faithful in the life and mission of the church; assist in the exercise of power and authority by the bishop or parish pastor; and assist the faithful in the church's embrace of the world, especially the poor. In fulfilling these needs, the deacon-intermediary would fortify the church's social foundations for the experience of communion and the practice of *koinonia* among the people of God.

Furthermore, accentuating the deacon as a symbol of *communitas,* rather than a rank in the hierarchy, could reinforce the Christological and ecclesial character of diaconal ministry. Deacons who embrace the spirit of humility resemble the Lord more closely and imbibe sentiments of mutual love and respect among the people of God. The perspective of the deacon as a symbol of *communitas* could elucidate the liturgical and administrative roles of the deacon as institutional means, patterned after the humble way of Jesus, which build up the body of Christ by leading people to greater personal conversion in the life of faith. As symbols of Christ the servant and as agents of the love of the Good Shepherd, deacons would fulfill their ordination charge to be ambassadors of God's love and mercy to the church and to the world in their service of charity.

Having come to this clearer definition of the deacon's role, the task remains to integrate these general notions into the specifics of twenty-first-century parish life and diocesan church order. This chapter will explore ways in which local churches could structure their diaconal ministry under the paradigm of social intermediary and symbol of *communitas.* I will take into consideration the structure of diaconal ministry that is presented in the *Directory for the Ministry and Life of Permanent Deacons* from the Congregation for the Clergy.[1] The *Directory*

---

1. Congregation for Catholic Education and Congregation for the Clergy, *Basic Norms.*

is fairly recent (1998), universally authoritative in nature, and the most extensive treatment of diaconal ministry by the Magisterium. It provides a certain amount of stability for the diaconate, serving as a template from which local norms are to be established by the episcopal conferences.[2] I will also look at the *National Directory for the Formation, Life and Ministry of Permanent Deacons in the United States* promulgated by the United States Conference of Catholic Bishops (in December 2004) to "guide and harmonize the formation programs drawn up by each diocese of the conference," as well as to implement the *Directory* from the Congregation for the Clergy.[3]

Using insights gained from the study of intermediate social structures, the history of the diaconate, and the significance of the deacon's ritual ministry, I will build upon elements within the *Directory* that favor the deacon as social intermediary and symbol of *communitas*. I will reference the *National Directory* when it provides a particular emphasis or specificity. It will be important to note the difference between what deacons *can* do (both theologically and canonically) and what is most *fitting* for diaconal ministry. Following the pattern established in this book, we will draw attention to the ways in which the deacon facilitates the participation of the faithful in the life of the church, and the ways in which the deacon inspires care and concern among the people of God for the poor.

When deacons function as intermediaries between the bishop or pastor and the laity, the first avenue of their mediation requires access to the decision-makers of the diocese: the bishop and his primary delegates at the diocesan level, and the pastor at the parish level.[4] Familiarity with the needs, desires, and charisms of the laity represents the other side of effective mediation. In

---

2. The *Directory* provides the general structure of diaconal ministry for the entire world. The *Joint Declaration* states: "The growth of the permanent Diaconate, however, gives rise to a need for a certain unity of direction and clarification of concepts, as well as for practical encouragement and more clearly defined pastoral objectives. The total reality of the Diaconate—embracing its fundamental doctrinal vision, discernment of vocation, as well as the life, ministry, spirituality and formation of deacons— calls for a review of the journey thus far made, so as to arrive at a global vision of this grade of Sacred Orders corresponding to the desire and intention of the Second Vatican Council" (page 7 of the official English translation publication).

3. United States Conference of Catholic Bishops, *National Directory for the Formation, Life and Ministry of Permanent Deacons in the United States* (Washington, D.C.: United States Conference of Catholic Bishops, 2005), no. 14 (7).

4. The "ordinary" of a diocese is required to delegate certain powers to auxiliary bishops or priests in the governance of the diocese; for example, the vicar general and the judicial vicar (see CIC, cc. 134, 475–481, 1420). Having the ear of one of these delegates or others like them will be, for the purposes of this thesis, considered the same as having the ear of the bishop.

the examination of offices suggested by the *Directory*, I shall note the sectors of the church's life and mission that pertain to the competence of the diaconate. I will then evaluate these offices insofar as they assist the relationship between the bishop or pastor and their people.

Under the general heading of "pastoral ministry outside the chancery," I will consider the possibilities suggested by the *Directory* for the deacon's second avenue of mediation between the people of God and those who fall through the cracks of societal structures. If deacons function as social intermediaries between the people of God and the poor, then deacons must be familiar with the needs of those on the "peripheries" of their communities. Mediation of this sort also requires familiarity with the charisms and resources of the people of God. Does the *Directory* suggest the creation or utilization of institutional structures that would make it possible for the deacon to fulfill this dimension of his ministry? My analysis of the *Directory* will show to what extent Paul VI's vision of the diaconate as an intermediate order has already become a reality in the church today. Following my examination of the *Directory*, I shall present new concrete possibilities for the diaconate today as an intermediate institution at various levels of the diocese.

The Structure of the Deacon's Ministry in the Directory

According to the *Directory*, the office of deacon requires special charisms in addition to those of baptism. Rooted in the sacrament of holy orders, the deacon "finds the point of reference for his own ministry in hierarchical communion with the bishop."[5] Sharing in the one ministerial *ordo* with the bishop, deacons "participate in the same pastoral functions, but exercise them differently in serving and assisting the bishop and his priests."[6] "Serving and assisting the bishop" may not seem at first glance to be a function worthy of ordination. Indeed, it would not be worthy if it were no more than the service of a lackey. But deacons are not to "be relegated to marginal duties, be made merely to act as substitutes, nor discharge duties normally entrusted to non-ordained members of the faithful."[7] The deacon is not ordained simply to serve the bishop and his presbyterate as menial labor, but has a special ministry of promoting

---

5. USCCB, *Directory*, no. 48 (113–14).
6. Ibid., no. 37 (101).
7. Ibid., no. 40 (104).

full, conscious, and active participation of all the faithful in the life and mission of the church.[8]

Stable Offices Inside the Chancery

The offices in the chancery expressly forbidden for the deacon are membership on the presbyteral council and the offices reserved to presbyters: judicial vicar, adjunct judicial vicar, and vicar forane. The offices of vicar general and moderator of the curia are also beyond the sphere of the deacon, even though the *Directory* does not mention this.[9] However, for deacons who have the necessary skills, there are multiple opportunities in the chancery to assist the bishop closely in his ministry. A deacon who is well qualified "may exercise the office of chancellor, judge, assessor, auditor, promotor iustitiae [promoter of justice], defensor vinculi [defender of the bond] and notary."[10] I shall examine these offices in detail below. Expressly linking charity with "appropriate service in administration of goods," the deacon may also be appointed to "the office of diocesan oeconomus [finance officer]."[11] Deacons may also participate in diocesan pastoral councils, finance councils, and diocesan synods. My concern, however, centers upon the stable offices in the curia. As these offices are canonical in nature, reference to the *Code of Canon Law* (hereafter "CIC") is necessary to explicate their particular functions and to point out their relevance to the deacon as an intermediary.

Notary, chancellor, and vice-chancellor

Notaries are those individuals, duly appointed by the bishop, "whose writing or signature establishes the authenticity of any acts whatsoever, of judicial acts only or of the acts of a certain case or transaction only."[12] Their duties include preparing decrees and dispositions, to record faithfully what has taken place

8. Ibid., no. 37 (101): "Their authority, therefore, exercised in hierarchical communion with the bishop and his priests, and required by the same unity of consecration and mission, is a service of charity which seeks to help and foster all members of a particular Church, so that they may participate, in a spirit of communion and according to their proper charisms, in the life and mission of the Church."

9. CIC, c. 478 §1, states that the vicar general and episcopal vicar must be presbyters. CIC, c. 473 §2, requires the moderator of the curia to be a priest.

10. USCCB, *Directory*, no. 42 (107). The *Directory* cites the CIC, cc. 482, 483 §1, 1421 §1, 1424, 1428 §2, and 1435.

11. USCCB, *Directory*, no. 38 (103).

12. CIC, c. 483 §1.

with all proper notations, and to declare copies to be in conformity with the original.[13] The *chancellor* (and by extension, the *vice-chancellor*), is the primary notary and secretary of the curia, "whose principal task is, unless particular law determines otherwise, to see to it that the acts of the curia are gathered, arranged and safeguarded in the archive of the curia."[14] They are appointed by the bishop and can be freely removed by him.[15] The 1917 CIC required that the chancellor be a priest, but the revised 1983 CIC permits the diocesan bishop to appoint any person—lay, religious, or cleric—to the office.[16] The office of chancellor or vice-chancellor does not, therefore, involve the broad exercise of governance but centers on the custody and transmission of information to and from the bishop.[17] At first appearance, the office of chancellor structured in this manner would seem to provide the opportunity for the deacon-chancellor to act as an intermediary. Considering the nature of the position, the deacon-chancellor would be aware of the concerns of the bishop and would be directly involved with the transmission of decisions to the faithful.

Only the bishop and the chancellor have a key to the chancery archive, and it is the duty of the chancellor to provide to interested parties "an authentic written copy or a photocopy of documents which are public by their nature and which pertain to the status of such persons."[18] This highly administrative work of the chancellor and notaries may at first seem rather remote from "ministry." It is, however, necessary to safeguard the rights of those involved in formal communications between the chancery and the people whom it serves. Without such administrative figures and processes it is hard to imagine how the service of the bishop to the rest of the people of God could be met, in view of the large number of faithful in a given diocese. The deacon as chancellor, vice-chancellor, and notary would serve to meet the need for a mediator of information.[19]

13. CIC, c. 484.

14. CIC, c. 482.

15. CIC, c. 485.

16. CIC 1917, c. 372 §1.

17. John P. Beal, James Coriden, and Thomas Green (eds.), *New Commentary on The Code of Canon Law: An Entirely New and Comprehensive Commentary by Canonists from North America and Europe, with a Revised English Translation of the Code. Commissioned by The Canon Law Society of America* (Mahwah, N.J.: Paulist Press, 2000), 635: "According to this introductory canon, the primary function of the chancellor is to maintain the curial records. However, the history and practice indicate otherwise, especially in the United States.... The canon itself allows for local adaptation of the role of the chancellor. In a larger diocese with many curial offices, the chancellor may play a supervisory role in relation to the records generated in the various offices. Such supervision would include the establishment of records management as well as retention and access guidelines."

18. CIC, c. 487.

19. For more on the history of keeping archives in the church, see William F. Louis, *Diocesan*

The tribunal

Within the curia there is the judicial branch of the chancery, the tribunal office. Within the tribunal are several functions available to the deacon. The deacon can be a judge, assessor, auditor, promoter of justice, or defender of the bond. An ecclesiastical *judge* is a person appointed by the diocesan bishop to hear and decide cases brought to the ecclesiastical court.[20] Judges possess judicial power, one of the three forms of the "power of governance."[21] This is the power of governance that concerns decisionmaking in the setting of a court. The object of judicial power is "to prosecute or vindicate the rights of physical or juridic persons," "to declare juridic facts," and "to impose or declare the penalty for offenses."[22] While the bishop is free to appoint those who have the requisite qualities and degrees, either cleric or lay, the lay judge can only serve as part of a collegiate tribunal with two other clerics.[23] This limitation does not apply to the deacon. Though the offices of judicial vicar and adjutant judicial vicar are reserved to priests, the deacon, as a cleric-judge, can hear and decide certain cases by himself. Thus, the CIC treats the deacon distinctly from both the laity and presbyters in this instance. Yet it hardly seems that a judge, standing over the parties to make a decision, is a fitting role for a social intermediary; I will take up this question more thoroughly in my theological reflection at the conclusion of this section.

Delegation of judicial power is forbidden by the CIC, except in a limited way in the appointment of an *assessor* or *auditor* "to carry out acts which are preparatory to a decree or decision."[24] The CIC provides the right for a single judge to appoint up to two assessors to help him with his task: "the assessor is to advise toward the correct direction of the process and the adequate evaluation of the proofs, whenever difficulties present themselves in these matters: not to decide the controversy together with the judge."[25] The deacon as as-

Archives: An Historical Synopsis and Commentary, Canon Law Studies 137 (Washington, D.C.: The Catholic University of America Press, 1941). For more on the history of the office of chancellor, which has its roots in civil and university administration, see John E. Prince, The Diocesan Chancellor: An Historical Synopsis and Commentary, Canon Law Studies 167 (Washington, D.C.: The Catholic University of America Press, 1942).

20. Lawrence Wrenn, Procedures (Washington, D.C.: Canon Law Society of America, 1987), 16.

21. The other two forms are the legislative and executive. See CIC, c. 135.

22. CIC, c. 1400.

23. CIC, c. 1421.

24. CIC, c. 135 §3.

25. Zenon Grocholewski, "Asesores del juez único," Commentario Exegético al Código de Derecho Canónico, ed. A. Marzoa, J. Miras, and R. Rodríguez-Ocaña, 2nd ed., Instituto Martín de Azpilcueta

sessor participates in the judicial process as a special assistant or clerk to the judge, not exercising full decisionmaking power but giving advice and helping the judge evaluate the proofs. The deacon-assessor does not hold the power of governance outright, but exercises a certain amount of influence through the advice he or she gives the judge.

The single judge or the president of a collegiate tribunal can designate an *auditor* to carry out the instruction of a case. The task of the auditor is to collect the proofs according to the mandate of the judge; the auditor can also be empowered to decide which proofs are to be collected and how they are to be collected.[26] Unlike the assessor, the auditor does not assist the judge in determining the direction of the process or the evaluation of the material of the case. The auditor is thus further removed from the decisionmaking authority of the judge than the assessor, but still plays a key role in the decisionmaking process by determining which proofs are to be collected and how they are to be obtained in the fulfillment of his or her mandate.

The auditor is not, in fact, the final word on the evidence to be considered in a case. The judge or president of a collegiate tribunal has the ability to add or exclude things gathered by the auditor prior to the decision.[27] The use of auditors has been a point of contention among canonists.[28] The concern of some canonists is about auditors interfering with the direct communication between the judge (decisionmaking authority) and those directly involved with the matter of the case. This concern touches upon the issue of the deacon as intermediary among the people of God. The number of people in the

---

Facultad de Derecho Canónico Universidad de Navarra (Pamplona: EUNSA, 1997) (hereafter CECDC), 4.1:795: "El cometido de los asesores es aconsejar en orden a la correcta direción del proceso y a la adecuada valoración de las pruebas, cuando se presenten dificultades en esas materias: no, en cambio, decidir la controversia juntamente con el juez" (author's translation).

26. CIC, c. 1428 §3.

27. Zenon Grocholewski, "De los auditores y ponentes," in CECDC, 808.

28. Beal, *New Commentary*, 1627–28: "Cardinal Roberti, one of the more prestigious of the commentators on the procedural law of the 1917 Code, was of the opinion that judge instructors [auditors] did more harm than good, since their involvement necessarily resulted in the principal judge losing that immediate contact with the parties and witnesses that is so important in deciding a case. The same argument was made in an attempt to suppress the office of auditor in the 1983 Code at the April 8, 1978 meeting of the consultors of the Commission. The office has, however, been retained in the 1983 Code, and it has indeed been found immensely useful in some courts for many years now. American tribunals employ a great many instructors who are responsible for collecting and presenting all the evidence to the defender of the bond and the judge, thus enabling the court to be of assistance to far more people than would ever be possible if the judge had to do all the auditing personally. Roberti's point is, of course, a valid one but must be weighed against the demands being made on tribunals today to serve such large numbers of petitioners."

community or local church is indeed a determining factor in the need for intermediary figures. As is rightfully pointed out by the CLSAC, one factor that necessitates intermediaries is the large number of petitioners for whom the tribunal is responsible. In the scenario of a small community, all other things being equal, the need for an intermediary would be less. But there are other factors that can necessitate intermediate figures regardless of size. Differences of culture and language may also require an intermediary of some sort. As the auditor is responsible for gathering proofs on behalf of the judge, certain skills are necessary to mediate differences that exist between the parties and the judge. The deacon-auditor who fulfills this role could function as a social intermediary.

The *promoter of justice* is an officer of the tribunal appointed "for contentious cases in which the public good could be at stake, and for penal cases; the promoter is bound by office to provide for the public good."[29] The promoter functions in a similar manner to that of a prosecuting attorney. In fact, the office of the promoter began in the thirteenth century with the Inquisition.[30] The definition of public welfare cannot be found in the CIC, although it generally covers the rights of all those not specifically represented at a specific trial.[31] It is the responsibility of the bishop to defend against abuses of the law and to provide for the common good in each and every case. The promoter, acting on behalf of the authority and power of the bishop, represents the bishop's interest in this regard. The promoter, either cleric or lay, must have an unimpaired reputation, possess at least a licentiate in canon law, and be proven in prudence and in zeal for justice.[32] Church law requires the involvement of a promoter in all penal cases. Trials concerning conflicting rights of two or more persons also requires the involvement of the promoter when (1) the bishop decides the public good is at stake, (2) the law requires it, as in marriage nullity cases, and (3) the matter is obviously public, as in a highly publicized matter involving well-known people.[33]

Some canonists regard the *defender of the bond* as a species of the promoter of justice.[34] The office of defender of the bond was established after the office

29. CIC, c. 1430.

30. Carmelo de Diego-Lora, "Promotor de justicia, defenso del vínculo y notario," in CECDC, 826.

31. See ibid., 817–18.

32. CIC, c. 1435.

33. Beal, *New Commentary*, 1629.

34. Matthaeus conte a. Coronata, *Institutiones iuris canonici ad usum ultriusque cleri et scholarum*, vol. 3: *De processibus*, 4th ed. (Rome: Marietti, 1956), 45.

of promoter, with the Apostolic Constitution *Dei Miseratione* of Pope Benedict XIV in 1741.[35] The CIC requires the same qualities and training for the defender as for the promoter, but assigns a more particular task. The defender is an officer of the tribunal appointed for cases that concern the nullity of an ordination, the nullity of marriage, or the dissolution of marriage. The defender is "to propose and clarify everything which can be reasonably adduced against nullity or dissolution."[36] The role of the defender serves to safeguard the dignity of the bonds of ordination and marriage in a trial process. While defenders are obliged to point out evidence for the validity of the sacred bonds, they are not to argue the case unreasonably.[37]

The offices of promoter and defender serve the tribunal, and therefore the bishop, to render justice in cases that involve the rights of the parties. The importance of these roles in the process of justice in the ecclesiastical courts is clear enough. They function to legitimate the juridic process as a whole, providing greater assurances that the decision rendered by the judge will be just. But can we consider them to be intermediate institutions as I have defined them? The historical origin of the promoter of justice and defender of the bond in the Inquisition as "prosecuting attorneys" or "devil's advocates" suggests they cannot. These offices do not have as their object the expression of care and concern of the higher authority for the parties of the case. Nor is it their duty to represent the individual parties to the judge. Nonetheless, the promoter and defender serve to legitimate the judicial process by representing the rights of the community as a whole in a contentious situation. In this manner the deacon-promoter and deacon-defender could be said to perform intermediate roles, but this type of mediation may not be what we desire for the ministry of the deacon.

Diocesan finance officer

The *finance officer* is yet another office in the chancery that is listed in the *Directory* as proper for the ministry of the deacon. Canon 494 demands the appointment of a finance officer by the bishop for each diocese. A term of the finance officer is fixed at five years by the law itself, providing an unusual measure of stability in the curia.[38] The concept of a finance officer for each diocese is al-

---

35. De Diego-Lora, "Promotor," 826: "La Const. Ap. de Benedictio XIV, *Dei miseratione*, de 3.XI.1741 introduce al defensor del vínculo en el sistema procesal canónico."

36. CIC, c. 1432.

37. See Wrenn's discussion of the defender's duty in *Procedures*, 21–22.

38. The finance officer is actually a more stable position than the vicars or chancellor, who can

most completely new and without counterpart in the former CIC promulgated in 1917. But canonists make the connection between the finance officer in the CIC and the office once held consistently by deacons and archdeacons down through the ages in the administration of ecclesiastical goods.[39]

The qualities established by CIC as necessary for the finance officer, whether lay or cleric, are that he or she "is to be truly skilled in financial affairs and absolutely distinguished for honesty."[40] Canon 494 further stipulates the function of the finance officer:

§3. It is the role of the finance officer to administer the goods of the diocese under the authority of the bishop in accordance with the budget determined by the finance council; from the income of the diocese the finance officer is to meet the expenditures which the bishop or others deputized by him have legitimately authorized.

§4. At the end of the year the finance officer must give to the finance council a report of receipts and expenditures.

The figure of the finance officer is somewhat like a comptroller, exercising discretionary authority within clearly defined limits. These limits are determined not by the finance officer but by the bishop in consultation with his finance council, his curial officials, and other consultative groups. Thus, the finance officer defrays diocesan expenses not by personal authority but on the basis of authorization.[41] Even though the finance officer does not exercise full decisionmaking authority, he or she is nonetheless critical in the implementation of decisions and policies that have already been determined. It would be overly simplistic to assert that the finance office does not hold any power or authority. A certain amount of power and authority is invested in the role of the finance officer, such that he or she can alert the bishop to necessary adjustments in the allocation of the church's financial resources to meet the needs of the life and mission of the church. The finance officer is not simply concerned about keeping financial records straight, but also to plan for the future financial needs of the diocese. The deacon-finance officer could very well

---

be freely removed by the bishop for only a just reason. Removal of the finance officer requires a grave cause and consultation with the finance council and the college of consultors. In this respect, the finance officer resembles the judicial vicar and adjutant judicial vicar, who retain their positions *sede vacante*. See Beal, *New Commentary*, 651–52.

39. Francisco J. Ramos, *Le Diocesi nel Codice di Diritto Canonico: Studio giuridico-pastorale sulla organizzazione ed i raggruppamenti delle Chiese particolari* (Roma: Millennium Romae, 1997), 389.

40. CIC, c. 494 §1.

41. Beal, *New Commentary*, 652.

fulfill an intermediate function in the governance of the diocese. This would be most especially true if the deacon-finance officer also had regular contact with sectors of the church and community that are burdened with material needs.

Theological Assessment

According to the *Directory*, there are many offices in the chancery open to the ministry of the deacon. None of them, however, is entrusted *especially* to the ministry of deacons. Having seen descriptions of what these offices entail, I will make a theological assessment about their appropriateness for the deacon, and to what degree they could be instances of social mediation. The more an office entails decisionmaking authority, the more problematic it is for the intermediate character of diaconal ministry.

The role of judge is particularly difficult for the deacon because it entails a direct exercise of the power of governance. As noted previously, the CIC makes a distinction between the lay-judge and the cleric-judge. The lay-judge can only function as a member of a collegiate tribunal, whereas the presbyter and deacon can act as sole judges.[42] During the revision process for the new CIC, some questioned the need for deacons to exercise the office of judge at all. The published record does not provide in detail the discussion that occurred among the consultors over the suitability or possibility of the deacon serving as an ecclesiastical judge. The mere fact that the laity had already been allowed by Pope Paul VI to serve as judges apparently resolved the doubts concerning the deacon's exercise of judicial power.[43] Without discerning the kind of cleric that the deacon is, the commission awarded the deacon the same status as the presbyter in the instance of serving as sole judge.[44]

---

42. The debate over lay participation in the exercise of jurisdiction was left unresolved in the text of CIC 1983. As the law currently stands, clerics are able to act as sole judges because their unique status as ordained ministers makes them capable of receiving such a mandate. C. 129 §1 states: "In accord with the prescriptions of law, those who have received sacred orders are capable of the power of governance, which exists in the Church by divine institution and is also called the power of jurisdiction." A very detailed description of the debate over the exercise of the power of governance by the laity is given in John Beal, "The Exercise of the Power of Governance by Lay People: State of the Question," *Jurist* 55 (1995): 1–92. Beal claims that the critical problem now is to determine which offices and ministries in the church are "intrinsically hierarchical and so are strictly reserved to ordained ministers, and which are not intrinsically hierarchical and so are open to lay members of the faithful." See also Elizabeth McDonough, "Jurisdiction Exercised by Non-Ordained Members in Religious Institutes," *Canon Law Society of America Proceedings* 58 (1996): 292–307.

43. Pontifical Council for Legislative Texts, *Communicationes* 10 (1978): 231.

44. Ibid.

One could argue that the judicial office is not the ideal or most important structure for the utilization of diaconal charisms. In the pre-Nicene church, deacons represented individuals to the decisionmaking authorities within the church. With the medieval archdeacon, the deacon became a decisionmaking authority figure himself. What we desire for the diaconate in a church that is organic and collegial are structures that center diaconal ministry closer to the people, while also providing the means to participate closely in the decision-making process. The office of judge does not seem to provide the necessary structure for the deacon to perform his role as an intermediary who represents the needs and desires of the people to those in authority over the community. As a judge, the deacon is the authority. While it is theologically and canonically possible for the deacon to serve as a judge in the church today, this structure does not fit well in our conception of the deacon as social intermediary.

The offices of promoter of justice and defender of the bond, however, do not involve the power of governance to the same extent as the office of judge. Thus, the natures of these offices seem better suited to the ministry of deacons. The degree to which these offices are appropriate for the deacon, however, must not be exaggerated. The CIC considers the laity, with proper training and delegation, as *ordinarily* competent to fulfill these tasks. Ordination does not, therefore, make one better suited than the laity to fulfill these roles. Deacons can perform these functions, but it is not theologically important for the church to have deacons carry out these tasks as an order among the people of God.

Furthermore, the historical origins of these offices caution against attributing an intermediate function to the deacon-promoter or deacon-defender. The deacon, as the "devil's advocate" or "prosecuting attorney," would serve to legitimate the judicial process for the church as a whole. They could mediate the concern of the larger community in the affairs of individuals before a church court. The type of mediation that I am looking for in the diaconate, however, envisions an advocate rather than a prosecuting attorney among the people of God.

Other offices within the tribunal are more intermediate in nature. In fulfilling the office of assessor, the deacon directly influences the decision made by the judge without possessing the power to make a judicial decision himself. An auditor exercises discretionary authority in gathering information necessary for the judge to make a good decision. The assessor and auditor are institutions developed within the church to expedite the judicial process more efficiently and fairly. These offices are mediating structures because they serve to overcome difficulties between the judge and the parties involved in a particular case. The assessor mediates expert knowledge to the judge, helping the judge to understand better the facts of the case, particularly in cases when the parties come from different linguistic and cultural backgrounds from the judge. Other obstacles (such as limited time) may also impede the judge from acting on his or her own to gather the necessary information for a good decision. The deacon-assessor or deacon-auditor could therefore serve as an intermediary in these structured roles.

Beyond the tribunal, the offices of chancellor, vice-chancellor, and notary are not all that appealing for diaconal ministry under the paradigm of social intermediary. These chancery positions are indeed important, for they assist the bishop directly in the administration of the diocese. They are not, however, entrusted to the diaconate in a special way today, nor should they be. Clericalization of the chancery is contrary to the general thrust of the Vatican II understanding of church and ministry. None of these offices are intrinsically part of the hierarchical ministry, unless the local ordinary structured them to entail more than what the CIC envisions. The desire to utilize the charisms of the people of God in a harmonious fashion suggests that offices like these should be left in the hands of the laity as much as possible, with due regard for the necessity of providing some structures for the ministry of the diaconate.

The historical origins of the finance officer, on the other hand, make this position appealing for diaconal ministry today. The finance officer is a key figure in the bishop's inner circle, but one who does not have the power of decisionmaking that is associated with the presbyterate and episcopacy. The finance officer is an auxiliary figure that nonetheless has considerable influence in the administration of the local church's goods. If the deacon as finance officer were to also have some sort of structured, ministerial contact with those in need, then the intermediary nature of his office would be even more secure. The deacon as finance officer could be a fitting way to shape the ministry of the deacon in the local church as a social intermediary.

To summarize, of all the offices of the chancery listed in the *Directory* for the deacon, only three seem especially suited for the deacon to fulfill his fundamental service of charity as a social intermediary: finance officer, assessor, and auditor. There are indeed many other ways the deacon could fulfill his ministry of service to the church and bishop within the chancery, some of which I will take up in the next chapter. But as John Paul II has taught, the diaconate should not replace lay involvement but enhance it.[45] The question is not whether

45. Pope John Paul II, "Catechesis at the General Audience (October 13, 1993)," no. 5, *Insegnamenti*

deacons can perform the roles mentioned in the *Directory,* but whether they *should.* An organic understanding of the church, and the desire for greater participation of the laity in the life and mission of the church, should prevent wide-scale "diaconization" of offices in the chancery.

The use of chancery positions to structure diaconal ministry actually occurs rather infrequently at present. A 2014–15 study on the permanent diaconate in the United States reported that 1.62 percent of the permanent deacons in the United States held a compensated, diocesan non-ministerial position (e.g., administration, business or finance), and 1.25 percent served in a compensated, diocesan ministerial position (e.g., youth ministry, religious education), with the vast majority having their primary duties in parish ministry.[46] According to an earlier study, most people perceive deacons as primarily sacramental ministers because of their experience of deacons assisting priests in a parish context.[47] Lay leaders show little evidence of thinking about the diaconate in any other context. A majority of deacons, their immediate supervisors, and parish lay leaders assume that diaconal ministry is supposed to be parish-based. An unfortunate consequence of the dominance of parish-based diaconal ministry is confusion about the identity of the deacon. The earlier report gives the following conclusion: "Except for the theologically sophisticated, it seems entirely natural that laity would view their deacons as either underqualified priests or overqualified laity."[48]

The parochialization of the diaconate seems to result from an intuitive sense that permanent deacons ought to exercise their ministry close to the people, rather than in a remote chancery office. For this reason, the *Directory*'s presentation of diaconal ministries outside the chancery is all the more important for my consideration of the deacon as a social intermediary and symbol of *communitas.*

XVI, 2 (1993): 1000–1004: "According to the Council the functions assigned to the deacon can in no way diminish the role of lay people called and willing to cooperate in the apostolate with the hierarchy. On the contrary, the deacon's tasks include that of 'promoting and sustaining apostolic activities of the laity.' To the extent that he is present and more involved than the priest in secular environments and structures, he should feel encouraged to foster closeness between the ordained ministry and lay activities, in common service to the kingdom of God."

46. Mary Gautier and Thomas Gaunt, *A Portrait of the Permanent Diaconate: A Study for the U.S. Conference of Catholic Bishops 2014–2015* (Washington, D.C.: Center for Applied Research in the Apostolate, 2015), 15.

47. National Conference of Catholic Bishops' Committee on the Permanent Diaconate, *A National Study on the Permanent Diaconate of the Catholic Church in the United States 1994–1995* (Washington, D.C.: United States Catholic Conference, 1996), 88.

48. NCCB, *National Study,* 8.

Pastoral Ministry Outside the Chancery

The *Directory* mentions other possible ministries for the deacon that are not as clearly defined as those offices found in the chancery. These other ministries, however, are more pastoral in nature, and can be diocesan or parochial.[49] The *Directory* offers several kinds of pastoral ministry that could be entrusted to the ministry of deacons. The pastoral care of families and the pastoral care of the sick are given special mention. The deacon can also be called upon to lead small communities or sectors of the local church. Finally, the *Directory* entrusts in a special way to the deacon the direction and promotion of charitable works among the faithful. In addition to the administrative duties that are associated with these pastoral tasks, the deacon assists the continual conversion of people by also teaching the apostolic faith and performing certain roles in liturgical rites related to these pastoral ministries. Through all of these tasks, the deacon carries on the work of evangelization in the church and in the world.

The Deacon and the New Evangelization

Under the heading of "Diaconia of the word," the *Directory* states that the principal function of the deacon "is to collaborate with the bishop and the priests in the exercise of a ministry which is not of their own wisdom but of the word of God, calling all to conversion and holiness."[50] The call to conversion and holiness is the work of evangelization. But as Pope Francis observed in the fourth chapter of *Evangelii Gaudium*, there is a social dimension to evangelization. "From the heart of the Gospel," he wrote, "we see the profound connection between evangelization and human advancement, which must necessarily find expression and develop in every work of evangelization."[51] Francis goes on to quote Pope Paul VI's foundational Apostolic Exhortation *Evangelii Nuntiandi*, "evangelization would not be complete if it did not take account of the unceasing interplay of the Gospel and of man's concrete life, both personal and social."[52] To evangelize society the church must challenge social factors, such

---

49. USCCB, *Directory*, no. 41 (104–5): "While assuming different forms, the diaconal ministry ordinarily finds proper scope for its exercise in the various sectors of diocesan and parochial pastoral action."

50. USCCB, *Directory*, no. 23 (89).

51. Pope Francis, *Evangelii Gaudium*, par. 178 (90).

52. Pope Paul VI, *Evangelii Nuntiandi*, Apostolic Exhortation, December 8, 1975, in AAS 68 (1976): 5–76; excerpted translation in *Origins* 5 (1976): 459–68. Par. 29 is quoted.

as excessive utilitarian individualism, that work against the conception of the self as belonging to others in the body of Christ. In linking human advancement with the transmission of faith, Paul VI pointed a way to understand the ministry of the deacon. In his service of charity, the deacon directly links the anthropological needs of the church and society with the theological power of the Gospel. It is the deacon's sphere of competence to safeguard the observance of social justice by Christians within the church (in terms of the exercise of power and authority) and within society (in terms of the obligation we have to those in need). The interior conversion of individuals, the maintenance of their identity as children of God, and the reinforcement of their belonging to others in the body of Christ require the social structures of the church to be in conformity with the Gospel she preaches to the world. The ministry of the deacon, as a social intermediary and symbol of *communitas*, could therefore be very important in the work of evangelization.

Contemporary society, states the *Directory*, requires a "new evangelization" which demands a greater and more generous effort on the part of deacons.[53] The specific language of a "new" evangelization was drawn from John Paul II's *Redemptoris Missio*.[54] The pope drew particular attention to the pressing need for the re-evangelization of people who have already heard the message of the Gospel, but have fallen away from the faith.[55] "Christian" societies that still exhibit deficiencies in the human order need the evangelization of society. Indeed, most of the world's Latin-rite deacons are found not in the missionary territories as envisioned by LG 29 and AG 16, but in the "Christian" societies of the West.[56] In other words, the ministry of most deacons falls within the context of the "new evangelization" described by John Paul II.[57] And in light of the link between the Gospel and human advancement, the United States Conference of Catholic Bishops, in the *National Directory*, articulated a "spe-

---

53. USCCB, *Directory*, no. 26 (92).

54. Pope John Paul II, *Redemptoris Missio*, Encyclical Letter, December 7, 1990, in AAS 83 (1991): 249–340; English translation: *Mission of the Redeemer* (Vatican City: Libreria Editrice Vaticana, 1991).

55. *Redemptoris Missio*, par. 33 (56): "There is an intermediate situation, particularly in countries with ancient Christian roots, and occasionally in the younger Churches as well, where entire groups of the baptized have lost a living sense of the faith, or even no longer consider themselves members of the Church, and live a life far removed from Christ and his Gospel. In this case what is needed is a 'new evangelization' or a 're-evangelization.'"

56. The *Kennedy Directory* (2016) records 18,972 permanent deacons in the United States alone, and the Pontifical Yearbook 2017 records 45,255 worldwide permanent deacons.

57. In the sixth chapter of *Redemptoris Missio*, permanent deacons are conspicuously absent in the discussion of leaders and workers in the missionary apostolate.

cial role" for the deacon "to promote communion and to counter the strong emphasis on individualism prevalent in the United States."[58] The delineation of structures for the ministry of the deacon, therefore, cannot ignore the contemporary context of the new evangelization within which the deacon carries out pastoral care.

The various dimensions of diaconal ministry are unified in the particular charism of the diaconate to support the communion of the church in how we live, how we pray, and what we believe as Christians. Thus, the administrative, liturgical, and catechetical dimensions of diaconal ministry are inseparably joined.[59] In previous chapters, I explored at length the significance of the administrative and liturgical dimensions of diaconal ministry; I add now the importance of catechesis in the ministry of deacons in the contemporary context of the new evangelization.

The Deacon and Catechesis

The deacon who actually functions as a social intermediary has a distinct expertise and authority with which to teach the faith. While he may not be as well trained as other clergy in the areas of scripture, theology, and liturgy, the deacon-intermediary has a certain wisdom from his personal contact with those whom he serves. His familiarity with the concrete connections between the content of faith and its implications for social life, both within the church and beyond it, provide the deacon-intermediary with a perspective that few have among the people of God. For this reason, the *National Directory* considers the diaconate to be a unique (and perhaps not yet fully utilized) resource for the new evangelization.[60]

As an assistant to the bishop and the presbyter, the deacon shares in their obligation to teach the faith. The *Directory* considers catechesis to be an essen-

58. USCCB, *National Directory*, no. 57 (31).

59. USCCB, *Directory*, no. 39 (103–4): "Together … they represent a unity in service at the level of divine Revelation: the ministry of the word leads to ministry at the altar, which in turn prompts the transformation of life by the liturgy, resulting in charity … 'these three ministries are inseparably joined in God's plan for redemption.'" The *Directory* cites John Paul II's address to the permanent deacons and their wives in Detroit, Michigan (September 19, 1987), that can be found in *Origins* 17 (1987): 327–29.

60. USCCB, *National Directory*, no. 58 (31): "The diaconate is lived in a particularly powerful way in the manner in which a deacon fulfills his obligations to his secular occupation, to his civic and public responsibilities, and among his family and neighbors. This, in turn, enables the deacon to bring back to the Church an appreciation of the meaning and value of the Gospel as he discerns it in the lives and questions of the people he has encountered."

tial part of the deacon's ministry of the word. Sensitive to the contemporary context, and reflecting the teachings of Paul VI and John Paul II, the *Directory* describes the pressing need for catechesis in general terms: "With growing secularization and the ever greater challenges posed for man and for the Gospel by contemporary society, the need for complete, faithful and lucid catechesis becomes all the more pressing."[61] In chapter 3, I pointed out the cultural phenomenon of excessive utilitarian individualism that pulls apart the social bonds that tie people together. Alienation and individualism are cultural forces in many contemporary societies that the church must challenge in her obligation to proclaim the Gospel.

The role of the deacon as catechist is not at all new. During the Golden Age of the diaconate, deacons provided continuing education of the faithful as well as catechesis for those entering the church. The AT testifies to deacons teaching in the early Roman church, where gatherings for the instruction of the congregation were held frequently throughout the week.[62] In roughly 400 A.D., Deogratias, a deacon from the church of Carthage, sent St. Augustine a written request to write something on catechizing inquirers.[63] Deogratias was a successful catechist who was desirous of further guidance in the ministry of catechizing, and was apprehensive of growing stale in his instructions.[64] Augustine responded with his *De catechizandis rudibus*, addressed to the deacon-catechist, outlining the content and methodology of his own catechesis.[65] In LG 29 and AG 16, the Second Vatican Council noted the possibility of permanent deacons taking up the task of catechesis, asserting the validity of such a ministry for the deacon.

The *Directory* offers a brief reference to the role of the deacon in the catechetical preparation of people for the celebration of the sacraments: "The ministry of deacons also includes preparation of the faithful for reception of the sacraments and their pastoral care after having received them."[66] While the deacon cannot be the presider of the most important liturgical ceremonies, the pastoral ministry that surrounds such celebrations is within the province of the deacon. It is unfortunate that the *Directory* does not develop more fully, for

61. USCCB, *Directory*, no. 25 (91).

62. See AT 39 and 41.

63. William Harmless, *Augustine and the Catechumenate* (Collegeville, Minn.: Liturgical Press, 1995), 107.

64. Joseph P. Christopher, introduction to *St. Augustine: The First Catechetical Instruction* [*De Catechizandis Rudibus*], trans. Joseph Christopher, ACW 2 (London: Longmans, Green and Co., 1962), 5.

65. *De catechizandis rudibus*, in CCSL 46:115–78.

66. USCCB, *Directory*, no. 30 (96).

example, the role of the deacon in the Rite of Christian Initiation of Adults.[67]

The *Directory* presumes the role of the deacon in the continuing education of the faithful without any exploration of the various possibilities in this ministry. Instead, the *Directory* highlights the importance of the deacon's witness of faith beyond the classroom or other formal structure:

[Deacons] should strive to transmit the word in their professional lives, either explicitly or merely by their active presence in places where public opinion is formed and ethical norms are applied—such as the social services or organisations promoting the rights of the family or life. They should always be aware of the great possibilities for the ministry of the word in the area of religious and moral instruction in schools, in Catholic and civil universities and by adequate use of modern means of social communication.[68]

The deacon is called to teach others not only with words, but also by his own presence and action. The unique character of the diaconate as an intermediate institution frees up the deacon to be an effective, clerical witness of the faith in the everyday structures of the world in ways that priest-presbyters and bishops cannot. While the other clergy are forbidden to assume public offices that entail the exercise of civil power, to conduct business or trade, to take an active part in political parties, or to govern labor unions, the deacon is free to do so with prior written permission of the diocesan bishop.[69] In his secular employment or professional service, the deacon models for the laity what they themselves are called to do in their mission of sanctifying the world. In order to teach others by way of example, the deacon must be part of the regular, ordinary world of society.

The Deacon and the Homily

Insofar as he assists the ministry of the bishop, the deacon bears a special responsibility to preach the Gospel. The homily is a particular kind of preaching, a "catechesis given in the setting of the liturgy, especially at the Eucharistic

---

67. See "Christian Initiation, General Introduction," nos. 14–15 (xviii), and "The Rite of Christian Initiation of Adults, Introduction," no. 15, in *The Rite of Christian Initiation of Adults* (New York: Catholic Book Publishing, 1988), 8: "Deacons should be ready to assist in the ministry to catechumens. Conferences of bishops that have decided in favor of the permanent diaconate should ensure that the number and distribution of permanent deacons are adequate for the carrying out of the steps, periods, and programs of the catechumenate wherever pastoral needs require."

68. USCCB, *Directory*, no. 26 (92).

69. See CIC, cc. 285–88; USCCB, *National Directory*, no. 91 (41).

assembly."[70] Reiterating the GIRM and *Praenotanda* of the Lectionary, the *Directory* states: "It is for the deacon to proclaim the Gospel and preach the word of God."[71] The CIC 1983 gives deacons the faculties to preach everywhere (in accordance with the conditions established by the law), which the *Directory* grounds in the deacon's participation in the Sacrament of Ordination.[72] This is a change from the CIC 1917, which required the deacon to receive faculties from his ordinary to preach.[73] The *Directory* goes on to say: "When the deacon presides at a liturgical celebration, in accordance with the relevant norms, he shall give due importance to the homily."[74] This rule derives from the directive in the *praenotanda* of the Lectionary that states: "As a rule it [the homily] is to be given by the one presiding."[75] This statement gives the impression that the deacon does not normally preach at the celebration of the eucharist because the deacon never presides at this liturgy. According to the GIRM, the homily at the eucharist "should ordinarily be given by the priest celebrant."[76] The deacon may, however, "sometimes give the homily, as occasion suggests."[77] Thus the deacon does not have an equal "right," all other things being equal, to preach the homily relative to the presider or concelebrating presbyters at the celebration of the eucharist.[78]

Ever since the time of Justin Martyr, the homily in the eucharistic celebration has normally been reserved to the same minister who presides, in continuity with his pastoral ministry within the community. "The close link between the two tables at the eucharistic celebration is ... seen in the fact that the Church entrusts the sacrament of the Word and the sacrament of the Eucharist, which form a single act of worship, to the same minister.... In the West, preaching the homily has always been considered a presidential function."[79]

70. John Paul II, *Catechesi Tradendae*, Apostolic Exhortation, October 16, 1979, in AAS 71 (1979): 1277–1340. Official English translation: *Apostolic Exhortation Catechesi tradendae of His Holiness Pope John Paul II to the Episcopate, the Clergy and the Faithful of the Entire Catholic Church on Catechesis in Our Time* (Vatican City: Vatican Polyglot Press, 1979), par. 48 (62).

71. USCCB, *Directory*, no. 24 (90); GIRM, no. 61; Congregation for Divine Worship and the Discipline of the Sacraments, *Missale Romanum, Ordo lectionum Missae, Praenotanda* (Vatican City: Typis Polyglottis Vaticanis, 1998), nos. 8, 24, 50.

72. CIC, c. 764.

73. CIC 1917, cc. 1328 and 1342 §1.

74. USCCB, *Directory*, no. 25 (91).

75. CDWDS, *Praenotanda*, no. 24.

76. GIRM, no. 42.

77. CDWDS, *Praenotanda*, no. 50.

78. Ibid., no. 24: "At a concelebration, the celebrant or one of the concelebrants as a rule gives the homily."

79. Domenico Sartore, "The Homily," in *Handbook for Liturgical Studies* (ed. Chupungco), 3:200.

Evidence from history is not clear as to whether preaching the homily at the eucharist was considered a normal function of the deacon. Barnett argues to the contrary.[80] Echlin, however, argues that the *Didache* attributes the function of preaching to deacons.[81] Despite Echlin's confidence, it is unlikely that the eucharistic homily was considered a regular part of the deacon's ministry of teaching in the early church. The deacon is, however, allowed to preach at the eucharistic celebration today "as the occasion suggests."

When the deacon preaches at Mass, his familiarity with the social needs of his culture should shape his preaching, such that the implications of social justice present in the Gospel are not slighted but emphasized by him. When the subject of the Lectionary readings directly pertains to themes of social justice, it might be appropriate for the deacon to preach to the eucharistic assembly. This would be a more fitting way to choose occasions for diaconal preaching than the practice found in some parishes of assigning the deacon a particular Sunday—say, the fourth Sunday of the month—to preach, regardless of the content of the readings. Still, occasional homilies from deacons are important to the diaconal ministry. They provide the deacon the occasional opportunity to address the entire assembly, something that would otherwise be an extremely rare opportunity for the deacon. The homily at the eucharist should not, however, become the mainstay of the deacon's ministry of the word. The deacon is directed outward and into the world, to be a minister of the word of God in the workplace and among the laity in their everyday lives.

The Deacon and Liturgy

Liturgy is another important element of evangelization that has special significance for the re-evangelization of those who are loosely connected to the church through simple attendance at liturgical rites. It has been shown in chapter 7 that the deacon functions as a symbol of *communitas* in the Mass. He has similar functions in the other important liturgies of the church. The deacon is a key symbol in the ritual reinforcement of the communion that already exists, and his symbolic presence points to the eschatological communion that all of Christ's

---

80. Barnett, *Diaconate*, 82–83: "The assertion that deacons preached as a matter of their office in the early Church is clearly contrary to the evidence. The function belonged normally to the president of the eucharistic assembly.… It is probable that preaching came to be thought of as a diaconal function in the Medieval period, when the diaconate had become largely an interim or transitional office on one's journey to the priesthood."

81. Echlin, *The Deacon in the Church*, 17.

followers are called to share. The liturgical functions of the deacon are therefore an integral part of the deacon's ministry of service of charity to the church.

The *Directory* characterizes the liturgical service of the deacon as assistance to the bishop and presbyter, the promotion of interior participation of the faithful in the liturgy and their exercise of the various ministries.[82] In connection with his service as an ordinary minister of Communion in the Mass, the deacon is an ordinary minister of Viaticum to the sick. He is also an ordinary minister of baptism, a rather new role for the deacon in an ordinary manner.[83] The CIC 1917 considered the deacon only an "extraordinary" minister of baptism, reserving this function ordinarily to the ministry of priests.[84]

In light of the confusion that often surrounds the ministry of deacons in the parish, it is worthwhile to ponder the wisdom of entrusting the ministry of baptism to the deacon on a regular basis. Outside of the cases of necessity due to proximate death or the lack of presbyters, it is not proper for the deacon to baptize adults. The integrity of the sacraments of initiation for adults demands that presbyters and bishops administer adult baptisms, as only they can immediately seal the newly baptized with the sacrament of confirmation. It therefore seems that the deacon is an ordinary minister of baptism only in the case of children, for whom confirmation does not take place immediately following baptism in the Roman rite. The discipline of entrusting baptisms to deacons has the unfortunate consequence of solidifying the separation of confirmation from baptism. Furthermore, the admittance of new members into the fold is normally a function of the head of the community. This is why bishops are the first ministers of baptism, and secondarily those presbyters who are heads of parish communities. Have we confused the ministry and image of the deacon by entrusting to him, in an ordinary fashion, the ministry of baptism? It would seem more beneficial to place emphasis upon the deacon's role in the preparation of parents or candidates for baptism, and the deacon's liturgical assistance at the liturgy of baptism presided over by the bishop or parish priest. In this way the image of the deacon as a distinct and unique intermediary figure would be better preserved. This assistance should not be merely ceremonial, but involve the deacon's interaction with the parents and godparents. The deacon's assistance as an intermediary will be especially fruitful in cases of linguistic or cultural differences between the priest or bishop and the faithful seeking baptism for their child.

82. USCCB, *Directory*, no. 30 (95).
83. Ibid., no. 31 (97); CIC, c. 861 §1.
84. CIC 1917, c. 738 §1.

The church entrusts other important liturgical functions that provide the deacon the opportunity to express the care and concern of the church in important moments of human life. The deacon is a minister of sacramentals, and it is for him to impart some blessings that are most closely linked to ecclesial and sacramental life.[85] The deacon can conduct funerals celebrated outside of Mass and lead the rites for Christian burial.[86] In all of these occasions, however, the *Directory* duly notes that these tasks must be given to a presbyter or bishop when they are present or available.[87]

It should not be discounted that the presbyter is given priority over the deacon in leading the blessings and rites of the church. In terms of his liturgical ministry, emphasis should be placed on the assistance the deacon provides the gathered assembly. As circumstances warrant, nonetheless, it is appropriate for the deacon to provide liturgical presidency, especially when the liturgies are closely related to his work as a social intermediary. If the liturgical leadership of the deacon were to flow from a specific ministry entrusted to him by the church, rather than the deacon simply taking his turn at the rites of baptism, matrimony, and funerals in a parish, it will be less likely that the deacon will be viewed as a "mini-priest" by the faithful.

Pastoral Care of the Family

One of the specific ministries the *Directory* offers as an example for the service of deacons is the pastoral care of the family. Exercised at the diocesan or parish level, the deacon's ministry entails counseling on "moral and liturgical questions, to difficulties of a social and personal nature," and include "catechesis on Christian marriage, the personal preparation of future spouses, the fruitful celebration of marriage, and help offered to couples after marriage."[88] The deacon as pastoral minister of the family very much satisfies my concern for placing the deacon in ministries that connect him with the people and the leader-

85. Congregation for Divine Worship and the Discipline of the Sacraments, *Rituale Romanum ex Decreto Sacrosancti Oecumenici Concilii Vaticani II Instauratum Auctoritate Ioannis Pauli II Promulgatum, De Benedictionibus* (hereafter De Benedictionibus), no. 18 (Vatican City: Typis Polyglottis Vaticanis, 1985).

86. Congregation for Divine Worship and the Discipline of the Sacraments, *Rituale Romanum ex Decreto Sacrosancti Oecumenici Concilii Vaticani II Instauratum Auctoritate Pauli PP. VI Promulgatum. Ordo Exsequiarum*, no. 19 (Vatican City: Typis Polyglottis Vaticanis, 1969); *Order of Christian Funerals*, no. 14.

87. USCCB, *Directory*, no. 36 (100).

88. Ibid., no. 33 (98–99).

ship of the local church. Pastoral care of the family can also utilize the personal experience of the married deacon as a husband and a father of children. The human gifts and talents of the married deacon, which are taken up in the Spirit at ordination, are thus placed at the service of the church. Entrusted with such a ministry the deacon can speak with a certain measure of credibility to those he prepares and counsels for marriage. It should also be recognized that the deacon has a certain obligation, in matters associated with the pastoral care of families, to speak up to the bishop and parish pastor, whom the *Directory* correctly identifies as "primarily" responsible for the pastoral care of families. Furthermore, the deacon can be delegated the faculty to officiate at wedding liturgies outside of Mass, in which he witnesses the exchange of vows and pronounces the nuptial blessing.[89]

The deacon can assist the bishop and the pastors of parishes to do a better job at meeting the concerns and needs of married couples and parents. Most importantly, the deacon could address the social pressures that negatively affect the Christian family. The deacon's personal experience of parenting and marriage is a great resource for both the church's leaders and members. The deacon assigned to family ministry should be capable of advising parents on how to raise children according to the Christian values of communion and responsibility for others in the contemporary social context, and help couples to understand their vocation of matrimony as a call to give sacrificially of themselves. In these ways the deacon works to counter the influence of the dominant social context of excessive individualism. Although the celibate presbyter has something important to say to married couples about living a sacrificial life of love, a married deacon can speak from personal experience of how to concretely lay down one's life for one's spouse and children.

A deacon who provides pastoral care to families utilizes administrative, liturgical, and catechetical dimensions of his ministry. This ministry requires the deacon to enter the homes of families and to know their needs and desires. In this way, the deacon bridges the needs of the family with the hierarchy, and he can be an ambassador of the Gospel when providing the comfort and assistance of pastoral counseling.

---

89. Congregation for Divine Worship and the Discipline of the Sacraments, *Rituale Romanum ex Decreto Sacrosancti Oecumenici Concilii Vaticani II Renovatum Auctoritate Pauli PP. VI Editum Ioannis Pauli PP. II Cura Recognitum. Ordo Celebrandi Matrimonium*, no. 24 (Vatican City: Typis Polyglottis Vaticanis, 1991). English Translation: International Commission on English in the Liturgy, *The Order of Celebrating Matrimony*, 2nd ed. (Totowa, N.J.: Catholic Book Publishing, 2016).

Pastoral Care of the Sick

Another ministry suggested by the *Directory* is the pastoral care of the sick. From the perspective of history, this ministry is particularly well-suited for the ministry of the deacon. Though sacred tradition reserves the sacrament of the anointing of the sick to the ministry of priests, there is still the need for the ministry of the deacon in the pastoral care of the sick.[90] The *Directory* encourages consideration of "service to alleviate the suffering of the sick, catechesis in preparation for the Sacrament of the Anointing of the Sick, preparing the faithful for death, and the administration of Viaticum."[91] As with the pastoral care of the family, ministry to the sick requires the deacon to be out among the people, visiting those who are suffering in hospitals and those who cannot leave their homes. He is obliged to make the leadership of the diocese and parish aware of the spiritual and physical needs of the sick. The deacon can also be responsible for animating the people to fulfill the church's obligation to visit and care for the sick. He can promote and coordinate visits, including the parish priest as needed. In preparing the sick for the celebration of the sacraments and assisting with their liturgical celebrations, a deacon provides valuable assistance to the parish priest or hospital chaplain. A deacon who takes this ministry seriously is an important bridge between the sick and dying, and the rest of the church. The deacon can voice the needs and concerns of the sick and suffering to the other members of the church, and he becomes the messenger of the love and concern of the church for those who are absent from the Sunday assembly because of their illness.

Pastoral Care of Parishes and Other Christian Communities

The *Directory* does not flesh out more fully what is only briefly mentioned in the CIC concerning the cooperation of a deacon with a presbyter in the pas-

---

90. Council of Trent, *Doctrina de sacramento extremae unctionis*, chap. 3 and c. 4, in *Decrees* (ed. Tanner), 1:713. History, however, provides instances of the deacon and even the laity of ministering the "oil of the sick" to those in need. While the fourth canon of the Council of Trent's teaching on the sacrament of the sick defends the church's practice of priests as "proper" ministers of the sacrament, some scholars hold that this teaching does not exclude the possibility that other, "extraordinary" ministers of anointing, such as the deacon, could be called. See Vorgrimler, *Sacramental Theology*, 232.

91. USCCB, *Directory*, no. 34 (99). CIC, c. 1003: "Unctionem infirmorum valide administrat omnis et solus sacerdos."

toral care of a parish.[92] Neither the *Directory* nor the CIC provide a stable structure or office for deacons in the parish, as the CIC does for pastors and parochial vicars. This is unfortunate for two reasons. First, it leaves the impression that the ministry of the deacon at the local level of the parish is not all that important. Secondly, there is a great need for stability in diaconal ministry, and the establishment of a universally recognized office for deacons would provide a framework of rights and obligations associated with their ministry in the parish. The lack of clarity in the CIC and the *Directory* concerning parochial deacons may very well be the reason why there is often ambiguity and role conflict surrounding the parish deacon. It may be the case that the assignment to a single parish is not the best way for the bishop to deploy some or all deacons, but I will save discussion of other possibilities to the next chapter. If deacons are to continue in parish ministry, greater specificity is needed for the purpose and function of the deacon in the parochial context. This lacuna in the CIC and *Directory* could be met with the structuring of the diaconate as an intermediate order among the people of God by the bishop. It is enough for now to be aware that the *Directory* recognizes the canonical possibility of diaconal appointments to the pastoral care of the parish, but offers no clarification as to how the parochial ministry of the deacon should be structured.

The issue of parochial deacons becomes even more complicated when they are appointed to parishes without a resident pastor. The *Directory* repeats the provision in the CIC for the administration of a parish by a deacon, and offers further clarifications.[93] First, the *Directory* specifies that the deacon has precedence over a layperson in the exercise of pastoral care of the parish. Second, the *Directory* clarifies the degree or manner to which the deacon cooperates with the pastor in the pastoral care of the parish: "In such cases, it is necessary to specify that the moderator of the parish is a priest and that he is its proper pastor. To him alone has been entrusted the *cura animarum*, in which he is assisted by the deacon."[94] The first clarification recognizes the significance of

---

92. CIC, c. 519: "The pastor is the proper pastor of the parish entrusted to him, exercising the pastoral care of the community committed to him under the authority of the diocesan bishop in whose ministry of Christ he has been called to share, so that for that same community he carries out the functions of teaching, sanctifying, and governing, also with the cooperation of other presbyters or deacons and with the assistance of lay members of the Christian faithful, according to the norm of law."

93. CIC, c. 517 §2: "If, because a lack of priests, the diocesan bishop has decided that participation in the exercise of the pastoral care of a parish is to be entrusted to a deacon, to another person who is not a priest, or to a community of persons, he is to appoint some priest who, provided with the powers and faculties of a pastor, is to direct the pastoral care."

94. USCCB, *Directory*, no. 41 (105).

the diaconate as part of the ecclesiastical *ordo*, and the second seeks to limit the extent to which the deacon becomes a stand-in for the parish priest in this extraordinary situation.[95] While the extraordinary provision for deacons to serve as pastoral administrators without resident pastors is necessary because of the lack of presbyters in some places, it should not be chosen lightly. Deacons serving as administrators (or quasi-pastors) increase the likelihood that they will be defined by the ministry of presbyters instead of their own distinct charism. Where there is a shortage of priests, it may be more appropriate for one priest to preside over multiple parishes, heavily assisted by the deacon and lay ministers, rather than appointing deacons as direct administrators. These are hard questions, but the value of the special role of the deacon should not be forgotten in dealing with difficult pastoral situations.

The *Directory* suggests what could be an ideal utilization of diaconal charisms when it mentions the possibility of calling deacons to guide specific sectors of the Christian community in the name of the bishop or parish priest. This would not involve the pastoral care of people to the degree that the office of parish administrator implies. The deacon's ministry to particular sectors of church membership would be a sort of missionary effort to those "social strata and groups where priests are lacking or cannot be easily found."[96] The *Directory* appears to recognize the potential for deacons to serve as intermediaries between the bishop or presbyter and specific segments of people in their care. This is particularly needed when the bishop or pastor has the pastoral care of people whose ethnic and cultural background he does not share. The *Directory* does not offer, however, any specific structures that might support the ministry of the deacon in this respect.

Direction and Promotion of Charitable Works

Another ministry specifically mentioned in the *Directory* for deacons concerns the obligation of the church to perform various works of charity. *Evangelii Nuntiandi* and *Evangelii Gaudium* are very clear in their insistence that the obligation of evangelization entails the transformation of societal structures. In like

---

95. The characterization of the deacon as a "cooperator" with the pastor in the *cura animarum* is still ambiguous in light of the teaching found in LG 29, where we find that deacons can "be appointed [*institui*] for the care of souls [*pro cura animarum*]." The teaching of the *Directory*, that only the parish pastor has the *cura animarum*, does not seem to be nuanced enough to account for the Second Vatican Council's teaching on the diaconate.

96. USCCB, *Directory*, no. 41 (105).

manner, the *Directory* and the *National Directory* hold the transformation of the social world as an objective for the ministry of the deacon. He is to be an agent of *communitas*. Part of the deacon's ministry in promoting active concern for others includes teaching about the transformation of the world "according to the Christian order," which requires transcending "all ideologies and narrow party interests."[97] Here, the *Directory* synthesizes for us what I have been arguing throughout this book: as ordained ministers of Christ and his church, deacons are commissioned to heal social divisions that plague our society, which may even affect the church by weakening her resolve to proclaim the Gospel of communion and solidarity.

The *Directory* expects deacons to be expert teachers in the promotion of human life in society. Respect for the dignity of human life is an essential characteristic of authentic community. As the spiritual and material needs of human society will only be fully met in the recognition of the basic human bond that is love, the deacon's social service is intrinsically tied with the motive of faith. The deacon is commissioned to communicate the dignity of those who are materially the least in society, and those who are least in a spiritual sense. The church commits to the ministry of the deacon, therefore, those who are separated from the community by sickness or sin. That the "sinful" are given special mention in the *Directory* points out that what is envisioned for the deacon is not simple philanthropy but evangelization. As ambassadors of God and the church, deacons are to bridge whatever distance there may be between the church and the world, and to mediate the care and concern of the people of God to those apart from them.

Teaching the dignity of human life and the importance of community is not enough. The promotion of active concern for others should be made concrete in the direction of charitable works. The church calls deacons to "dis-

---

97. Ibid., no. 38 (102): "Diocesan and parochial works of charity, which are among the primary duties of bishops and priests are entrusted by them, as attested by Tradition, to servants in the ecclesiastical ministry, that is, to deacons. So too is the service of charity in Christian education; in training preachers, youth groups, and lay groups; in promoting life in all its phases and transforming the world according to the Christian order. In all of these areas the ministry of deacons is particularly valuable, since today the spiritual and material needs of man, to which the Church is called to respond, are greatly diversified. They should, therefore, strive to serve the faithful without discrimination, while devoting particular care to the suffering and the sinful. As ministers of Christ and of his Church, they must be able to transcend all ideologies and narrow party interests, lest they deprive the Church's mission of its strength which is the love of Christ. Diaconia should bring man to an experience of God's love and move him to conversion by opening his heart to the work of grace."

charge the duties of charity and also provide social services."[98] To fulfill these functions, deacons should be organizers and animators. The administrative skills of the deacon could be utilized so that the people of God may have real opportunities to do their own part in fulfilling the church's obligation of care for the poor. The deacon is empowered to call into service the charisms of the baptized in organizing the practice of social justice.

The 1994 study on the permanent diaconate in the United States points out the great need that exists today to redirect the diaconate toward the work of social justice. Contrary to popular understanding, most deacons have little to do with the promotion of charitable works. While the deacons often mentioned "service to others" in their written comments in the survey, the category "to influence social change" rarely appeared. Few reported much training in the areas of Catholic social thought, ministries, or direct human services. Lay leaders wrote that they only very occasionally hear a deacon preach about social ministry or the social teaching of the church. Deacons did not appear familiar with diocesan agencies like Catholic Charities or the Family Life Office. The deacons themselves did not give as motivations for entering the diaconate a desire to better serve the community or to make the church's social teaching better known. Overwhelmingly, they said they were motivated by the opportunity for a mostly parochial ministry of service that might deepen their own spiritual life and give them a more powerful sense of purpose and place in life.[99]

It is no surprise that North American permanent deacons exhibit a degree of individualism in their motives for serving the church. The dominant American culture in which they live encourages looking out for one's self-interest over and against concern for others, even spiritual self-interest. Although it is no surprise, the results of the survey are troubling, given the fact that LG 29 specified the diaconate for the administration and direction of charity. Critical adjustments will need to be made in the structuring of the diaconate so that permanent deacons will, in the future, function as effective social intermediaries. It is inexplicable, for instance, that deacons usually have little training in Catholic social teaching. If there is the expectation that deacons be expert teachers in the realm of social justice, the church must provide the tools necessary for deacons to carry out this task.

---

98. USCCB, *Directory*, no. 38 (103).
99. This paragraph is a summary of the findings in NCCB, *National Study*, 8–9.

Summary

This examination of the *Directory* has uncovered ministries and offices by which the deacon could socially mediate the power, authority, gifts, and talents of the people of God. There are many possibilities for the deacon to engender concern for others in his work of evangelization, "to preserve the unity of the spirit through the bond of peace."[100] The positions of diocesan finance officer, as well as assessor and auditor, provide stable frameworks for the ministry of deacons, but these offices do not structure ministries that are ideal for the diaconate in particular. On the other hand, ministries such as the pastoral care of families, the sick, and other sectors of the church utilize a broad spectrum of diaconal charisms and place the deacon in close contact with the people he serves. While these ministries may be ideal for diaconal ministry, no structures exist in the CIC or the *Directory* that would allow the deacon to carry them out in a stable fashion.

Thus, the fundamental difficulty with the *Directory* is its inability to match specific ministries that are appropriate for the diaconate with structures that would allow deacons to carry them out. This weakness in the *Directory* is directly related to the confusion and role conflict associated with the permanent diaconate. The deacon's relationship with the laity and the pastor, for example, remains ambiguous for the parish deacon. Yet, at what other level of church organization could the deacon fulfill the most appropriate ministries identified in the *Directory*? In short, the ministry of deacons needs to be structured by offices that are particular to deacons themselves. As the CIC does not provide assistance in this regard, creativity is needed on the part of the local church to construct the right kind of offices for deacons to exercise their ministry at parochial and diocesan levels.

Among the offices and ministries suggested for the deacon, some are particularly suited for the deacon as a social intermediary among the people of God. Offices in the chancery open to the ministry of deacons would provide a certain measure of access to and influence of those with pastoral governance of the diocese. Their close proximity to the bishop and the primary decision-makers of the diocese (a position that is strongly attested in history of the early church for the deacon) would allow chancery deacons to participate in the decisionmaking process. These stable structures, however, do not ensure daily contact with people, nor is it clear how they provide the means for the dea-

---

100. Eph 4:3.

con to exercise the non-administrative dimensions of diaconal ministry on a stable basis. For example, how would the liturgical ministry of the deacon be utilized in an appointment to an office in the tribunal? Obviously, additional ministries (and consequently, other structures or offices) would need to be given the chancery deacon to exercise his other ordination charisms. While parochial ministry can supplement chancery positions, it is better to identify single structures that would utilize to a fuller extent the various charisms of the diaconate. The desire is not for several offices for each deacon, but individual offices that respect the character of the deacon as a social intermediary and symbol of *communitas*.

The *Directory* offers several ministries and offices that could be helpful in structuring the diaconate for the distribution of knowledge, power, resources, and charity among the people of God. It is up to the local churches, at the levels of national conferences and individual dioceses, to decide within the limits established by the *Directory* and the CIC how best to shape the ministry of their deacons in the concrete. I shall look forward in the next chapter by offering some examples that could stabilize the ministry of the deacon as a social intermediary, ways in which the diaconate could link the needs and concerns of the people with the structures of power operative in the local church. By adopting these structures, local churches could bring into clearer focus the new portrait of the deacon begun by the Second Vatican Council.

CHAPTER 9

Restructuring the Diaconate as an Intermediate Institution

Taking a fresh look at the deacon as a social intermediary and symbol of *communitas* provides a clearer perspective for the resolution of many ambiguities commonly associated with the diaconate. Now that I have evaluated the present structures of the diaconate in the previous chapter, I will develop the image of the deacon as a social intermediary by the articulation of possible new structures for diaconal ministry today. I will illustrate the concrete ramifications of the abstract conception of the deacon as a social intermediary and symbol of *communitas*. Fine-tuning the structure of the diaconate in the local church requires the consideration of possibilities not considered in the 1998 *Directory* from the Congregation of the Clergy, possibilities that are nonetheless in accord with the *Directory*'s established principles and canon law.

Some of these structures include offices that are exercised in close proximity to the bishop. The desire to keep the diaconate close to the people, however, makes it best not to have a majority of deacons associated with the juridic power-center of the diocese that is the chancery. Reducing the ambiguity of the diaconate in the local church also demands clarifying the role of the deacon in relation to the parish. To achieve this aim, I will propose some guidelines for structuring the parochial ministry of the diaconate. The parish-based diaconate is not problem-free. The parochial deacon is too often seen as a mini-priest, for it is in the parish context that the ministry of the deacon is often confused with, and defined in terms of, presbyteral ministry. For these reasons, the ideal structure for the diaconate would center the majority of diaconal ministry outside the chancery but not necessarily within parishes.

The main thrust of this chapter is the advocacy and utilization of inter-parochial structures that are or can be made available to the diaconate. The ministries appropriate for the diaconate today, and the structures for the exercise of these ministries in a stable manner, will be delineated in three general areas of the local church: the chancery, the parish, and institutions and regional areas of the diocese. This new portrait of the deacon will be drawn from existing ministries and structures that are not presently especially associated with deacons, as well as proposals for the creation of new structures. In the end, the proposed configuration of diaconal ministry will provide a concrete plan for structuring the diaconate to facilitate the relationship between the bishop and the laity, as well as to engender among the people of God a sense of solidarity with the poor.

Chancery Positions

The desire for the deacon to support the relationship between the bishop (and his chief delegates) and his people as a social intermediary should influence the shape of diaconal ministry in the chancery office. The presence of deacons in the chancery remains rare, but there are a number of positions presently mentioned for the deacon in the *Directory* and the CIC. As discussed in the previous chapter, fitting positions include finance officer, assessor, auditor, and procurator-advocate in the tribunal. But other offices not specifically mentioned in the CIC may be appropriate for the ministry of a deacon.

In many dioceses, offices have been created to address the social context of the church's work of evangelization. Diocesan organizations for social services and other offices concerned with advocating social justice are complementary institutions that seek the transformation of the social order. The institutions that provide social services focus on the organization of concrete charitable works. The other offices are specialized institutions that advocate the incorporation of Catholic social teaching in the policies and actions of church membership and society at large. In light of the prominence of the pastoral care of the family in the *Directory*, the position of director of the Family Life Office is yet another office often created at the local level that is worthy of our consideration. The above structures are noteworthy for they support ministries already shown to be appropriate for the deacon. Each of them provides stability for the ministry of the deacon in his assistance to the bishop in the pastoral care of the diocese. This is not an exhaustive list of possibilities for diaconal ministry; it only offers further examples of how the deacon can serve as a social intermediary in the chancery.

Procurator-Advocate

My examination of the tribunal positions in the *Directory* found the offices of assessor and auditor to have qualities of intermediate institutions. The offices of judge, defender of the bond, and promoter of justice were found not particularly desirable for the ministry of a deacon because these offices are too much associated with the direct exercise of judicial authority and power. Deacons have, in history, represented individuals before the bishop in matters that required his judgment.[1] It is this form of mediation that is desired today for the ministry of the deacon in the tribunal. The offices of *procurator* and *advocate* are structures by which the deacon could exercise the function of a judicial intermediary.[2] A procurator is someone who has been given a mandate by a party to act on his or her behalf in a judicial case.[3] An advocate, on the other hand, is someone approved by ecclesiastical authority who safeguards the rights of a party in a canonical process by arguments regarding the law and the facts.[4] The advocate gives technical assistance, examining and drawing up the different documents, undertaking the written and oral defense, and prepares evidence.[5] This function requires the advocate to be an expert in canon law and approved by the bishop.[6]

It is the responsibility of the tribunal to provide, as far as possible, permanent legal representatives who receive a salary from the tribunal and whom parties in judicial cases can choose for their representation.[7] If appointed to such office, qualified deacons could provide the assistance of a mediator in the

---

1. See Pokusa, *A Canonical-Historical Study*, 121–22.

2. Although these offices are distinct, they are often performed by the same person in the same case.

3. Ernest Caparros et al. (eds.), *Code of Canon Law Annotated* (Montreal: Wilson and Lafleur Limitée, 1993), 924: "The procurator is, in short, an *alter ego* of the party in whose name and for whom he presents written documents to the tribunal with the petitions, receives notifications, etc. Except for those activities that require the direct participation or a special mandate of the party, the procurator acts in his place, and may even create—by his conduct in the process—procedural responsibilities for the party he represents as if the latter had incurred them himself."

4. Lawrence Wrenn, "Procurators for the Trial and Advocates [cc. 1481–1490]," in *The Code of Canon Law: A Text and Commentary*, ed. James Coriden, Thomas Green, and Donald Heintschel, Canon Law Society of America (New York: Paulist Press, 1985), 967 (hereafter CLSAC).

5. *Code of Canon Law* (ed. Caparros), 924.

6. CIC, c. 1483.

7. CIC, c. 1490: "As far as possible, legal representatives are to be appointed in a stable manner in each tribunal, who receive a stipend from the tribunal and are to exercise, especially in marriage cases, the function of advocate or procurator on behalf of parties who wish to select them."

judicial process on a stable basis. With the office of the procurator-advocate there are the benefits of stability and a ministry well-suited for the deacon as a social intermediary. In addition to the administrative and juridic assistance to the party, the deacon-procurator/advocate would more than likely be in a position to utilize other dimensions of his ministry. In cases concerning the nullity of a marriage, the deacon could assist individuals by providing catechesis and pastoral counseling to help them deal with the reality of their divorce and their prospects for a future marriage. If an annulment is granted, the deacon may even be asked to perform a future marriage ceremony for one of the parties.

Director of Social Services

Many dioceses have created institutions for providing social services in a stable and efficient manner (often called "Catholic Charities" in the United States). The importance of this work in evangelization may be a reason to consider deacons for leadership of these charitable institutions. As an ordained minister of the church, the presence of a deacon in this position would be a structured way of connecting the transformation of the social order with the preaching of the Gospel. The daily work of institutions that provide social services complements the deacon's significance in the liturgy as a symbol of *communitas*. There is also the historical basis for such a diocesan-wide ministry for the deacon, most solemnly memorialized in the Feast of St. Lawrence. Furthermore, having a cleric in this position would tie the bishop more closely to the charitable distribution of the church's resources. The deacon would visibly function as the bishop's hands in directing the social services provided by the church. A qualified layperson who has the mandate of the bishop could, in a pragmatic sense, do the same work. His or her representation of the bishop, however, would not be of the same degree as that of a deacon. In light of the importance of social work in the mission of the church, and in light of the particular charisms of the diaconate, the local church might justifiably fill the position of director of social services with a deacon.

Director of the Office of Social Justice

The charism of the deacon may also be helpful in the fulfillment of the church's obligation to seek the transformation of the social world in her work of evangelization through teaching. The Office of Social Justice usually has a catechetical mission to make members of the local church and the wider community more aware of the fundamental principles of Catholic social teaching. The office is a specialized organ of the church for influencing civic decisions that affect the incorporation of Gospel values in societal structures and policies. The Office of Social Justice could also be concerned with the observance of communion values *within* the church. A deacon entrusted with an office to assist the bishop in safeguarding the church's apostolic identity and integrity would have an influential voice in decisions concerning the apportionment of human and financial resources among the members of the body of Christ. He would function, in this capacity, as the bishop's eyes, ears, and hands. A deacon entrusted with the Office of Social Justice should enjoy the right to speak up, in a respectful manner, to the bishop and his presbyterate on matters of social justice within the local church.

Director of the Family Life Office

Many dioceses have created offices that focus on the important work of evangelizing the family. The scope of the Family Life Office can be very broad: from preparing couples for marriage, marital counseling, and issues related to parenting, to the promotion of the spirituality of marriage and the pastoral care of the divorced and remarried. The *Directory* pointed out how fitting such a ministry is for a married deacon. In light of the fact that many bishops require or strongly recommend that engaged couples participate in certain programs before the celebration of matrimony, a deacon could oversee marriage preparation programs at the diocesan level as director of the Family Life Office. In this position the deacon could also be given the pastoral authority to initiate catechetical programs, retreats, and workshops to assist families in the many difficulties that challenge them today. A married deacon as Family Life director would serve an important and official link between lay organizations like Marriage Encounter or Engaged Encounter and the hierarchy. Because of his experience as a husband and father, the married deacon would naturally be familiar with the needs and concerns of families in the local church. For this reason, and for the expertise gained from his training, the deacon's advice to the bishop and presbyterate on matters related to the evangelization of the family should carry the weight of a recognized authority. The local church could therefore deem the office of the director of the Family Life Office fitting for the ministry of a married deacon.

Parochial Structures

Although a large majority of deacons are assigned to a parish for the entire scope of their ministry, it is not theologically necessary that this form of diaconal ministry continue to be the norm. Rather, pastoral necessity should determine whether or not one or more deacons are appointed to a particular parish. Small, culturally homogenous parishes that have relatively few pastoral or administrative burdens for the pastor might not be appropriate for a parochial deacon's entire ministry. It is the larger parishes—where the pastor and parochial vicar(s) are vastly outnumbered by the size of the congregation— that could warrant the whole ministry of a parochial deacon. Where there is such a pastoral need for one or more deacons, the bishop should strongly consider the possibility of training some deacons specifically for parochial ministry. Because there is no structure for the pastoral office of the deacon in the CIC or *Directory*, careful discernment is needed to structure the appointment of deacons to parishes.

No office exists for the ministry of a deacon in a parish except that which the bishop specially creates. It is a significant fact that the appointment of the deacon to the parish comes from the bishop. The parish deacon exercises his ministry with the mandate of the bishop, not the mandate of the pastor. History evidences that the diaconate thrives only in an organic and collegially structured church, where deacons have a direct connection to the bishop and are not fully subordinate to presbyters in all things. This fact should influence the way the pastor and parochial vicars, as well as the people of the parish, relate to the deacon: the parochial office created by the bishop for the deacon should reinforce the right and obligation of the deacon to share in the pastoral care of the parish, although under the presidency of the pastor. The official appointment letter of a deacon to a parish should provide as much as possible a framework that ensures this shape of ministry for the deacon in the parish. The bishop's letter could identify general areas of ministry that are more particular to the charisms of the diaconate, while leaving the specific determination of the deacon's ministry to the pastor.

One way to structure support for the deacon as a social intermediary in the parish would be to encourage the pastor to consult the parochial deacon on important matters that concern the pastoral care and temporal goods of the parish.[8] The deacon should be an *ex officio* member of pastoral coun-

---

8. The CIC already requires the pastor to consult the parish and finance councils and parochial vicars. For the rights and obligations of parochial vicars, see CIC, cc. 545–52.

cils.[9] If the pastor utilizes the assistance of the deacon in the administration of the parish, the deacon should also be an *ex officio* member of the finance council.[10] These small adjustments in structure would go a long way to clarify the status and position of the deacon in the parish. If these structures were in place, the deacon would have some authority with which to exercise his ministry of assistance to the operative *episkopé* in the parish. The deacon would enjoy a structured access to the head of the parish, allowing the deacon to bring the concerns and desires of the faithful into the decisionmaking process.

Although there are many ways for the deacon to cooperate with the presbyters in the pastoral care of the parish, confusion over the identity of the deacon has impeded the proper utilization of diaconal charisms in the parish. The greatest mistake has been the employment of the deacon as a stand-in or relief support for the presbyters assigned to the parish. Unless the deacon has a specific ministry all his own within the parish, it is likely that he will be defined in terms of the presbyter. The entrustment of the following ministries to the parochial deacon could fortify his identity in distinction from the presbyter.

Social Justice Ministry

An ideal ministry for the deacon in the parish is the promotion of social justice and the direction of charitable works. The deacon could be given the task of developing and implementing initiatives that come from the pastor or pastoral council in order to animate the members of the parish in social justice causes. Catechesis by a deacon who is well-trained in the social teachings of the church would support the social consciousness of the parishioners. Recognized as an agent of communitas, the deacon would be expected to point out the connections between the faith of the Gospel and the everyday life of parishioners. Seeking to heal the fractures of utilitarian individualism, the deacon would bring particular social issues facing the local community to the awareness of parishioners. The deacon's administrative skills could be utilized by entrusting the organization of parish charitable works to him. In this manner, the parochial deacon could provide the necessary institutional requirements for parishioners to get involved with the mission of church. The deacon would have to

---

9. CIC, c. 536 §1: "A pastoral council is to be established in each parish, over which the pastor presides and in which the Christian faithful, together with those who share in pastoral care by virtue of their office in the parish, assist in fostering pastoral activity."

10. Even though the CIC does not require parochial vicars or deacons to be on the finance council (c. 537), it would only make sense to have parochial deacons who serve as finance officers for the parish on this council.

be familiar with the needs of the poor in the local community, especially the needy that belong to the parish. In order to match the needs of the poor with the resources of the parish, the deacon would also have to be acquainted with the gifts and talents of all his parishioners.

If the deacon were to be entrusted with social justice ministry of this nature, his presence on the parish finance council would be beneficial. He could serve as a watchful eye, seeking to guarantee the practice of charity through proper stewardship of the parish's temporal goods. By entrusting the deacon with the promotion of social concern among the parish, the administrative, liturgical, and catechetical dimensions of the deacon's ministry could be harmoniously orchestrated into action.

Parish Administration

Due to a shortage of parish priests in many areas, there has been much discussion concerning the burden of administration that the pastor must carry. Parish business managers are becoming more commonplace, especially in the larger parishes that have schools. The history of the diaconate points to the possibility of entrusting the temporal administration of the parish to a permanent deacon. But in a parish where a business manager is needed, there are typically ministries for the deacon that are just as pressing and more suitable for the ministry of deacons today. The ministry of a deacon assigned to a parish should not impede the involvement of professional laity in the administration of the parish.

The care and administration of a parish cemetery, however, might be particularly appropriate for the deacon. In addition to overseeing the upkeep of the grounds, the deacon could share in the pastoral care of bereaving families. The deacon would provide liturgical assistance at the funeral rites, and perhaps even regularly preside over the rites of burial. In charge of coordinating the various liturgical and pastoral needs that surround the occurrence of death, the deacon could promote the active participation of parishioners and instill concern for those who grieve the loss of a loved one by organizing and training a bereavement committee of parishioners. In this capacity, the deacon could be a great help to the pastor and the parishioners in meeting the needs of people at such a critical pastoral moment.

Catechesis

It is difficult to conceive of a situation in which a deacon, whose entire ministry has been structured for a particular parish, would not have some catechetical function. Because deacons are the primary assistants for the liturgy, they are also important figures in the preparation of candidates for the sacraments. Co-operating with the parish priests and the laity, married deacons could be an important element in a team effort to prepare couples for the sacrament of matrimony. Married deacons might also be preferred over celibate presbyters by some parishioners who seek pastoral counseling for marital problems. Deacons could also serve as procurator-advocates for divorced parishioners who seek the benefit of a church annulment. In all of these pastoral cases, the deacon would have plenty of opportunity to catechize the faithful on the Catholic perspective of the sacrament of marriage.

As already noted above, the early history of the church attests the appropriateness of assigning the catechesis of converts to deacons. The *Didascalia Apostolorum* presents the deacon as a midwife in the spiritual birthing process known as baptism.[11] While respecting the role of the godparent, it would not be unusual to expect parochial deacons to know personally those seeking to join the church, accompanying them closely through the rites of conversion. The presence of the parochial deacon on the parish RCIA formation team would help the catechumens internalize an organic and collegial model of the church.

Parochial deacons could also be entrusted with the task of catechizing parents when they present their child or children for baptism. This particular ministry would place the deacon in close contact with many "marginal" Catholics who rarely attend the Sunday liturgies, but who tend to be quite faithful when it comes to the anthropologically significant rites of passage. A parochial deacon would be a key figure in the work of the new evangelization by exercising such a ministry.

In addition to the proximate preparation for the sacraments, deacons could also provide continuing catechesis at the parochial level. It would be entirely appropriate for pastors to delegate a deacon to teach sections that concern the social teachings of the church, or even entire courses on such a subject for which few Catholics have an adequate understanding or appreciation. Through parish catechesis, the deacon could carry on the work of the new evangelization by teaching the social implications of the Gospel.

11. DA, chap. 16, no. iii, 12; Connolly, *Didascalia*, 146–47.

Pastoral Care of the Sick

Parochial deacons who are assigned the pastoral care of the sick can significantly assist the presbyters and the people of their parish to remedy the alienation and suffering that accompanies illness. To meet the human and spiritual needs of the sick, the parish deacon may be given the responsibility of making regular visits to the hospitals and homes of shut-ins, offering pastoral counseling, the opportunity for prayer, and the sacrament of Communion or Viaticum. The parochial deacon may also coordinate visits by other members of the parish, working to maintain human relationships between the sick and the parish. The deacon would also be the likely figure to arrange, on behalf of the sick, visits by the pastor or parochial vicar for their priestly sacramental ministry. In the more solemn celebration of the liturgy of anointing during a parish Mass, the parochial deacon could be responsible for the logistics of getting the sick to and from the church, as well as the extra arrangements and directions necessary during the liturgy itself.

Inter-Parochial Structures

Authentic pastoral needs may call for the ministry of deacons in the chancery and in parishes. It is not theologically necessary, however, to limit the structure of diaconal ministry to these specific areas. In fact, the development of structures for deacons outside the chancery, and not particular to an individual parish, would better clarify the nature and function of the diaconate as an intermediate institution. The history of the diaconate reveals other appropriate avenues for deacons to perform their unique ministry under the direction of the bishop and in cooperation with the presbyterate. The early church of Rome entrusted deacons with the administration of sacred sites like cemeteries. The early church also entrusted the administration of the church's temporal goods and organization of charitable works to several regional deacons who were responsible for distinct territorial divisions of the church. Inter-parochial structures such as these could provide stability for the ministry of deacons and define more clearly their distinct ministry among the people of God today.

No provisions exist in the CIC or the *Directory* for inter-parochial deacons, therefore positioning the deacon in a stable manner outside the chancery but not in parishes would require careful creativity. Not only does the CIC forbid the positions of pastor and parochial vicar to deacons, but also the titles "chaplain" and "rector."[12] In the inter-parochial structures, the deacon would not exercise a power of governance that pertains to the presbyterate, but he would have greater freedom to initiate and coordinate programs of pastoral care for the people that fall between the cracks of society. They would mediate the care and concern of the people, not only from the bishop and his chancery, but also from the pastors and their parishes. In this "middle territory" of the diocese as their primary domain, deacons would regain a historic basis for the fulfillment of their sociologically significant function of preserving unity and solidarity among the people of God.

Inter-parochial structures could reinforce the distinct character of the diaconate, marking out more concretely its theoretical distinction as an intermediate institution. Entrusting a specific ministry and a specific sector of the local church to deacons would allow them to develop expertise in facilitating the distribution of power and authority among the people of God. Limiting their territory would make it possible for them to become familiar with the people in their pastoral charge. Specifying a particular ministry would allow the deacon to develop and perfect the skills and knowledge necessary to meet the needs of the church that have been entrusted to him. With the development of their abilities in these areas would come the natural authority to speak out on issues associated with their pastoral charge. Inter-parochial assignments should therefore entail a commitment on the part of the bishop and the deacon that is long-term, providing the necessary institutional stability for the proper development of diaconal charisms.

Furthermore, these inter-parochial structures would avoid difficulties that often arise between the presbyter-pastor and the parochial deacon. The deacon who exercises one of the offices I suggest below would work alongside presbyters assigned to the parishes in their district, but relate more directly to the bishop. Because of their mandate from the bishop, deacons would be natural liaisons for the chancery to the people and ministries in their charge. In virtue of their practical knowledge, inter-parochial deacons would be a valuable source of information for those making decisions in the chancery.

In the ministries proposed, the position of the deacon would need to be

---

12. CIC, c. 556: "Rectors of churches are understood here as priests [*sacerdotes*] to whom is committed the care of some church which is neither parochial nor capitular nor connected to a house of a religious community or society of apostolic life which celebrates services in it." CIC, c. 564: "A chaplain is a priest [*sacerdos*] to whom is entrusted in a stable manner the pastoral care, at least in part, of some community or particular group of the Christian faithful, which is to be exercised according to the norm of universal and particular law."

clearly spelled out. The relationship of the deacon with the chancery office, as well as the other clergy of his territory, should be stipulated in writing. The relation between the inter-parochial deacon and parish priests would not necessarily subordinate the deacon to the parish pastors. Presbyters may very well depend upon the authority that the inter-parochial deacon receives from the bishop in providing ministry on behalf of the poor, a ministry specially entrusted to the diaconate by the universal church.[13] To avoid the problems that were associated with the archdiaconate of the late-medieval period, however, it must be made clear that deacons in inter-parochial structures only carry out ministries befitting the charisms of the diaconate. Deacons should only be entrusted with a share but not the whole of pastoral care for the sector under their charge.

Pastoral Care in Existing Institutions

Before the consideration of territorial structures for the ministry of deacons in the diocese, it is important to make note of the need for diaconal ministry at specific and important sites throughout the diocese. Hospitals and prisons are truly sacred sites for Christians, for Christ is present among the suffering and neglected of those institutions. Diocesan cemeteries are also sacred sites for Christians, as it is in them that the hope for the resurrection is made visible by the respect and honor given to the relics of the dead. The local church could benefit from the ministry of deacons in these "in between" places of the diocese. The sacramental presence of the deacon at these institutions would communicate the church's awareness of them as special places for the witness and practice of Gospel values.

Hospital ministry

Catholic hospitals usually make provisions for the pastoral care of the sick, both in their accepted mission and in their establishment of pastoral care departments staffed with employee chaplains. It can be difficult to offer pastoral care in hospitals that are not Catholic, for in these institutions pastoral care

---

13. In general, deacons have auxiliary functions in service to the *episkopé* exercised by the bishop and his presbyterate. In some concrete circumstances, however, deacons exercise functions in accordance with their charisms that place the deacon before individual presbyters in terms of the authority to exercise the mandate received from the bishop. See the arguments made by Herve Legrand and Karl Rahner examined in chapter 6, above.

may or may not be a recognized part of the hospital mission and structure. Although parochial deacons may be charged to visit the sick of their own parishes in hospitals such as these, there are many Catholics and others at the hospital who are not actively involved in their church. Deacons could be assigned by the bishop to hospitals in order to meet, with due discretion, the spiritual needs of all individuals, whether or not they adhere to the Catholic faith or are "active" in another faith system. In addition to bringing Communion, certain sacramentals, and the opportunity for pastoral counseling, deacons assigned to hospitals could function as mediators for the sick and their particular parish church or congregation. As the situation demands, deacons could be on hand to arrange for the ministry of priests or pastors of other denominations at the hospital, facilitating their introduction to the patients. Deacons could also take the lead in animating the faithful to fulfill their part in the church's obligation to visit, assist, and pray for the sick. This could include evangelizing the faithful about the local church's special obligation to people with HIV/AIDS, addictions, or mental illness, people for whom sympathy and charity are not always found among the members of society or the local community of faith.

We must not forget the special pastoral care required for the medical staff members who take care of the sick and dying. A deacon who has special training in helping other people deal with the pressures of working in an environment where suffering and death are common could be of great spiritual benefit to them. A deacon in this ministry could also challenge the medical and administrative staffs of hospitals and care facilities to adopt an understanding of their work as a vocation and not simply a health profession.

Prison Ministry

There could be many opportunities for deacons in prison ministry as well. Although they could not fulfill all the roles of presbyter-chaplains, deacons could function in a similar manner according to the charisms they have. Deacons could be given the regular faculties to preach and lead Communion services, as well as provide pastoral counseling, catechesis, bible studies, and prayer services to prisoners and to staff. In addition to facilitating the ministry of the presbyter or pastor when they come to celebrate the eucharist or other sacraments, deacons could serve as an important link between prisoners and the Christian community outside the walls of the jail or prison. Because of the limited number and nature of visitors at prisons, the presence of the deacon could be very important in maintaining personal contact between prisoners and the Christian community. Deacons who serve in places where death-row inmates are imprisoned would have an important duty in the realm of social justice. They could be key figures for the diocesan office of social justice on the particular issue of capital punishment. Without doubt, assignment for prison ministry would require special skills and training on the part of the deacon.

Diocesan or Regional Cemeteries

For a certain period in the church's history (from at least the time of the episcopal deacon Callistus) the local church regularly entrusted the administration of cemeteries to deacons. The same could happen again if the local church were to deem such a ministry worthwhile for the diaconate. As was mentioned above concerning the administration of parish cemeteries, deacons could be placed in charge of cemeteries that are owned and operated by the diocese or are shared by two or more parishes. In their positions as directors of cemeteries, deacons would ordinarily be available to perform Christian burial for the deceased who have no one to bury them, or for those who have fallen away from participation in a particular congregation. The local church may very well deem such a position proper for the ministry of the deacon.

Territorial "Deaconries"

One of the greatest obstacles to clarifying the role of the deacon is the absence of any meaningful, defined diaconal structures in the church. Bishops have dioceses and priests have parishes, but what does the deacon have that is uniquely his? The structure similar to "deaconries" of old could provide an ideal framework for diaconal ministry. In this institution, the deacon could be allowed to specialize in the exercise of a charism at the heart of his order, all the while avoiding the subordination of deacons to parish priests.

The establishment of territorial deaconries would supply a concrete means of clarifying more precisely the identity and role of the deacon among the people of God. In this inter-parochial structure, the deacon would be more directly connected to his bishop. As the hands of the bishop, the deacon would represent the care and concern of the bishop for his people. As the eyes of the bishop, the deacon would relate to the bishop and the major decisionmakers in the chancery the needs and desires of the poor in his sector of the church. The inter-parochial deacon assigned to a deaconry would also have an intrinsic relationship to the parishes of his territory. The deacon would be familiar with people and clergy of the parishes within his territory, coordinating the ministry of charitable works and social justice among them. The inter-parochial deacon would thus serve as an intermediate institution between the parishes and the poor among them. The relationship between deaconries and parishes needs to be delicately considered because the CIC already provides structures for the coordination of pastoral care among parishes within various regions in the diocese.

For the territorial limits of the deaconries, the local church may decide to follow regional divisions that already exist in the form of deaneries or "vicariates forane."[14] If this were the case, then the place of the vicar forane must be taken into account when structuring the office of the inter-parochial deacon. The vicar forane has the duty and right to promote and coordinate common pastoral activity in the vicariate, and he has some authority over the clergy in his vicariate.[15] For these reasons, the inter-parochial deacon would be under the authority of the vicar forane. One benefit of having the deaconries coincide with the vicariates forane would be the elimination of any possibility for powerful "archdeaconries" to develop within the local church. The provision in the CIC for the office of vicar forane reinforces the authority of the presbyterate and prevents deaconries from developing power and authority beyond the scope of diaconal ministry.

The ministry of the inter-parochial deacon assigned to a deaconry could entail administrative, catechetical, and liturgical functions. Administratively, the regional deacons could be the primary promoters and directors of the church's charitable works. As urban areas tend to already have institutions for the distribution of social services, the local church may identify less populated areas as the sphere of diaconal ministry. Alternatively, deacons could be entrusted with promoting and directing charitable activities among people for whom the local church is weakest in meeting the social obligations of evangelization.[16] Working alongside the pastors, the deacons would call forth the gifts and talents of the laity in his region. The regional deacon would build up the body of Christ by encouraging the exercise of baptismal charisms of the people of God, who sanctify the world in the work of evangelization through the human advancement of society.

14. CIC, c. 374 §2: "To foster pastoral care through common action, several neighboring parishes can be joined into special groups, such as vicariates forane."

15. CIC, c. 555.

16. An Italian author promotes the idea of utilizing permanent deacons to evangelize the social world of the laborer. Although this may not require a structure like that of a deaconry, it provides yet another possibility for the ministry of deacons today in a specific social context. See Nicola Ceci, *Il Ministero del Diacono nel mondo del lavoro* (Rome: Editrice Rogate, 1999).

Deacons are much freer than priests to work in secular structures, and therefore the deacon can be a key player in advancing social development through political and other civic activities and institutions.[17] For the evangelization of the faithful, the regional deacon would need structured avenues that provide him an entry into the parishes of his territory. He would need forums in which to address the social needs of the people of the community, to preach the social teachings of the church and Gospel, and animate the laity to take their part in the work of social development. If more than one deacon were assigned to a particular deaconry, then they could divide the parishes of their territory among themselves in programs of catechesis. The deaconry could also have its own forums for catechesis and social debate, perhaps holding discussions that are more difficult to have in the parish context.

Regional deacons could also be present for the Sunday liturgies of the various parishes in their territory. Making visits to parishes at regular intervals, regional deacons would be expected to provide liturgical assistance, thereby manifesting the relationship between the work they do in promoting and directing charitable works and the nature of the Mass as a passage to communion. The liturgical assistance of regional deacons would be most appropriate at episcopal liturgies that take place within their deaconry, such as the celebration of confirmation, the installation of a pastor, or other special Masses. Although regional deacons would not be placed directly within the parochial structures of ministry, the administrative, catechetical, and liturgical dimensions of their ministry would necessitate avenues into the life and work of the parish. The interplay of the parish and the deaconry would manifest the unity and diversity of the church that exists at higher levels.[18]

Leadership of Various Sectors
within the Church

Deacons could also be assigned to particular groupings of people within the diocese that are not territorially based. For example, the multicultural character of the local church has encouraged many bishops to establish important links between themselves and the various ethnic or cultural groups that are

17. The CIC does not prohibit deacons from holding public office or other political offices, including participation in labor unions. This sort of activity is normally forbidden for other clergy. See CIC, c. 288.

18. In addition to the various levels of organization of the church between the papacy and the diocese, religious orders and societies of apostolic life overlap the structures of the diocese and parish.

present in the local church. Economic and language barriers often make participation in the local church very difficult for some of these groups. While the full pastoral care for these people demands charisms beyond the diaconate, qualified deacons could nonetheless serve as personal liaisons between the bishop and the various cultural communities.[19] The deacon's charisms allow him to hold liturgies of the word, to preach and teach in the language of the people to whom he is called to minister. The deacon could provide administrative service by coordinating programs of evangelization, and making members of the dominant culture aware of the presence of other cultures in their midst. The deacon could play a crucial role in making sure the sacramental needs of the people in his charge are met. Classes of people like migrant workers pose a special difficulty for the bishop and his priests. In order to meet the spiritual needs of a people who are continually "on the move," flexible structures are required. Several deacons entrusted with the leadership of smaller communities within the larger church could help make the pastoral care of the bishop and his priests more effective for these people.

Conclusion

The offices and ministries proposed in this section for the diaconate in the local church provide the necessary structures for the deacon to exercise a ministry at the heart of the diaconate: to serve as a social intermediary and symbol of *communitas* among the people of God. The proposed ministries, and the institutional structures for them, follow the theological outlines established by the Second Vatican Council, the CIC, and the *Directory*. The creation of specific offices for the ministry of deacons in the local church is key to firming up the identity of the deacon and his fundamental role among the people of God. Not only is it important to discern the proper ministries for the deacon in the local church, but it is also important to provide the right structures that allow deacons to perform the function that has roots going back to the early church of Rome. The implementation of some or all of the above suggestions for the ministry of deacons would restore historical structures for the ministry of the deacons, but in a form that is needed for today. In light of the cultural forces in

19. The CIC calls for the appointment of presbyter-chaplains to provide pastoral care for special groups within the diocese. See CIC, c. 568: "As far as possible, chaplains are to be appointed for those who are not able to avail themselves of the ordinary care of pastors because of the condition of their lives, such as migrants, exiles, refugees, nomads, sailors."

modern societies that tear apart the basic human bond, the role of the deacon could be an important element of the church's new evangelization.

In accomplishing these proposed pastoral tasks, the deacon would continue to function as an apostolic minister, seeking to safeguard the apostolic identity of the local church in terms of right teaching, right worship, and just living. The deacon's participation in the work of evangelization includes his ministry of proclaiming the Gospel and teaching its social implications. The symbolic role of the deacon in the liturgy reinforces sentiments of belonging to one another as people of the New Covenant. The ritual functions of the deacon call attention to the fact that our union with God is bound up with our communion with one another. The deacon's concern for right worship, therefore, not only concerns the active participation of the people during the liturgical ceremony, but also their worship in daily life. The deacon thus works for the healing of social fractures, resisting the cultural forces that work against authentic human communion by reinforcing sentiments and actions of sacrificial love. The source and summit of diaconal ministry structured for social mediation is none other than the Paschal mystery.

Configured to Christ the servant, the deacon serves the bishop and the church as a whole. In the ministries and structures proposed above, the deacon would ultimately have as his objective the full participation of the laity in the life and mission of the church. In representing both the people and the pastoral authorities within the church in his mediating functions, the deacon also assists the legitimation of the exercise of authority among the people of God. Stronger bonds of communion within the local church are the fruits of diaconal ministry structured according to an organic and collegial model of the church. Having structured access to the decisionmaking process, deacons can express the needs and desires of the Christian faithful at the table where decisions are made. Structured closely to the people in their pastoral ministry, deacons would also able to express the love and concern of the bishop (and the pastor) for his flock. This is an important function not only for social reasons, but most of all because it is the desire of the Good Shepherd for his bishops and priests to feed and tend his sheep.

Conclusion

An inadequate role description for Latin-rite deacons hampers the effectiveness of their ministry. For the diaconate to become successful it must have a specialized ministry that is well-defined and important to the life and mission of the church. Deacons know they are called to serve as ordained ministers, and they have some concrete guidance regarding what they are allowed to do, but pastoral demands and a lack of clarity pull them in various directions. We should not assume that, because the ranks of permanent deacons have been growing and the pastoral need is great, the diaconate will simply flourish now that it has been restored. The original Golden Age of the deacon in the history of the church, as we have seen, occurred before the legalization of Christianity in the Roman Empire, before the church grew to its large present structure of dioceses and parishes. In a sense, the diaconate as a distinct ministry failed, over centuries, to find its place in a church structure where bishops manage a large territory and individual pastors hold sway in far-flung parish communities. The Second Vatican Council has given the permanent diaconate a second chance, in a modern world where transportation and communication allows for greater contact among the church's ordained ministers than has been seen since the early days of the church. But we are also in a time of a growing "priest shortage," in which the temptation is strong to use permanent deacons simply as priest stand-ins or "mini-priests." Instead, we should be looking at what is unique and necessary to the charisms of deacons as "ordained to the ministry, not the priesthood."

For the diaconate to thrive, bishops, priests, the laity, and the deacons themselves must understand what deacons are called to do and whether a particular ministry is appropriate for the diaconate. The deacon's role cannot be reduced to a simple set of tasks, whether charitable or liturgical. Such limitations of the deacon's scope occurred after the Golden Age of the diaconate in the church's history, and the result was the gradual diminishment of the diaconate to a mere stepping stone to the priesthood—the very situation that the Second Vatican Council sought to remedy by restoring a "permanent" diaconate. Instead, deacons need a focal understanding of their role that organizes many potential activities, encouraging some and discouraging others.

By examining the diaconate from a variety of angles, I have uncovered what is and ought to be the role of deacons for a church in the modern world. The deacon has been, and could still be, a symbol of *communitas* and social intermediary among the people of God. As a social intermediary, he should work to connect the people of God with their local leader, the bishop, and the church with the needs of the poor; not as a barrier standing in the way of direct contact, but as a bridge-builder drawing church leaders, ordinary believers, and people on the margins of society closer together. As a symbol of *communitas*, he should encourage the faithful to see each other in their shared humanity, more basic than all social roles and distinctions.

Deacons already often play such a role and can already begin to live this understanding in their ministry. But the evidence suggests that they do not often have this self-understanding, especially when it comes to promoting the social teaching of the church in word and deed. So the first key step is a change in understanding the role of the diaconate, not only for deacons themselves but for bishops, priests, and the laity.

Furthermore, the diaconate also needs to be structured in such a way as to serve the social distribution of power and material resources among the people of God. I have given many such suggestions in the latter part of this book, and I will give a few more at the end of this chapter, but the essential point is not any of the individual suggestions provided. Rather, it is essential for the structure of the diaconate to flow out of its central charisms, rather than being pasted together *ad hoc*. Only then will it be fully empowered to be a ministry at the heart of the church.

Recapitulation

The terms *communitas* and "social intermediary" are drawn from social sciences, but in articulating the deacon's role using these terms, I am not intending to reduce the deacon or the church to merely human, sociological terms. Rather,

I introduced these terms through an analysis of some sociological and anthropological sources in order to provide a lens through which to make better sense of the underdeveloped theology and varied history of the diaconate. My search for a specialized, diaconal ministry could not have begun with an immediate evaluation of the historical functions given to the deacon. At the start of my inquiry, I had no clear means of determining which roles were appropriate for diaconal charisms and which were not. The historical forms of the diaconate are a mixture of consistent patterns and divergent irregularities, which cautions against a rigid formulation of the diaconate to the last detail. Consequently, the inherent flexibility of the diaconate has made it very difficult to grasp its essential core beyond that of the general statement, "the ministry of charity."

The Second Vatican Council and Earliest Sources

Nor have Magisterial pronouncements on the diaconate provided the specificity that we seek. Of all the Magisterial teachings on the diaconate, the Second Vatican Council is paramount, and it produced only minimal descriptions of the diaconate. The teaching found in *Lumen Gentium* on the diaconate was very important: it opened the doorway for a stable order in the Latin rite, "ordained not to the priesthood, but to the ministry." But the Council's teaching does not provide greater precision about the relationship between the charisms given at the ordination of deacons and the type of ministry they are to perform among the people of God. We still needed a new way of interpreting the various functions that had been entrusted to them over time. The methodology of my study provides the ability to relate the theological charisms of the diaconate, as currently understood, with a concrete recognizable structure and function that is found in the earliest sources of the church.

The very earliest sources, and those given special reference in the teaching on the diaconate found in *Lumen Gentium*, are the biblical writings that use the words *diakonos, diakonia,* and *diakonein.* I found minimal information about the office of deacon in the pages of the New Testament. I discovered, however, that *diakonia* is more than a "humble servant"; it connotes the function of mediation, the work of a herald, messenger, ambassador, or go-between. I also ascertained that biblical *diakonia* must be understood within Christological, pneumatological, and ecclesial dimensions. *Diakonia* flows from a gift of the Spirit, is rendered in conformity to the way of Christ, and is in service to the church as a whole and not for one's personal gain. While scripture does not provide a ready-made answer to contemporary questions about the diaconate, it does provide the theological framework within which the diaconate operates. The Second Vatican Council applied the biblical concept of *diakonia* to the diaconate in its affirmation that deacons are strengthened with sacramental grace, namely that they are to model their ministry after the humble service of Christ, and that they are dedicated to the people of God in communion with their bishop and his presbyterate.

My investigation of the teaching in *Lumen Gentium* led also to a consideration of the patristic text known as the *Apostolic Tradition* and attributed to St. Hippolytus. This document is of great value as it is one of the earliest sources that goes into some detail about the nature and ministry of the diaconal office. The author's commentary on the ordination rite for deacons makes explicit the distinction between the deacon and the presbyter: the deacon, unlike the presbyter, is ordained "not to the priesthood, but to the ministry." Maintaining this theological distinction is important in our attempt to safeguard the charism of the diaconate in our day. The more that deacons are viewed as sacral mini-priests, the more likely they are to be confused with the order of presbyters. It is unfortunate that the scholastic notion of the diaconate as a particular degree of participation in, or a step toward, the ministerial priesthood still influences the conceptualization of the deacon in the minds of many people in the church today.

Although it is necessary to maintain an adequate distinction from the presbyterate, clarity cannot be found for the order of deacon apart from the other ecclesiastical orders, especially the episcopacy. The teaching of *Lumen Gentium* ties the ministry of the deacon closely to the ministry of the bishop. Collegiality, collaboration, and communion are the backdrop for the Second Vatican Council's teaching on the ecclesiastical *ordo*. The deacon has a share in the apostolic ministry of the bishop, though not in the same manner as that of the presbyter.

It is true that deacons share with the bishop and presbyters the task of safeguarding the apostolic faith, worship, and moral life among the people of God in their charge. But deacons are different from the rest of the clergy because they do not have the responsibility of oversight of the local church. The position of deacons in the organizational structure of the church provides them with a unique way to serve out the ministries of administration and charity. Devoted to the ministry of charity without the responsibility of presidency, deacons are institutionally less impeded to bear the presence of Christ to those on the margins of society and the church. The natural separation that occurs with the exercise of institutional power and authority does not hamper them.

Thus, deacons are free to challenge and exhort the people of God in a way that bishops and presbyters are not. Furthermore, the structure of the diaconate makes it well-suited for the role of mediating between the higher clergy and the rest of the Christian faithful.

Following the close of the Council, Pope Paul VI implemented the Council's desire to make possible the permanent diaconate. Prophetically, Paul VI stated in *Ad Pascendum* that the "intermediate order" known as the diaconate is an expression of the needs and desires of the Christian communities, and is a driving force for *diakonia*. My research of the theological material on the diaconate points to the apex that is Paul VI's statement. From this point forward, my study sought to comprehend the significance of the diaconate as an "intermediate order," and to appreciate this insight more completely from the perspective of sociology.

Insights from Sociology

The next section turned more directly to an exploration of the social need for mediation among the people of God. The more complex a society is, the greater the need for social institutions that tie the individuals of the society together. I brought to light the excessive forms of individualism that sociologists have identified in contemporary cultures. Porous institutions, loose commitments, and the experience of alienation are the contemporary "signs of the times" that the church is called to interpret in light of the Gospel.

The perspective of sociology was not only useful to comprehend better the world that the church is called to serve, it also helped to elucidate the human dimension of the church itself. As the body of Christ in which the Spirit dwells, the church has a social reality that cannot be ignored. The way in which the members of the body of Christ relate to one another in terms of power, authority, and influence is a concern of the Gospel. My research found that intermediate structures are necessary to ensure the sufficient distribution of knowledge and power. Intermediate institutions satisfy the need to legitimate authority within a given society when they are effective in making the leadership aware of the needs of the people and when they communicate the concern of the leadership back to the people. These intermediate institutions alleviate tensions and break down barriers that might develop between those who have the ultimate responsibility to make final decisions, and those who must follow the decisions that are made.

I concluded that the role of an intermediary figure between the bishop and the people, and between the people of God and the individual in need, is consistent with the theological foundations of the ministry of the deacon. The ultimate work of the church in transforming human society into a true communion with God and one another can only be accomplished through the personal participation of individuals. But while the choice to "love one another" is made within the recesses of the heart, it is not made without the assistance of institutions. The community of the church, with its social structures in service to the Spirit, provides the necessary social and theological environment for the individual to exercise his or her choice for the Christian way of life. If the diaconate were structured to mediate the relationships between the bishop and his flock, or between the people of God and individuals in need, the deacon would not only serve to bring about greater social cohesion but also greater personal conversion. The performance of diaconal ministry not only manifests the unity of the church, but also manifests her love through the active engagement of her members.

In my endeavor to delineate the nature and purpose of a social intermediary in the church, we uncovered a relationship between social structure and the life and mission of the church. The diaconate as an intermediate order among the people of God touches upon the constitution of the church, her very nature and purpose. With the concept of social intermediary as our tool of interpretation in hand, we were ready to examine the historical functions of the diaconate down through the centuries.

The History of the Diaconate: From the Golden Age to Sacralization

I then journeyed through the history of the church, searching for precedents of the deacon as social intermediary. I made historical connections between diaconal charisms and mediating functions in the exercise of the diaconate. In the Golden Age of the diaconate during the third and fourth centuries, deacons were very important to the life of the church. They were the chief liaisons between the bishop and the laity. The deacon was responsible for the care of the sick, feeding the poor, burial of the dead, the extension of hospitality, and the administration of temporalities. In performing these tasks deacons were essential in the bishop's exercise of pastoral care for his flock. The deacon was also important in animating the laity to fulfill their obligations to those in need. It was the deacon's role to build up the community of faith by reminding them of their obligation to serve. They were not only effective agents of communion, but also visible, everyday reminders of the Gospel command to love one another.

As the idea of cult came to have a primary position for the ordained ministry, so the non-cultic functions of the deacon were relegated to a lower importance. The sacralization of the ministry, with the consequent disciplines of mandatory celibacy and the *cursus honorum*, deprived the diaconate of its original vigor. No longer were some men ordained to the priesthood, and others to the diaconate, but all clergy passed through the diaconate to the presbyterate and few, if any, persevered in the order of deacons for a lifetime, let alone exercised the unique social roles of the diaconate. Though it had been important for the life and mission of the church, the diaconate was virtually removed from the social structure of the church during the Middle Ages, except for the figure of the archdeacon. During this era of the diaconate, the social function of the deacon as a mediator of power and authority among the people of God was not expressly recognized or practiced. Most deacons no longer worked in close proximity to the bishop and were instead directly subordinate to the presbyter under whom they performed their ministry.

The office of archdeacon in the Middle Ages was unique in that a deacon in this office did maintain a close connection with the bishop. The office of archdeacon accumulated so much power and authority over time, however, that the archdeacon could no longer be said to function as a social intermediary as we understand it. Though he was nominally the spokesman for the poor and all others under him, including the other clergy, he was not all that distinct sociologically from the bishop. He was too much like the bishop and not enough like the people for whom he was making decisions. But even the history of the archdeacon supports my thesis that the deacon is still, at root, a social intermediary among the people of God. There is a direct correlation between the practice of appointing presbyters to the office of archdeacon and the disengagement of the office of the archdeacon from an authentic, intermediate social function. History shows that the diaconate was vital to the life and mission of the church when it served as an intermediate institution among the people of God in the Golden Age. But the transformation of the diaconate into other functions during the Middle Ages left little reason for deacons to hold the offices they were now occupying. Eventually, even the office of archdeacon no longer required a deacon to fulfill its tasks.

Ritual Roles

Although the history of the decline of the permanent diaconate suggested that deacons must not be restricted to a liturgical role, I did not mean to imply that deacons do not need a robust involvement in the liturgy to fulfill their call and ministry. "Social intermediary" by itself is an incomplete understanding of the deacon's role, which cannot be reduced to that of a social worker. Hence, I next turned to examine the symbolic role of the deacon. I sought to understand the significance of the liturgical ministry of deacons, and found a link between their ritual functions around the altar and their ministry of social mediation in daily life. Studies in anthropology indicate that ritual is a powerful tool for the reinforcement of social cohesion. Through the ritual act, people reconnect with the source of community at a fundamental level. Ritual's dialectical relationship with society does not, however, guarantee its effectiveness. Ritual needs the supportive environment of an already existing community life to be effective. Ritual and the experience of community are linked together.

Turner's anthropological theory of ritual includes the concept of "symbols of *communitas*" that work to connect individuals with their community. Symbols of *communitas* induce a desire for community and enable individuals to encounter one another at a level deeper than their normal social statuses. My investigation of the deacon's paradigmatic roles in the eucharist in light of Turner's theory provided a means to evaluate the liturgical ministry of the deacon. During key *communitas* moments of the Mass, deacons function as symbols of *communitas* when they draw the assembly's attention to the presence and needs of others. The role of the deacon in the general intercessions, the procession of the gifts and their preparation, the sign of peace, the distribution of communion, and dismissal symbolically manifest the deacon's role as a social intermediary among the people of God.

Implications for Today

Finally, I considered the common functions entrusted to the deacon today, and proposed the creation of new ones to better structure the diaconate according to diaconal charisms. I found that the revised Code of Canon Law (CIC) does not adequately capture the vision of the diaconate as espoused by the Second Vatican Council. Still locked in the scholastic mode of ministry, the CIC lacks the necessary nuance that upholds the unique character of the diaconate in distinction from the presbyterate and the episcopacy until its modification by Pope Benedict XVI. Furthermore, the CIC does not offer a unique structure for the ministry of the deacon either in the parish, alongside the parish, or at the diocesan level. The latest document from Rome concerning the life and ministry of deacons improves upon the treatment of the deacon in the CIC by explaining the ministry of the deacon in greater depth without collapsing it into the ministerial priesthood. But the *Directory* does not fully enflesh the unique social quality of the diaconate as an intermediate order. I therefore took it upon myself to spell out possible new structures for the ministry of deacons in the contemporary church.

The suggested structures are born from my appreciation for the unique character of the diaconate as an institution for social mediation. I advocated for the creation of new offices for deacons parallel to the parochial structure so as to avoid confusion with presbyteral ministry and to better utilize the charisms of the diaconate. Structures similar to the deaconries of old might be of benefit to the church today, while certain diocesan offices already hold promise for the ministry of deacons. But if deacons are to continue functioning primarily in the parochial context, then a standardized office for the parish deacon needs to be created in order to stabilize the rights and obligations awarded the deacon in this context.

While I would recommend the encouragement of such structures from the highest levels of the church hierarchy, the local diocese should have the requisite freedom to discern the particular offices and ministries which it desires to entrust to the ministry of deacons. The bishop, in consultation with his presbyterate and the people of his diocese, needs to be careful in the selection of functions for his deacons. I provided many suggestions in chapters 8 and 9 as to which ministries and functions seem to be in keeping with the charisms of the diaconate, but these are meant to be illustrative, not exhaustive. As a diocese discerns with its deacons what they are to do, it should keep in mind that the success of the diaconate depends upon the ability of deacons to function as symbols of *communitas* and social intermediaries among the people of God. The choice of candidates to the diaconate would then be determined most by the candidates' gifts, talents, and abilities in fulfilling the particular ministries already chosen for them.

In summary, my examination of the theological foundations of the diaconate, and the social need for mediation among the people of God, identifies the deacon's position in the organizational structure of the church. Taking into consideration the renewal begun by the Second Vatican Council, I conclude that a conscious restructuring of diaconal ministry along the lines of social mediation is in order. I have found that the nature of the diaconate is well-suited for the necessary function of social mediation, and that there are a variety of roles that could be entrusted to the order of deacons to accomplish this specialized ministry among the people of God.

Further Implications

The description of the deacon as a symbol of *communitas* and social intermediary among the people of God clarifies adequately the role of the diaconate for a church in the modern world. But what is the relationship of the diaconate to other institutions of social mediation within the church? The necessity of social mediation has produced many other structures in the church apart from the diaconate, such as, councils, synods, and other offices that can be fulfilled by the laity. How is the deacon unique among them?

The Ministry of *Diakonia* and the Priesthood

The deacon functions both in a personal and symbolic manner. As a personal agent and promoter of *diakonia* among the people of God, the deacon performs his ministry in a stable, day-to-day manner. In this his ministry is distinct from other periodic forms of mediation. And in distinction to the laity, who can be empowered to fulfill tasks akin to social mediation, only the deacon is an enduring, sacramentally configured icon of Christ the servant.

The unique sacramental character of deacons distinguishes them among the laity and the members of the other clerical orders. In the process of ordination, candidates for the order of deacon receive special charisms to be industrious imitators of the Lord in the humble way of charity. With the reception of these gifts comes the obligation, on the part of deacons, to fulfill the ministry for which they are given. In ordaining candidates to the order of deacon, the local church obliges itself to deploy them well. They are to be a concrete manifestation of Christ among us, bearing the presence of Christ to those they meet in the everyday affairs of their ministry.

The deacon does not enact diaconal ministry in place of the laity or the bishop; rather, deacons represent the diaconal dimension of the church as a whole. There is a need for this special sacramental presence among us. As the presence of bishops and presbyters reminds the *ekklesia* of its dependence upon Christ the head, the presence of deacons reminds us of our dependence on Christ the servant. Only by allowing Christ to serve us can we respond to his command to be self-emptying servants of one another.

My concept of the deacon as a social intermediary affirms a distinction within the unity of the sacrament of holy orders. I have found that the expression "sacerdotal character" is inexact when it is applied to this sacrament in general. It is better to speak of a "ministerial character" or *diakonia*, as did the Second Vatican Council. Bishops, priests, and deacons are together charged with bringing the *diakonia* of Jesus Christ to the poor and needy, and to further develop it within the church. This is expressly stated for the bishop, and the deacon shares in the diaconal task of the bishop in a special way. Presbyters have a different sharing in the ministry of the bishop, one that includes the *episkopé*. The presbyters represent the bishop in their parishes and have the final responsibility for leadership in the communities in their charge. This is why they alone preside at the eucharist. Consequently, presbyters have a greater share of the apostolic mission of the bishop than do deacons.

But deacons have a share in the apostolic mission of the bishop, too. Deacons represent the bishop in the performance of *diakonia*, for which the bishop is ultimately and directly responsible. As the presbyter shares in the presidential leadership of the bishop, deacons are called to conduct their ministry not only in unity with the bishop, but also in communion with the presbyterate. The following diagram best illustrates the relationship of the deacon to the clergy of the other orders:

FIGURE 10.1

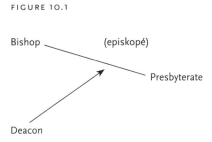

By contrast, the scholastic notion of ministry requires either the rejection of the sacramental character of the diaconate or an intrinsic association of it with the ministerial priesthood. Neither of these adequately accounts for what we know of the deacon from history and the sources of Catholic belief. I have already shown that reducing diaconal ministry to a participation in the ministerial priesthood contradicts the earliest sources of the faith and prolongs the confusion of the diaconate with the presbyterate. The Second Vatican Council taught that deacons are "strengthened by sacramental grace," alluding to the sacramental character of the diaconate itself. Though the ministerial priesthood is central to the sacrament of holy orders (and indeed, we could even say the diaconate is oriented to its fruitful exercise), the sacrament is not limited to the spiritual powers of the priesthood.[1] It also includes other gifts of the Holy Spirit given to the clergy for building up the church. In short, we have deacons *because* we have priests and bishops.

But in the schema of a "middle priesthood," the diaconate would be a step directly above the baptized and confirmed laity, and a step directly beneath the presbyter. This schema contradicts the organic and collegial understanding of ministry found in the teachings of the early Church Fathers and the Second Vatican Council. It also effectively evaporates the uniqueness of diaconal ministry into the ministry that pertains to the presbyter. The idea of a "middle priesthood" should be recognized as an innovation, rather than a true description of the Catholic belief concerning the diaconate. As the diaconate entails a sacramental character, and does not entail a participation in the *sacerdotium* of the bishop, the fundamental element of the sacrament of holy orders must be *diakonia*. In this perspective, there are no contradictions between the ecclesiastical ministry of the ordained and the ecclesial ministry of the baptized.

Needed Adjustments to Church Law and Documents

In order to manifest more clearly the true character of diaconal ministry, changes need to be made in some of the established texts that greatly influence the understanding of the deacon in the minds of people. I investigated the deacon as presented in the CIC, pointing out that there is still a need to make provisions for the special ministry of the deacon. I noted that the CIC forbids the title of "chaplain" or "vicar" to the deacon, and yet offers no particular office in the parish open for the ordinary ministry of the deacon. If deacons are to be utilized in the parish, then there ought to be some official office for them similar in status to that of parochial vicar for the presbyter. Clearly established expectations and rights for deacons in the parochial context are needed. Even

---

1. I do not, in this book, explore the question of whether women could be ordained to the order of the diaconate, which remains a lively question at the time of publication. The proper exclusion of the diaconate from the priesthood would bear directly on that question.

the simple title of "parish deacon" with a stipulation of the requisite universal rights and responsibilities would be beneficial. This would go a long way
to alleviate confusion over diaconal and presbyteral ministry. Furthermore,
as deacons cannot have the title or office of "chaplain" when they are given
the responsibility of providing pastoral care in institutions such as hospitals or
prisons, some other stable office or title should be created for the ministry of
deacons in these situations.[2]

Another important text that greatly influences our conception of diaconal
ministry is the Rite of Ordination of Deacons, which does not envision a participation in the ministerial priesthood. Sacerdotal language is noticeably and
thankfully absent, with only a fleeting and subdued reference given to the *ministerium* of the sons of Levi in the anamnetic section of the ordination prayer.
While the ordination rites of bishops and presbyters link their ministries with
the *tria munera* (office of priest, prophet, and king), the diaconal rite of ordination does not make the same association.[3] Yet there is still room for improve-
ment in the most recent ritual text of the ordination of deacons.[4]

The ritual text would be improved by the addition of clear and precise language about the nature of the diaconate. A specific element within the ordination liturgy needs attention, the promises made by the candidates for the
order of deacon. There are now either five or six ritual questions (depending

2. For a canonical analysis of the ministry of permanent deacons as military chaplains, see William Ditewig, "The Permanent Deacon as Military Chaplain: Canonical Reflections," *Jurist* 51 (1991):
340–63.

3. In the ordination homily for a bishop, we read: "Our Lord Jesus Christ, who was sent by the
Father to redeem the human race, in turn sent twelve Apostles into the world. They were filled with
the power of the Holy Spirit, to preach the Gospel, and to sanctify and govern all the peoples gathered
into one flock." Congregation for Divine Worship and the Discipline of the Sacraments, *Pontificale
Romanum ex Decreto Sacrosancti Oecumenici Concilii Vaticani II Renovatum Auctoritate Pauli PP.VI Editum Ioannis Pauli PP. II Cura Recognitum. De Ordinatione Episcopi, Presbyterorum et Diaconorum*, editio
typica altera (Vatican City: Typis Polyglottis Vaticanis, 1990), no. 75 (38) (hereafter OEPD). English
translation: International Commission on English in the Liturgy, *The Roman Pontifical as Renewed by
Decree of the Second Vatican Ecumenical Council Published by Authority of Pope Paul VI and Further Revised at the Direction of Pope John Paul II. Rites of Ordination of a Bishop, of Priests, and of Deacons*, second
typical edition (Washington, D.C.: United States Conference of Catholic Bishops, 2003), no. 75 (46)
(hereafter ROBPD). In the ordination homily of priests, we read: "For your part, you will exercise
the sacred duty of teaching in the name of Christ the Teacher.... Likewise you will exercise in Christ
the office of sanctifying.... Finally, dear sons, exercising for your part the office of Christ, Head and
Shepherd" (no. 123 [75–76]).

4. For a comparison of the *editio typica* and *editio typica altera* of the rites of ordination, see Jan
Michael Joncas, "The Public Language of Ministry Revisited: *De Ordinatione Episcopi, Presbyterorum
et Diaconorum* 1990," *Worship* 68 (1994): 386–403.

on whether the candidate is married) that deacon-candidates are expected to answer in the affirmative. There were only four questions in the first ritual text following the Second Vatican Council. The four original questions are present in the new ritual in exactly the same form. The first, second, and third questions of both the old and new ritual are general questions that lack any real specificity concerning diaconal charisms. They deal with the candidates' willingness: (1) to be "consecrated" [*consecrari*] for the ministry; (2) to fulfill the *munus* of the diaconate by assisting the priestly orders and by assisting the Christian people to advance in humble charity; (3) and to hold and preach the mystery of faith by word and deed.[5] The previous fourth ritual question, which corresponds to the last promise in the new rite, asks the candidates if they are willing to conform their lives to Christ in light of their proximate ministry at the altar.[6] Three of the four original questions touch upon the concept of biblical *diakonia* in terms of pneumatological (1), ecclesiological (2), and Christological (4) principles. As such, these questions are legitimate and are somewhat helpful in the process of internalizing a correct understanding of the diaconate. None of them, however, explicate well what is unique about diaconal ministry.

A fifth ritual question was inserted in the new rite to highlight the commitment to celibacy required of candidates who are not married.[7] Between the publication of the *editio typica* and the *editio typica altera*, the subdiaconate was suppressed. The new ritual, therefore, incorporated the commitment to celibacy within the ordination ritual of deacons. No ritual promise is demanded of the married deacon for a commitment to celibacy upon the death of his wife, but the fifth ritual question, as it now stands, is unfortunate because it draws attention to the value of celibacy for the diaconate without giving requisite attention to the value of a married diaconate. Marriage, as well as the commitment to celibacy, can enrich diaconal ministry. We should avoid giving the

5. OEPD, no. 200 (130): "Do you resolve to be consecrated for the Church's ministry by the laying on of my hands and the gift of the Holy Spirit?" ROBPD, no. 200 (130): "Do you resolve to discharge the office of deacon with humble charity in order to assist the priestly Order and to benefit the Christian people?" Ibid.: "Do you resolve to hold fast to the mystery of faith with a clear conscience, as the Apostle urges, and to proclaim this faith in word and deed according to the Gospel and the Church's tradition?"

6. ROBPD, no. 200 (131): "Do you resolve to conform your way of life always to the example of Christ, of whose Body and Blood you are ministers at the altar?"

7. Ibid.: "Those of you who are prepared to embrace the celibate state: do you resolve to keep for ever this commitment as a sign of your dedication to Christ the Lord for the sake of the Kingdom of Heaven, in the service of God and man?"

appearance in the ordination liturgy that married deacons are second-class to celibate deacons (or vice-versa). A simple remedy that would not require the elimination of the question on celibacy would be the addition of a corresponding question pertaining to the married candidate.

The second additional question in the new ritual, asked of celibate and married candidates alike, concerns their willingness to take on the obligation of prayer.[8] Far be it from me to naysay an encouragement for deacons to have a spiritual life, but why was the decision made to insert a promise about prayer and not about the activity of deacons that is supposed to be most characteristic of their order? No explicit recognition is given to the distinctive character of the order of deacon as identified by *Lumen Gentium*: works of charity and administration. In light of my thesis, there needs to be more than a general reference to the ambiguous designation of the deacon as a "worker of charity." The ritual promises could explicate the nature of the deacon's service to bishops, presbyters, and the people of God. The identity of the deacon would be made more clear by asking the candidates two questions: (1) if they are willing to mediate the care and affection of the church to the poor in body and spirit, and (2) if they are willing to serve the communion of the church by expressing the needs and desires of the laity to the bishop and his presbyters. Simple questions such as these would help to clarify the deacon's position within the church more than the promises currently demanded of candidates.

Ecumenical Implications

The parameters of this book prevented an investigation of the diaconates of other rites, churches, and ecclesial communities. My conclusions about the nature and ministry of the Latin-rite deacon, however, should have a broader appeal because they are rooted in the study of human nature. There is a need for social mediation within every Christian community, regardless of theology or history, and there can be no authentic Christian community without a commitment to solidarity with the poor. Ecumenical discussions on diaconal ministry are important because they bring to the surface fundamental elements of that faith which are common to all Christians. The renewal of the diaconate in the Latin rite required a change in thinking about ministry as a whole, accomplished by the Second Vatican Council, and the presence of the renewed diaconate con-

---

8. Ibid.: "Do [all of] you resolve to maintain and deepen the spirit of prayer that is proper to your way of life and, in keeping with this spirit and what is required of you, to celebrate faithfully the Liturgy of the Hours with and for the People of God and indeed for the whole world?"

tinues to function as a corrective to the concept of ministry focused solely on the ministerial priesthood. In like manner, thinking about the diaconate in an ecumenical context may help to clarify some stumbling blocks that remain in the way of consensus on the nature and function of the ordained ministry.

The Latin-rite deacon, as I have understood him, is an ordained minister who is entirely devoted to the work of social mediation through symbolic and active service. Affirming the need for a diaconal ministry that is both liturgical and active beyond the sanctuary poses a challenge to other forms of the diaconate that only have one dimension of service but not the other.[9] For many of the Eastern churches, the diaconate is mostly liturgical in form. The ministry of the deacon in these churches is often related to the ministry of angels in worship.[10] While their liturgical ministry is important, attention should also be paid to the active social role of deacons as manifested in the early history of the churches in the East. Mainstreaming diaconal ministry into the other dimensions of church life would accentuate the place of charitable deeds in the mission of the church. From their unique position, deacons could effectively tie the liturgical worship of the assembly to their practice of social justice.

Among the ecclesial communities of the West various forms of a "diaconate" exist, most of which shy away from any observance of ritual functions or sacramental ordination. A greater appreciation for the human need for ritual could assuage reluctance by many Christian communities for a sacramental form of the diaconate. My thesis offered this perspective, pointing out the necessity for symbolic reinforcement of social ties. Concerns on the part of some Christian communities that do not recognize a ministerial priesthood need not involve the sacramentality of the diaconate. Though Christians are not in agreement over the ministry of bishops and presbyters, discussions on the order of deacon could provide common ground. As the Roman Catholic church and the World Council of Churches already recognize *diakonia* as the fundamental context of the sacrament of holy orders, a mutually acceptable statement on the diaconate need not be too far away.[11] Mutual acceptance of

---

9. World Council of Churches, *Baptism, Eucharist and Ministry*, Faith and Order Paper No. 111 (Geneva: World Council of Churches, 1982), no. 24 (25) (hereafter BEM): "The function of deacons has been reduced to an assistant role in the celebration of the liturgy: they have ceased to fulfill any function with regard to the diaconal witness of the Church"; BEM, *Commentary*, no. 31 (27): "In many churches there is today considerable uncertainty about the need, the rational, the status and the functions of deacons."

10. Gregory Mansour, "Role of the Deacon in the Maronite Church," *Diakonia* 29 (1996): 130.

11. BEM, no. 15 (22): "Because Jesus came as one who serves ... to be set apart means to be consecrated to service."

a symbolic and social role for the deacon in the church and the world could give new life to discussions surrounding episcopal and presbyteral ministry. The renewed figure of the Latin-rite deacon, as articulated in my thesis, is an adequate response to some of the challenges posed by the landmark ecumenical statement popularly known as "BEM." *Baptism, Eucharist and Ministry* calls for "Churches maintaining the threefold pattern" to ask themselves "how its potential can be fully developed for the most effective witness of the Church in this world."[12] Acceptance of the Latin-rite deacon as a social intermediary and symbol of *communitas* fulfills this request, providing the Roman Catholic church with another crucial point of convergence with the teaching found in BEM.

Placing strong emphasis "on the active participation of all members in the life and the decision-making of the community," BEM recognizes that ordained ministry "requires the community's effective participation in the discovery of God's will and the guidance of the Spirit."[13] Our thesis highlights the role of the deacon, from the perspective of the Catholic tradition, in mediating power and authority among the people of God. This understanding of the diaconate also fulfills BEM's desire for an ordained ministry described in the following way: "[One] that is bound to the faithful in inter-dependence and reciprocity. Only when they seek the response and acknowledgment of the community can their authority be protected from the distortions of isolation and domination."[14] Thus, the diaconal model proposed by BEM is very much in line with my thesis. There can be nothing but wholehearted affirmation of BEM's articulation of the nature and ministry of the diaconate: "*Deacons* represent to the Church its calling as servant in the world. By struggling in Christ's name with the myriad needs of societies and persons, deacons exemplify the interdependence of worship and service in the Church's life."[15] My thesis articulates how the Roman Catholic church can find agreement with BEM's statement on the diaconate, and it provides a well-reasoned argument for the reception of BEM's teaching by the other ecclesial communities and churches.

Diaconal ministry also places deacons in many concrete ecumenical contexts of pastoral importance. Deacons who minister in the hospital setting serve the religious needs of patients and medical staff of differing faiths. Prison ministry performed by a Latin-rite deacon is not only in service to prisoners

12. BEM, no. 25 (25).
13. BEM, no. 27 (26); no. 26 (26).
14. BEM, "Ministry," no. 16 (23).
15. BEM, "Ministry," no. 30 (27).

and staff who are Catholic, but to all who desire the helping hand and consoling ear of the clergy. Deacons who serve in family ministry will often encounter couples who do not share the same faith. Moreover, deacons are natural bridges between the various Christian communities in the direction and promotion of charitable work. The ministry of deacons, therefore, could not only serve the communion of the Roman Catholic church, but also the communion that exists among the various churches and ecclesial communities.

My study of the Latin-rite deacon, therefore, has implications beyond the Latin rite and the Roman Catholic communion. The diaconate has the potential to be an influential *ordo* among all the people of God. As we continue into the next millennium of the church's history, an effective diaconal presence would help us face the particular troubles of an alienated world and a divided church. My conception of deacons as social intermediaries and symbols of *communitas* renders intelligible the way in which their ministry is fundamental for the life of the church: it is the task of deacons to make sure that the social structure of the church truly functions as an instrument of the Spirit. Christian communities throughout the world must discern whether they are ready to allow the ministry of deacons to really influence the way decisions are made and material resources are shared. It remains to be seen how this model of the diaconate can be adopted in the church, helping her to manifest the *diakonia* of Jesus Christ.

Final Conclusion

How can the church become "poor and for the poor," in Pope Francis's phrase, with its ordained "ministers of charity" failing to serve as a central symbol in the church of radical love and service?[16] Or failing to connect the ordinary faithful and the church leaders alike to the needs of those on the "peripheries"? The modern world cries out for the presence and ministry of deacons as a symbol of *communitas* and as an intermediary between the people of God and the poor. But we should not neglect the final aspect, intermediary between the people of God, including the poor, and the bishop. Francis writes in *Evangelii Gaudium:* "If something should rightly disturb us and trouble our consciences, it is the fact that so many of our brothers and sisters are living without the strength, light and consolation born of friendship with Jesus Christ, without

16. Pope Francis, "Address to Representatives of Communications Media," March 16, 2013; available at www.vatican.va.

a community of faith to support them, without meaning and a goal in life."[17] As we have seen in my sociological analysis, it is not enough to share the Gospel with individuals, but to connect them to a community, a community that in the Roman Catholic church is structured around the symbol of unity, the bishop.

The church ought to encourage deacons to become specialists in her mission to overcome the alienation that plagues so many people of the world's societies, and to heal the divisions that afflict the church. Functioning as symbols of *communitas* and social intermediaries among the people of God, deacons could serve the communion of the church and promote compassion for the poor in body and spirit.

In the final analysis, my understanding of the nature and purpose of the diaconate as a social intermediary and symbol of *communitas* is important not only because it solves the problem for the diaconate of its own distinct identity: it also provides the diaconate with an important ministry fundamental for the accomplishment of the church's mission. To adapt a line from John Paul II, it is time for the church to say, "Deacons, become what you are."[18]

---

17. Pope Francis, *Evangelii Gaudium*, par. 49.

18. Pope John Paul II, *Familiaris Consortio*, Apostolic Exhortation, November 22, 1981, par. 17: "Family, become what you are."

BIBLIOGRAPHY

Sources

Biblical Texts

Aland, Kurt, and Barbara Aland. *The Greek New Testament*. Stuttgart: Deutsche Bibelgesellschaft, 1994.

Brenton, Lancelot Charles Lee. *The Septuagint with Apocrypha: Greek and English*. Peabody, Mass.: Hendrickson Publishers, 1995.

Confraternity of Christian Doctrine and the United States Catholic Conference of Catholic Bishops. *The New American Bible*. Revised edition. Washington, D.C.: United States Conference of Catholic Bishops, 2015.

Fischer, Bonifatius, and Robert Weber. *Biblia sacra iuxta Vulgatam versionem*. Stuttgart: Deutsche Bibelgesellschaft, 1983.

Holy Bible. Revised Standard Version. London: Thomas Nelson and Sons, 1959.

Joint Committee on the New Translation of the Bible. *The New English Bible with the Apocrypha*. London: Oxford University Press, 1970.

Metzger, Bruce M., and Roland E. Murphy. *The New Oxford Annotated Bible: with the Acpocrypal/Deuterocanonical Books*. New York: Oxford University Press, 1991.

Wansbrough, Henry. *The New Jerusalem Bible: Study Edition*. London: Darton, Longman and Todd, 1994.

Early Christian Sources

Schaff, Philip, ed. *A Selected Library of the Nicene and Post-Nicene Fathers of the Christian Church: First Series*. 14 volumes. Grand Rapids, Mich.: Eerdmans, 1952–56.

Schaff, Philip, and Henry Wace, eds. *A Selected Library of the Nicene and Post-Nicene Fathers of the Christian Church: Second Series*. 14 volumes. Grand Rapids, Mich.: Eerdmans, 1952–56.

Ambrose. "De Officiis Ministrorum." In *St. Ambrose: Select Works and Letters*, in NPNF-II 10.

Ambrosiaster. "De jactantia romanarum levitarum." In PL 35:2301–3.

The Apostolic Tradition of Hippolytus. Translated by Burton S. Easton. Ann Arbor, Mich.: Cushing-Malloy, 1924–62.

Augustine of Hippo. *De catechizandis rudibus*. In CCSL 46:115–78.

Botte, Bernard. *La tradition apostolique de Saint Hippolyte: essai de reconstitution.* Edited by Albert Gerhards and Sabine Felbecker. Fifth edition. Münster: Aschendorffsche Verlagsbuchhandlung, 1989.

Brock, Sebastian P., and Michael Vasey, eds. *The Liturgical Portions of the Didascalia.* Liturgical Study 29. Bramcote: Grove Books, 1982.

Christopher, Joseph P. *S. Avreli Avgvstini Hipponiensis Episcopi De Catechizandis Rvdibvs Liber Vnvs. Translated with an Introduction and Commentary.* The Catholic University of America Patristic Studies 8. Washington, D.C.: The Catholic University of America Press, 1926.

Clement of Rome. "The Epistle of S. Clement to the Corinthians." In Lightfoot (ed.), *Apostolic Fathers* 2:5–188, 271–305.

———. "Epistle of Clement to James." In ANF 8:218–22.

Connolly, Richard Hugh, ed. and trans. *Didascalia Apostolorum: The Syriac Version Translated and Accompanied by the Verona Latin Fragments. With an Introduction and Notes.* Oxford: Clarendon Press, 1929.

Corpus Christianorum. Series Latina. 211 volumes. Turnhout: Brépols, 1953–.

Cuming, Geoffrey J. *Hippolytus: A Text for Students.* Liturgical Study 8. Bramcote: Grove Books Limited, 1976.

Cyprian of Carthage. "Cyprianus Rogatiano Fatri S." In CCSL 3b, *Sancti Cypriani Episcopi Opera,* Pars III, 1:9–16. Edited by Gerardus Dierck. Turnhout: Brepols, 1954.

———. "De Opere et Eleemosynis." In CCSL 3a, *Sancti Cypriani Episcopi Opera,* 55–72.

———. "Epistle XII." In ANF 5:293.

———. "Epistle XXXV." In ANF 5:314.

———. "Epistle LI." In ANF 5:327–35.

———. "Epistle LXIV." In ANF 5:365–66.

Deiss, Lucien. *Springtime of the Liturgy. Liturgical Texts of the First Four Centuries.* Translated by Matthew J. O'Connell. Collegeville, Minn.: Liturgical Press, 1979.

Denzinger, Heinrich, ed. *Sources of Catholic Dogma.* Translated by Roy Deferrari. Thirtieth edition of *Enchiridion Symbolorum.* St. Louis, Mo.: Herder, 1957.

Didache. Translated by James Kleist. Edited by Johannes Quasten. ACW 6. Westminster, Md.: Newman Press, 1948.

Dix, Gregory. *The Treatise on the Apostolic Tradition of St. Hippolytus of Rome, Bishop and Martyr.* Second revised edition. London: SPCK, 1937–68.

Eusebius Pamphili. *The Church History of Eusebius.* Translated by Arthur C. McGiffert. In NPNF-II 1:81–387.

Grisbrooke, W. Jardine. *The Liturgical Portions of the Apostolic Constitutions: A Text for Students.* Grove Liturgical Study 61. Bramcote: Grove Books Limited, 1990.

Hippolytus. *The Refutation of All Heresies (Philosophumena).* In ANF 5:9–153.

Ignatius of Antioch. *Letter to the Ephesians.* Text and translation in Lightfoot (ed.), *Apostolic Fathers* 2:21–89, 543–50.

———. *Letter to the Magnesians.* Text and translation in Lightfoot (ed.), *Apostolic Fathers* 2:105–40, 550–54.

———. *Letter to the Philadelphians.* Text and translation in Lightfoot (ed.), *Apostolic Fathers* 2:248–82, 563–66.

———. *Letter to the Smyrnaeans.* Text and translation in Lightfoot (ed.), *Apostolic Fathers* 2:287–326, 567–71.

———. *Letter to the Trallians.* Text and translation in Lightfoot (ed.), *Apostolic Fathers* 2:150–82, 554–62.

Irenaeus of Lyons. *Adversus Haereses.* In ANF 1:315–567.

Jerome. "Letter to Evangelus." In NPNF-II 6:288–89.

———. "Letter to Sabinianus." In NPNF-II 6:289–95.

Jurgens, William. *The Faith of the Early Fathers.* 3 volumes. Collegeville, Minn.: Liturgical Press, 1970–79.

Justin Martyr. *Apologia I.* In *Patrologia Cursus Completus, Series Graeca,* ed J.-P. Migne, 6:327–470. Paris: 1857–66. English translation in ANF 1:163–93.

Lightfoot, Joseph, ed. and trans. *The Apostolic Fathers: Clement, Ignatius, and Polycarp.* Second edition. 5 volumes. Peabody, Mass.: Hendrickson, 1989.

Migne, Jacques-Paul, ed. *Patrologia Cursus Completus. Series Graeca.* 161 volumes. Paris: Excudebat Migne, 1856–66.

———. *Patrologia Cursus Completus. Series Latina.* 221 volumes. Paris: Excudebat Migne, 1844–64.

Neuner, Josef, and Jacques Dupuis, eds. *The Christian Faith in the Doctrinal Documents of the Catholic Church.* Revised edition. New York: Alba House, 1982.

Osiek, Carolyn. *The Shepherd of Hermas: A Commentary.* Edited by Helmut Koester. Minneapolis, Minn.: Fortress Press, 1999.

Polycarp of Smyrna. *Letter to the Philippians.* In Lightfoot (ed.), *Apostolic Fathers,* 3:321–50, 471–76.

Roberts, Alexander, and James Donaldson, eds. *The Ante-Nicene Fathers: Translations of the Writings of the Fathers Down to A.D. 325.* 9 volumes. Grand Rapids, Mich.: Eerdmans, 1951–57.

Sperry-White, Grant, ed. and trans. *The Testamentum Domini: A Text for Students. With Introduction, Translation, and Notes.* Grove Liturgical Study 66. Bramcote: Grove Books Limited, 1991.

Tertullian. *On Baptism.* In ANF 3:669–79.

———. *On Monogamy.* In ANF 4:59–72.

Theodoret. *Ecclesiastical History.* In NPNF-II 3:33–159.

Ritual Texts

Andrieu, Michel. *Les "Ordines Romani" du haut moyen âge.* 5 volumes. Études et documents 11, 23, 24, 28, 29. Louvain: Spicilegium Sacrum Lovaniense, 1931–.

Congregation for Divine Worship and the Discipline of the Sacraments. *Pontificale Romanum ex Decreto Sacrosancti Oecumenici Concilii Vaticani II Instauratum Auctoritate Pauli PP. VI Promulgatum. De Ordinatione Diaconi, Presbyteri et Episcopi.* Editio typica. Vatican City: Typis Polyglottis Vaticanis, 1968. English translation: International Commission on English in the Liturgy. *The Roman Pontifical Revised by Decree of the Second Vatican Council and Published by Authority of Pope Paul VI. Rites of Ordination of Deacons, Priests and Bishop.* Typical edition. Washington, D.C.: ICEL, 1978.

———. *Rituale Romanum ex Decreto Sacrosancti Oecumenici Concilii Vaticani II Instauratum Auctoritate Pauli PP. VI Promulgatum. Ordo Exsequiarum.* Vatican City: Typis Polyglottis Vaticanis, 1969. English translation: International Commission on English in the Liturgy.

The Roman Ritual Revised by Decree of the Second Vatican Ecumenical Council and Published by the Authority of Pope Paul VI. Order of Christian Funerals. New York: Catholic Book Publishing, 1989.

——. *Rituale Romanum ex Decreto Sacrosancti Oecumenici Concilii Vaticani II Renovatum Auctoritate Pauli PP. VI Promulgatum. Ordo Initiationis Christianae Adultorum.* Editio typica altera. Vatican City: Typis Polyglottis Vaticanis, 1974. English translation: International Committee on English in the Liturgy. *RCIA: Rite of Christian Initiation of Adults.* Study edition. Washington, D.C.: United States Catholic Conference, 1988.

——. *Caeremoniale Episcoporum ex Decreto Sacrosancti Oecumenici Concilii Vaticani II Instauratum Auctoritate Ioannis Pauli II Promulgatum.* Vatican City: Libreria Editrici Vaticana, 1984. English translation: International Commission on English in the Liturgy. *Ceremonial of Bishops. Revised by Decree of the Second Vatican Ecumenical Council and Published by Authority of Pope John Paul II.* Collegeville, Minn.: Liturgical Press, 1989.

——. *Rituale Romanum ex Decreto Sacrosancti Oecumenici Concilii Vaticani II Instauratum Auctoritate Ioannis Pauli II Promulgatum, De Benedictionibus.* Vatican City: Typis Polyglottis Vaticanis, 1985. English translation: International Commission on English in the Liturgy. *The Roman Ritual Revised by Decree of the Second Vatican Ecumenical Council and Published by Authority of Pope John Paul II, Book of Blessings.* New York: Catholic Book Publishing, 1989.

——. *Pontificale Romanum ex Decreto Sacrosancti Oecumenici Concilii Vaticani II Renovatum Auctoritate Pauli PP.VI Editum Ioannis Pauli PP. II Cura Recognitum. De Ordinatione Episcopi, Presbyterorum et Diaconorum.* Editio typica altera. Vatican City: Typis Polyglottis Vaticanis, 1990. English translation: International Commission on English in the Liturgy. *The Roman Pontifical as Renewed by Decree of the Second Vatican Ecumenical Council Published by Authority of Pope Paul VI and Further Revised at the Direction of Pope John Paul II. Rites of Ordination of a Bishop, of Priests, and of Deacons.* Second typical edition. Washington, D.C.: United States Conference of Catholic Bishops, 2003.

——. *Rituale Romanum ex Decreto Sacrosancti Oecumenici Concilii Vaticani II Renovatum Auctoritate Pauli PP. VI Editum Ioannis Pauli PP. II Cura Recognitum. Ordo Celebrandi Matrimonium.* Editio typica altera. Vatican City: Typis Polyglottis Vaticanis, 1991. English Translation: International Commission on English in the Liturgy. *The Order of Celebrating Matrimony.* Second typical edition. Totowa, N.J.: Catholic Book Publishing, 2016.

——. *Missale Romanum, Ordo lectionum Missae, Praenotanda.* Editio typica altera. Vatican City: Typis Polyglottis Vaticanis, 1998. English translation: International Commission on English in the Liturgy. *Lectionary for Mass: Introduction,* In *The Liturgy Documents. A Parish Resource,* 1:119–62. Fourth edition. Chicago: Liturgy Training Publications, 2004.

——. *Institutio Generalis Missalis Romani.* Editio typica tertia. Vatican City: Typis Polyglottis Vaticanis, 2001. English translation: International Committee on English in the Liturgy. *General Instruction of the Roman Missal.* Third typical edition. Liturgy Documentary Series 2. Washington, D.C.: United States Conference of Catholic Bishops, 2003.

Mohlberg, Leo, Leo Eizenhöfer, and Petrus Siffrin, eds. *Missale Francorum.* Rerum ecclesiasticarum documenta, series maior, fontes 2. Rome: Herder, 1957. English tanslation by Paul F. Bradshaw, *Ordination Rites of the Ancient Churches of East and West,* 223–30. New York: Pueblo, 1990.

——. *Sacramentarium Veronense.* Rerum ecclesiasticarum documenta, series maior, fontes 1. Third improved edition. Rome: Herder, 1978. English translation: Paul F. Bradshaw. *Ordination Rites of the Ancient Churches of East and West,* 215–18. New York: Pueblo, 1990.

Magisterial, Legislative, and Ecumencial Texts

Acta et Documenta Concilio Oecumenico Vaticano II Apparando, Series I: *Antepraeparatoria*. 4 volumes. Rome: Typis Polyglottis Vaticanis, 1960–61.

Acta et Documenta Concilio Oecumenico Vaticano II Apparando, Series II: *Praeparatoria*. 3 volumes. Rome: Typis Polyglottis Vaticanis, 1964.

Acta Synodalia Sacrosancti Concilii Oecumenici Vaticani II. 4 volumes. Rome: Typis Polyglottis Vaticanis, 1970–78.

Benedict XV, Pope. *Codex Iuris Canonici Pii X Pontificis Maximi iussu digestus Benedicti Papae XV Auctoritate Promulgatus*. Vatican City: Typis Polyglottis Vaticanis, 1933. English translation and commentary: T. Lincoln Bouscaren and Adam C. Ellis, eds. *Canon Law: A Text and Commentary*. Third revised edition. Milwaukee, Wis.: Bruce Publishing, 1958.

Benedict XVI, Pope. *Deus Caritas Est*. Encyclical Letter. December 25, 2005. Available at www.vatican.va.

———. *Sacramentum Caritatis*. Apostolic Exhortation. February 22, 2007. Available at www.vatican.va.

———. *Caritas in Veritate*. Encyclical Letter. June 29, 2009. Available at www.vatican.va.

———. *Omnium in Mentem*. Encyclical Letter. October 26, 2009. Available at www.vatican.va.

Catechism of the Catholic Church. Washington, D.C.: United States Catholic Conference, 1994.

Concilium Tridentinum: Diariorum, actorum, epistolarum, tractatum. Nova Collectio. Societas Goerresiana. Freiburg: Herder, 1965.

Congregation of Catholic Education and Congregation for Clergy. *Ratio fundamentalis institutionis diaconorum permanentium: Directorium pro ministerio et vita diaconorum permanentium*. AAS 90 (1998): 835–927. Official English translation: *Basic Norms for the Formation of Permanent Deacons: Directory for the Ministry and Life of Permanent Deacons. With Joint Declaration and Introduction*. Vatican City: Libreria Editrice Vaticana, 1998.

Congregation for Divine Worship and the Discipline of the Sacraments. *Concerning dispensation from the diriment impediment of entering into a second marriage and remaining in the ministry on the part of permanent deacons who are widowed (cc. 1087–1088)*. Circular Letter. June 6, 1997. Prot. N. 263/97. English translation in William Woestman. *The Sacrament of Orders and the Clerical State. A Commentary on the Code of Canon Law*, "Appendix IV," 338–40. Ottawa: St. Paul University, 1999.

Congregation for the Doctrine of the Faith. *Inter insigniores*. Declaration. October 15, 1976. AAS 69 (1979): 98–116. Official English translation in *Origins* 6 (1977): 517–24.

———. "A Commentary on the Declaration." *Origins* 6 (1977): 524–31.

———. "Response to the *dubium* concerning the teaching contained in the Apostolic Letter *Ordinatio Sacerdotalis*." AAS 87 (1995): 1114. English translation in *Origins* 25 (1995): 401, 403.

Corpus Iuris Canonici. Editio lipsiensis secunda post Aemilii Ludouici Richteri curas ad librorum manu scriptorum et editionis romanae fidem recognouit et adnotatione critica instruxit Aemilius Friedberg. Pars prior: *Decretum Magistri Gratiani*. Pars secunda: *Decretalium Collectiones*. Graz: Akademische Druck u. Verlagsanstalt, 1879–1955.

Council Nicaea I. *Canones*. Greek and Latin texts with English translation in Tanner (ed.), *Decrees*, 1:6–15.

Council of Chalcedon. *Canones*. Greek and Latin texts with English translation in Tanner (ed.), *Decrees*, 1:87–103.

Council of Trent. *Sessio XXIII, July 15, 1563, Vera et catholica doctrina de sacramento ordinis ad condemnandos errores nostri temporis.* [Session 23, July 15, 1563, *The true and catholic doctrine of the sacrament of order, to condemn the errors of our time.*] Latin and English text in Tanner (ed.), *Decrees,* 2:742–53.

———. *Sessio XIV, November 25, 1551, Doctrina de sanctissimis poenitentiae et extremae unctionis sacramentis.* [Session 14, November 25, 1551, *Teaching concerning the most holy sacraments of penance and last anointing.*] Latin and English text in Tanner (ed.), *Decrees,* 2:703–18.

Council Vatican II. *Sacrosanctum Concilium.* December 4, 1963. Latin and English text in Tanner (ed.), *Decrees,* 2:820–43.

———. *Ecclesia Orientalium.* November 21, 1964. Latin and English text in Tanner (ed.), *Decrees,* 2:900–907.

———. *Lumen Gentium.* November 21, 1964. Latin and English text in Tanner (ed.), *Decrees,* 2:849–900.

———. *Christus Dominus.* October 28, 1965. Latin and English text in Tanner (ed.), *Decrees,* 2:921–39.

———. *Apostolicam Actuositatem.* November 18, 1965. Latin and English text in Tanner (ed.), *Decrees,* 2: 981–1001.

———. *Ad Gentes.* December 7, 1965. Latin and English text in Tanner (ed.), *Decrees,* 2:1011–42.

———. *Gaudium et Spes.* December 7, 1965. Latin and English text in Tanner (ed.), *Decrees,* 2:1069–1135.

———. *Sacrosanctum Oecumenicum Concilium Vaticanum II: Constitutions, Decreta, Declarationes.* Roma: Typis Polyglottis Vaticanis, 1974.

Flannery, Austin, ed. *Vatican Council II.* In *The Conciliar and Post Conciliar Documents,* vol. 1. New revised edition. New York: Costello Publishing, 1996.

Francis, Pope. *Evangelii Gaudium.* Apostolic Exhortation. November 24, 2013. Available at www.vatican.va.

———. *Laudato Si'.* Encyclical Letter. May 24, 2015. Available at www.vatican.va.

Innocent I, Pope. *Epistola 25.* In PL 20:551–64.

John XXIII, Pope. *Mater et Magistra.* Encyclical Letter. May 15, 1961. AAS 53 (1961): 401–64.

———. *Pacem in Terris.* Encyclical Letter. April 11, 1963. AAS 55 (1963): 257–304.

John Paul II, Pope. *Catechesi Tradendae.* Apostolic Exhortation. October 16, 1979. AAS 71 (1979): 1277–1340. Official English translation: *Apostolic Exhortation* Catechesi tradendae *of His Holiness Pope John Paul II to the Episcopate, the Clergy and the Faithful of the Entire Catholic Church on Catechesis in Our Time.* Vatican City: Vatican Polyglot Press, 1979.

———. *Laborem Exercens.* Encyclical Letter. September 14, 1981. AAS 73 (1981): 577–647. English translation: *On Human Work.* Washington, D.C.: United States Catholic Conference, 1982.

———. *Familiaris Consortio.* Apostolic Exhortation. November 22, 1981. AAS 74 (1982): 81–191. English translation: *The Role of the Christian Family in the Modern World.* Boston: Pauline Books and Media, 1982.

———. *Sacrae Disciplinae Leges.* Apostolic Constitution. January 25, 1983. In *Code of Canon Law. Latin-English Edition. New English Translation,* xxvii–xxxii. Washington, D.C.: Canon Law Society of America, 1999.

———. *Address on Permanent Deacons.* March 16, 1985. In *Insegnamenti* 13.1:649. Vatican City: Libreria Editrice, 1985.

———. *Sollicitudo Rei Socialis.* Encyclical Letter. December 30, 1987. AAS 80 (1988): 513–86. English translation: *On Social Concern.* Washington, D.C.: United States Catholic Conference, 1988.

———. *Address to the Permanent Deacons and their Wives Given at Detroit, MI.* September 19, 1987. *Origins* 17 (1987): 327–29.

———. *Christifideles Laici.* Apostolic Exhortation. December 30, 1988. AAS 81 (1989): 393–521. English translation: *Apostolic Exhortation on the Vocation and the Mission of the Lay Faithful in the Church and in the World.* London: Catholic Truth Society, 1988.

———. *Codex Iuris Canonici Auctoritate Ioannis Pauli PP. II Promulgatus.* Vatican City: Libreria Editrice Vaticana, 1989. English translation: *Code of Canon Law Latin-English Edition. New English Translation.* Washington, D.C.: Canon Law Society of America, 1999.

———. *Redemptoris Missio.* Encyclical Letter. December 7, 1990. AAS 83 (1991): 249–340. English translation: *Mission of the Redeemer.* Vatican City: Libreria Editrice Vaticana, 1991.

———. *Centesimus Annus.* Encyclical Letter. May 1, 1991. English translation: *On the One Hundredth Anniversary of Rerum Novarum.* Washington, D.C.: United States Catholic Conference, 1991.

———. *Catechesis at the General Audience.* October 13, 1993. In *Insegnamenti,* 14.2:1000–1004. Vatican City: Libreria Editrice, 1993.

———. *Crossing the Threshold of Hope.* Edited by Vitorrio Messori. Translated by Jenny McPhee and Martha McPhee. London: Jonathan Cape, 1994.

———. *Ordinatio Sacerdotalis.* Apostolic Letter. May 22, 1994. AAS 76 (1994): 545–48. Official English translation in *Origins* 24 (1994): 51–53.

———. *Evangelium Vitae.* Encyclical Letter. March 25, 1995. AAS 87 (1995): 401–522. English translation: *The Gospel of Life.* Origins 24 (1995): 689–725.

———. *Catechismus Catholicae Ecclesiae.* Editio typica. Città del Vaticano: Libreria Editrice Vaticano, 1997. Official English translation: *Catechism of the Catholic Church. Revised in accordance with the official Latin text promulgated by Pope John Paul II. Contains glossary and analytical index.* Second English edition. Washington, D.C.: United States Catholic Conference, 1997.

———. *Dies Domini.* Apostolic Letter. May 31, 1998. AAS 90 (1998): 713–66.

Leo XIII, Pope. *Rerum Novarum.* Encyclical Letter. May 15, 1891. Available at www.vatican.va.

Mansi, Joseph, ed. *Sacrorum Conciliorum Novae et Amplissima Collectio.* 53 volumes. Florentiae (volumes 1–35), 1758–98; Parisiis (volumes 36–53), 1901–27.

Munier, Charles, ed. *Statuta Ecclesia Antiqua.* Concilia Galliae. CCSL 148.

Munier, Charles, and Bernard Botte, eds. *Les Statuta ecclesiae antiqua: edition, etudes critiques.* Biblothèque de l'Institut de Droit canonique de l'Université de Strasbourg 5. Paris: Presses Universitaires de France, 1960.

Neuner, Josef, and Jacques Dupuis, eds. *The Christian Faith in the Doctrinal Documents of the Catholic Church.* Revised edition. New York: Alba House, 1982.

Optatus. *De Schismate Donatistarum.* In PL 11:884–1104.

Paul VI, Pope. *Populorum Progressio.* Encyclical Letter. March 26, 1967. AAS 59 (1967): 257–99.

———. *Sacrum Diaconatus Ordinem.* Apostolic Letter. June 18, 1967. AAS 59 (1967): 697–704. English translation: *Canon Law Digest* 6 (1967): 577–84.

———. *Sacerdotalis Caelibatus*. Encyclical Letter. June 24, 1967. AAS 59 (1967): 657–97. English translation in Woestman, *Sacrament of Orders*, 238–67.

———. *Pontificalis Romani Recognitio*. Apostolic Constitution. June 18, 1968. AAS 60 (1968): 369–73.

———. *Ad Pascendum*. Apostolic Letter. August 15, 1972. AAS 64 (1972): 534–40. English translation in Flannery, *Vatican II*, 433–40.

———. *Ministeria Quaedam*. August 15, 1972. AAS 64 (1972): 529–34. English translation in Flannery, *Vatican II*, 427–32.

———. *Evangelii Nuntiandi*. Apostolic Exhortation. December 8, 1975. AAS 68 (1976): 5–76. English translation in *Origins* 5 (1976): 459–68.

———. *We write in answer*. Letter to Archbishop Coggan of Canterbury. November 30, 1975. AAS 68 (1976): 599–600.

Pius XI, Pope. *Quadragesimo Anno*. Encyclical Letter. May 15, 1931. AAS 23 (1931): 177–228.

Pius XII, Pope. *Sacramentum Ordinis*. Apostolic Constitution. November 30, 1947. AAS 40 (1948): 5–7.

Pontifical Council for the Interpretation of Legistlative Texts. *Communicationes*. Vatican City: Tipografia Vaticana, 1969–.

Tanner, Norman, ed. *Decrees of the Ecumenical Councils*. 2 volumes. Washington, D.C.: Georgetown University Press, 1990.

United States Conference of Catholic Bishops. *National Directory for the Formation, Ministry and Life of Permanent Deacons in the United States*. Washington, D.C.: United States Conference of Catholic Bishops, 2005.

World Council of Churches. *Baptism, Eucharist and Ministry*. Faith and Order Paper 111. Geneva: World Council of Churches, 1982.

Reference Texts

Brunotte, Heinz, and Otto Weber, eds. *Evangelisches Kirchenlexikon*. 4 volumes. Göttingen: Vandenhoeck and Ruprecht, 1961.

Catholic University of America Editorial Staff, ed. *New Catholic Encyclopedia*. 17 volumes. Palatine, Ill.: Jack Heraty and Associates, 1981.

Cross, Frank L., and Elizabeth A. Livingston, eds. *The Oxford Dictionary of the Christian Church*. Third edition. New York: Oxford University Press, 1997.

Hatch, Edwin, and Henry Redpath. *A Concordance to the Septuagint and the Other Greek Versions of the Old Testament (Including the Apocryphal Books)*. Oxford: Clarendon Press, 1897.

Moulton, William F., and Alfred S. Geden. *A Concordance to the Greek New Testament*. New York: Charles Scribner's Sons, 1897–1957.

National Conference of Catholic Bishops' Committee on the Permanent Diaconate. *A National Study on the Permanent Diaconate of the Catholic Church in the United States 1994–1995*. Washington, D.C.: United States Catholic Conference, 1996.

New Webster's Dictionary and Thesaurus of the English Language. Revised and updated. Danbury, Conn.: Lexicon Publications, 1993.

Newman, Barclay M. *A Concise Greek-English Dictionary of the New Testament*. Stuttgart: Deutsche Bibelgesellschaft/German Bible Society, 1993.

O'Donnell, Christopher. *Ecclesia: A Theological Encyclopedia of the Church*. Collegeville, Minn.: Liturgical Press, 1996.

Official Catholic Directory. Anno Domini 2016. Jubilee Year of Mercy. New Providence, N.J.: P. J. Kennedy and Sons, 2016.

Theological Dictionary of the New Testament. Translated by Geoffrey W. Bromiley. Volumes 1–4 edited by Gerhard Kittel; volumes 5–9 edited by Gerhard Friedrich; volume 10 compiled by Ronald E. Pitkin. Grand Rapids, Mich.: Eerdmans, 1964–76.

Zerwick, Maximillian, and Mary Grosvenor. *A Grammatical Analysis of the Greek New Testament*. Roma: Editrice Pontificio Istituo Biblico, 1996.

Studies

Scripture

Abbott, Thomas K. *A Critical and Exegetical Commentary on the Epistles to the Ephesians and to the Colossians*. The International Critical Commentary 36. Edinburgh: T. and T. Clark, 1897–1974.

Banks, Robert J. "Church Order and Government." In *Dictionary of Paul and His Letters*, edited by Gerald F. Hawthorne, Ralph Martin, and Daniel Reed, 131–37. Downers Grove, Ill.: InterVarsity Press, 1993.

Barclay, William. *The Letters to Timothy, Titus and Philemon*. Revised edition. The Daily Study Bible. Edinburgh: St. Andrew Press, 1975.

Barrett, Charles K. *A Critical and Exegetical Commentary on the Acts of the Apostles*, volume 1: *Preliminary Introduction and Commentary on Acts I-XIV*. Edinburgh: T. and T. Clark, 1994.

Bartlett, David L. *Ministry in the New Testament*. Minneapolis, Minn.: Fortress Press, 1993.

Baumert, Norbert. *Woman and Man in Paul: Overcoming a Misunderstanding*. Translated by P. Madigan and L. Maloney. Collegeville, Minn.: Liturgical Press, 1996.

Beyer, Herman. "διακονέω, διακονία, διάκονος." TDNT 2:81–93.

Bieringer, Reimund. "Paul's Understanding of Diakonia in 2 Corinthians 5.18." In *Studies on 2 Corinthians*, edited by Reimund Bieringer and Jan Lambrecht, 413–28. Bibliotheca Ephemeridum Theologicarum Lovaniensium 112. Leuven: Peeters, 1994.

Bornkamm, Günther. "πρεσβυτερος." In TDNT 6:651–83.

Brandt, Wilhelm. *Diakonie und das Neue Testament*. PhD diss., University of Münster, 1923.

———. *Dienst und Dienen im Neuen Testament*. Gütersloh: Bertelsmann Verlag, 1931.

Brown, Raymond. *Priest and Bishop: Biblical Reflections*. New York: Paulist Press, 1970.

———. *The Gospel According to John (i-xii)*. Anchor Bible 29. London: Geoffrey Chapman, 1971.

———. "Episkopê and Episkopos: The New Testament Evidence." *Theological Studies* 41 (1980): 322–38.

———. *The Gospel and Epistles of John: A Concise Commentary*. Collegeville, Minn.: Liturgical Press, 1988.

Brown, Raymond, Joseph Fitzmyer, and Roland Murphy, eds. *The New Jerome Biblical Commentary*. Englewood Cliffs, N.J.: Prentice-Hall, 1968 and 1990.

Bruce, Frederick F. "The New Testament and Classical Studies." *New Testament Studies* 22 (1975–76): 229–42.

Brueggemann, Walter. *The Covenanted Self: Explorations in Law and Covenant*. Edited by Patrick D. Miller. Minneapolis, Minn.: Fortress Press, 1999.

Byrne, Brendan. *Romans*. Sacra Pagina 6. Collegeville, Minn.: Liturgical Press, 1996.

———. "The Letter to the Philippians." In NJBC, 791–97.

Campbell, Robert A. *The Elders: Seniority with Earliest Christianity*. Edinburgh: T. and T. Clark, 1994.

Collins, John N. "Georgi's 'Envoys' in 2 Cor 11:23." *Journal of Biblical Literature* 93, no. 1 (1974): 88–96.

———. *Diakonia: Re-interpreting the Ancient Sources*. New York: Oxford University Press, 1990.

———. "Ministry as a Distinct Category among Charismata (1 Corinthians 12:4–7)." *Neotestamentica* 27, no. 1 (1993): 79–91.

———. "Forum: God's Gifts to Congregations." *Worship* 68 (1994): 242–49.

———. "A Ministry for Tomorrow's Church." *Journal of Ecumenical Studies* 32 (1995): 159–78.

———. "Did Luke Intend a Disservice to Women in the Martha and Mary Story?" *Biblical Theology Bulletin* 28, no. 3 (1998): 104–11.

———. "A Monocultural Usage: διακον-words in Classical, Hellenistic, and Patristic Sources." *Vigiliae Christianae* 66 (2012): 287–309.

Collins, Raymond F. *First Corinthians*. Sacra Pagina 7. Collegeville, Minn.: Liturgical Press, 1999.

Denzer, George A. "The Pastoral Letters." In NJBC, 350–61.

Dibelius, Martin, and Hans Conzelmann. *The Pastoral Epistle: A Commentary on the Pastoral Epistles*. Philadelphia: Fortress Press, 1972.

Dillon, Richard J. "Acts of the Apostles." In NJBC, 722–71.

Dunn, James D. G. *The Acts of the Apostles*. Epworth Commentaries. Peterborough: Epworth, 1996.

———. *The Theology of Paul the Apostle*. Edinburgh: T. and T. Clark, 1998.

Dunn, James D. G., and David A. Fiensy. "The Composition of the Jerusalem Church." In *The Book of Acts in its Palestinian Setting*, edited by Richard Bauckham, 213–36. Grand Rapids, Mich.: Eerdmans, 1995.

Fitzmyer, Joseph. "The Letter to the Romans." In NJBC, 830–68.

Foerster, Wendelin. "ἔξεστιν/ἐξουσία." In TDNT 3:560–75.

Fretheim, Terrence E. "Genesis." In *The New Interpreter's Bible: A Commentary in Twelve Volumes*, 1:319–674. Nashville, Tenn.: Abingdon Press, 1994.

Friedrich, Gerhard. "Die Problematik eines Theologischen Wörterbuchs zum Neuen Testament." *Studia Evangelica* 73 (1959): 481–86.

Getty, Mary Ann. *Philippians and Philemon*. Dublin: Veritas Publications, 1980.

Giles, Kevin. *The Patterns of Ministry among the First Christians*. Melbourne: Collins Dove, 1989.

———. "Church Order, Government." In *Dictionary of the Later New Testament & Its Developments*, edited by Ralph Martin and Peter Davids, 219–26. Downers Grove, Ill.: InterVarsity Press, 1997.

Grayston, Kenneth. *The Letters of Paul to the Philippians and to the Thessalonians*. Cambridge: Cambridge University Press, 1967.

Grundmann, Walter. "δύναμαι/δύναμις." In TDNT 2:284–317.

Haenchen, Ernst. *The Acts of the Apostles: A Commentary.* Philadelphia: Westminster Press, 1971.

Hanson, Anthony T. *The Pastoral Letters.* Cambridge Bible Commentary. Cambridge: Cambridge University Press, 1966.

Hawthorne, Gerald F. *Philippians.* World Biblical Commentary 43. Waco, Tex.: Word Books, 1983.

Hillers, Delbert R. *Covenant: The History of a Biblical Idea.* Baltimore, Md.: Johns Hopkins University Press, 1969.

Houlden, John L. *The Pastoral Epistles.* London: Penguin, 1976.

Jeremias, Joachim. *New Testament Theology.* Translated by John Bowden. New York: SCM Press, 1971.

———. "παις Θεου." In TDNT 5:654–717.

Johnson, Luke Timothy. *The Acts of the Apostles.* Sacra Pagina 5. Collegeville, Minn.: Liturgical Press, 1992.

Käseman, Ernst. *Essays on New Testament Themes.* London: SCM Press, 1964.

Kelly, John N. D. *A Commentary on the Pastoral Epistles: 1 Timothy, 2 Timothy, Titus.* New York: Harper and Row, 1963.

Lambrecht, Jan. *Second Corinthians.* Sacra Pagina 8. Collegeville, Minn.: Liturgical Press, 1999.

Lécuyer, Joseph. "Les diacres dans le nouveau testament." In *Les diacre dans l'Eglise et le monde d'aujourd'hui,* edited by Paul Winninger, Joseph Lécuyer, and Yves Congar, 15–26. Unam Sanctam 59. Paris: Cerf, 1966.

Lienhard, Joseph T. "Acts 6:1–6: A Redactional View." *Catholic Biblical Quarterly* 37 (1975): 228–36.

MacDonald, Margaret Y. *The Pauline Churches: A Socio-Historical Study of Institutionalization in the Pauline and Deutero-Pauline writings.* Society for New Testament Studies Monograph Series 60. Cambridge: Cambridge University Press, 1988.

Marshall, I. Howard. "Lord's Supper." In *Dictionary of Paul and His Letters,* edited by Gerald F. Hawthorne, Ralph P. Martin, and Daniel G. Reid, 569–75. Downers Grove, Ill.: InterVarsity Press, 1993.

McKenzie, John L. "Aspects of Old Testament Thought." In NJBC, 1284–1315.

Murphy, Roland E. "Second Isaiah: The Servant of the Lord." *Catholic Biblical Quarterly* 9 (1947): 273–74.

Murphy-O'Connor, Jerome. "Eucharist and Community in First Corinthians." In *Living Bread, Saving Cup: Readings on the Eucharist,* edited by R. Kevin Seasoltz, 1–29. Collegeville, Minn.: Liturgical Press, 1982.

———. *1 Corinthians.* New Testament Message 10. Dublin: Veritas Publications, 1979.

O'Grady, John J. "Authority and Power: Issues for the Contemporary Church." *Louvain Studies* 10 (1984): 122–40.

Radcliffe, Timothy. "As One Who Serves." *The Tablet* 246 (July 11, 1992): 865–66.

Robertson, Archibald, and Alfred Plummer, eds. *A Critical and Exegetical Commentary on the First Epistle of St. Paul to the Corinthians.* Second edition. The International Critical Commentary. Edinburgh: T. and T. Clark, 1911–71.

Robinson, John A. T. *Re-dating the New Testament.* London: SCM Press, 1976.

Schnackenburg, Rudolf. *The Epistle to the Ephesians: A Commentary.* Translated by Helen Heron. Edinburgh: T. and T. Clark, 1991.

Schweizer, Eduard. *Church Order in the New Testament*. Studies in Biblical Theology. London: SCM Press, 1961–63.

Sim, David C. *Apocalyptic Eschatology in the Gospel of Matthew*. Society for New Testament Studies: Monograph Series 88. Cambridge: Cambridge University Press, 1996.

Stiefel, Jennifer H. "Women Deacons in 1 Timothy: A Linguistic and Literary Look at 'Women Likewise …'. (1 Tim 3.11)." *New Testament Studies* 41 (1995): 442–57.

Theissen, Gerd. *The Social Setting of Pauline Christianity: Essays on Corinth*. Edited and translated by John H. Schütz. Philadelphia: Fortress Press, 1982.

Turner, Nigel. "Jewish and Christian Influence on New Testament Vocabulary." *Novum Testamentum* 16 (1974): 149–60.

Vincent, Marvin R. *The Epistle to the Philippians and to Philemon*. Edited by Samuel R. Driver. The International Critical Commentary. Edinburgh: T. and T. Clark, 1972.

Weiser, Artur. "διακονέω, διακονία, διακονος." In *Exegetical Dictionary of the New Testament*, edited by Horst Balz and Gerhard Schneider, 1:302–4. Grand Rapids, Mich.: Eerdmans, 1994.

Westermann, Claus. *Genesis 1–11: A Commentary*. Translated by John J. Scullion. London: SPCK, 1984.

Young, Frances M. "On ΕΠΙΣΚΟΠΟΣ and ΠΡΕΣΒΥΤΕΡΟΣ." *Journal of Theological Studies* 45 (1994): 142–48.

Liturgy

Andrieu, Michel. "La carrière ecclésiastique des papes et les documents liturgiques du moyen âge." *Revue des sciences religieuses* 21, no. 3 (1947): 90–120.

Botte, Bernard. "L'Esprit Saint et l'Église dans la *Tradition Apostolique* de S. Hippolyte." *Didascalia* 2 (1972): 221–33.

Bradshaw, Paul F. *Ordination Rites of the Ancient Churches of East and West*. New York: Pueblo, 1990.

———. *The Source for the Origins of Christian Worship: Sources and Methods of the Study of Early Liturgy*. London: SPCK, 1992.

Bradshaw, Paul F., and Charles Whitaker. *Essays on Hippolytus*. Edited by Geoffrey J. Cuming. Grove Liturgical Studies 15. Bramcote: Grove Books, 1978.

Brakmann, Heinzgerd. "Zum Dienst des Diakons in der Liturgischen Versammlung." In *Der Diakon: Wiederentdeckung und Erneuerung seines Dienstes*, edited by Josef G. Plöger and Hermann J. Weber, 147–63. Freiburg: Herder, 1981.

Bugnini, Annibale. *The Reform of the Liturgy 1948–1975*. Translated by Matthew J. O'Connell. Collegeville, Minn.: Liturgical Press, 1990.

Cabié, Robert. *The Eucharist*. Translated by Matthew J. O'Connell. The Church at Prayer 2. Collegeville, Minn.: Liturgical Press, 1986.

Chupungco, Anscar J., ed. *Handbook for Liturgical Studies*. 5 volumes. Collegeville, Minn.: Liturgical Press, 1997–2000.

Citrini, Tullio. "Dalla Liturgia di ordinazione alla ministerialità diaconale." In *Le Liturgie di Ordinazione: Atti della XXIV Settimana di Studio dell'Associazione Professori di Liturgia Loreto (AN), 27 agosto—1 settembre 1995*, 241–54. Studi di liturgia 29. Rome: C. L. V. Edizioni Liturgiche, 1996.

Connolly, Richard H. *The So-called Egyptian Church Order and derived Documents.* Texts and Studies 8.4. Cambridge: Cambridge University Press, 1916.

Dix, Gregory. *The Shape of the Liturgy.* Westminster: Dacre Press, 1945.

Folsom, Cassian. "The Liturgical Books of the Roman Rite." In Chupungco, *Handbook*, 1:245–314.

Gros, Miguel. S. "Les plus anciennes formules romaines de benediction des diacres." *Ecclesia Orans* 5 (1988): 45–52.

Gy, P. M. "Ancient Ordination Prayers." *Studia Liturgica* 13 (1979): 70–93.

Hibbard, John R. "The Role of the Deacon at the Eucharist." *National Bulletin on the Liturgy* 32 (1999): 220–24.

Hoffman, Lawrence A. "Jewish Ordination on the Eve of Christianity." *Studia Liturgica* 13 (1979): 11–41.

Hovda, Robert W. "Pastoral Guidelines." In *It Is Your Own Mystery: A Guide to the Communion Rite,* edited by Melissa Kay, 16–34. Washington, D.C.: Liturgical Conference, 1977.

Jasper, Ronald C. D., and Geoffrey J. Cuming. *Prayers of the Eucharist: Early and Reformed.* Second edition. New York: Oxford University Press, 1980.

Joncas, Jan M. "The Public Language of Ministry Revisited: *De Ordinatione Episcopi, Presbyterorum et Diaconorum 1990.*" *Worship* 68 (1994): 386–403.

Jounel, Pierre. "Ordinations." In *The Church at Prayer,* vol. 3: *The Sacraments,* edited by Aimes G. Martimort et al., 139–79. Collegeville, Minn.: Liturgical Press, 1992.

Jungmann, Josef A. *The Mass of the Roman Rite: Its Origins and Development (Missarum Sollemnia).* New revised and abridged edition in one volume. Translated by Francis A. Brunner and revised by Charles K. Riepe. London: Burns and Oates, 1951–61.

Kavanagh, Aidan. "Textuality and Deritualization: The Case of Western Liturgical Usage." *Studia Liturgica* 23, no. 1 (1993): 70–77.

Keifer, Ralph. "Preparation of the Altar and the Gifts or Offertory?" *Worship* 48 (1974): 595–600.

Kiesling, Christopher. "Liturgy and Social Justice." *Worship* 51 (1977): 351–61.

Kleist, James A. "The Didache." Introduction and text in ACW 6, edited by Johannes Quasten and Joseph Plumpe, 13–25. Westminster: Newman, 1948.

Lameri, Angelo. *La Traditio Instrumentorum e delle insegne nei riti di ordinazione. Studio storico-liturgico.* Studi di liturgia 35. Roma: C. L. V. Edizioni Liturgiche, 1998.

Legrand, Hervé. "The Presidency of the Eucharist According to the Ancient Tradition." *Worship* 53 (1979): 413–38.

McManus, Frederick. "The Roman Order of Mass: From 1964 to 1969: The Preparation of the Gifts." In *Shaping English Liturgy: Studies in Honor of Archbishop Denis Hurley,* edited by Peter C. Finn and James M. Schellman, 107–38. Washington, D.C.: Pastoral Press, 1990.

Metzger, Marcel. "The History of the Eucharistic Liturgy in Rome." In Chupungco, *Handbook,* 3:103–31.

Palazzo, Eric. *A History of Liturgical Books from the Beginning to the Thirteenth Century.* Translated by Madeleine Beaumont. Collegeville, Minn.: Liturgical Press, 1998.

Reynolds, Roger E. *Clerical Orders in the Early Middle Ages: Duties and Ordination.* Variorum Collected Studies Series cs670. Brookfield: Ashgate, 1999.

———. *Clerics in the Early Middle Ages: Hierarchy and Image.* Variorum Collected Studies Series cs669. Brookfield: Ashgate, 1999.

Sartore, Domenico. "The Homily." In Chupungco, *Handbook*, 3:189–208.

Searle, Mark. "The Notre Dame Study of Catholic Parish Life." *Worship* 60 (1986): 312–33.

Serra, Domenic E. "The Greeting of Peace in the Revised Sacramentary: A New Pastoral Option." In *Liturgy for the New Millennium. A Commentary on the Revised Sacramentary: Essays in Honor of Anscar J. Chupungco, O.S.B.* Translated by Mark Francis and Keith Pecklers, 97–110. Collegeville, Minn.: Liturgical Press, 2000.

Studer, Basil. "Liturgical Documents of the First Four Centuries." Translated by Edward Hagman. In Chupungco, *Handbook*, 1:199–224.

Taft, Robert. *Beyond East and West: Problems in Liturgical Understanding.* Second revised and enlarged edition. Rome: Edizioni Orientala Christiana, 1997.

Van Unnik, Willem C. "*Dominus Vobiscum*: The Background of a Liturgical Formula." In *New Testament Essays: Studies in Memory of Thomas Walter Manson*, edited by Angus J. Higgins, 270–305. Manchester: Manchester University Press, 1959.

Vogel, Cyrille. *Medieval Liturgy: An Introduction to the Sources.* Translated and edited by William Storey and Neils Rasmussen. Washington, D.C.: Pastoral Press, 1986.

Windels, Olivier. "Le ministère diaconal en liturgie." *Nouvelle revue théologique* 119, no. 3 (1977): 397–404.

Witczak, Michael. "The Sacramentary of Paul VI." In Chupungco, *Handbook*, 3:133–75.

History

Alberigo, Giuseppe, and Franca Magistretti, eds. *Constitutionis Dogmaticae Lumen Gentium: Synopsis Historica.* Bologna: Istituto per le Scienze Religiose, 1975.

Altaner, Berthold. *Patrology.* Translated by Hilda Graef. Freiburg: Herder and Herder, 1958.

Amanieu, Alain. "Archidiacre." In *Dictionnaire de Droit Canonique contenant tous les termes du droit canonique avec un Sommaire de l'Histoire et des Institutions et de l'état actuel de la discipline, Volume 1: Abamita – Azzon*, edited by Raoul Naz, 948–1004. Paris: Librairie Letouzey et Ané, 1935.

Anonymous. "Thomas of Celano." In *Oxford Dictionary of the Christian Church*, edited by Elizabeth Livingston and Frank Cross, 1617. Third edition. New York: Oxford University Press, 1997.

———. "Consalvi, Ercole." In *The Oxford Dictionary of the Christian Church*, edited by Elizabeth Livingston and Frank Cross, 401. Third edition. New York: Oxford University Press, 1997.

Arendzen, John P. "An Entire Syriac Text of the 'Apostolic Church Order.'" *Journal of Theological Studies* 3, no. 9 (1902): 59–60.

Aubert, Roger. "Antonelli, Giacomo." In *New Catholic Encyclopedia*, 1:641–42.

Barnard, Leslie W. *Studies in The Apostolic Fathers and Their Background.* Oxford: Basil Blackwell, 1966.

Bartlet, James V. *Church Life and Church-Order during the First Four Centuries.* Oxford: Oxford University Press, 1943.

Bettenson, Henry, ed. and trans. *The Early Christian Fathers: A Selection from the Writings of the Fathers from St. Clement of Rome to St. Athanasius.* New York: Oxford University Press, 1969.

Bevilacqua, Anthony J. *Procedure in the Ecclesiastical Courts of the Church of England with Its*

Historical Antecedents in the Roman and Decretal Law. Rome: Pontificia Universitas Gregoriana, 1956.

Bligh, John. "Deacons in the Latin West Since the Fourth Century." *Theology* 58, no. 425 (1955): 421–29.

Brox, Norbert. "Church Orders." In *Sacramentum Mundi: An Encyclopedia of Theology*, edited by Karl Rahner et al., 1:373–75. London: Burns and Oates, 1968.

Campbell, D. R. "Pius III, Pope." In *New Catholic Encyclopedia*, 11:394–95.

Cayre, Fulbert. *Manual of Patrology and History of Theology*. Volume 1 translated by H. Howitt. Paris: Desclée, 1935.

Chadwick, Henry. *The Early Church*. Grand Rapids, Mich.: Eerdmans, 1967.

Christopher, Joseph P. Introduction to *St. Augustine: The First Catechetical Instruction [De Catechizandis Rudibus]*, translated and edited by Joseph Christopher, 3–11. ACW 2. London: Longmans, Green and Co., 1962.

Colson, Jean. *La Fonction Diaconale aux Origines de l'Église*. Paris: Desclée de Brouwer, 1960.

Coxe, A. Cleveland. "Introductory Notice to Cyprian." In ANF 5:263–65.

Croce, Walter. "Die Niederen Weihen und ihre hierarchische Wertung; eine geschichtliche Studie." *Zeitschrift für Katholische Theologie* 70, no. 3 (1948): 257–314.

———. "From the History of the Diaconate." In U.S. Bishops' Committee on the Diaconate, *Foundations for the Renewal of the Diaconate*, translated by David Bourke, Karl H. Kruger and William F. Schmitz, 61–89. Washington, D.C.: United States Conference of Catholic Bishops, 2003.

Dale, Alfred W. W. *The Synod of Elvira and Christian Life in the Fourth Century: An Historical Essay*. London: Macmillan and Co. Press, 1882.

De Bertier de Sauvigny, Guillaume A. "Consalvi, Ercole." In *New Catholic Encyclopedia*, 4:191–92.

Dix, Gregory. "Ministry in the Early Church c. A.D. 90–410." In *The Apostolic Ministry: Essays on the History and Doctrine of Episcopacy*, edited by Kenneth E. Kirk, 183–304. London: Hodder and Stoughton, 1946.

Domagalski, Bernhard. "Römische Diakone im 4. Jahrhundert." In *Der Diakon: Wiederentdeckung und Erneuerung seines Dienstes*, edited by Josef Plöger and Herman Weber, 44–56. Freiburg: Herder, 1981.

Echlin, Edward P. "The Origins of the Permanent Diaconate." *American Ecclesiastical Review* 163 (1970): 92–105.

———. "The Deacon's Golden Age." *Worship* 45 (1971): 37–46.

Faivre, Alexandre. *Naissance d'un hiérarchie: Les premières étapes du cursus clérical*. Paris: Beauchesne, 1977.

———. *Ordonner la fraternité: Pouvoir d'innover et retour à l'ordre dans l'Église ancienne*. Paris: Cerf, 1992.

Favazza, Joseph A. *The Order of Penitents: Historical Roots and Pastoral Future*. Collegeville, Minn.: Liturgical Press, 1988.

Fuellenbach, John. *Ecclesiastical Office and the Primacy of Rome: An Evaluation of Recent Theological Discussion of First Clement*. The Catholic University of America Studies in Antiquity 20. Washington D.C.: The Catholic University of America Press, 1980.

Gaudemet, Jean. *L'Église dans L'Empire Romain (IVᵉ–Vᵉ siècles)*. Histoire du Droit et des Instituions de l'Église en Occident, Tome III. Paris: Sirey, 1990.

Gryson, Roger. *The Ministry of Women in the Early Church*. Translated by Jean Laporte and Mary Louise Hall. Collegeville, Minn.: Liturgical Press, 1976.

Hardick, Lothar. "Francis of Assisi, St." In *New Catholic Encyclopedia*, 6:28–31.

Hardy, Edward R. "Deacons in History and Practice." In *The Diaconate Now*, edited by Richard T. Nolan, 11–36. Washington, D.C.: Corpus Books, 1968.

Harmless, William. *Augustine and the Catechumenate*. Collegeville, Minn.: Liturgical Press, 1995.

Harnack, Adolf von. *Sources of the Apostolic Canons*. Translated by John Owen. London: F. Norgate and Co., 1895.

Hsia, Ronnie P. *The World of Catholic Renewal 1540–1770*. New Approaches to European History. Cambridge: Cambridge University Press, 1998.

Lee, Frederick G. *Reginald Pole, Cardinal Archbishop of Canterbury: An Historical Sketch with an Introductory Prologue and Practical Epilogue*. New York: G. P. Putnam's Sons, 1888.

Leon, Harry J. *The Jews of Ancient Rome*. Revised edition. Peabody, Mass.: Hendrickson, 1995.

Lynch, John E. "Power in the Church: an Historico-critical Survey." In *Power in the Church*. Edited by James H. Provost and Knut Walf, 13–22. Concilium 197/3. Edinburgh: T. and T. Clark, 1988.

MacDonald, Allan J. *Hildebrand: A Life of Gregory VII*. London: Methuen, 1932.

Mortimort, Aimé G. *Deaconesses: An Historical Study*. Translated by K. D. Whitehead. San Francisco, Calif.: Ignatius Press, 1986.

Muir, Edward. *Ritual in Early Modern Europe*. New Approaches to European History. Cambridge: Cambridge University Press, 1997–99.

Munier, Charles. *L'Église dans l'Empire Romain (IIe-IIIe): IIIe partie Église et Cité*. Histoire du Droit et des Institutions de l'Église en Occident, tome II, volume 3. Paris: Cujas, 1979.

Murphy, F. "Catacombs." In *New Catholic Encyclopedia*, 3:197–201.

Osiek, Carolyn. "The Early Second Century through the Eyes of Hermas: Continuity and Change." *Biblical Theology Bulletin* 20, no. 3 (1990): 116–22.

Pokusa, Joseph W. *A Canonical-Historical Study of the Diaconate in the Western Church*. The Catholic University of America Canon Law Studies 495. Washington, D.C.: The Catholic University of America Press, 1979.

———. "The Diaconate: A History of Law Following Practice." *Jurist* 45 (1985): 95–135.

Prat, Ferdinand. "Les prétentions des diacres romains au quatrième siècle." *Recherches de Science Religieuse* 3, no. 5 (1912): 463–75.

Quasten, Johannes. *Patrology*. 3 volumes. Westminster, Md.: Newman Press, 1953–64.

Reynolds, Roger E. *Clerical Orders in the Early Middle Ages: Duties and Ordination*. Variorum Collected Studies Series cs670. Brookfield: Ashgate, 1999.

———. *Clerics in the Early Middle Ages: Hierarchy and Image*. Variorum Collected Studies Series cs669. Brookfield: Ashgate, 1999.

Rowland, Christopher. *Christian Origins: An Account of the Setting and Character of the Most Important Messianic Sect of Judaism*. London: SPCK, 1985.

Schenk, William. *Reginald Pole: Cardinal of England*. New York: Longmans, Green and Company, 1950.

Schwartz, Eduard. *Über die Pseudoapostolischen Kirchenordnungen*. Strasbourg: K. J. Trübner, 1910.

Staniforth, Maxwell. *Early Christian Writings: The Apostolic Fathers*. New York: Dorset Press, 1968.

Thomas of Celano. *The First Life of St. Francis*. In *St. Francis of Assisi, Writings and Early Biographies: English Omnibus of the Sources for the Life of St. Francis*, translated by Marion A. Habig. Chicago: Franciscan Herald Press, 1972.

Vagaggini, Cipriano. "L'ordinazione delle diaconesse nella tradizione greca e bizantina." *Orientalia Christiana Periodica* 40 (1974): 146–89.

Wallach, Luitpold. "Alcuin." In *New Catholic Encyclopedia*, 1:279–80.

Wright, J. Robert. "The Emergence of the Diaconate." *Liturgy* 2, no. 4 (1982): 17–23, 67–71.

Zardoni, Serafino. "La storia del diaconato permanente." *Seminarium* 37 (1997): 733–51.

Philosophy and Human Sciences

Adams, Richard N. *Energy and Structure: A Theory of Social Power*. Austin: University of Texas Press, 1975.

Alexander, Bobby C. *Victor Turner Revisited: Ritual as Social Change*. American Academy of Religion Academy Series 74. Atlanta: Scholars Press, 1991.

Arendt, Hannah. *On Violence*. New York: Harcourt, Brace and World, 1970.

Bell, Catherine M. "Ritual, Change, and Changing Rituals." *Worship* 63 (1989): 31–41.

———. *Ritual Theory, Ritual Practice*. New York: Oxford University Press, 1992.

———. *Ritual: Perspectives and Dimensions*. New York: Oxford University Press, 1999.

Bell, Catherine M., and Thomas Luckmann. *The Social Construction of Reality: A Treatise in the Sociology of Knowledge*. New York: Anchor Books, 1967.

Bell, Catherine M., Richard Madsen, William Sullivan, Ann Swidler, and Steve Tipton. *Habits of the Heart: Individualism and Commitment in American Life. Updated Edition with a New Introduction*. Los Angeles: University of California Press, 1985–96.

———. *The Good Society*. New York: Vintage Books, 1991.

Bellah, Robert N. "Religion and the Shape of National Culture." *America* 181, no. 3 (August 7, 1999): 9–14.

Berger, Peter L. *The Sacred Canopy: Elements of a Sociological Theory of Religions*. First edition. Garden City, N.Y.: Doubleday, 1967.

———. *A Rumor of Angels: Modern Society and the Rediscovery of the Supernatural*. Garden City, N.Y.: Doubleday, 1969.

———. *The Heretical Imperative: Contemporary Possibilities of Religious Affirmation*. Garden City, N.Y.: Anchor Press, 1979.

———. *A Far Glory: The Quest for Faith in an Age of Credulity*. New York: Anchor Books, 1992.

Berger, Peter L., and Richard J. Neuhaus. *To Empower People: The Role of Mediating Structures in Public Policy*. Washington, D.C.: American Enterprise Institute, 1977.

———. *To Empower People: From State to Civil Society*. Second edition. Edited by Michael Novak. Washington, D.C.: AEI Press, 1996.

Bernstein, Basil. "Social Class, Speech Systems and Psycho-therapy." *British Journal of Sociology* 15, no. 1 (1964): 54–64.

———. "Elaborated and Restricted Codes: Their Social Origins and Some Consequences." In *Communication and Culture: Readings in the Codes of Human Interaction*, edited by Alfred G. Smith, 427–41. New York: Holt, Rinehart and Winston, 1966.

———. "Linguistic Codes, Hesitation Phenomena and Intelligence." In *Class, Codes, and Control*, vol. 1: *Theoretical Studies Towards a Sociology of Language*, edited by Basil Bernstein, 76–94. London: Routledge and Kegan Paul, 1971.

———. "Social Class, Language, and Socialization." In *Theoretical Studies Towards a Sociology of Language*. Volume 1 of *Class, Codes, and Control*, edited by Basil Bernstein, 170–89. London: Routledge and Kegan Paul, 1971.

———. "A Sociolinguistic Approach to Socialization; with Some Reference to Educability." In *Directions in Sociolinguistics: The Ethnography of Communication*, edited by John J. Gumperz and Dell H. Hymes, 465–97. New York: Holt, Rinehart, and Winston, 1972.

Bouyer, Louis. *Rite and Man: Natural Sacredness and Christian Liturgy*. Translated by M. Joseph Costelloe. University of Notre Dame Liturgical Studies 7. Notre Dame, Ind.: University of Notre Dame Press, 1963.

Buber, Martin. *Between Man and Man*. Translated by Ronald G. Smith. London: Fontana Library, 1961.

Collins, Mary. "Ritual Symbols and the Ritual Process: The Work of Victor W. Turner." *Worship* 50 (1976): 336–52.

Crocker, J. Christopher. "Ritual and the Development of Social Structure: Liminality and Inversion." In *The Roots of Ritual*, edited by James D. Shaughnessy, 47–86. Grand Rapids, Mich.: Eerdmans, 1973.

DeRego, Frank R., and James D. Davidson. "Catholic Deacons: A Lesson in Role Conflict and Ambiguity." In *Religion in a Changing World: Comparative Studies in Sociology*, edited by Madeleine Cousineau, 89–98. Westport, Conn.: Praeger, 1998.

Douglas, Mary. *Purity and Danger: An Analysis of the Concepts of Pollution and Taboo*. London: Routledge, 1966–96.

———. *Natural Symbols: Explorations in Cosmology*. Revised edition. London: Routledge, 1973–96.

———. *How Institutions Think*. Syracuse, N.Y.: Syracuse University Press, 1986.

Eisenstadt, Shmuel N., ed. *Max Weber on Charisma and Institution Building*. Chicago: The University of Chicago Press, 1968.

———. "Comparative Liminality: Liminality and Dynamics of Civilization." *Religion* 15, no. 3 (1985): 315–38.

Elshtain, Jean Bethke. *Democracy on Trial*. New York: BasicBooks, 1995.

Fardon, Richard. *Mary Douglas: An Intellectual Biography*. New York: Routledge, 1999.

Farwell, Lyndon J. *Betwixt and Between: The Anthropological Contributions of Mary Douglas and Victor Turner Toward a Renewal of Roman Catholic Ritual*. PhD diss., Claremont Graduate School, 1976.

Fichter, Joseph H. *A Sociologist Looks at Religion*. Theology and Life Series 23. Wilmington, Del.: Michael Glazier, 1988.

Gaillardetz, Richard. "North American Culture and the Liturgical Life of the Church: The Separation of the Quests for Transcendence and Community." *Worship* 68 (1994): 403–16.

Geertz, Clifford. "Religion as a Cultural System." In *Anthropological Approaches to the Study of Religion*, edited by Michael Banton, 1–46. Association of Social Anthropologist Monographs 3. London: Tavistock, 1966.

Gelpi, Donald L. "Conversion: Beyond the Impasses of Individualism." In *Beyond Individualism: Toward a Retrieval of Moral Discourse in America*, edited by Donald L. Gelpi, 1–30. Notre Dame, Ind.: University of Notre Dame Press, 1989.

Gennep, Arnold van. *The Rites of Passage*. Translated by Monika Vizedom and Gabrielle Caffee. Chicago: University of Chicago Press, 1909–88.

Goldsmith, Malcolm C. "Power, Authority and Conflict." In *Sociology, Theology and Conflict*, edited by Denys E. H. Whiteley and Roderick Martin, 48–60. Oxford: Basil Blackwell, 1969.

Granfield, Patrick. "Legitimation and Bureaucratisation of Ecclesial Power." In *Power in the Church*, edited by James H. Provost and Knut Walf, 86–93. Concilium 197/3. Edinburgh: T. and T. Clark, 1988.

Greeley, Andrew. *The Catholic Myth: The Behavior and Beliefs of American Catholics*. New York: Touchstone, 1997.

———. *The Catholic Imagination*. Berkeley: University of California Press, 2000.

Grimes, Ronald. "Victor Turner's Definition, Theory, and Sense of Ritual." In *Victor Turner and the Construction of Cultural Criticism: Between Literature and Anthropology*, edited by Kathleen Ashley, 141–46. Indianapolis: Indiana University Press, 1990.

———. "Liturgical Supinity, Liturgical Erectitude: On the Embodiment of Ritual Authority." *Studia Liturgica* 23 (1993): 51–69.

Hemrick, Eugene. "The Need to Define Roles." *Origins* 10 (August 1980): 151–54.

Hengel, Martin. *The Charismatic Leader and His Followers*. New York: Crossroad, 1981.

Hoge, Dean. *The Future of Catholic Leadership: Responses to the Priest Shortage*. Kansas City, Mo.: Sheed and Ward, 1987.

Holmes, Urban. "Liminality and Liturgy." *Worship* 47 (1973): 386–97.

Isenberg, Sheldon, and Dennis Owen. "Bodies, Natural and Contrived: The Work of Mary Douglas." *Religious Studies Review* 3, no. 1 (1977): 1–17.

Kaufmann, Franz-Xaver. "The Sociology of Knowledge and the Problem of Authority." *Journal of Ecumenical Studies* 19, no. 2 (1982): 18–31.

Kavanagh, Aidan. "Life-Cycle Events, Civil Ritual and the Christian." In *Liturgy and Human Passage*, edited by David Power and Louis Maldonado, 14–24. Concilium 112. New York: Seabury Press, 1979.

Kertzer, David I. *Ritual, Politics & Power*. New Haven, Conn.: Yale University Press, 1988.

Mette, Norbert. "Decline or Transformation in Solidarity?" In *Faith in a Society of Instant Gratification*, edited by Maureen Junker-Kenny and Miklos Tomka, 81–90. Concilium 1999/4. London: SCM Press, 1999.

Mitchell, Nathan, ed. "Revisiting the Roots of Ritual." *Liturgy Digest* 1, no. 1 (1993): 4–36.

———. *Liturgy and the Social Sciences*. American Essays in Liturgy. Collegeville, Minn.: Liturgical Press, 1999.

National Conference of Catholic Bishops. *A National Study of the Permanent Diaconate in the United States*. Washington, D.C.: United States Catholic Conference, 1981.

———. *A National Study on the Permanent Diaconate of the Catholic Church in the United States 1994–1995*. Washington, D.C.: United States Catholic Conference, 1996.

Pistone, John. "Among Brothers." *Deacon Digest* (March/April 1997): 7–8.

Rappaport, Roy A. *Ritual and Religion in the Making of Humanity*. Cambridge Studies in Social and Cultural Anthropology 110. Cambridge: Cambridge University Press, 1999.

Ricoeur, Paul. *The Symbolism of Evil*. Translated by Emerson Buchanan. Religious Perspectives 17. New York: Harper and Row, 1967.

Seasoltz, R. Kevin. "Anthropology and Liturgical Theology: Searching for a Compatible

Methodology." In *Liturgy and Human Passage*, edited by David Power and Louis Maldonado, 3–13. Concilium 112. New York: Seabury Press, 1979.

Stringer, Martin D. "Liturgy and Anthropology: The History of a Relationship." *Worship* 63 (1989): 503–21.

Swatos, William H., ed. "Anomie," in *Encyclopedia of Religion and Society*, 23. Walnut Creek, Calif.: Altamira Press, 1998.

———. "Turner, Victor W(itter)." In *Encyclopedia of Religion and Society*, 527–28. Walnut Creek, Calif.: Altamira Press, 1998.

Tomka, Miklos. "Individualism, A Change in Values, the Experience Society: Converging Trends in Sociology." In *Faith in a Society of Instant Gratification*, edited by Maureen Junker-Kenny and Miklos Tomka, 25–35. Concilium 1999/4. London: SCM Press, 1999.

Tracy, David. *The Analogical Imagination: Christian Theology and the Culture of Pluralism*. New York: Crossroads, 1981.

Turner, Victor. *The Forest of Symbols: Aspects of Ndembu Ritual*. Ithaca, N.Y.: Cornell University Press, 1967.

———. *The Drums of Affliction: A Study of Religious Processes Among the Ndembu of Zambia*. Oxford: Clarendon Press, 1968.

———. *The Ritual Process: Structure and Anti-Structure*. New York: Aldine De Gruyter, 1969–95.

———. "Passages, Margins, and Poverty: Religious Symbols of Communitas. Part One." *Worship* 46 (1972): 390–412.

———. "The Center Out There: Pilgrim's Goal." *History of Religions* 12, no. 3 (1973): 191–230.

———. *Dramas, Fields, and Metaphors: Symbolic Action in Human Society*. Ithaca, N.Y.: Cornell University Press, 1974–96.

———. *Revelation and Divination in Ndembu Ritual*. Ithaca, N.Y.: Cornell University Press, 1975.

———. "Ritual, Tribal and Catholic." *Worship* 50 (1976): 504–26.

———. "Sacrifice as Quintessential Process: Prophylaxis or Abandonment?" *History of Religions* 16, no. 3 (1977): 189–215.

———. "Variations on a Theme of Liminality." In *Secular Ritual*, edited by Sally F. Moore and Barbara G. Meyerhoff, 36–52. Assen: Van Gorcum, 1977.

———. "Images of Anti-Temporality: An Essay in the Anthropology of Experience." *Harvard Theological Review* 75, no. 2 (1982): 243–65.

———. *On the Edge of the Bush: Anthropology as Experience*. Edited by Edith Turner. Tucson: University of Arizona Press, 1985.

———. *The Anthropology of Performance*. New York: PAJ Publications, 1987–88.

Wackenheim, Gerard. "Ecclesiology and Sociology." In *The Church as Institution*, edited by Gregory Baum and Andrew Greeley, 32–41. Concilium 91. New York: Herder and Herder, 1974.

Ward, Hannah. "Boundary-Dwellers." *The Way* 33, no. 2 (1993): 97–105.

Weber, Max. *The Theory of Social and Economic Organisation*. New York: Oxford University Press, 1947.

———. *Economy and Society*. Edited by Günther Roth and Claus Wittich. 3 volumes. New York: Bedminster Press, 1968.

Wuthnow, Robert. *Loose Connections: Joining Together in America's Fragmented Communities*. Cambridge, Mass.: Harvard University Press, 1998.

Theology

Armbruster, Carl J., and John J. Begley. "The Hidden Thorns." *Commonweal* (March 26, 1971): 60–64.

Aquinas, Thomas. *Summa Theologiae*. Edited by Billaurt Rubeis et al. Rome: Marietti, 1953. English translation: *Summa Theologica*. Translated by the Fathers of the English Dominican Province. 3 volumes. New York: Benziger, 1947–48.

Audet, Jean P. *Structures of Christian Priesthood: A Study of Home, Marriage, and Celibacy in the Pastoral Service of the Church*. Translated by Rosemary Sheed. New York: MacMillan, 1968.

Auer, Johann, and Joseph Ratzinger. *Dogmatic Theology*, vol. 6: A *General Doctrine of the Sacraments and the Mystery of the Eucharist*. Translated by Erasmo Leiva-Merikakis, translation edited by Hugh M. Riley. Washington, D.C.: The Catholic University of America Press, 1995.

Barnett, James M. *The Diaconate: A Full and Equal Order*. Revised edition. Valley Forge, Penn.: Trinity Press International, 1979–95.

Bishops' Committee on the Diaconate. *Foundations for the Renewal of the Diaconate*. Washington, D.C.: United States Conference of Catholic Bishops, 1993.

Borras, Alphonse, and Bernard Pottier. "Le diaconat exercé en permanence: restauration ou rétablissement?" *Nouvelle revue théologique* 118, no. 6 (1996): 817–38.

———. *La grâce du diaconat: Questions actuelles autour du diaconat latin*. Bruxelles: Cerf, 1998.

Botte, Bernard. "Collegiate Character of the Presbyterate and Episcopate." In his *The Sacrament of Holy Orders*, 83–92. Collegeville, Minn.: Liturgical Press, 1962.

Brockman, Norbert. *Ordained to Service: A Theology of the Permanent Diaconate*. Hicksville, N.Y.: Exposition Press, 1976.

Brovelli, Franco, ed. "Ordine e ministeri." In *I Sacramenti: teologia e storia della celebrazione*, 243–300. Fourth edition. *Anàmnesis* 3/1. Genova: Marietti, 1995.

Buckley, Joseph C. "The Permanent Diaconate." *Furrow* 23, no. 8 (1972): 476–82.

Butler, Sarah. "Women's Ordination and the Development of Doctrine." *Thomist* 61, no. 4 (1997): 501–24.

———. "Women as Deaconesses." *Josephinum Diaconal Review* (Fall 2015): 33–52.

Catholic Theological Society of America. "Tradition and the Ordination of Women: CTSA Resolution." *CTSA Proceedings* 52 (1997): 197–204.

Ceci, Nicola. *Il Ministero del Diacono nel mondo del lavoro*. Rome: Editrice Rogate, 1999.

Chaback, Michael J. *Love Become Service: The Integration of the Sacraments of Matrimony and Holy Orders in the Ministry and Life of the Married Permanent Deacon*. Chester Springs, Penn.: Dufour Editions, 2013.

Chauvet, Louis-Marie. *Du symbolique au symbole: Essai sur les sacrements*. Paris: Cerf, 1979.

———. *Symbol and Sacrament: A Sacramental Reinterpretation of Christian Existence*. Translated by Patrick Madigan and Madeleine Beaumont. Collegeville, Minn.: Liturgical Press, 1995.

Collins, John N. *Are All Christians Ministers?* Collegeville, Minn.: Liturgical Press, 1992.

———. "A Ministry for Tomorrow's Church." *Journal of Ecumenical Studies* 32, no. 2 (1995): 159–78.

———. *Diakonia Studies: Critical Issues in Ministry*. New York: New York University Press, 2014.

Congar, Yves. *Lay People in the Church: A Study for a Theology of the Laity.* Translated by Donald Attwater. Revised edition with additions by the author. Philadelphia: Fortress Press, 1976.

Cooke, Bernard. *Ministry to Word and Sacraments: History & Theology.* Philadelphia: Fortress Press, 1976.

———. "'Fullness of Orders': Theological Reflections." *Jurist* 41 (1981): 151–67.

Coppenrath, M. "Les ordres inférieurs à la prêtrise: degrés du sacerdoce ou étapes vers la prêtrise?" *Nouvelle revue théologique* 81, no. 5 (1959): 489–501.

Coriden, James A. "The Permanent Diaconate/Meaning of Ministry." *Origins* 7, no. 4 (1978): 653–56.

Croghan, Leo M. "The Theology and the Spirit of the Diaconate's Restoration." *American Ecclesiastical Review* 161 (1969): 293–301.

Crowley, Patrick. "The Diaconate for the Present Age: A Theological Assessment." *Clergy Review* 59 (1974): 787–803.

Cummings, Owen F. *Deacons and the Church.* Mahwah, N.J.: Paulist Press, 2004.

———. *Saintly Deacons.* Mahwah, N.J.: Paulist Press, 2005.

Cummings, Owen F., William T. Ditewig, and Richard Gaillardetz. *Theology of the Diaconate: The State of the Question.* Mahwah, N.J.: Paulist Press, 2004.

Dallen, James. *The Dilemma of Priestless Sundays.* Chicago: Liturgy Training Publications, 1994.

Dassman, Ernst. "Diakonat und Zölibat." In *Der Diakon: Wiederentdeckung und Erneuerung seines Dienstes,* edited by Josef Plöger and Hermann Weber, 57–67. Freiburg: Herder, 1981.

Dianich, Severino. *Teologia del ministero ordinato: Una interpretazione ecclesiologica.* Third edition. Prospettive teologiche 4. Milan: Edizioni Paoline, 1993.

Ditewig, William T. *101 Questions and Answers on Deacons.* Mahwah, N.J.: Paulist Press, 2004.

———. *The Emerging Diaconate: Servant Leaders in a Servant Church.* Mahwah, N.J.: Paulist Press, 2007.

Doshner, J. A. "The Deacon: A Man of Service." *Dominicana* 49, no. 4 (1964): 322–31.

Dulles, Avery. "L'ordinazione delle donne. I motivi per dire no." *La Civiltà Cattolica* 149 (1998): 119–28.

Echlin, Edward. "The Deacon in the Secular Age." *Worship* 43 (1969): 154–58.

———. *The Deacon in the Church: Past and Future.* New York: Alba House, 1971.

Epagneul, Michel D. "Du rôle des diacres dans l'Église d'aujourd'hui." *Nouvelle revue théologique* 79 (1957): 153–68.

Florovsky, Georges. "The Problem of Diaconate in the Orthodox Church." In *The Diaconate Now,* edited by Richard T. Nolan, 81–98. Washington, D.C.: Corpus Books, 1968.

Franzelin, John B. *Theses de Ecclesia Christi.* Rome: Typographia Polyglotta, 1887.

Gaillardetz, Richard. "Shifting Meanings in the Lay-Clergy Distinction." *Irish Theological Quarterly* 64, no. 2 (1999): 115–39.

Grillo, Andrea. *Teologia Fondamentale e Liturgia: Il rapporto tra immediatezza e mediazione nella riflessione teologica.* Edited by R. Cecolin, A. N. Terrin, and F. Trolese. Caro Salutis Cardo, Studi 10. Padova: Edizioni Messaggero Padova, 1995.

———. *Introduzione alla teologia liturgica: Approccio teorico alla liturgia e ai sacramenti cristiani.* Edited by R. Cecolin, A. N. Terrin, and F. Trolese. Caro Salutis Cardo, Studi 3. Padova: Edizioni Messaggero Padova, 1999.

Gula, Richard M. "Theology of the Diaconate—Part One." *American Ecclesiastical Review* 169, no. 9 (1975): 621–35.

———. "Theology of the Diaconate—Part Two." *American Ecclesiastical Review* 169, no. 10 (1975): 669–80.

Gy, P. M. "La notion chrétienne d'initiation. Jalons pour une enquête." *La Maison-Dieu* 132 (1977): 33–54.

Hannaford, Robert. "Towards a Theology of the Diaconate." In *The Deacon's Ministry*, edited by Christine Hall, 25–44. Herefordshire: Gracewing, 1992.

Haquin, André, and Philippe Weber, eds. *Diaconat XXIe siècle.* Bruxelles: Lumen Vitae, 1997.

Hauke, Manfred. "Diakonat der Frau?" *Forum Katholische Theologie* 12 (1996): 36–45.

———. "Observations on the Ordination of Women to the Diaconate." In *The Church and Women: A Compendium*, edited by Helmut Moll and translated by G. Harrison, 117–39. San Francisco, Calif.: Ignatius Press, 1988.

Horvath, Tibor. "Theology of a New Diaconate." *Revue de l'Université d'Ottawa* 38 (1968): 248–76, 495–523.

International Theological Commission. "Christianity and the World of Religions." *Origins* 27 (1997): 150–66.

———. *From the Diakonia of Christ to the Diakonia of the Apostles.* International Theological Commission Historico-Theological Research Document. Chicago: Hillendbrand Books, 2003.

Joncas, Jan M. "The Public Language of Ministry Revisited: *De Ordinatione Episcopi, Presbyterorum et Diaconorum 1990.*" *Worship* 68 (1994): 386–403.

Jubany, Narciso. "El Concilio de Trento y la renovación de los ordenes inferiores al presbiterado." *Estudios Ecclesiasticos* 36, no. 136–37 (1961): 127–44.

Kasper, Walter. *Leadership in the Church: How Traditional Roles Can Serve the Christian Community Today.* New York: Crossroad, 2003.

Kavanagh, Aidan. "Confirmation: A Suggestion from Structure." In *Living Water, Sealing Spirit: Readings on Christian Initiation*, edited by Maxwell Johnson, 148–58. Collegeville, Minn.: Liturgical Press, 1995.

Kennedy, Robert T. "Shared Responsibility in Ecclesial Decision-Making." *Studia Canonica* 14 (1980): 5–23.

Kerkvoorde, Augustinus. "The Theology of the Diaconate." In his *Foundations for the Renewal of the Diaconate*, translated by William F. Schmitz, 90–138. Washington, D.C.: United States Catholic Conference, 2003.

Kilmartin, Edward J. "Ministry and Ordination in Early Christianity against a Jewish Background." *Studia Liturgica* 13 (1979): 42–69.

———. "Lay Participation in the Apostolate of the Hierarchy." *Jurist* 41 (1981): 343–70 [89–116 of original pagination].

Kmiec, Edward. "The Profile and the Discernment of Candidates for the Permanent Diaconate." *Seminarium* 37 (1997): 763–78.

Kraus, Theodore. *The Order of Deacons: A Second Look.* Hayward, Calif.: Folger Graphics, 1997.

Küng, Hans. *The Church.* Translated by Ray Ockenden and Rosaleen Ockenden. London: Burns and Oates, 1967.

———. *Why Priests?* Translated by Robert Collins. Garden City, N.Y.: Doubleday, 1972.

Lamb, Matthew. "Solidarity." In *The New Dictionary of Catholic Social Thought*, edited by Judith Dwyer, 908–12. Collegeville, Minn.: Liturgical Press, 1994.

Lambrecht, Jan. "Power as Service." *Louvain Studies* 12, no. 1 (1987): 54–61.

LaPiana, George. "The Roman Church at the End of the Second Century." *Harvard Theological Review* 18, no. 3 (1925): 201–77.

Lécuyer, Joseph. *What Is a Priest?* Translated by Lancelot Sheppard. New York: Hawthorne Books, 1959.

Legrand, Hervé-Marie. "Vocation au diaconat et interpellation: réflexion ecclésiologique à partir de la tradition." In *Documents Episcopat: Bulletin du Secrétariat de la Conférence Episcopale Française*, 3:407–84. Paris: Paris Secrétariat, 1985.

———. "Le diaconat dans sa relation à la théologie de l'Église et des ministères. Reception et devenir du diaconat depuis Vatican II." In *Actes du Colloque Diaconat XXIe siècle*, 13–41. Paris: Cerf, 1997.

Macy, Gary. "The Ordination of Women in the Early Middle Ages." *Theological Studies* 61, no. 3 (2000): 481–507.

Mansini, Guy. "On Affirming a Dominical Intention of a Male Priesthood." *Thomist* 61, no. 2 (1997): 301–16.

Mansour, Gregory. "The Role of the Deacon in the Maronite Church." *Diakonia* 29 (1996): 128–32.

Martos, Joseph. *Doors to the Sacred: A Historical Introduction to Sacraments in the Catholic Church*. Expanded edition. Ligouri, Mo.: Triumph, 1991.

Maso, Alberto dal. *L'Efficacia dei sacramenti e la «performance» rituale: Ripensare l'«ex opere operato» a partire dall'antropologia culturale*. Edited by R. Cecolin, A. N. Terrin, and F. Trolese. Caro Salutis Cardo, Studi 12. Padova: Edizioni Messagero Padova, 1999.

McCaslin, Patrick, and Michael Lawler. *Sacrament of Service: A Vision of the Permanent Diaconate Today*. New York: Paulist Press, 1986.

McKenzie, John L. *Authority in the Church*. New York: Sheed and Ward, 1966.

McKnight, William Shawn. *The Latin Rite Deacon: Symbol of Communitas and Social Intermediary among the People of God. A Theological Description of the Permanent Diaconate Utilizing Studies in Sociology and Anthropology*. STD diss., Pontificium Athenaeum S. Anselmi de Urbe, 2001.

———. "Ritual and the Call to Service: How the Eucharist Promotes the Practice of Social Justice." *Newman Review* 2 (2001): 79–96.

———. "The Diaconate as *Medius Ordo*: Service in Promotion of Lay Participation." In *The Deacon Reader*, edited by James Keating, 78–98. New York: Paulist Press, 2006.

———. "The Deacon in the Liturgy: An Epiphany of Service." *Josephinum Diaconal Review* (Fall 2015): 3–23.

———. "The Uniqueness of the Deacon." In *The Character of the Deacon. Spiritual and Pastoral Foundations*, edited by James Keating, 61–84. Mahwah, N.J.: Paulist Press, 2017.

Mette, Norbert. "Solidarity with the Lowliest: Parish Growth Through the Witness of Practical Service." In *Diakonia: Church for Others*, edited by Norbert Greinacher and Norbert Mette, 76–83. Concilium 198. Edinburgh: T. and T. Clark, 1988.

Militello, Cettina. "La progressiva «crescita» del ministero ordinato." *Rivista Liturgica* 83 (1996): 29–42.

Miralles, Antonio. "Le Diaconesse: Bilancio di Dodici Anni di Pubblicazioni." *Ricerche Teologiche* 7 (1996): 161–76.

———. "Lo Status Quaestionis della Teologia del Diaconato Permanente." *Seminarium* 37 (1997): 715–32.

Mitchell, Nathan. *Mission and Ministry: History and Theology in the Sacrament of Order.* Message of the Sacraments 6. Wilmington, Del.: Glazier, 1982.

Mohler, James A. *The Origin and Evolution of the Priesthood.* New York: Alba House, 1970.

Müller, Gerhard L. *Priestertum und Diakonat: Der Empfänger des Weihesakramentes in schöpfungstheologischer und christologischer Perspektive.* Einsiedeln: Johannes Verlag, 2000.

Nowell, Robert. *The Ministry of Service: Deacons in the Contemporary Church.* New York, N.Y.: Herder and Herder, 1968.

O'Meara, Thomas. "Karl Rahner on Priest, Parish and Deacon." *Worship* 40 (1966): 103–10.

———. *Theology of Ministry.* New York: Paulist Press, 1983.

Oro, F. Dell'. "La «*Editio typica altera*» del Pontificale Romano delle Ordinazione. I nuovi «*Praenotanda*»." *Rivista Liturgica* 78 (1991): 281–335.

Osborne, Kenan. *Ministry. Lay Ministry in the Roman Catholic Church: Its History and Theology.* New York: Paulist Press, 1993.

———. *The Diaconate in the Christian Church: Its History and Theology.* Chicago: National Association of Diaconate Directors, 1996.

———. *The Permanent Diaconate: Its History and Place in the Sacrament of Orders.* Mahwah, N.J.: Paulist Press, 2007.

Pagé, Roch. *Diaconat permanent et diversité des ministères.* Montréal: Paulines, 1988.

Paul, R. "The Deacon in Protestantism." In *The Diaconate Now,* edited by Richard T. Nolan, 37–56. Washington, D.C.: Corpus Books, 1968.

Philips, Gérard. "History of the Constitution." In *Commentary on the Documents of Vatican II,* edited by Herbert Vorgrimler, 1:105–37. New York: Herder and Herder, 1966–69.

———. *La chiesa e il suo mistero: Storia, testo e commento della lumen gentium.* Milano: Jaca, 1975–93. [Italian translation of *L'Église et son mystère.* Paris: Desclée de Brouwer, 1967].

Plöger, Josef, and Hermann Weber, eds. *Der Diakon: Wiederentdeckung und Erneuerung seines Dienstes.* Freiburg: Herder, 1981.

Pottier, Bernard. "La sacramentalité du diaconat." *Nouvelle revue théologique* 119, no. 1 (1997): 20–36.

Powell, Douglas. "Ordo Presbyterii." *Journal of Theological Studies* 26, no. 2 (1975): 290–328.

Power, David N. *Gifts That Differ: Lay Ministries Established and Unestablished.* Studies in the Reformed Rites of the Catholic Church 8. New York: Pueblo, 1980–85.

———. "The Basis for Official Ministry in the Church." *Jurist* 41 (1981): 314–42.

———. "Church Order: The Need for Redress." *Worship* 71, no. 4 (1997): 296–309.

———. "Theology of Eucharistic Celebration." In Chupungco, *Handbook,* 3:321–66.

———. *Sacrament: The Language of God's Giving.* New York: Herder and Herder, 1999.

Puglisi, James. *The Process of Admission to Ordained Ministry: A Comparative Study,* vol. 1: *Epistemological Principles and Roman Catholic Rites.* Translated by Michael S. Driscoll and Mary Misrashi. Collegeville, Minn.: Liturgical Press, 1996.

Rahner, Karl. "Theology of Power." In his *Theological Investigations,* vol. 4: *More Recent Writings,* translated by Kevin Smyth, 391–409. Baltimore, Md.: Helicon Press, 1966.

———. *Servants of the Lord.* New York: Herder and Herder, 1968.

———. "The Teaching of the Second Vatican Council on the Diaconate." In his *Foundations for the Renewal of the Diaconate,* translated by David Bourke, 182–92. Washington, D.C.: United States Conference of Catholic Bishops, 2003.

———. "The Theology of the Restoration of the Diaconate." In his *Foundations for the Renewal of the Diaconate*, translated by Karl Kruger, 139–81. Washington, D.C.: United States Conference of Catholic Bishops, 2003.

———. "On the Diaconate." In his *Foundations for the Renewal of the Diaconate*, translated by David Bourke, 193–212. Washington, D.C.: United States Conference of Catholic Bishops, 2003.

Rahner, Karl, and Herbert Vorgrimler, eds. *Diaconia in Christo: Über die Erneuerung des Diakonats*. Freiburg: Herder Verlag, 1962.

Reese, James M. "Patterns of Ministry in the New Testament as Interpreting the Role of the Permanent Diaconate." *American Ecclesiastical Review* 166, no. 3 (1972): 174–84.

Renken, John A. *The Deacon in Vatican Council II: A Consideration of the Conciliar Teaching in View of the Historical Development of the Office*. PhD diss., Pontifical University of St. Thomas, 1981.

Rice, Nick. "Will the Diaconate Become Parochialized?" *Origins* 26 (1997): 745 and 747–49.

Riquet, Michel. *Christian Charity in Action*. Translated by P. Hepburne-Scott. Twentieth Century Encyclopedia of Catholicism 105. New York: Hawthorn Books, 1961.

Ritt, P. "Twenty-Five Years of Restored Diaconate." *Church* 9 (1993): 42–45.

Ross, J. M. "Deacons in Protestantism." *Theology* 58, no. 425 (1955): 429–36.

Rouillard, Philippe. "From Human Meal to Christian Eucharist." In *Living Bread, Saving Cup: Readings on the Eucharist*, edited by R. Kevin Seasoltz, 126–57. Collegeville, Minn.: Liturgical Press, 1982–87.

Schamoni, Wilhelm. *Married Men as Ordained Deacons*. London: Burns and Oates, 1955.

Scheffczyk, Leo. "Laypersons, deacons, and priests: A difference of ministries." *Communio* 23, no. 4 (1996): 639–55.

Schillebeeckx, Edward. "Catholic Understanding of Office." *Theological Studies* 30 (1969): 567–86.

Scorci, P. "Il Diaconato: ordine o ministero?" *Rivista Liturgica* 83 (1996): 583–99.

Seasoltz, R. Kevin. "Justice and the Eucharist." In *Living Bread, Saving Cup: Readings on the Eucharist*, edited by R. Kevin Seasoltz, 305–23. Collegeville, Minn.: Liturgical Press, 1982–87.

Semmelroth, Otto. "The Priestly People of God and Its Official Ministers." In *The Sacraments in General: A New Perspective*, edited by Edward Schillebeeckx and Boniface Willems, 87–100. Concilium 31. New York: Paulist Press, 1968.

Senn, Frank. "The Servant Church and the Diaconate." *Lutheran Forum* 19 (1985): 17–23.

———. "The Ecclesiological Basis of the Office of Deacon: The Contribution of Sven-Erik Brodd." *Pro Ecclesia* 3 (1994): 197–205.

Sepe, Crescenzio. "Il diaconato segno visibile dell'azione dello Spirito Santo." *Notitiae* 30 (1994): 472–86.

Shugrue, Timothy J. *Service Ministry of the Deacon*. Washington, D.C.: United States Catholic Conference, 1988.

Siebel, Wigand. "The Exercise of Power in Today's Church." In *Power in the Church*, edited by James Provost and Knut Walf, 39–49. Concilium 197/3. Edinburgh: T. and T. Clark, 1988.

Singles, D. "The Permanent Deacon in France." *Chicago Studies* 25 (1986): 117–31.

Starkloff, Carl F. "Church as Structure and Communitas: Victor Turner and Ecclesiology." *Theological Studies* 58, no. 4 (1997): 643–68.

Sykes, Stephen. "Power and Authority in Ecumenical Theology." In *Ecumenism: Present Realities and Future Prospects. Papers Read at the Tantur Ecumenical Center, Jerusalem, 1997*, edited by Lawrence Cunningham, 169–83. Notre Dame, Ind.: University of Notre Dame Press, 1997.

Tavard, George. *A Theology for Ministry.* Theology and Life Series 6. Wilmington, Del.: Glazier, 1983.

———. *The Church, Community of Salvation: An Ecumenical Ecclesiology.* New Theology Studies 1. Collegeville, Minn.: Liturgical Press, 1992.

Theodorou, Evangelos. "The Institution of Deaconesses in the Orthodox Church and the Possibility of Its Restoration." In *The Place of the Woman in the Orthodox Church and the Question of the Ordination of Women: Interorthodox Symposium. Rhodes, Greece 30 October—7 November 1988,* edited by Gennadios Limouris and translated by S. Harakas, 207–38. Katerini: Tertios Publications, 1992.

Tillard, Jean-Marie R. *Chiesa di Chiese: L'ecclesiologia di communione.* Brescia: Queriniana, 1989.

Vanzan, Piersandro. "Diaconato permanente femminile. Ombre e luci." *La Civiltà Cattolica* (1999): 439–52.

Vorgrimler, Herbert. "The Hierarchical Structure of the Church, with Special Reference to the Episcopate, Article 29." In *Commentary of the Documents of Vatican II,* edited by Herbert Vorgrimler and translated by Lalit Adolphus, Kevin Smyth, and Richard Strachan, 1:226–30. New York: Crossroad, 1967–89.

———. *Sacramental Theology.* Translated by Linda M. Maloney. Collegeville, Minn.: Liturgical Press, 1992.

Wainwright, Geoffrey. *Eucharist and Eschatology.* London: Epworth Press, 1971–73.

Winninger, Paul. *Vers un Renouveau du Diaconat.* Paris: Desclée de Brouwer, 1958.

Woods, Susan K. *Sacramental Orders.* Collegeville, Minn.: Liturgical Press, 2000.

Zagano, Phyllis. *Holy Saturday: An Argument for the Restoration of the Female Diaconate in the Catholic Church.* New York: Herder and Herder, 2000.

Zizioulas, John. *Being as Communion: Studies in Personhood and the Church.* Crestwood, N.Y.: St. Vladimir's Seminary Press, 1985.

Canon Law

"Acta Comissionis: Adunatio diei 7 Aprilis 1978." *Communicationes* 10 (1978): 227–32.

Beal, John. "The Exercise of the Power of Governance by Lay People: State of the Question." *Jurist* 55 (1995): 1–92.

Beal, John P., James A. Coriden, and Thomas J. Green, eds. *New Commentary on the Code of Canon Law: An Entirely New and Comprehensive Commentary by Canonists from North America and Europe, with a Revised English Translation of the Code.* Commissioned by The Canon Law Society of America. Mahwah, N.J.: Paulist Press, 2000.

Bertrams, Wilhelm. "Communio, communitas et societas in Lege Fundamentali Ecclesiae." *Periodica* 61 (1972): 553–604.

Borras, Alphonse. "Les effets canoniques de l'ordination diaconale." *Revue Théologique de Louvain* 28 (1997): 453–83.

Bouscaren, T. Lincoln. "Canon 453." *Canon Law Digest* 1 (1934): 246.

Canon Law Society of America. "Canonical Implications: Ordaining Women to the Permanent Diaconate." *Origins* 25 (1995): 344–52.

Caparros, Ernest, et al., eds. *Code of Canon Law Annotated*. Montréal: Wilson and Lafleur Limitée, 1993.

Coriden, James, Thomas Green, and Donald Heintschel, eds. *The Code of Canon Law: A Text and Commentary*. Canon Law Society of America. New York: Paulist Press, 1985.

Coronata, Matthaeus conte a. *De processibus*. Volume 3 of *Institutiones iuris canonici. ad usum utriusque cleri et scholarum*. Editio Quarto Aucta et Emendata. Rome: Marietti, 1956.

DePaolis, Velasio. "De natura sacramentali potestatis sacrae." *Periodica* 65 (1976): 59–105.

Diego-Lora, Carmelo de. "Promotor de justicia, defenso del vínculo y notario: Comentario." In CECDC, 817–22.

Ditewig, William. "The Permanent Diaconate as Military Chaplain: Canonical Reflections." *Jurist* 51 (1991): 340–63.

Green, Thomas. "Shepherding the Patrimony of the Poor: Diocesan and Parish Structures of Financial Administration." *Jurist* 56 (1997): 706–34.

Grocholewski, Zenon. "Asesores del juez único." In CECDC, 795.

———. "De los auditores y ponentes." In CECDC, 806–8.

Instituto Martín de Azpilcueta Facultad de Derecho Canónico Universidad de Navarra. *Commentario Exegético al Código de Derecho Canónico*. Edited by A. Marzoa, J. Miras, and R. Rodríguez-Ocaña. Volume 4.1. Second edition. Pamplona: EUNSA, 1997.

Justinian. *Corpus iuris civilis*, vol. 3: *Novellae*. Fifth edition. Edited by Rudolf Schöll and Wilhelm Kroll. Berlin: Weidmann, 1928.

Louis, William F. *Diocesan Archives: An Historical Synopsis and Commentary*. Canon Law Studies 137. Washington, D.C.: The Catholic University of America Press, 1941.

McDonough, Elizabeth. "Jurisdiction Exercised by Non-Ordained Members in Religious Institutes." *Canon Law Society of America Proceedings* 58 (1996): 292–307.

Orsy, Ladislas. "The Congregation's 'Response': Its Authority and Meaning." *America* 173, no. 19 (December 9, 1995): 4–5.

Prince, John E. *The Diocesan Chancellor: An Historical Synopsis and Commentary*. Canon Law Studies 167. Washington, D.C.: The Catholic University of America Press, 1942.

Ramos, Francisco J. *Le Diocesi nel Codice di Diritto Canonico: Studio giuridico-pastorale sulla organizzazione ed I raggruppamenti delle Chiese particolari*. Rome: Millennium Romae, 1997.

Robleda, O. "Iurisdictio-Officium ecclesiasticum." *Periodica* 59 (1970): 661–89.

Woestman, William. *The Sacrament of Orders and the Clerical State: A Commentary on the Code of Canon Law*. Ottawa: St. Paul University, 1999.

Wrenn, Lawrence. *Procedures*. Washington, D.C.: Canon Law Society of America, 1987.

———. "Procurators for the Trial and Advocates [cc. 1481–1490]." CLSAC, 967–68.

Book Reviews

Danker, Frederick W. *Critical Review of Books in Religion*. Atlanta: Scholars Press, 1991.

Frend, W. H. C. "Book Review: *Diakonia: Re-interpreting the Ancient Sources*." *Theology* 94 (1991): 464–66.

Giles, Kevin. "Book Review: *Are All Christians Ministers?*" *Christian Book Newsletter* (Melbourne) 11 (1993): 8–9.

Grayston, Kenneth. "Book Review: *Diakonia: Re-interpreting the Ancient Sources*." *Journal of Theological Studies* 43, no. 1 (1992): 198–200.

Imbelli, Robert P. "Book Review. *Diakonia: Re-interpreting the Ancient Sources.*" *Commonweal* 120, no. 5 (March 12, 1993): 20–22.

Neyrey, Jerome H. "Book Review. *Diakonia: Re-interpreting the Ancient Sources.*" *Biblical Theology Bulletin* 21, no. 4 (1991): 166–67.

Murphy-O'Connor, Jerome. "Book Review: *Diakonia: Re-interpreting the Ancient Sources.*" *Revue Biblique* 102, no. 1 (1995): 152–53.

Reumann, John. "A New Review Revising Deacons and the 'Servant Church' on the Basis of Greek and Early Christian Usages." *The Patristic and Byzantine Review* 10, nos. 1–2 (1991): 65–66.

Tavard, George. "Book Review: *Diakonia: Re-interpreting the Ancient Sources.*" *Worship* 66, no. 4 (1992): 378–82.

Wright, J. Robert. "Book Review: *Diakonia: Re-interpreting the Ancient Sources.*" *Anglican Theological Review* 74, no. 1 (1992): 108–10.

INDEX

RELATED TITLES FROM
CUA PRESS

Called to Holiness
On Love, Vocation, and Formation
Pope Emeritus Benedict XVI

Priestly Celibacy
Theological Foundations
Gary Selin

The Ideal Bishop
Aquinas's Commentaries on the Pastoral Epistles
Michael G. Sirilla

A Service of Love
Papal Primacy, the Eucharist, and Church Unity,
with a New Postscript
Paul McPartlan

Apostolic Religious Life in America Today
A Response to the Crisis
Edited by Richard Gribble, CSC

A Spiritual Theology of the Priesthood
The Mystery of Christ and the Mission of the Priest
Dermot Power